Peace, Justice and Freedom: Human Rights Challenges in the New Millennium

Peace, Justice

Edited by
Gurcharan S. Bhatia
J.S. O'Neill
Gerald L. Gall &
Patrick D. Bendin

Human Rights Challenges
for the New Millennium

and Freedom

The University of Alberta Press

Published by
The University of Alberta Press
Ring House 2
Edmonton, Alberta T6G 2E1

Canadian Cataloguing in Publication Data

Main entry under title:
Peace, justice and freedom

Papers from the conference, Universal rights and human values: a blueprint for peace, justice and freedom, held at the University of Alberta, Nov. 26-28, 1998.

Includes bibliographical references.
ISBN 0-88864-339-X

1. Human rights—Congresses. 2. Human rights advocacy—Congresses. I. Bhatia, Gurcharan S. (Gurcharan Singh), 1931–
JC571.P39 2000   323   C99-911304-6

Peace, Justice and Freedom: Human Rights Challenges for the New Millenium is a publication for the book trade from the University of Alberta Press.
Editorial: Carol Berger
Proofreading: Jill Fallis
Printed and bound in Canada by Hignell Book Printing Ltd., Winnipeg, Manitoba.
∞ Printed on acid-free paper.

The University of Alberta Press gratefully acknowledges the support received for its program from the Canada Council for the Arts. The Press also acknowledges the financial support of the Government of Canada through the Book Publishing Industry Development Program for its publishing activities.

Contents

Acknowledgements

Mᴀɴʏ ᴘᴇᴏᴘʟᴇ ᴄᴏɴᴛʀɪʙᴜᴛᴇᴅ to the organization and running of the November 1998 conference on Universal Rights and Human Values: A Blueprint for Peace, Justice and Freedom. The Canadian Human Rights Foundation and the University of Alberta, major sponsors of the conference, wish to acknowledge the following people: the conference's executive committee of Patrick Bendin, Gurcharan S. Bhatia, Jim Edwards, Bob Fagan, Jean Forest, Gerald Gall, Nancy Hannemann, Robinson Koilpillai, J.S. (Jack) O'Neill and Cathy Anne Pachnowski; the planning committee of James Leitch, Charlach Mackintosh, Chaldeans Mensah, Hai Nguyen, Christine Rapp and Bruce Uditsky; the staff including Linda Robertson, Sonia Sinha, Madhvi Russell, Minla Sadasiwan, Susan Spronk, Doug Raynor, Sabrina Park, Bob LePage and his security staff, G.J. Manegre, Pascale Lagacé, Frank Calder, Doodie Cahill, Gene Zwozdesky (MLA), Randy Palivoda, Claudette Tardif, Fil Fraser, Myrna Howell, Diane Wilson, Sara Coumantarakis and Ruth Bertelsen. Our thanks also go to the youth conference committee, including Diana Coumantarakis, Eleanor Colver, Wendy Gall, Jacquie O'Neill, Ann Marit Johnson, Greg Mossman, Cherie Klassen, Jordan Sharon, Rene Salazar, Ailing Shih, Yamit More, Catherine Dextrase and Shampa Chakraborty. More than one hundred Edmontonians volunteered their time during the conference to ensure its success. Special thanks are reserved for conference participants who have kindly agreed to the publication of their presentations in this book. We also appreciate the support and assistance of Glenn Rollans, director of the University of Alberta Press, and text editor Carol Berger. We thank you all.

The Sponsors

Canadian Human Rights Foundation
University of Alberta

Co-Sponsors

Alberta Law Review
Amnesty International Canada
Canadian Committee to Protect Journalists
Canadian Council for International
    Cooperation
Canadian Council of Churches
Canadian Teachers' Federation
Centre for Constitutional Studies, University
    of Alberta
Faculty of Law, University of Alberta
Faculté Saint-Jean, University of Alberta
International Centre, University of Alberta
International Centre for Human Rights and
    Democratic Development
International Commission of Jurists
Office of Human Rights, University of Alberta
Provincial Human Rights Commissions of
    Canada
The Edmonton Journal
The Lester B. Pearson Canadian Peacekeeping
    Training Centre
The Volunteer Centre of Edmonton

Funding Sponsors

Canadian Heritage, Government of Canada
Human Rights, Citizenship and
    Multiculturalism Education Fund,
    Government of Alberta
Canadian International Development Agency
TELUS
United Nations Association in Canada,
    Edmonton Chapter
Canadian Multicultural Education Foundation
Department of Justice, Government of Canada
Canadian Human Rights Commission
Amoco Canada Petroleum Company Ltd.
Clifford E. Lee Foundation
TransCanada Pipelines Ltd.
Canadian Airlines
Hole's Greenhouses and Gardens Ltd.
Syncrude Canada Ltd.
Wild Rose Foundation
Royal Bank of Canada
City of Edmonton
Health Canada
Alberta Association for Community Living
Edmonton Chinese Lions Club
Edmonton Community Foundation
Alberta Professional Reporters Inc.
National Film Board
Power Industry
Quality Color Press Inc.
Tanner Young Marketing
Vision TV

Honorary Financial Advisors, KPMG
Honorary Legal Advisors, Field Atkinson
    Perraton

Introduction

IN 1996 THREE PEOPLE—a Sikh, a Jew and a Christian—decided to hold an international conference on human rights in Edmonton, Alberta, to mark the fiftieth anniversary of the United Nations Universal Declaration of Human Rights. This followed the holding of a conference the previous year, the theme of which was Human Rights and Changing Global Values: The Universal Declaration, the Vienna Conference and Beyond. These three persons were directors of the Canadian Human Rights Foundation which was established in 1968 by the late John Humphrey. Humphrey, a professor of law at McGill University in Montréal, was a co-author of the Universal Declaration twenty years earlier. He sought to educate the world about human rights, to promote the principles and the values of the Declaration. This too was the purpose of the international conference held in Edmonton.

One of the great educational institutions in the world, the University of Alberta, joined the Canadian Human Rights Foundation as a major sponsor of the conference. The university's support and that of our many co-sponsors made it possible to fulfil our plans. Our vision for the conference, which was held on 26–28 November 1998, was to refocus the world's attention on the Universal Declaration of Human Rights. We wanted to gather together human rights figures from around the world and create an opportunity for discussion and debate. In this we were successful. Delegates left the conference with a sense of purpose and dedication, a sense of direction at the dawn of a new millennium.

The following pages contain words that were spoken during those three days in Edmonton. They stand as a testament to the struggle of people around the world to better their lives, to end conditions of war and repression. South African Archbishop Desmond Tutu shares his country's experience of reconciliation, of coming to terms with the history of apartheid. Mary Robinson, the UN high commissioner for human rights, speaks of her visit to a First Nations reserve in central Alberta and cautions against celebrating the Declaration when so many of the world's people continue to suffer from grave human rights abuses. Antonio Lamer, chief justice of the Supreme Court of Canada, emphasizes the need to promote a culture of human rights.

There are other voices which are not as well known, from Africa and Asia, Europe and the Americas. Some have escaped war and torture. Others are former political prisoners forced into exile because of their calls for freedom of speech and democracy. Senior jurists speak of the history of law and how the courts have tried to grapple with the trial and punishment of those accused of crimes against humanity. Bioethicists ask what the future of genetic research holds and aboriginal voices question the cost of resource development in their home territories. There are also contributions from participants in the conference's youth session, the new generation of decision-makers. Canadian member of Parliament David Kilgour, who was present at the conference but was not a speaker, has contributed his thoughts about the Declaration of Human Rights in light of international events which have unfolded in the year since the conference.

We met together in November of 1998 to learn from one another, to examine and discuss the human rights challenges of our planet as we enter a new century. Now, with the publication of this book, the powerful messages of the conference can be brought to the four corners of the world. Peace, justice and freedom—the conference and the ideas it generated will move us closer towards those elusive goals.

Gurcharan S. Bhatia, chair and J.S. (Jack) O'Neill, co-chair

Peace, Justice and Freedom

HUMAN RIGHTS CHALLENGES IN THE NEW MILLENNIUM

Message to the International Conference on Universal Rights and Human Values

Aung San Suu Kyi is a Burmese dissident and Nobel Prize laureate. Since 1988 she has led the pro-democracy movement against the authoritarian rule of Burma's State Law and Order Committee (SLORC). In 1995 she was released from six years of house arrest in Rangoon but continues to be denied the freedom to travel. Every week thousands of people gather at her home to hear her informal speeches calling for reform, civil freedoms and an end to tyranny. Her peaceful crusade against her country's military rulers has led her to be compared to Nelson Mandela, Vaclav Havel and Mahatma Gandhi. She is the daughter of independence leader General Aung San, modern Burma's most famous martyr, who was assassinated in 1947 when Suu Kyi was two years old.

MAY I BEGIN BY EXPRESSING MY SINCERE REGRETS that I am unable to join you in Edmonton today. I would have wished to take part in the discussions at this conference which, I have little doubt, will provide valuable ideas and suggestions for making our planet a safer, happier home for all of us. Largely due to the sad situation of human rights in my own country, I am unable to attend this conference in person and must therefore be content with sending a short message.

The title of this conference could well be turned inside out without distorting its true sense or diminishing its potency: peace, justice and freedom could be viewed as universal values which form the foundation of our demand for those basic human rights that should be recognized by the international community and guaranteed by every state in the world.

Few rational human beings anywhere, regardless of their race, religion or culture, would deny the supreme value of peace, justice and freedom in their positive, vigorous aspects. It is now widely seen that peace should be more than the mere absence of war: it should be a positive force that counters violence as a means of resolving the problems of human society. Justice should not only aim at controlling the negative traits in human nature. It should work to promote a sense of fairness, compassion and universal brotherhood. Freedom should be more than a lack of shackles. It should mean an environment where the right to develop one's own potential, without curbing that of others, can be exercised without fear.

The articles of the United Nations Universal Declaration of Human Rights are aimed at creating a human environment which will foster peace, justice and freedom. Its preamble spells out the indissoluble link between universal rights and human values, or between universal values and human rights. This link will surely become better established as a result of the endeavours of conferences such as this, where scholars and statesmen, international human rights activists and representatives of the United Nations agencies gather to focus attention on this most important of subjects: the right of all peoples to live full lives, secure in their dignity as free and respected members of the human race.

May I conclude by thanking those who have made it possible for me to send this message and by extending my warm wishes for the success of this conference to its organizers and participants.

DESMOND M. TUTU

What Comes After Conflict and Repression?

Desmond M. Tutu is archbishop emeritus of Cape Town. In 1995 he was appointed to chair the Truth and Reconciliation Commission in South Africa by President Nelson Mandela. He was awarded the Nobel Peace Prize in 1984 in recognition of his contribution to the crusade for justice and racial conciliation in South Africa.

WHEN WE SURVEY OUR VULNERABLE EARTH HOME, we must be appalled that its soil has been soaked with so much bloodletting and its landscape littered with hundreds of thousands of the casualties of the abuse of power.

And yet we should not be so despondent, thinking that tales of woe and gloom are all that characterize this, the last century of the millennium. It would be too one-eyed and negative in the extreme. For there has been another side of the sombre picture we must undoubtedly paint of our times. We have also seen how resilient the human spirit can be as it has triumphed against all kinds of odds. We have seen dictatorships bite the dust and freedom and justice prevail, rising from the ashes of repression and injustice like the proverbial phoenix.

Yes, we have had the Holocaust but we have also had the defeat of Nazism, fascism and the fall of the Berlin Wall. Freedom has broken out in all kinds of even the most unlikely places. Yes, we have had the excesses of Pol Pot in Cambodia and injustice and oppression in other places, but we have also seen the end of colonialism and the emergence of new nation states. And, wonder of wonders, we have thrilled at the end of apartheid in South Africa and the establishment of a new dispensation—democratic, nonracial and nonsexist—in place of what most churches, including the white NGK (Nederduitse Gereformeerde Kerk—the largest of the three major Dutch Reformed churches) in South Africa, have condemned as sinful in and of itself and what senior judges in a deposition to the Truth and Reconciliation Commission have denounced as itself a gross violation of human rights. We must celebrate that such a vicious system has been replaced by a constitutional democracy with a Bill of Rights that is enforceable

5

by the courts and where attempts are being made to cultivate a culture of respect for human rights and the rule of law.

That is a wonderful achievement. It is a spectacular victory over the forces of darkness and evil and inhumanity and cruelty. Dear friends, that victory would have been totally impossible without your love, prayers and support. We are the beneficiaries of that support. We are deeply indebted to you for making the miracle of April 1994 happen. Therefore, our victory is your victory. On behalf of millions of my fellow South Africans, I have the great privilege of saying, thank you, thank you, thank you. It is thanks to you that Nelson Mandela is free today. It is thanks to you that we are free in South Africa today. Thank you, thank you.

Whilst it is true that the story of our world is not just unrelieved gloom and despair, we have to be honest and admit that there are far too many conflicts going on. Far too many of God's children still suffer unnecessarily and suffer untold misery and anguish. And most of the conflict is civil conflict or it is internal repression—in Sri Lanka, Northern Ireland, the Middle East, Afghanistan, Rwanda, the Democratic Republic of Congo, Bosnia, Kosovo, Cyprus, Turkey, Sierra Leone, Sudan, Somalia, Burundi, Nigeria, Burma, Angola.

These and other countries like them will sooner or later have to deal with the problems of postconflict, postrepression transition and how are they going to cope? Are there models from which to choose about how to tackle what will be an increasingly common phenomenon?

The first, and perhaps somewhat instinctive reaction in the postrepression, postconflict period, is to wreak revenge. Those who were the victims seek to settle scores with the perpetrators who violated their rights in the period now passed. This is an atavistic throwback to an earlier period in our evolution, when the laws of the jungle held sway, when it was survival of the fittest.

In order to survive one had to dispatch one's enemies or negotiate as soon as possible and as effectively as possible if one did not want to run the risk of being wiped out. That is what happened in Rwanda. The Tutsis returned to settle scores with their Hutu compatriots for the outrages and violations they had suffered three decades earlier. The sectarian strife in Northern Ireland is fuelled by attack and counterattack between Roman Catholics and Protestants—fellow Christians and fellow Ulster citizens.

The option holds out no prospect whatsoever of peace and stability but is a sure recipe for ongoing violence and bloodletting, each new incident on one side being the provocation of a reprisal from the other, which in its turn provokes its own counter-reprisal *ad nauseum*. It was an option considered by some at home.

On the day following our handing over of the Truth and Reconciliation Commission report to Nelson Mandela, we were at a banquet hosted by the Johannesburg Press Club. One of those who spoke there was Saki Macozoma. He had as a youth been jailed on Robben Island. He told the banquet audience that many of his youthful contemporaries on the island used to dream of the day when they would be prison warders, to pay back to the jail warders what they had been made to endure. Mercifully for us, this is an option that was rejected and Saki did not become a prison warder but today heads up the parastatal Transnet responsible for our national rail, air and sea transportation network.

Another option was the Nuremberg Trial option, where the perpetrators of the repressive regime or those involved in the conflict are brought to trial. It was possible for this to happen after World War II because the Allies had inflicted a comprehensive defeat on the Nazis and their allies. So they were able to apply so-called victor's justice. The judges and prosecutors after the trial were able to pack their bags and return to their respective homes.

We in South Africa were unable to consider this as a real and viable option. There was no clear winner, no clear loser. The apartheid government did not defeat the liberation movements and they, in their turn, had not succeeded to topple the apartheid regime. There was a military stalemate. This option was unacceptable for other compelling reasons as well.

The country was not able to afford the time and money resources that would be required to ensure that the judicial process would operate efficiently. As it is, it is labouring under very considerable pressure. It would have meant that the country would be mired for a long time in a process in which gruesome and distressing details would be publicized which would have a traumatic and divisive effect on a fragile and deeply wounded and polarized society.

Perhaps the most important reason was that the members of the security establishment, who still controlled the guns, would not have supported the relatively peaceful transition from repression to democratic rule if they knew that they would afterwards run the gauntlet of the judicial process. They had the capacity to derail the entire transformation process. We would have had no democratic South Africa today had negotiated settlement not been made. So the Nuremberg Trial option was rejected as well.

A third option was to do nothing. There were those who glibly said, "Let bygones be bygones. Let us forget the past and now concentrate on the present and the future." This was seductive. In most other countries, e.g., Chile, the military dictators had given themselves a blanket amnesty before handing power over to civilian rulers.

This option too, mercifully, was rejected. First of all, we cannot by mere fiat make bygones be bygones. The texture of the universe and our own make-up render this impossible. Those bygones, unless properly and adequately dealt with, are not pliable, conveniently going away and lying down. No, they have an uncanny habit of returning to haunt us. At Dachau, the site of the former concentration camp, at the entrance to its museum, are those haunting words, "Those who forget the past are doomed to repeat it."

Another reason is that amnesia of this kind is victimizing the victims a second time round. The Chilean playwright Dorfmann, in his *Death and the Maiden*, has the woman whose husband has just been appointed as chairperson of their country's Truth Commission recognize the voice of the man who has come to her home for help after his car has broken down. She recognizes him as the man who tortured and raped her when she was in detention. She somehow manages to tie him up and is ready to kill him when he denies he had done these things to her. Finally, he admits the truth and she lets him go free. His lie undermined her integrity, her identity, her memory. His admission acknowledges her and rehabilitates her identity.

When you want to destroy a people, you destroy their history, their memory and so, their identity. And that is true also of individuals. We found that telling their story to a sympathetic audience was something cathartic, something therapeutic, for many of those who came before the commission. One young man who had been blinded after police action in his township said after testifying, "You have given me back my eyes."

So we in South Africa said, "No to amnesia, no to general or blanket amnesty" and, "Yes to individual amnesty—freedom in exchange for the truth, for full disclosure." Some have said that this encouraged impunity. But we contend differently. The applicants must accept responsibility for the deeds for which amnesty is sought. They must accept accountability—amnesty is not granted to those who are innocent or who claim to be innocent. You apply for amnesty because you are guilty. So this provision in fact rules out impunity. And the application is heard in the case of gross violations of human rights (killing, abduction, torture and severe ill-treatment) in an open public hearing, not behind closed doors. It is in the full glare of TV lights and media publicity.

Some have held that justice is sacrificed for the sake of reconciliation. I contend that this is not entirely the case. There is a kind of punishment in the public humiliation for quite a few and it is often the first time that their wives or community learn that their seemingly decent men were in fact members of a death squad. Some have been divorced as a consequence. We would argue though that retributive justice is not the only kind of justice. We believe that there is what we call restorative justice, where the primary purpose is the healing of a rupture, the restoration of harmony, the redressing of the balance.

We believe we have uncovered much truth about our past. No one can ever again say that they did not know that the apartheid state used torture routinely, or that it did not have elements who believed they were carrying out the orders of the highest in government when they abducted and killed and buried secretly many of the then government opponents, or that the liberation movements were also guilty of gross violations of human rights, e.g., through torturing those even of their membership who were suspected of being enemy agents or of killing innocent civilians and noncombatants.

Now we know who bombed Knotso House, the headquarters of the South African Council of Churches. At the time it happened the then Minister of Law and Order, Mr. Vlok, had announced unashamedly and blatantly that it was the work of the ANC and he accused Mrs. Shirley Gunn, who as a consequence was detained for six months. Mr. Vlok, to his credit in his amnesty application for ordering this terrorist act, did apologize handsomely to Mrs. Gunn. We now know what happened to Steve Biko, to the Cradock Four, the African National Congress-aligned activists whose charred bodies were found in their burnt-out car.

We have exhumed over fifty remains of those who were abducted, killed secretly and buried secretly, and returned their remains to their relatives who have given them decent burials. They have thanked the Truth and Reconciliation Commission for helping them to experience closure. We now know that the apartheid government had a Chemical and Biological Warfare Program that was not just defensive as they had claimed. It was also offensive. Some of the perpetrators have said that they had projects aimed at reducing the fertility of black women. They were looking for toxins that would target only black people. They wanted to poison Nelson Mandela in prison so that his brain would be damaged and he would not survive too long after his release. Mercifully, they were often inept and they failed in their nefarious scheme.

Can you imagine what would have happened to reconciliation had they succeeded? They nearly succeeded in poisoning Dr. Frank Chikane, now director general in the deputy president's office. How many other attempts of this sort were there and how many did succeed? We don't know. They produced Ecstasy tablets. Is it accidental that there is a drug problem in some black areas?

Reconciliation is not cheap or easy and it is not something that a Truth and Reconciliation Commission can achieve with the wave of a magic wand. It is going to be a long haul, a slow and demanding process to which every South African would be expected to contribute. It should be a national project. The Truth and Reconciliation Commission operated under the auspices of an act entitled The Promotion of National Unity and Reconciliation Act. The Truth and Reconciliation Commission was conceived to promote, not achieve, reconciliation. And yet there have been some moving instances when perpetrator and victim have been reconciled, when the one asked for and the other gave forgiveness.

The head of the Ciskei Homeland government declared the Ciskei a no-go area for the African National Congress which protested this ban by marching on Bisho, the Ciskeian capital. The Ciskeian Defence Force (CDF) opened fire on the demonstrators, killing several and wounding many others. We held a hearing on this Bisho massacre. The first witness was the former head of the CDF. He riled us all by how he said whatever he said.

The next set of witnesses was a quartet of CDF former officers, three blacks and one white, their spokesperson. He said to this jam-packed hall, filled with those who had been injured or had lost loved ones in the massacre, "Yes, we ordered the troops to open fire." And you could feel the tension in the room rising. Then he turned to the audience and said, "Please forgive us. Please accept my colleagues back into the community."

Do you know what that audience did? It broke out into deafening applause. When it had subsided, I said, "Let's keep quiet for a while. We are in the presence of something holy." Yes, you have sometimes felt that the only right response would have been to remove your shoes because you were standing on holy ground.

Or Mr. Smit, an Afrikaner father of an eight-year-old who was killed by a bomb attack by the African National Congress at a Wimpy bar. He said he wasn't angry. If he was angry it was not at the African National Congress, but at the previous apartheid government. He believed that his son's death had somehow contributed to the transformation happening in the country. We really do have some remarkable people.

We see in the South African example a people trying to come to terms with their often horrendous plight, eschewing the options of revenge, Nuremberg trials, amnesia through blanket amnesty, opting for the novel way of seeking reconciliation through the truth. It is not going to be easy for we are past masters and mistresses at rationalization, at self-justification and at entering the denial mode.

We are a traumatized and wounded nation seeking healing through truth and reconciliation and dealing with the postconflict, postrepression in this unique way. Perhaps South Africa will be a beacon of hope. The divine sense of humour is exquisite. Who could ever have thought of South Africa as a sign of anything except the most awful ghastliness? Precisely. God wants us to succeed for the sake of God's world so that God can point those many trouble spots in the world to South Africa and say, "They are such an unlikely, so unprepossessing a bunch. They had a nightmare called apartheid. It has ended. Your nightmare will end too. They used to say their problem was intractable, well they are solving it." Nowhere can anyone ever say again that a problem is intractable.

It is possible to move from conflict to peace and stability relatively peacefully. It is possible to negotiate the rapids of transition from repression to democracy and the rule of law and respect for human rights. It is possible to do so without unleashing destructive and destabilizing counter forces. Yes, the South African Truth and Reconciliation Commission is a model worth trying.

The Challenge
of the Future for
Human Rights

Mary Robinson is the United Nations high
commissioner for human rights and the former
president of Ireland. Upon taking office as Ireland's
president in 1990, she became a powerful catalyst for
change, strengthening Ireland's economic, political
and cultural links with other countries. She is considered the most influential and most popular president in
Irish history. In recognition of her work on behalf of
developing countries, she was awarded the Special
CARE Humanitarian Award.

11

I WELCOME THE OPPORTUNITY TO ADDRESS this important international
conference here in Edmonton on Universal Rights and Human Values: *Les
Droits Universels et les Valeurs Humaines*. It is a conference that touches on
many issues that need to be addressed, especially during this anniversary year. I
am glad to be in the company of two fellow speakers whom I have met before
and with whom I have had very valuable exchanges. In the case of Chief Justice
Lamer, we only had one meeting, when I came to Canada on a previous occasion
as president of Ireland, and he gave me a talking stick. He told me that if I was
holding it nobody else could speak, but I tried it out from time to time on family
and friends and it doesn't work!

I recall many meetings with Archbishop Desmond Tutu and it is a pleasure to
see him again this evening. I particularly remember one evening, the night
before the inauguration of President Nelson Mandela, when I sat beside
Archbishop Desmond Tutu and his wife. While we were waiting for the last
speech of President De Klerk and the last speech of President Elect of Nelson
Mandela, before he became president the following day, Archbishop Tutu
turned to me and said, "Do you really understand what has happened here?"

I remember feeling very humbled and feeling that I could understand intel-
lectually that it was a wonderful moment for human rights, for the new South
Africa, and for all that was going to be put in place later, but you would have to

have been a South African to have truly appreciated what a momentous day it was.

I saw something of what the change meant in action in the work of the Truth and Reconciliation Commission, which Archbishop Tutu has chaired so courageously and which has been a wonderful example of a country coming out of conflict into generosity and trying to build peace and reconciliation, while not always getting the kind of response that it deserved. In the long struggle to embed a culture of human rights throughout the world, we should cherish our victories and the transition to a new South Africa must be regarded as one of the great modern triumphs for human rights.

Turning to this year, I have maintained that the fiftieth anniversary of the Universal Declaration is an occasion to be marked rather than one for celebration. We cannot celebrate when millions are still victims of torture, repression, hunger and terrible poverty; when millions of children are dying because they do not have access to safe water or to basic health care; when trafficking in women and children is on the increase in many places; when discrimination on the basis of race, ethnicity and religion denies populations all round the world their most basic dignity; when we know that horrors like those that moved the framers of the Declaration—including John Humphrey to whom I pay particular tribute here in Edmonton—to say "Never again" still exist.

These very horrors have revisited the people of Cambodia, Rwanda and Bosnia not so long ago. And we don't have to look outside any particular country to find human rights problems. It is important that I bring home the message, as High Commissioner for Human Rights, that all countries have human rights problems, including Canada.

I learned today, during what was an enjoyable, memorable visit to Hobbema First Nations reserve outside Edmonton, about some of the issues of discrimination. There was pain among the people I met, flowing particularly from the past, but also a sense of exclusion in the present as they combat those problems.

I was presented with a publication that impressed me greatly: *The Rights Path—Alberta*. It is published by the Aboriginal Human Rights Committee and was presented to me by Muriel Venn. The publication is an extraordinarily good way of educating about human rights, which is a subject I wanted to touch on briefly in the context of looking towards the future. It shows us that when we talk about human rights education, it is all about participation and empowerment. It is about knowing not only what the rights are but how to access them, how to follow through. What do these rights really mean? How can I stand up for my rights? How can I stand up for the rights of others? What are the duties and the obligations involved? What impressed me was the simple language and yet the empowerment in this booklet and that it reflects the quality of access here in Canada to knowing your rights.

Access is not necessarily so easy in many countries. There is not, first of all, access to education itself, access to literacy. We have a long way to go and that is our challenge. The vision of fifty years ago demands that we implement change through human rights education—especially in this decade of human rights education, which began in 1995. We are actively pursuing our goals especially during this anniversary year but it must go beyond this year.

Predicting what lies ahead is a difficult task. Who would have foreseen fifty years ago the technological advances that have taken place, the information revolution, the conquest of space? Every generation feels that the times are changing and uncertain, but the present generation is experiencing change at a dizzying speed. Many wonders undoubtedly await us. Radical changes are already underway in the scientific and health fields, and the issues they raise will have to be faced up to. It may be that new horrors lie ahead as well. The pessimist would point to the dangers of conflict between cultures, of environmental catastrophe, of an ever-widening and destabilizing chasm between rich and poor. This is our world of 1998 and, coming to the new millennium, this is what we have to educate our young about. We are not powerless in the face of these challenges. Strength can be drawn from the fact that what seemed strange at one time is later accepted as the norm.

The Universal Declaration of Human Rights was viewed with scepticism when it first appeared because there was no enforcement mechanism. No one foresaw what an inspiration it would be, for example, to President Nelson Mandela. He has spoken of the Declaration as a light in the dark days, an inspiration in very difficult times. The power of its message won through. The notion of rights as universal and indivisible was regarded as impossibly idealistic, but today that is the cornerstone of our human rights philosophy. And today we have enforcement mechanisms, we have an International Court, we have the range of monitoring mechanisms of my office.

The task we face on this fiftieth anniversary is to breathe new life into the Universal Declaration so as to face the challenges of the future while remaining true to its basic aims. There may be less consensus today on moral and ethical values but that should not deter us. We should start from the same point as the framers of the Declaration started: that all human beings are born free and equal in dignity and rights.

If we build on that foundation, if all the young people here today relate that to their world, and to the means of communication within their world, reaching out to those who do not have the same starting point or life chances; if we build on that foundation and on the principles of respect for the individual and for each other's cultures and an acknowledgement of our interdependence on the planet, we will be on the right path to fulfilling the vision of fifty years ago. And that is our challenge. Not just to honour but to implement in a real, practical way, the vision of fifty years ago.

ANTONIO LAMER

Towards a Human Rights Culture

Antonio Lamer is the chief justice of Canada. He is also chairman of the Canadian Judicial Council, the Advisory Council of the Order of Canada and the Board of Governors of the National Judicial Institute. He was awarded the Order of Merit by the University of Montréal and the Knight of Justice by the Order of St. John.

FOR ME, AS CHIEF JUSTICE OF CANADA, the development, ratification and widespread implementation of the Universal Declaration and the ideas it contains is one of the great triumphs of the 20th century. When we recognize the impact of this document on the global legal culture, we are really celebrating a phenomenon of extraordinary proportions. The Universal Declaration of Human Rights is the embodiment of a profound set of ideals as to how all human beings should interact with one another. It counsels respect for their dignity and worth, their equality of status, and the protection of their autonomy from state interference and abuses of state authority. It represents, therefore, the transformation of a humanistic philosophy into a legal instrument of deep and enduring global significance.

Just think of the magnitude of the impact that this document has had over the five decades since 1948. Starting just with the instruments promulgated within the United Nations system, we have the 1966 Covenants on Civil and Political Rights, and Economic, Social and Cultural Rights. Along with those very fundamental documents, of enormous significance in their own right, we have witnessed the issuance of further international human rights conventions, such as the International Convention on the Elimination of All Forms of Racial Discrimination, the Convention on the Elimination of All Forms of Discrimination Against Women, the Convention Against Torture and Other Cruel, Inhuman or Degrading Treatment or Punishment, and the Convention on the Rights of the Child. Parallel to the United Nations human rights measures, yet traceable still to the Universal Declaration, are the regional human rights systems, such as those in Europe and the Americas. Many nations of the world have enacted their own domestic human rights standards that derive in whole or in part from the Universal Declaration.

As a Canadian jurist I feel a special affinity for the Universal Declaration, in part because of the involvement of a great many Canadians in it, beginning, of course, with former Professor John Humphrey of McGill University whose contribution to the drafting of the Universal Declaration of Human Rights was so important. I had the pleasure and honour of working with Professor Humphrey when he chaired the Canadian Human Rights Foundation and, I am proud to say, I was on his board of directors. In the field of human rights, he was a giant. His death in 1995 was a great loss to the Canadian human rights community. But the other reason for my affinity for the Universal Declaration is because that Declaration, and the treaties that followed it, provided much of the inspiration for the adoption of the legal instruments that protect human rights in Canada—our federal and provincial human rights statutes, the federal statutory Bill of Rights of 1960 and, finally and most importantly, the Canadian Charter of Rights and Freedoms.

The Universal Declaration sparked the beginning of the international human rights movement and the growth, both internationally and within many individual states, of what I like to refer to as a culture of human rights. Let me describe what I mean by a human rights culture. To my mind, a human rights culture describes a state of affairs in which three basic conditions obtain. First, there must be an acknowledgement by the state that the rights and powers that it possesses are those that have been yielded to it by individuals who are, by virtue simply of their membership in the human race, born with a constellation of universal rights and freedoms. A human rights culture cannot exist where the state believes that human rights are something that it, in its beneficence, bestows on individuals. Second, citizens must be secure in the knowledge that they are free to assert their rights against the state without fear of reprisal. Third, there must exist an appropriate forum for the resolution of human rights issues which is competent, enjoys independence and acts impartially—in other words, an independent and impartial judiciary applying the rule of law.

It is only where these conditions exist that individuals, leaders, lawyers, judges, governments and institutions will come to regard the norms laid down in human rights instruments as being authoritative and worthy of respect. Human rights law can only be effective where it is supported by a firm and deep-seated commitment to the importance of human rights in our world.

Such a human rights culture has taken hold in many countries of the world and the global community has also gone a long way towards it. Again, I see this as an outgrowth of the Universal Declaration of Human Rights. Its recognition by the community of nations and its progeny at the international and domestic levels have provided widely accepted reference points from which we now tend to evaluate alleged human rights violations. This, in my view, is a phenomenon of supreme importance in the history of the modern world.

But we still have far to go. As Mary Robinson recently said, "The moment is ripe for momentous change" in the promotion and protection of human rights. We have a long way to go to achieve full implementation of the noble ideals contained in the Universal Declaration of Human Rights. In particular, the development of a culture of human rights in many countries, for historical, social, political and economic reasons, will be very difficult and very slow. We all have to do our part to assist those countries in every way we can. In this respect I am very proud of the efforts the Canadian judiciary has made over recent years to assist various countries in improving their legal systems generally and, more particularly, assuring the independence of their judiciary. We shall continue in this vein because the cause is a good one and we have already seen the fruits of our labours.

I urge you all to do what you can to further the growth of a human rights culture around the world so that the ideals and values contained in this marvellous document, the Universal Declaration of Human Rights, can be enjoyed by those who have not yet benefited from them.

ANTONIO LAMER

ANNE McLELLAN

Vision and Reality

The Declaration Fifty Years Later

Anne McLellan is Canada's minister of justice and attorney general. She is a former minister of natural resources and professor of law at the University of Alberta.

IN SOME WAYS IT IS PERHAPS IRONIC that an official of a government should be given the honour of addressing a conference on human rights since the human rights movement has been largely about individuals seeking protection from the abuses of the state. The progress that the world has made in advancing human rights in the last half century is largely due to the efforts of nongovernmental players—human rights activists, nongovernmental organizations, legal scholars and international civil servants.

If he were still alive, John Humphrey, the Canadian law professor who headed the UN's Human Rights Division during its first twenty years—and who was a leading proponent and a principal architect of the Declaration—might be addressing this gathering in my place. Indeed, it would have been appropriate for any number of prominent human rights activists to tender these opening remarks.

But if there is a reason for asking a government official to launch a conference celebrating the Declaration's fiftieth birthday, it is that the adoption of the Declaration represents the moment in history when a large number of governments—forty-eight in all—voluntarily and in writing agreed to forgo part of their sovereignty in order to advance the rights of individuals. They did so after the most terrifying tragedy of this century, the Holocaust, had revealed its full horror.

The drafting and signing of the Declaration was itself an act of collective imagination that seized on what is best in us—hope, reason and compassion. And we are still captivated by its promise today.

▰▰▰ Birth of a Vision

Although it is generally acknowledged that these forty-eight governments never intended to incur a legal obligation to guarantee the rights set forth in the Declaration, that's ultimately what they did. By adopting the Universal Declaration, the members of the UN General Assembly approved the blueprint for a colossal construction project that continues to this day and has forever changed the international legal landscape.

From the beginning the Declaration quickly became in inspiration for legally binding human rights treaties. This was despite the fact that the onset of the cold war had dramatically slowed the drafting of those covenants that were to complete the International Bill of Human Rights. The Declaration's provisions began almost immediately to influence national constitutions and regional instruments. Within two years of the Declaration's adoption, the countries of western Europe had transformed most of its provisions into conventional law by signing the European Convention for the Protection of Human Rights and Fundamental Freedoms (1950).

In the last thirty years, the Declaration has spawned a whole body of international law—binding legal standards—that details the rights of individuals and the obligations of governments; treaties that refine and elaborate the lofty principles set out in the Declaration. Some of those treaties, like the more recently adopted Convention on the Rights of the Child, have received near universal ratification.

Others, including the International Covenant on Economic, Social and Cultural Rights and Political Rights, have been ratified by about three-quarters of United Nations' members. The number of ratifications of these treaties continues to grow, and impending anniversaries of the Universal Declaration still have the power to coax new signatures from reluctant governments.

When officials from 171 nations gathered in Vienna for an international conference on human rights in June 1993, the timing was intended to galvanize action by governments to make good on the promise of the Universal Declaration in the five years leading up to its fiftieth anniversary. In their Program of Action, the delegates in Vienna called on all governments to ratify the main international human rights treaties, with the result that more than one thousand new ratifications or accessions to these treaties have been deposited in the last five years alone.

But the ratification of a human rights treaty, important as it is, is only a first step. It is not enough for governments to sign a contract pledging to safeguard the rights of individuals in their jurisdictions. They must go further. They must give practical effect to those guarantees—in judicial interpretation, domestic legislation, public policy and executive action. And they must promote dialogue, education and training, taking concrete steps to ensure that the values and principles set out in international treaties are institutionalized in civil society.

Even in Canada, where we pride ourselves on our broad acceptance of international human rights norms, work remains to be done to move from the promise to the performance of our international obligations. The challenge for lawmakers and law enforcers everywhere in the next fifty years will be to translate the growing body of paper commitments into the actual daily enjoyment of human rights by even more individuals.

From Vision to Reality: The Canadian Experience

The signing of the UN Declaration was the starting point of the international human rights movement. Canada's commitment to the legislative protection of rights and freedoms was signalled in 1958 when a draft Canadian Bill of Rights was presented to Parliament.

The prime minister at the time, the late John Diefenbaker, told the House of Commons that he saw the Bill of Rights as a first step for Canada to live up to the UN Declaration. As he said, "This measure...is the first step on the part of Canada to carry out the acceptance either of the international declaration of human rights or of the principles [contained in] that noble document."

While an important achievement, the Canadian Bill of Rights was soon viewed, particularly in the decades that saw rapid growth within the human rights movement, as but a stepping stone. Since the bill was enacted in 1960, we have built a solid domestic human rights framework, including federal and provincial human rights legislation, and finally, the Canadian Charter of Rights and Freedoms.

For Canada, the Charter has done more to make international human rights law a domestic reality than any other Canadian achievement. Both the drafting history of the Charter and its final text exhibit the rich influence of the Universal Declaration and other international human rights instruments, and Canadian courts have not failed to take notice. At least 135 reported judicial decisions have cited the Declaration or other international human rights instruments as aids in interpreting Canadian human rights legislation, including the Charter.

Perhaps one of the most inspiring of these statements was made by the late Chief Justice Brian Dickson in a 1987 decision of the Supreme Court of Canada (Reference Re: Public Service Employee Relations Act [1987] 1 S.C.R. 313) where he wrote: "A body of treaties (or conventions) and customary norms now constitute an international law of human rights under which the nations of the world have undertaken to adhere to the standards and principles necessary for ensuring freedom, dignity and social justice for their citizens. The Charter conforms to the spirit of this contemporary international human rights movement, and it incorporates many of the policies and prescriptions of the various international documents pertaining to human rights. [These] must, in my opinion, be relevant and persuasive sources for interpretation of the Charter's provisions."

Elsewhere in that judgement, he said: "I believe that the Charter should generally be presumed to provide protection at least as great as that afforded by similar provisions in international human rights documents which Canada has ratified."

The growing tendency of Canadian courts to consider international human rights standards in interpreting Canadian law is a development to be encouraged. Consider the Supreme Court decision in the *Keegstra* case, a landmark decision respecting a state's ability to take measures to combat hate speech in light of freedom of expression.

In this case, the Supreme Court of Canada deemed the negative consequences of derision, hostility and abuse encouraged by hate propaganda on individual self-worth to be irreconcilable "in a nation that prides itself on tolerance and the fostering of human dignity through...respect for the many racial, religious and cultural groups in our society." The Court cited various international human rights instruments which called upon states to prohibit incitement to hatred and noted that such international condemnation of hate speech buttressed the objective behind Canada's prohibition.

The government has a responsibility to promote and uphold human rights by ensuring the federal legislation respects international human rights obligations and the Charter. Through legislative review, officials in my department are involved in reviewing new legislation, policies and programs for consistency with the Charter and, in certain circumstances, for consistency with Canada's international human rights obligations.

But expecting government to safeguard human rights on its own, even in a democratic society as open and tolerant as ours, is insufficient. It is for this very reason that we have the good fortune to have so many institutions—the courts, federal and provincial human rights commissions and other administrative tribunals—whose mandates and responsibilities are to ensure that Canadian citizens are protected from human rights abuses.

And here is where domestic and international human rights mechanisms play a critical role. I note with pride that the Canadian Human Rights Commission, one of these mechanisms, celebrates its twentieth anniversary this year, and the Alberta Human Rights and Citizenship Commission, its twenty-fifth.

In the past decade or so, the government of Canada has also sought to advance our understanding of equality and official language minority rights under the Charter of Rights and Freedoms through a program that enables individuals and groups to challenge federal legislation in the courts. The Court Challenges Program has been used to strike down federal legislation found to be discriminatory, and it has done much to foster and promote a human rights culture in Canada.

But such domestic mechanisms are still not enough. That is precisely why we have international human rights regimes with their monitoring mechanisms.

One monitoring mechanism is the requirement that states report on the extent to which they have complied with their obligations under human rights treaties. In this way, states are put under the uncomfortable spotlight of international scrutiny. Another monitoring mechanism is the individual petition system that enables individuals to petition the UN directly when they believe their rights have been violated. It is important that governments recognize the jurisdiction of the various treaty bodies to hear such petitions.

So far, the act of according recognition has not been as whole-hearted as one might hope, for reasons that are perhaps understandable. No government wants to be hauled before an international tribunal for failing to live up to its international obligations. Yet, if human rights guarantees are to have any real meaning, alleged violations by a state must be reviewable by an international tribunal. One of the most important aspects of individual complaint procedures is that it allows state practices to be scrutinized at the international level—where domestic scrutiny has been exhausted. States, including Canada, need to be open to such scrutiny and be prepared for potential criticism. This is one of the ways that human rights law improves at home.

Since Canada signed the Optional Protocol to the International Covenant on Civil and Political Rights, recognizing the jurisdiction of the UN Human Rights Committee to receive and rule on human rights complaints from individual Canadians, we have had the dubious distinction of being much complained against. But if I may turn that criticism into a compliment, I think this is indicative of a healthy and active human rights culture in Canada. Most cases are dismissed as inadmissible or for not revealing a violation. However, one of the first Canadian complaints heard by the UN Human Rights Committee resulted in Canada repealing a provision of the Indian Act. This sent a clear signal to all Canadians: the right to address human rights issues does not stop at national borders.

All of these mechanisms, domestic and international, are the institutional after-effects of the Universal Declaration and we should embrace and use them. But, in saying this, I don't mean to minimize the difficulty for governments to do so.

This brings me to one final point about implementation. If we are really to make progress on some of the emerging human rights issues of the day, governments must do even more than revise their laws, set up domestic redress mechanisms and recognize the jurisdiction of international tribunals.

This is especially true when it comes to addressing issues such as social and economic equality. Achieving a great measure of economic and social equality in an era of economic globalization has proven to be a significant challenge for all governments. This includes Canada, where we too face issues such as the growing disparity between rich and poor, child poverty, homelessness and the unacceptable living conditions of many aboriginal peoples on First Nations reserves. Increasingly in Canada, federal and provincial governments are working together in areas such as social services, health programs and employment equity to turn international commitments into action.

One example is Canada's National Children's Agenda, with its equalization payments to disadvantaged families and an Aboriginal Head Start program that seeks to achieve not only equality of opportunity for aboriginal children, but equality of results.

All of us, rich countries as well as poor, still have a great deal of work to do to fulfil the promise of the Universal Declaration. Our work may even increase in the future. This is partly because our concept of human rights is evolving, encompassing, for some, issues that were not even conceived of by the drafters of the Universal Declaration. As recently as ten years ago, violence against women was considered by all but a few radical feminists to be a matter for criminal law, not human rights law. Yet by 1993 at the World Conference on Human Rights, governments had made the elimination of violence against women "in public and private life" a central plank of the Vienna Declaration and Program of Action.

■■■■ Conclusion

In 1948 could we possibly have imagined the world in which the Universal Declaration would be tested fifty years later? Could we fifty years ago have foreseen the human rights implications of economic globalization? Could we have perceived the issues that new reproductive technologies might one day raise, or divine the extent to which communications technologies might one day threaten individual privacy?

These issues are being placed on the rights agenda because of pressure from social justice groups, women's groups, disability rights activists, environmental groups, artists and writers the world over. And the pressure is growing at an ever-accelerating pace, in a phenomenon the *Globe and Mail* recently called "the globalization of conscience."

As this human rights consciousness gains strength, government action and inaction will come under growing public scrutiny. And this is good. History shows that governments don't relinquish their sovereignty graciously. One of the great accomplishments of the international human rights movement is the steadiness with which it has held a mirror up to our actual, not our idealized, social and political lives.

Fifty years ago, the UN Declaration gave us our benchmarks and now, after a period of reflection, celebration and accounting for our actions, we look to individuals like you to take us to the next step, to the next level. In choosing these steps, remember that an International Criminal Court was one of the unrealized goals of the original drafters of the Declaration. We now have an International Criminal Court to deal with the Rwandas and Kosovos of the next millennium.

Remember also that for some years we fought for a UN High Commissioner for Human Rights and now we have her—Mary Robinson.

Let me conclude by reflecting on a speech given by Karl Popper, an Austrian philosopher, to the Institut des Arts in Brussels in the wake of World War II. Karl Popper offered an insight that should appeal as much to the prodders as it does to government officials: "The appeal of utopianism arises from our failure to realize that we cannot make heaven on earth. What I believe we can do instead is to make life a little less terrible and a little less unjust in each generation. A good deal can be achieved in this way."

Fifty years—two generations—after the signing of the Universal Declaration, we can share, perhaps rejoice, in the prudent optimism of Karl Popper. Life is a little less terrible, life is a little less unjust. This is in large part because of the committed people, men and women around the world, who have an unwavering commitment to human rights and to the inherent dignity, value and equality of all persons, regardless of where they live.

DAVID KILGOUR

Half a Century of Human Rights

David Kilgour has served as a member of the Canadian
Parliament since 1979 and is currently the secretary of
state for Latin America and Africa. He has authored
several books on politics and received numerous
awards, including the B'nai Brith Canada
Human Rights Award.

THE CONCEPT OF UNIVERSALITY is what makes the UN Declaration of
Human Rights so important. Although some nations still try to sweep human
rights abuses under the outdated carpet of national sovereignty, this has become
less and less accepted. More and more, human rights are a universal concern. As
UN Secretary General Kofi Annan has said, "It is the universality of human
rights that gives them their strength and endows them with the power to cross
any border, climb any wall, defy any force."

While the declaration itself was not legally binding in the sense of imposing
sanctions on nations that violated its principles, it nonetheless asserted those
principles as a yardstick against which both governments and peoples could be
measured. It also provided the impetus for many legal documents, both international and domestic, including Canada's own Charter of Rights entrenched in
our constitution.

The idea that there should be universal standards of human rights has become
much more broadly accepted in the past fifty years, but it has always faced
difficulties. Some governments use phrases such as "cultural relativism" to
suggest that certain human rights are somehow a Western standard imposed on
them from outside. Yet some rights are so fundamental they must be common
to all of humanity. Again, to quote Annan: "Human rights, properly understood
and justly interpreted, are foreign to no culture and native to all nations."

27

■ Dangerous Developments in the 1990s

The collapse of communism and the end of the cold war by no means ended the catalogue of 20th-century violations of human dignity. The world is no longer divided between two opposing camps facing each other in a nuclear stand-off, but we now find ourselves struggling with the ugliest forms of nationalism, interethnic hatred and religious rivalries released from the constraints of a bipolar world.

State sovereignty and the doctrine of noninterference in the internal matters of another state have long provided a convenient cover for tyrants to carry out human rights abuses with impunity. As present events in Kosovo show, that era is ending. Vaclav Havel, president of the Czech Republic, enunciated a newer vision when he addressed Canada's Parliament in April 1999:

> The alliance of which both Canada and the Czech Republic are now members is waging a struggle against the genocidal regime of Slobodan Milosevic. It is neither an easy struggle nor a popular one, and there can be different opinions on its strategy and tactics. But no person of sound judgement can deny one thing: This is probably the first war ever fought that is not being fought in the name of interests, but in the name of certain principles and values. If it is possible to say about a war that it is ethical, or that it is fought for ethical reasons, it is true of this war. Kosovo has no oil fields whose output might perhaps attract somebody's interest; no member country of the alliance has any territorial claims there; and Milosevic is not threatening either the territorial integrity, or any other integrity, of any NATO member. Nevertheless, the alliance is fighting. It is fighting in the name of human interest for the fate of other human beings. It is fighting because decent people cannot sit back and watch systematic, state-directed massacres of other people. Decent people simple cannot tolerate this, and cannot fail to come to the rescue if a rescue action is within their power.

Despite the sovereignty shibboleth of some governments, recent initiatives by the United Nations demonstrate that it is quite capable of intervening in a nation's affairs, often in the name of protecting human rights or providing humanitarian assistance, even if the nation concerned is vehemently opposed to the intervention. The transformation of South Africa, the Gulf war, the democratization of Namibia, the UN efforts in Cambodia and Bosnia, and the NATO intervention in Kosovo—all demonstrate that the wider international community now has an opportunity to introduce order, peace and relief where there is chaos, conflict and vast human suffering.

Canada and Rights

Canada is an active participant in the promotion of human rights. Our immigration policies that have done much to build a more tolerant country have also provided refuge for many victims of oppression and have given special importance to the unification of families, but there remains room for concern.

An effective foreign policy on human rights does not have to entail drastic cuts in foreign aid budgets, severance of trade agreements or altruistic forgiveness of debt (although Canada and other countries who have forgiven some debt of the poorest nations should be applauded for doing so). Commonwealth governments, as an important international community, could vote against multilateral agency loans to oppressive regimes; we might as individual governments push harder against human rights violators within the UN, francophone and Commonwealth countries generally.

DAVID KILGOUR

LLOYD AXWORTHY

Human Rights and Foreign Policy

Lloyd Axworthy is Canada's minister of foreign affairs.
He has been a member of Parliament for twenty years
and is also a member of the Privy Council. He received
the Council of Europe's 1998 North–South Peace Prize
for his work in securing an international treaty to ban
anti-personnel mines.

HUMAN RIGHTS HAVE BEEN MUCH IN THE NEWS RECENTLY. During his visit to Asia this month (November 1998), Prime Minister Chrétien highlighted the human rights dimension of our foreign policy. He called attention to some of Canadians' concerns about repressive governments. The current visit to Canada of the United Nations high commissioner for human rights, Mary Robinson, has further focused attention on international human rights challenges. Two days ago (24 November 1998), the British House of Lords denied Chilean General Augusto Pinochet immunity from prosecution for serious human rights violations. This is a milestone decision. It marks a major step in the battle against impunity and gives renewed impetus to the creation of an International Criminal Court.

The world is a different place than it was fifty, twenty-five or even ten years ago. Over the past decade, the course of global events has shifted from the stale impasse of the cold war to a new, evolving, still uncertain path towards the next century. The face of war has changed—civilians, especially the most vulnerable, are increasingly the main victims and targets of violent conflict. Many of the challenges we face are transnational: protection of children, arms proliferation, illicit drugs. These threats have no borders and have a direct impact on daily lives everywhere. In a wired world of instantaneous communications and a global economy, our lives are more interdependent than ever.

We continue to grapple with how to deal with these changes. However, one thing is certain. These new realities put the individual—the security of the individual—at the centre of our concerns. The old conventional wisdom that international matters were a dialogue between states, has now shifted to focus on promoting and advancing the interests of the individual. Promoting humanitarian objectives, increasing protection from abuse, reducing risks of physical endangerment, improving quality of life and creating the tools to guarantee these goals are providing a new impetus for concerted global action.

For fifty years Canada has been committed to advancing international human rights. This legacy is now helping to shape a human security approach to our foreign policy. We have built an impressive international human rights record. Ever since Canadian John Humphrey drafted the first version of the Universal Declaration of Human Rights, Canada has played a prominent role in advancing, defending and expanding the reach of human rights at the UN and elsewhere on the international stage. First, we have worked hard to strengthen the human rights system, notably, through the creation of the UN High Commissioner for Human Rights and support for human rights treaty bodies. At the United Nations we proposed and moved forward the creation of special rapporteurs to focus on specific threats, such as those to freedom of opinion and expression and violence against women. We advocated the inclusion of women's human rights as an integral part of the global human rights agenda. And we obtained international agreement on a binding convention to protect human rights defenders.

These achievements were made in partnership with others but we can be justifiably proud of the Canadian contribution in giving form and life to the lofty principles of the Universal Declaration. They reflect an impulse for toler-ance, democracy and respect—important features of Canadian society. They also highlight our belief in shared values and standards, as well as a sense of a common human community. The Universal Declaration has served as the model for an expanding web of international human rights norms and mecha-nisms. The assertion of state sovereignty—which for so long served as a pretext to hide human rights abuses—is losing its potency and credibility. Some states have shown a new willingness to accept scrutiny of their human rights records. International organizations are finding new courage to probe those records, through on-site visits by monitors and special rapporteurs and the establish-ment of international human rights offices in the field.

Undeniably, there has been progress since the Universal Declaration was concluded. And there are positive trends. However, our approach to human rights must continue to evolve. Our human rights activities must keep pace with the changes around us. As Prime Minister Chrétien recently noted, the respect for human rights is an increasingly crucial actor in stability, security and good governance everywhere, and upon which our own well-being resides.

For these reasons we must attempt to broaden the range and scope of human rights initiatives. This means sustaining efforts at the United Nations, while making new efforts at the regional and bilateral levels. This means main-streaming human rights into all other aspects of our global activities. This means establishing and expanding partnerships with civil society. Finally, this means developing innovative tools with which to advance human rights goals.

Canada, as a member of the bureau of the UN Commission on Human Rights in 1998, has worked with the Office of the High Commissioner to ensure that the international human rights mechanisms are strong enough to fulfil the tasks we have given them. Canada has announced a contribution of $500,000 to the work of the High Commissioner in Colombia to build lasting peace by strengthening human rights. We will maintain our active engagement at the United Nations to ensure human rights decisions are implemented effectively. We must also pursue human rights goals at the regional level. In the Americas we have made human rights and democracy a central pillar of the Summit of the Americas process, as well as at the Organization of American States (OAS). At the Asia Pacific Economic Conference (APEC) Summit in Kuala Lumpur, we put a motion on the table to ensure that the APEC discussions would also be accompanied by the direct involvement of civil societies in the Pacific Rim area. And in the Commonwealth, through the Commonwealth Ministerial Action Group (CMAG), we are working with others to advance democracy in Nigeria and Sierra Leone.

We have reached out at the bilateral level too, retooling our approach with a number of countries to develop civil society initiatives, construct democratic institutions and engage in serious human rights dialogue. This is the objective behind the establishment of bilateral human rights mechanisms with countries such as China, Cuba and Indonesia. Such agreements have led to substantive engagement on human rights issues and the opportunity to invest in building up human rights groups and institutions in these countries. For instance, with China, we have created a Joint Committee on Human Rights. It recently met in Winnipeg and Whitehorse to exchange views on a range of human rights issues. We held a plurilateral symposium on human rights, which included independent human rights institutions from the region. We are currently working on projects relating to legal reform and economic, social and cultural rights. As we broaden the "where" of human rights, we must also work on the "how" by integrating human rights concerns into other areas of foreign policy, including peace and security, disarmament, development and trade.

Respect for human rights is an important condition for lasting peace and security. Canada assumed its seat on the Security Council in January 1999. I have discussed with High Commissioner Mary Robinson how we can push for a more human-centred approach to the council's peace and security mandate. Human rights and humanitarian concerns should be better woven into the council's activities, for example, through greater consideration of the impact of conflict on civilians. Elsewhere, we are building on our traditional commitment to peacekeeping by including human rights and humanitarian assistance components in peace-support operations. The Organization for Security and Co-operation in Europe (OSCE) Kosovo Mission, involving military, civilian police and human rights monitors working side by side, is only the most recent example.

LLOYD AXWORTHY

The land mines treaty points to a new norm for global efforts in the area of disarmament. Concern about the devastating impact of these weapons on human security provided the main motivation for international action. For the first time, arms control concerns were combined with elements of humanitarian and human rights law. Canada has been looking at international development assistance through a human rights lens. Our development assistance includes extensive programming—$62 million in 1997 through 460 projects—in support of human rights goals and democratic development, the emergence of participatory and pluralistic societies, for governments that respect the rule of law and human rights, and through activities that promote economic, social, cultural rights, civil and political rights.

Perhaps the most contentious area in terms of mainstreaming human rights is the relationship between trade and human rights. The issue has never been a crude trade-off between promoting commerce or human rights. They are not mutually exclusive but mutually reinforcing. The promotion of good governance, democracy and human rights are essential to the creation of a climate for sustainable economic development which benefits everyone. Economic prosperity, in turn, enhances the prospects for stable societies which allow human rights to flourish. The Asian crisis shows what can happen when this equation is out of balance.

Almost three years ago, when I addressed our annual consultations with non-governmental organizations (NGOs) for the first time, I underlined the need to fold human concerns into commercial and financial issues. This is still the case. But we have been making progress. We have been working to establish rules that strengthen the link between trade and the respect for human rights. At the International Labour Organization (ILO), Canada actively worked for the adoption of the Declaration on Fundamental Principles and Rights at Work. We support Organization for Economic Co-operation and Development efforts to examine corporate codes for the ethical conduct of business abroad, while working with Canadian businesses to facilitate the development of voluntary codes of conduct.

I mentioned our efforts at APEC to address the human face of the crisis and to make globalization work better. The human impact, whether of financial crises or trade liberalization, cannot be ignored. I recently met with the Canadian directors at the International Financial Institutions to talk about how to reinforce good governance and democracy as a consideration in lending decisions. We need to better and more actively integrate human concerns into international forums that deal with commerce and trade. This is not utopian nonsense, it is simply good business sense. Human rights concerns are climbing out of their traditional box. As we integrate human rights concerns into other areas of international activities, we must also expand our horizons for co-operation.

The cast of actors on the international scene is expanding. States now share the stage with a growing number of NGOs, business associations and individuals. These actors can play a positive role, bringing new tools, resources and experience to the table. New creative partnerships with civil society are needed to move forward human security goals, including the international human rights agenda. A few examples come to mind. In regions where there is no intergovernmental human rights infrastructure, Asia for instance, regional networks of human rights defenders can help create a space for discussion of human rights. In isolationist regimes where human rights abuses might otherwise remain invisible—Burma, for instance, or Nigeria under the former regime—it is human rights NGOs that get information out to the international community and insist on action. In Cuba, we are working to expand the capacity for local NGOs to advance human rights goals. In many cases, government channels are still the best route for addressing human rights concerns and for pressing human rights themes onto the international agenda. However, in other instances, NGOs will be better placed than governments to make inroads and build local capacity for human rights.

Our past experience has provided valuable lessons about creating effective partnerships in the future. One of the most important is that those who have the most at stake should be closely involved. The most compelling voices during the land mines campaign were those of people who had survived land mine explosions. The most powerful advocates against child labour are the children who have suffered because of it. That is why Canada is committed to strengthening the field of human rights, to ensure that the vulnerable and the disenfranchised can find empowerment and express themselves. In Indonesia, for example, we have fostered the growth of an independent human rights institution through the Canadian Human Rights Commission. But we need to build capacity at home, too, something we have been doing through the Youth Internship Program and CANADEM, our stand-by force of human rights experts which is always ready to be deployed around the world.

The human rights of populations living in countries emerging from or at risk of conflict are particularly vulnerable. That is why we launched the Canadian Peacebuilding Initiative in 1996. It has supported over forty projects, from Central America to the African Great Lakes region to East Asia. The aim is to rebuild institutions and societies, thereby allowing countries to deal with conflict before it spills over into violence and leads to human rights abuses. New global instruments that expand the reach of international criminal law will also serve to advance international humanitarian and human rights law. The other side of human security is human responsibility.

The situation of General Pinochet has renewed focus on the problem of impunity for serious violations of international humanitarian law. Impunity impedes reconciliation—a prerequisite for lasting peace. Sooner or later, matters which are left unresolved will resurface. The expectation of impunity also encourages violators. It is an Achilles heel in efforts to promote human rights. The decision of the House of Lords makes clear the global dimension of this challenge and our collective responsibility to address the issue. It is precisely with this in mind that Canada is working to establish the International Criminal Court. The time has come for a permanent institution to deter some of the most egregious breaches of humanitarian law. The court will help ensure the respect for fundamental minimum standards of humanity. It will be an effective tool to ensure that those who commit abuses are held accountable. The Pinochet decision reaffirms the need for an International Court to help develop a framework with which national courts can work.

We recognize the need to constantly reevaluate and reassess our approaches. To that end, I announced an examination of our human rights strategy in December 1997. The objective was not to prepare another report, but to launch on ongoing dialogue—with the NGO community in particular—to maintain an open-ended process to reformulate and recalibrate our human rights approaches. This leads me to identify those areas that we believe need greater attention and resolution.

In an uncertain world it is the most vulnerable, in particular children, who are most at risk and who pay the highest price and, as a result, require special attention. There are three issues of particular concern: the sexual exploitation of children, child labour and war-affected children. We are working to conclude a protocol to the Convention on the Rights of the Child to address sexual exploitation while we attempt to better implement our own domestic legislation. Concerning child labour, efforts are underway at the ILO to develop a new convention aimed at eliminating the worst forms of child labour. At the same time, we will continue to pursue efforts to involve the private sector more actively in the development of codes of conduct. Our approach to war-affected children is multidimensional, with a focus on issues relating to child soldiers. In all areas, peace-building and development projects are underway to meet the needs of children victimized and traumatized by these abuses.

The reaction of some to the stresses of a world in transition is to retreat to more traditional, sometimes extreme, values as a way of asserting their identities. Freedom of religion appears particularly vulnerable in situations like these. No faith is exempt. Wherever religious intolerance appears—as it has recently in different forms in Indonesia, Russia, India or Iran—it must be opposed.

We are pursuing the issue on several fronts. This will be a priority subject at our consultations with NGOs in February 1999, in preparation for the UN Human Rights Commission. In the coming months the Centre for Foreign Policy Development is supporting a number of roundtables with Canadian civil society to address different aspects. As a follow-up to the Oslo Interfaith Declaration, we have been exploring a partnership on religious freedom with

Norway at both the government and civil society levels. Finally, the subject is part of the agenda in our bilateral human rights dialogues with China, Indonesia and Cuba. We are working hard to foster dialogue between Chinese and Canadian civil society groups. In Cuba, the progress made by the Catholic Church—most recently with Cuba's authorization for forty foreign religious workers to go there—results in no small part from the emphasis Canada and others have put on the issue.

The media remains at risk either by its use as an instrument for hate and division or through efforts to suppress access. We do not need to look far for examples. In November 1998, in British Columbia, newspaper editor Tara Singh Hayer was slain defending the right to free media in Canada. We must remain vigilant in exposing violations while taking measures to defend the principle of an independent media and the security of the individuals at risk. The UN Special Rapporteur on Freedom of Opinion and Expression was created for this purpose. These efforts need to be complemented by concrete assistance that nurtures a free and independent media. To this end, we have supported projects through the Canadian Peacebuilding Initiative in Bosnia, South Africa and, most recently, on the margins of APEC, where we are supporting the initiation of a regional network of journalists to defend and promote free media in the region.

If "the medium is the message," diversity in the medium is essential. Yet in an increasingly interconnected world, ownership of the medium is concentrated in fewer and fewer hands. We need to be wary that the range of information, opinion and viewpoints—the messages—are not diminished as a result. While the information superhighway can transport the best, it can also transport the worst. Hate speech, child pornography and child prostitution have moved onto the Internet. They have to be dislodged. The aim is not to control the Internet *per se,* but to take aim at those who would misuse it for criminal and other illegal activities that can hurt or harm.

Some months ago I received a wonderful gift, a talking stick, from Phil Fontaine, the head of Canada's Assembly of First Nations. It is a millennia-old technology. When handed to a speaker, it is supposed to imbue that person's words with courage, honesty and wisdom. We must sustain efforts to ensure that today's talking stick—cyberspace technology and the Internet—contributes to the common good and advances human rights while denying those who would foment hatred, crime or exploitation. The human rights website created by the Department of Foreign Affairs and International Trade, with hyperlinks to our new report, For the Record 1997: The UN Human Rights System, is a contribution to this effort.

For fifty years, Canada's commitment to advancing international human rights has been clear and consistent. We have accomplished a good deal. This legacy has helped to shape the human security approach to our foreign policy. Canada's human rights policy is an indispensable part of moving the human security agenda forward. Our objective now is to adapt this policy to keep up with and make the most of a changing global environment. I have outlined some of the emerging challenges and some of the ways we are responding. Canada has a special role to play. Given our own record, our history and our experience of building bridges with each other, we can also learn how to build better, more effective bridges around the world. Using ideas, shared values and partnerships we can influence events and promote human rights around the world.

Let me remind you of the words that were presented to John Humphrey to convince him to work on the Charter of the United Nations some fifty years ago. He was told, *"Ce sera là une grande aventure"*—this will be a great adventure. The fiftieth anniversary of this inspirational document is an appropriate occasion to reflect on the achievements, struggles and lessons learned in moving human rights forward. It is also the right time to think about how to continue "the great adventure."

Human Rights and Transnational Corporations

PEOPLE OR PROFITS?

People Before Profits

The Ogoni Experience and Shell

Owens Wiwa is coordinator of MOSOP-Canada
(Movement for the Survival of Ogoni People) and a
research scientist at the University of Toronto.
Detained and tortured by the Nigerian government
while working for MOSOP, he continues the work of his
late brother Ken Saro-Wiwa, campaigning for better
environmental practices and respect for human rights
by oil companies and governments in the
developing world.

IN MAY 1995 I WAS CONFRONTED WITH A SITUATION that demanded that I had to do something: I had to talk to business officials. I had been avoiding doing this for some time. What I'm going to talk about now illustrates exactly the choice between profit and people, a choice that the company had to make at the time. And I'll talk about what the company's decision was. It was a very trying period for me. My home, called Ogoni, was under military siege. Thirty villages out of 426 villages had come under attack by the military people.

Women were raped. Houses were burned down. Some people who could not run were shot at. My brother and many of my friends were in detention, held in very bad conditions in Nigeria. And we had to do something to stop it. We had appealed to Amnesty International, to The Body Shop, Sierra Club, Greenpeace— to organizations all over the world. And they were doing campaigns for the freedom of these people or at least for the human rights abuses that were being done on the children, on the women, to stop. But it did not stop.

So I went to see the acting Canadian High Commissioner in Nigeria and he introduced me to the Irish ambassador to Nigeria. And the Irish ambassador had a party and invited me and introduced me to the American ambassador to Nigeria. And the American ambassador then took me and introduced me to the British ambassador. This was happening because I had mentioned that I wanted to speak to the head of Shell in Nigeria.

Why did I want to speak to the head of Shell in Nigeria? We had talked with the top leaders in Nigeria. We had talked to the press. We had talked to the human rights group in Nigeria. Everybody was saying "Stop the violence against the people," but they also advised me to go and talk to Shell. Luckily, the British high commissioner arranged a meeting with the head of Shell. He told me that the head of Shell said he was going to discuss anything I wanted but that he did not want to discuss human rights abuses or reparations for the environmental damage done to the Ogoni people. I agreed that I wasn't going to discuss the issue of reparations. But, of course, the reason why I was going to meet him was the human rights abuses.

I was surprised when I was hiding in Lagos at a very secret location, when a car came up one day with diplomatic plates, and somebody came out and came to where I was hiding from the Nigerian military, and I was given an invitation to attend the Queen's birthday party in Nigeria. And I went there and I met the head of Shell, Brian Anderson, the head of Shell Nigeria. Over three meetings I literally begged him to use his influence on the Nigerian government to see that my brother and my colleagues were free or at least that they had a fair trial in a number of courts. He told me that that was a difficult thing for him to do but he would try if—and only if—I wrote a statement saying that no environmental damage had been caused by Shell in Ogoni. The story did not end there.

I managed to write this request to my brother. And my brother wrote back a letter in which he said I should show Brian Anderson, the head of Shell, our regional damage. And I went and showed him my brother's letter, which I have. And my brother said in his letter that there was no way we were going to tell a lie. He did actually say that if Shell did what they are supposed to do—respecting the people, dealing with the people, consulting with the people, instead of military dictators—then there would be no bad press for them and then there would be no need for one to write this sort of statement.

Having said that, I would say that traditionally the promotion and protection of human rights has focused on the relationship between the state and the individual. Most reports are based on protecting the individual against excesses which constitute barbarous acts, which outrage the conscience of mankind. Many institutions and especially transnational corporations do influence the capacity of states for the realization and promotion of these rights. They also profit from the abuse of these rights, yet they allude state control or even international sanctions. There is now a growing focus on the activities of transnational corporations on these particular regimes.

Recently in Nigeria a Shell manager said that companies require stability for them to make profits and dictatorships provide that stability in Africa. That is exactly the core of the problem we are having in not only in Africa but in many countries around the world where there are resources that are wanted by these transnationals, resources that we all need to live day by day.

The globalization of trade and the increase in power of transnational corporations has made them economically and politically more powerful than many nation states. This has added urgency to the need for monitoring the human rights impacts of the decisions and processes of transnational corporations. Pierre Pearsons of Amnesty International recently said, "Human rights need to be an explicit determinant in corporate decisions and the existence of human rights principles will increasingly be a criteria on which a standard judgement of corporate performance will be measured." I agree with this statement. But I also believe that until we make it unprofitable for businesses to be doing business with despotic regimes, they will continue to do that. After all, business is about competition.

Unless there is a system whereby we as consumers or organizations like the United Nations can put clear-cut sanctions against businesses that continue to support or to act as the pillars of dictatorship, they will continue to do their corrupt practices. They will say that this company from this country is doing it and why shouldn't they since they don't want to lose out. We are not against companies creating wealth. We are against the fact that we should die because they want to create wealth for themselves. This has happened for a long time.

Looking at Africa, this has been occurring since the period of the slave trade. International businesses actually came to our home, supplied the weapons and supplied all the reasons for communities to fight each other in order for them to have people to be sold as slaves, to make money. Profit was the motivation of the slave trade.

Some of the human rights abuses that happened during the colonial period were also because some companies wanted to make profits. There was the Belgian Congo, where more than ten million people are said to have either been killed or been abused one way or the other. Apartheid in South Africa also benefited business. Recently we had the Truth and Reconciliation Commission submitting its reports. In one of the reports it was very clear that businesses were the ones who profited most from the apartheid system. It was the corporations that profited. This has now made it very, very important for us not to look at just the leaders or the governments who are committing human rights abuses, but the system and the businesses that are supporting these governments. In some cases, like in the case in Nigeria, these humans rights abuses were committed so that a business could continue to make profit.

It is true that Nigeria depends on oil for most of its money. But if we talk of depending on oil, depending on oil for what? If you go back to 1963, when oil constituted only about five per cent of our foreign income, there were no human rights abuses like we have now, when oil constitutes about ninety-five per cent of our income. Our leader, Abacha, actually killed people, the way he killed my brother, just so that business could continue to make money.

Could it be different? Yes, it could be very, very different—the way it is here. What I'm talking about is the double standards that companies use. The standard they use here is markedly different from the standard they use in the developing world. Will business sanction or support human rights abuses in the West, even if there were no stringent laws or a good system? I do not think so. I would think twice before I would do anything that would harm my brother or people from my village or people from my country.

The issue is, will businesses in the West do the same thing that they are doing here in Africa? Is there a way that we can these double standards stop? If these double standards do not stop, if people do not find a way to stop the double standard, then I think what we are seeing now will continue up to the next millennium. We are doing some things to see that they stop, and what we are doing we are starting from a very young age. By "we," I mean the movement of the survivors of the Ogoni people. At schools we have been talking to those who will be working in international corporations in the future. In high schools we go to talk about human rights, values that they should absorb at an early age so that by the time they start to work in transnational corporations, they will know that the decisions they take might have an impact, a negative impact on the rights of people very far away. We are also trying to get to workers of transnational corporations, to let them know that sitting down in an office and making a decision does have an impact on quite a lot of people, and this impact can result in refugees, and the refugee situation can lead in people dying or not being able to do what they were trained to do.

We also look at consumers, the ones who buy from transnational corporations. As I said earlier, we all need some of these products. We appeal to consumers to ask the companies how these products came here, to ask how many people were killed before this oil reached their cars. To ask if there is a better way that the company can operate so that people do not die for them to drive their cars.

We're trying to encourage countries to put legal instruments into place that will punish transnational corporations that violate the rights of people in distant lands. Financial compensation should be collected from the transnational corporations to be used as aid to communities that have had their rights violated. We believe that if countries put effective sanctions against the products of these companies it may be helpful to us.

■■■■

I'm looking back at what happened during the slave trade, when Britain actually had to use its power to stop British companies from continuing in their slave trade. We may need that sort of thing to happen now because, at the end of it, who are the beneficiaries of these profits that transnational corporations make? They pay taxes to governments here so governments here do have a moral obligation to see that the money they get from these transnational corporations is not money that has come because of the deprivation of the rights of other people.

At the international level we propose that international courts should also try individuals—individuals this time—from transnational corporations which are implicated in human rights abuses in other countries. The guns that are bought by these companies that are used for mass killings, we should also look at this. Those who are involved in buying these guns should be accountable for the actions of these guns. In this aspect I'm thinking about what happened in Nigeria. In 1993, three hundred thousand people from Ogoni came up to demonstrate against the environmental problems we were having. We called on to Shell to have a dialogue with us to see what they can do to resolve the problem.

Three weeks after our demonstration the head of Shell in Nigeria signed a contract to import weapons into Nigeria. We have the documents. Instead of talking to us, the company decided to go for the guns. We think that the individuals who take these decisions, where we have the proof, should be called on to explain to the world why they have done what they have.

The country of origin of the transnational corporation should also be held accountable at the level of the UN. Britain and Holland get a lot of the taxes, money, that comes out of the destruction of our home. These governments should be asked questions at the level of the United Nations. If these things are done we believe that transnational corporations will be more careful in deciding between people and profits.

WARREN ALLMAND

Globalization and Ethical Profits

Warren Allmand is president of the International
Centre for Human Rights and Democratic Development.
For more than three decades he was a member of the
Canadian Parliament and held numerous portfolios,
including solicitor general and minister of Indian affairs
and northern development. He is Queen's Counsel and
a member of the Privy Council.

THE INTERNATIONAL CENTRE FOR HUMAN RIGHTS AND DEMOCRATIC DEVELOPMENT is an independent Canadian institution with an international mandate. Our mission is to defend and promote all those rights set out in the Universal Declaration, including economic and social rights. For this reason we have established a priority program to deal with the impact of globalization on these rights.

Most, but not all, transnational corporations think that this choice is unavoidable and act as if they must choose between people and profits. That is not the case. There is no essential contradiction between human rights and profits. There can be even larger profits when people and human rights are respected. It is correct, however, that if there are global or regional trade arrangements—such as the North America Free Trade Agreement (NAFTA), Asia Pacific Economic Conference (APEC) and the World Trade Organization (WTO)—without effective social charters, without minimum standards for labour and social program, then there will be pressures in the countries concerned to lower taxes, slash social program and to reduce labour and environmental standards to the lowest common denominator in order to attract and accommodate international business. In this sense they put profits before people.

The result of all of this is that the rich get richer and the poor poorer. These policies have resulted in obscene situations, with people sleeping on frozen streets, eating out of garbage cans and dying of preventable disease. Of course all of this is happening during a time when our GDP and national wealth is increasing. The pie is getting bigger but the majority of the population is getting less. They're getting smaller pieces. Consequently, in the context of global free trade, one can say that the transnational corporations are choosing profits over people and human rights. They and the countries which agreed to these trade arrangements are in fact violating Articles 22 to 26 of the Universal Declaration of Human Rights, which provide for the rights to food, housing, education and pensions and protection against unemployment. The Universal Declaration declares these to be rights—not options, not preferences or a wish list—but rights. This was confirmed by 170 nations, including Canada, in the Vienna Declaration and Programme of Action in 1993. Despite this there is a tendency in most nations, in the West as in the East, to marginalize these rights almost out of existence.

With such globalized trade agreements, there is pressure for nations to reduce and ignore human rights, especially economic and social rights, and pressures for transnational corporations to do the same. However, it is not necessary that all nations and all transnationals succumb to these pressures in order to make a profit, and some do not. The Body Shop is an excellent example of this latter group and I would like to publicly congratulate the company for the work it has done on human rights, ranging from funding organizations, to campaigning on human rights in Tibet and Nigeria, to accepting the advice of human rights organizations and to seeing that the human rights of its own employees are respected.

In our human rights work, many of us focus on governments, for it is states that sign international human rights treaties and states that are accountable for their provisions. But the preamble to the Universal Declaration is in fact very clear: it applies to "all peoples and all nations" and to "every individual and every organ of society." That, my friends, includes business. In this increasingly globalized world, where the most important economic actors are in fact not sovereign states but private corporations, we simply cannot ignore their involvement with human rights.

Of the one hundred largest economic entities in the world today, fifty-one are corporations; only forty-nine are states. Consequently, I would like to focus on the relevance of international human rights law to the world of business. More and more businesses operating in the global market are being forced to look at the human rights implications of their daily operations. Most people now recognize that business has responsibilities beyond the bottom line. They are expected to be good corporate citizens. In a survey of Canadian firms which our centre did in 1997, in cooperation with the Canadian Lawyers' Association for International Human Rights (CLAIHR), forty-two per cent of the firms which responded said they believed that corporations had a role to play in protecting international human rights and promoting sustainable development. I will return to this survey shortly because there is often a considerable gap between what companies say they should do and what they actually do.

I would now like to refer to two case studies—Nike and Shell. Nike went from being a cool brand name for young people around the globe to a brand name that was synonymous with sweatshops, with the result that trade unions, students and human rights groups organized a campaign against it. Nike went from being an invincible corporate empire (revenues close to $10 billion, bigger than seventy countries in the world) to a company whose profits were cut in half between May 1997 and May 1998. It went from denying there were problems to gradually admitting some "mistakes" and finally turning around its corporate strategy in a desperate bid to change its image.

I am not here to say that Nike has solved all its problems or that we should stop pressuring this company. But Nike's revision of its code of conduct, the raising of the minimum age for its employees, its tentative steps to accept independent monitoring with NGOs and the announcement that it was increasing the wages of its Indonesian workers should be seen as a victory for human rights. Furthermore, the impact of the Nike campaign was not only effective against that company. Senior executives from other brands were watching and wondering how long they would be able to escape the same kind of scrutiny.

Another example is Shell, whose human rights record became notorious in 1995 when the assassination of Ogoni writer and activist Ken Saro-Wiwa received worldwide attention. The international focus on Shell's activities in Nigeria, the support for the Ogoni people around the world and the picketing of Shell's gas stations seem at last to be having an effect. Shell is now the only international petroleum company to have a human rights policy as part of its business mission, the only company on record as supporting the Universal Declaration of Human Rights and to issue a human rights and business primer for its employees. Shell and Nike are just two well-known examples but they are not alone.

Companies have to understand, however, that while their interest in human rights may have been provoked by a public relations or PR problem, the solution is not to be found in a PR exercise. Any company that tries to treat human rights as some kind of gloss to put on a fancy corporate brochure will end up in even more trouble. Human rights must be a commitment throughout the entire organization, not just window-dressing located in its department of public relations. Of course it is unreasonable to expect that we can solve the problem of corporate human rights abuse by going after firms one at a time.

We obviously need legislation, national and international, which will govern the behaviour of states and companies. But such rules are difficult to get in a world obsessed with competitive advantage and deregulation. Nevertheless, we must continue to campaign for better international rules, social charters and codes of conduct in bodies like the World Trade Organization or within regional trade agreements such as NAFTA and APEC. Those are long-term battles to establish some new form of global governance. In the meantime, what can we do immediately? There is an initiative in the UK which I think holds considerable promise for Canada. It is called the Ethical Trade Initiative, or ETI. Similar initiatives are underway in the Netherlands and the United States. The Ethical Trade Initiative, funded and facilitated by the UK government, is a partnership of about fifteen companies and about the same number of NGOs and trade unions. Together over the past year they have reached some agreement about standards for ethical trade and how such standards should be monitored.

The ETI is exciting precisely because it brings together many of the key actors, bases its principles on existing international standards (ILO standards) and has enormous scope. Combined, the companies involved in the ETI have a turnover of more than £50 billion and deal with tens of thousands of suppliers in over fifty countries. Similar developments are happening elsewhere. Recently the organization Business for Social Responsibility, with 1,400 corporate members in the US, held a conference attended by 850 business people. The Council on Economic Priorities, an American NGO, has set up an agency to audit companies for compliance with a code of conduct developed by trade unions, NGOs and businesses—again, based on international standards.

So what about Canada? The sad fact is that Canada is very much behind its European and American counterparts on this issue, at least as far as business and government is concerned. Why do I say Canada is behind? Consider the following facts. For over a year a coalition of Canadian groups and trade unions have been calling for a task force on sweatshop abuses in the apparel industry. This call has been endorsed by over 30,000 Canadians, as well as a number of important companies and the Retail Association of Canada. Government, despite promises last summer that action was forthcoming, has yet to convene a meeting. The BC government struck a legislative committee to look at the human rights and social implications of the Multilateral Agreement on Investment. Despite invitations to many businesses and business associations, not a single one came forward to offer its views. Our centre was planning to host a conference on human rights and ethical business practices in January 1999. We sent out over 2,500 invitations, mainly to Canadian businesses. After two months, only eleven had registered. We felt it necessary to cancel.

In the survey I mentioned earlier, done with CLAIHR, we found that only one in seven of Canada's one hundred largest corporations had codes of conduct with minimum human rights provisions. So there is a lot of work to be done in Canada. We need corporate leaders who are prepared to take risks and encourage others to follow suit. We need a firm commitment from government to make sure that business respects human rights internationally, just as it is required to respect human rights nationally and provincially. On the NGO side, we need to ensure that our campaigns are coordinated and effective in order to have maximum impact.

In the 1995 report of the Commission on Global Governance, titled Our Global Neighbourhood, the authors state that for globalization to be a positive process, it needs an effective system of global governance. They said that global decision-making needs to build on institutions at many levels and that the creation of adequate governance mechanisms must be more inclusive and participatory—that is, more democratic—than in the past. Global governance will foster global citizenship and will work to include the alienated and marginalized segments of national and international society. Finally, it will work to subject the rule of arbitrary power—economic, political or military—to the rule of law within global society. That is what we are attempting to do. That is how transnational corporations can respect human rights and still make profits.

JIM BUTLER

The Environmental and Civil Rights Movements

Their Similarities and Challenges

Jim Butler is a professor of conservation biology and wildlife at the University of Alberta in Edmonton, Canada.

THE ENVIRONMENTAL AND CIVIL RIGHTS MOVEMENTS have many parallels in their history. Both have struggled with the same underlying issues of injustice, morality, quality of life, the dissonance of human values and the evolving concept of "natural rights." Both movements employ similar approaches of education, lobbying, public protest and civil disobedience. All environmental issues are social issues and all civil rights issues have an ecological connection.

53

The naturalist and philosopher Henry David Thoreau published the first essay to justify civil disobedience in 1849. It was titled "The Relation of the Individual to the State." Tolstoy admired it in 1900. Gandhi circulated the essay in South Africa and India. Martin Luther King used it in the civil rights movement and stated, "As a result of Thoreau's writings we are heirs of a legacy of creative protest."

The environmental movement followed and built upon the spirit and success of the civil rights protests of the 1950s and 1960s and anti-war protests of the 1960s. The spirit of questioning and challenging injustice was the basis of the emerging environmental movement of the 1970s. This was the decade which began with the first Earth Day Celebrations, the first view of the earth from space and the birth of a more radical environmental front symbolized by Friends of the Earth and the media-conscious Greenpeace formed in Vancouver, BC.

As environmental demonstrations continued into the 1980s, the linkage to the civil rights movement as a source of inspiration was acknowledged. On 3 November 1987 activists from Earth First, considered the most radical of all environmental groups, were arrested after unfurling a banner at the Lincoln Memorial in Washington, DC. The banner read: "Equal rights for all species." In an article published by the *Earth First Journal* in 1988, Mike Roselle wrote: "This new civil rights movement is our only hope... We must shift the focus from land management to civil rights for all people. The Tree People, Rock People, Deer People, Grasshopper People and beyond." In another Earth First demonstration on 16 January 1989, on the holiday of Martin Luther King, activists unfurled a banner in front of the US Department of Fish, Wildlife and Parks which read: "Equal rights for all species—We have a dream."

The quality of our environment and the quality of human life are inextricably interconnected. Every assault and compromising degradation in the name of progress upon our landscape, forests, water, atmosphere and the diversity of life is an assault upon human health and lifestyle and diminishes the human spirit. In an Alberta government growth summit opinion poll (24 July 1997), Albertans stated that they value nature higher than any other measure of quality of life. They rated nature two and a half times more important than available jobs. Unpolluted air was ranked number three in priority, three times higher than quality education. Meanwhile, the air pollution of Hinton in central Alberta was described by that town's mayor as the "smell of money." This comment exemplifies the clash in priorities between the economic and public sectors.

The environment and people must always be viewed as our primary assets. We most often sacrifice the unique in favour of the commonplace. Far too often the special, rare and unique portions of our land have been compromised to support the dominant, traditional, visible, most powerful or most financed alternatives. Unique and rare portions of our landscapes, wild and scenic places, flora and fauna are easily compromised as they become lost in broad-based land allocations.

We must recognize, list, celebrate and protect our unique environmental aspects and allow the fullest expression of their diversity to lead and inspire us and serve to mould our internal and external identity. We have experienced compromise for so long that it is difficult, if not impossible, to distinguish between right and wrong. We tend now to readily accepted the best of the wrongs in the fragmentation of our ideals.

Quality of life and experience is linked to wild places, wildlife and outdoor recreation opportunities and this access must be protected. The outdoor pursuits of Albertans have been much studied and show a powerful preference for visiting parks, lakes, rivers and undeveloped land for widely diverse reasons. Available camping, fishing, recreational areas and wilderness opportunities are projected to be in severe short supply by the turn of the century.

Growth must be redefined (apart from the common utilization of the corporate or business sector) in favour of quality of life, human potential, environmental wellness, social empowerment and diversification of opportunity. There is also the matter of the "hypocrisy of growth," where enterprises that might well create jobs and contribute to the formal economy may suppress, at home or abroad, populations of people, their freedoms and dignity, depreciate land, ecology and threaten wildlife species and traditional ways of life. The hypocrisy is that we must not pretend as a people that we can in good conscience reap benefits of growth in a global economy while the extended measure of that activity suppresses the health and well-being of people and the environment. All people and governments should pledge to conduct their affairs as a model of excellence, integrity and extended ethical consistency.

We might aspire that our internal conduct serve as an example to other jurisdictions and trade partners. This moral position will be achieved when we have the courage to reject offending corporations and their products in favour of others who conduct their affairs according to social and environmental responsibility. Growth in a modern paradigm is far more than an expansion of trade. There can be no measure of acceptable growth without global social justice, non-oppression of affected peoples and the extension of rights to the land and its wildlife.

The model and engine currently driving our society is outdated, regretfully favouring competitive market economics fuelled by large corporate sector initiatives that operate with short-range parameters and a narrow vision of their need to contribute to society. The immediate tangible benefits often override long-term opportunities which could offer a greater range of sustainable employment.

Limits to growth are essential. There needs to be an understanding that economic growth is not the be-all and end-all but rather pales in comparison with the sustainability of an economy. Quality of life is linked to the recognition that there must be defined limits to growth. The current prevalent model sees an economy as an unconstrained system with nature contained therein. In this paradigm, growth is a normative value. However, a sustainable economy recognizes that economy is only a subsystem within the larger and finite ecosystem. Growth should stop when the optimal scale of the human niche is achieved and the capacity for environmental quality is retained on a sustainable basis. In essence, our natural capital should be the limiting factor to growth.

The principal gap which separates the underlying philosophy of the environmental movement and human rights movement centres around the issue of the importance of extension of rights for humans to non-humans. Civil rights leaders have naturally focused on social injustice and inequality as they relate to human beings. This "homocentric" (human-centred) priority has granted little expression for the biocentric or ecocentric (human beings are only a part of the broad ecosphere). Biocentrism is a fundamental concept for biologists and environmentalists who are concerned with the loss of biodiversity and the health of the ecosystem, not just the effects of environmental deterioration on human beings.

Religious leaders who are often the inspiration behind social reforms possess no more knowledge of ecology and biodiversity than scientists possess of religion or morality. The linkages have always been present, however, and, because of this, environmentalists no longer viewing environmental destruction solely in terms of ecological viability. They are increasingly addressing issues in terms of what is right or wrong. These are matters of morality and central precepts to the civil rights movement. It may be legal to shoot the last grizzly bears, kill whales or clear-cut the last old-growth forests. But this does not make it right. Being guided by higher moral prerogatives calls upon a higher authority, one above the perceived tyranny of central authorities they have become disillusioned with. Following a course that is perceived as ethical and maintaining the moral high ground, is the path forged by the civil rights movements of the 1950s and 1960s.

In the 1940s a hero to the North American ecology movement, Aldo Leopold, wrote an essay known as "Land Ethic." In it, he states: "A thing is right when it tends to preserve the integrity, stability and beauty of the biotic community. It is wrong when it tends otherwise." Leopold was viewing our relationship to land in terms of morality: a thing is right or wrong. From the perspective of eastern religions and philosophy, none of this would be anything new. Wisdom to a Taoist is to conform to the rhythm of the universe, the natural order. In Shinto, evil was defined as that which disrupts the natural order of things. Buddhism never fostered a homocentric perspective towards non-human life forms. And the Buddha in the Sutta-Nipata warned his disciples that if they destroyed or contaminated water resources they did so "at great Karmic peril." The Penan people of Borneo have a word for law, *adat*. The basic premise is that humans are part of a larger ecological community and that the rights of all life forms must be recognized, including those yet to arrive in the next generation and long-dead ancestors.

The underlying challenge that the environmental and the civil rights movements share is responding to the shifting of values. There is a dissonance in perception and belief systems. Values evolve over time in a society as subsequent generations view the world and themselves in different ways. It is not a clash between the enlightened and the unenlightened, the good and the bad, the power-elite and the middle class. It is a conflict over values and the complex variables that shape them.

Human Rights and Responsibilities

History
Repeats Itself

Wei Jingsheng is a visiting scholar at Columbia
University. He was exiled to the US in 1997 after being
imprisoned for eighteen years in China as a "counter-
revolutionary." He is the recipient of the Olof Palme
Memorial Prize (1994), the Robert F. Kennedy Memorial
Human Rights Award (1996) and the National
Endowment for Democracy Award (1997). His letters
from prison to his family and communist leaders were
published in a book called *The Courage to Stand Alone.*

EVERYONE WANTS TO TALK ABOUT the responsibility of government to
protect human rights. My feeling is that this is a very simple issue. The worst
human rights offenders actually come from governments. The best protectors of
human rights are also our governments. However, our governments are usually
not the correct forces to make sure that human rights are protected in our
society. That is why we need democratic systems to protect and guarantee that
these human rights are protected by our governments.

When it comes to domestic policies, it is very easy for us to make sure that
these systematic protections are in place. But we face many more difficulties in
terms of protecting human rights, because human rights are universal and are
not confined to only one country. So it is very important, in our struggle to
protect human rights around the world, that we assume our own responsibilities for human rights.

We need to make sure that we have enough ways and means to protect our
own human rights within our own country. Of course, we all care about our own
human rights within our own country. But no matter whether you are
protecting human rights or violating human rights, it is not confined within the
boundaries of one's own country. Before World War II many of us thought we
could just worry about our own human rights, and that we didn't have to worry
about what was happening in Nazi Germany at that time. Because of this, the
Nazi government not only committed violations within its own country, but also
spread these violations around the world.

59

What we are seeing today is a repeat of history. We see our own governments saying, "Well, we don't need to worry about what's happening in Vietnam, what's happening in Malaysia and what's happening in China. All we need to do is worry about our own human rights in our own backyard." But I have to tell you, dictators don't just violate human rights within their own countries. Their influence exceeds far and wide, even to Canada. For example, whenever I conduct my political activities or human rights activities in Canada, I am affected, of course, by our communist government in China. Many foreign reporters in China have been expelled for reporting the truth. Even your students at the Asian Pacific Economic Conference who protested against Suharto and Yan Su Ming had their human rights violated. So even though we live in Canada, we not only have to worry about the protection of our own human rights, but also that of human rights around the world. Defending human rights is a worldwide phenomenon.

In the 1980s, due to the South African apartheid policy, the level of concern for human rights in the world was raised a notch. Not only have human rights activists helped out in the South African situation, making sure that South Africa is free, but in doing so they have also raised a lot of concerns about human rights around the globe. But since 1989 a lot of human rights defenders have come across a very difficult and very capable opponent. China is one of the few big countries in this world. Although it was roundly criticized by Western governments during the Tiananmen Square massacre, these voices of criticism have diminished over the last few years.

In fact, we have seen in the last couple of years that a lot of Western countries—Canada included—have not, for example, supported the United Nations resolution to criticize China's human rights violations. What gets hurt is not just human rights in China but human rights around the world. If you are concerned about human rights, you should be concerned only about human rights and not worry about where it happens. We should strive to protect human rights no matter whether the offences are occurring in South Africa, in China or even in Canada.

Vietnam and Human Rights

A Call for International Pressure

Doan Viet Hoat is a scholar-in-residence at Catholic University, Washington, DC, where he lectures on international human rights. In the 1970s he taught at the University of Saigon and edited *Freedom Forum,* an underground magazine which published pro-democracy views. He was arrested and detained without charge for his promotion of democracy and pluralism and adopted as a prisoner of conscience by Amnesty International in 1981. In 1992 he was named Man of the Year by Vietnamese newspapers in the US and overseas. He is the recipient of the Press Freedom Award (1993) from the Committee to Protect Journalists based in New York, the Robert F. Kennedy Human Rights Award (1995) and the Golden Pen of Freedom (1998) from the World Association of Newspapers.

FIFTY YEARS AGO, on 10 December 1948, the founding members of the United Nations signed the Universal Declaration of Human Rights. I want to call your attention to two paragraphs of the preamble of this historical document. In the second paragraph of the preamble the founding countries make it clear that "disregard and contempt for human rights have resulted in barbarous acts which have outraged the conscience of mankind, and the advent of a world in which human beings shall enjoy freedom of speech and belief and freedom from fear and want has been proclaimed as the highest aspiration of the common people." Paragraph six of the preamble underlines the responsibility of the UN member states "to achieve, in cooperation with the United Nations, the promotion of universal respect for an observance of human rights and fundamental freedoms."

These two affirmations are closely related. Disregard and contempt for human rights can only be avoided if government officials make themselves advocates and defenders of human rights. Similarly, freedom of speech and freedom from fear and want cannot become reality without government's concrete and continuous efforts to create administrative and legal avenues and an environment that support the freedom of exchange of ideas and information, as well as labour and products.

With these observations in mind I would like to give you my knowledge about the present human rights situation in Vietnam. The Vietnamese government recently released some political prisoners. This positive event is welcomed by all human rights activists and organizations, both Vietnamese and around the world. However, I would like to call your attention to the following three points.

First, most of the recently released political prisoners are the beneficiaries of international intervention, which implies that international pressure has a positive impact on the present Vietnamese administration and, as such, should be continued on other unsolved human rights problems.

Second, there are still hundreds of oppressed political and religious dissidents in Vietnam who are either incarcerated or harassed or under house arrest. Most of them are unknown by the international community. For those detained, the conditions of their imprisonment is miserable, with forced labour and humiliation. For those under house arrest or under the close watch of the police, harassment, infringement of privacy, violation of fundamental human rights, disregard and contempt of human dignity—all those barbarous acts—are committed by government officials and the police every day and in every place around the country.

Thirdly, the communist government in Vietnam has always rejected the term "political prisoners." Neither do they accept the term "prisoners of conscience." They instead persist on using terms like "criminals," "delinquents" or "law violators" to refer to those detained for political dissident activities.

This is alarming because the government will continue to suppress political dissidents under the pretext of law enforcement and social order and stability. This reality also urges human rights activists to have a closer look at the legal system and laws in Vietnam. I strongly believe that the recent release of some well-known political detainees marks an important step towards the liberalization and democratization of Vietnam. With such a belief in mind, I propose that the international community pay more attention to the government's responsibility to create the sociopolitical and legal foundations required to realize freedom of the press and freedom of political expression.

Transparency and openness are two *sine qua non* conditions of progress in a civil society. And yet openness can only become a reality with a free press and a democratic political system. Freedom and democracy, as such, have not existed in Vietnam. The Communist Party of Vietnam still has a powerful control over all aspects of social life. The communist leaders have made it clear that they will not share power with any other individuals or with any other party. They still affirm that they have the historical responsibility and right to "direct" the people towards socialism and communism.

Being an advocate of freedom and democracy, I campaign for equality of opportunity in Vietnam, for every citizen to have the equal right to contribute to the development of the country—no matter what party he or she belongs to and what ideology he or she supports. The government's responsibility is not to direct the people as to what they should do and what they should support. No one, no matter how wise and how powerful he may be, has the right to tell others what they should do and what they should not do, what they should believe and what they should not believe. This conviction is the foundation not only of the Universal Declaration of Human Rights but also of civilization itself.

The most important duty of the present Vietnamese government is to give back to the people their right to master their own lives and the life of their country. The Vietnamese people should have the right to determine who they want to govern their country and what policy they support. No such fundamental civil right can exist without a free press and free elections. A free press can only come about if the government allows nongovernmental, noncommunist mass media to exist. Free elections can never come about in a one-party political system. If the present communist government wants to build a "civilized and equal society," as it always states, it should accept free and equal opportunity of political and cultural activities for all Vietnamese people, regardless of their divergent political opinions.

"Diversity in Unity" has nowadays become the guiding principle for developing a civilized and equal society. This principle should apply not only for economic activities, but also for those which are cultural and political. I challenge the Communist Party and the communist government in Vietnam to accept free and equal competition in political and cultural activities in the same way that they have accepted free competition in the economy.

Vietnam, as a member of the United Nations, is bound to abide by the international human rights codes. Yet abuses of political and civil rights are committed by government officials, especially by the police, almost every day. There are no legal avenues which allow for peaceful protest against the government's misconduct. Only freedom of expression and the freedom to gather allows for that.

I call on international opinion to campaign for freedom of the press and the right to peaceful demonstration in Vietnam. Vietnamese human rights activists at home and abroad believe that they will continue to receive international support for freedom and democracy. They also believe that, with international support, their campaign for a democratic and prosperous Vietnam will become a reality in the near future.

J. EDWARD BROADBENT

The Case of International Trade Agreements

J. Edward Broadbent holds the J. S. Woodsworth Chair
in Humanities at Simon Fraser University in Vancouver,
BC. He was a member of the Canadian Parliament from
1968–89, leader of the New Democratic Party from
1975–89 and the first president of the Montréal-based
International Centre for Human Rights and Democratic
Development. He was a participant in the 1993
International Tribunal on the Violation of Women's
Human Rights in Vienna and a member of the panel of
experts at the International Tribunal on Rights in Haiti in
1994. He is a member of the Privy Council and an
Officer of the Order of Canada.

DURING THE PAST YEAR Canadians have witnessed the unfolding of what could be called the "APEC story." The focus during the fall of 1998 has been on civil and political rights. More specifically, it has been on allegations that political and civil rights of Canadians were violated by members of the RCMP and by the government of Canada, including, it has been claimed, by the Prime Minister himself. These alleged violations occurred during demonstrations at the time the leaders of countries attending the Asia Pacific Economic Conference (APEC) were meeting at the University of British Columbia in Vancouver.

Much to the chagrin of many of the demonstrators, the importance of what their protests were all about in the first place has been largely ignored by the Canadian media. Indeed, had it not been for the harsh action taken against some of the demonstrators, there would have been virtually no stories about the cruel, systematic and violent denial of human rights that was being waged by a number of APEC governments against their own citizens. The Canadian demonstrators were protesting for specific reasons: they were objecting to the fact that democratic governments, including that of Canada, were promoting the expansion of trade with brutal dictatorships while ignoring throughout the trade discussions and agreements any reference to the impact such commercial and industrial development would have on the human rights of the millions of men and women who live in APEC countries.

The students and other protesters were of course right in their judgement. During the past fifteen years, democratic governments have joined with others in regional and global trade agreements which have strengthened the international commercial rights of corporations while ignoring their obligations to protect and promote the human rights of people whose lives are profoundly affected by those same agreements.

Before elaborating on the nature of state human rights obligations in the context of trade, let me briefly illustrate by a few examples that what is involved is not simply an abstract principle. Human rights are not abstractions. They refer to the real-life experience of men, women and children. As the UN covenants indicate, they refer to entitlements based on the inherent claim of human beings to a life of dignity.

It has been asserted by our own Prime Minister, among others, that by concentrating on the promotion of dynamic industrial economies, we simultaneously promote democracy. It is difficult to know what is more alarming—the inaccuracy of the claim of this direct link between dynamic economies and democracy or the possibility that Mr. Chrétien might actually believe it. If the generalization were true, Germany, by far the most productive and fully employed economy in 1938, would have also been a thriving democracy.

But what about rights in the countries taking part in Vancouver's APEC meeting? I mention three that I had visited not long before the APEC summit. Canadians had the opportunity to witness the clash between two agendas in Vancouver. On the one hand, the governments, whether democratic or not, focused on their commercial interests and their stipulated goal of reaching free trade by 2020. At the same time, NGOs, including health workers, environmentalists, women's groups, and workers' and other human rights advocates, talked about what was not on the table—their concerns and their rights as affected by the first agenda. I will restrict my comments to workers' rights because they are the rights most pertinent to new capital investment and because, as Virginia Leary, the US human rights scholar, has noted, they are an excellent indicator of the condition of rights in general.

Let me give you some examples taken from countries who send representatives to Vancouver, countries with market-based economies, whose GNPs were very high and whose governments either threaten or deny the rights of their people: China, Thailand and Indonesia.

China

As we know, major economic reforms were introduced in China in the 1980s. One of the results was increased pressure for democracy. However, instead of responding positively to demands for more rights, the autocratic Communist government ordered the tanks onto Tiananmen Square and the world witnessed a bloody massacre followed by arrests. Among others, a railway worker, Han Dongfang, was imprisoned without charge. He was tortured but subsequently released. When I visited China he was living in exile in Hong Kong. His only crime has been to demand the right of freedom of association, the right to an independent union—independent from control by the Communist Party. In the fall of 1997, the recently established Communist authority in Hong Kong abolished labour laws guaranteeing workers' rights. Indicative of his continuing courage, Han Dongfang has decided to stay to continue with the struggle.

While all major civil and political rights are repressed, the government of China has been especially harsh when it comes to trade union rights. According to the internationally credible Asia Watch, following the events of April–June 1989, no student or intellectual was sentenced to death. But forty-five workers were. Among others active in the democratic movement, more workers also disappeared into labour camps and a higher percentage of workers were tried and received longer sentences when convicted. The practice continues. Last month (October 1998), the day after Mary Robinson, the UN high commissioner for human rights, left Beijing, Zhu Rui, a woman labour rights activist, and several other so-called dissidents were taken into custody.

▄▄▄ Thailand

I met with young workers one night after their shift in factories outside Bangkok. They told me of dangerous levels of sawdust in toy factories and cotton dust in textile mills. Also, they spoke of routine compulsory overtime. One woman told how she would have been forced to quit if she had decided to look after her seriously ill husband for more than one day. As a consequence, he was left at home alone. A Kader factory worker (188 were killed in a Kader factory fire in April 1993) told me she survived the fire, in spite of being locked in, by jumping from the fourth storey onto the bodies of friends. Moving from factory to factory, she now works as an organizer to inform workers of their completely unenforced health and safety rights. Following this tragedy, other toy factories in two of China's export zones have had almost identical fires. In one of these, eighty-seven lost their lives. In every case, the barbarous excuse is the same: Management claims it is necessary to lock workers in to stop them from stealing and to prevent them from leaving work early.

▄▄▄ Indonesia

In August 1995, I met with labour and other human rights activists outside of Jakarta. The meeting had been called to talk about the impact of globalization and the need for rights (assembly, association, speech). That gathering, however, was held in secret because in Indonesia any meeting of over five people requires government approval. Among other matters referred to that evening was the recent tragedy of Marshinah, a young woman who had attempted to exercise her right of association by organizing an independent union. One weekend she was taken in by the security forces and tortured, raped and murdered. Her body was dumped on the streets as a warning to others.

Last fall, Muchtar Pakpahan, the courageous national leader of an independent union, was being held under house arrest in the hospital, where he was critically ill. He was on trial for his life on trumped-up charges. In 1994 he had been charged with "criminal" behaviour after demanding that factory workers' minimum wage be doubled to four dollars a day. Today his national union, with 250,000 members, has at last the right to hold a national congress. Following the overthrow of Suharto, the once alleged criminal has now become a national hero widely embraced by democratic governments. I was pleased that Foreign Minister Lloyd Axworthy, during the 1997 APEC meeting, obtained permission for a British Colombian physician to visit him in hospital.

These stories from only three developing countries are not isolated incidents in the global economy. In 1996, according to official figures alone, over four thousand people were arrested or questioned for trying to exercise the right of association in connection with trade union activity. During the same period, 264 men and women were actually murdered for pursuing the same right (ICFTU Annual Report on Violation of Trade Union Rights, 1997). I am not aware of a figure even in the same league for activists in other areas of human rights.

As the 20th century has unfolded, empirical studies have shown that there is a strong correlation between the presence of vital independent unions and the presence of democracy. Globally today, the ways in which worker rights are respected or denied in a given country is a very good indicator of the condition of other democratic rights and institutions in that country.

A central point to be made about globalization is that at the very time governments are making it easier through trade agreements for business to trade, invest, build alliances and establish associations so that they can profit, many of the same governments reduce, hold back or totally violate the freedom of working people to build alliances and associations so they can survive. Rather than furthering the democratic process in these instances, globalization is doing the opposite. The spread of international law must entail protection of the human rights of workers, as well as the commercial rights of companies. Otherwise, as Adam Smith, the first theorist of capitalism, pointed out in his *Wealth of Nations*, the rule of law "so far as it is instituted for the security of property, is in reality instituted for the defence of the rich against the poor, of those who have some property against those who have none at all."

What can be done? Regrettably, the problem with trade agreements negotiated since the North American Free Trade Agreement (NAFTA), or proposed, like the Multilateral Agreement on Investment (MAI), is that they include only rights important to corporations. Rights such as those of intellectual property are very well protected. It is the human rights of people subject to the impact of that capital that remain ignored. Canada cannot continue to put to one side obligations it has as a signatory to international human rights treaties, while it negotiates trade agreements.

Democratic governments should start to practice what they preach about the importance of both trade and rights. More specifically, trade agreements must be seen for what they are: namely, legally binding commitments which affect not only the commercial interests of corporations but also, inescapably, the men and women who work for these corporations. By improving the position of corporations in international trade agreements, we increase their mobility. Without related action on behalf of working people, we thus intensify the competitive economic struggle on the side of the corporations. Existing trade agreements, in short, are not neutral in their effects. It's for this reason that all trade agreements should include clauses protecting those basic human rights most pertinent to economic life. In this respect at least NAFTA was a start. NAFTA has side agreements on labour and the environment, and one of its stated objectives is to "protect, enhance, and enforce basic workers' rights." While the side agreement is weak in substance, it has established the important precedent of linking trade and human rights.

The inclusion of rights for workers should be a priority in all regional and global trade negotiations. While there must be a concern for all human rights, we must insert a social clause with a minimum core of rights in the heart of all trade regulations. Such a clause, when implemented, would enable working men and women in developing countries to bring about a more equitable distribution of economic benefits, just as earlier the same rights were used by millions of men and women in Europe and North America to obtain a higher level of economic justice.

▰▰ The Social Clause

The basic purpose of a social clause is to ensure that working men and women will not be forced to work in conditions where their human rights are denied. At the heart of such a clause would be freedom of association and, specifically, the right to establish independent trade unions. As I have mentioned, the right to an independent trade union is the only human right found in both the Covenant on Civil and Political Rights (Article 22) and the Covenant on Economic, Social and Cultural Rights (Article 8).

A social clause would not regulate wages. Such international wage regulation would unfairly discriminate against poorer countries. A social clause would regulate process, not guarantee monetary outcomes. It would significantly strengthen the ability of ordinary people to use internationally recognized rights to improve their conditions of life. The most effective use of such a clause would be to entrench it in the World Trade Organization (WTO) agreement.

Why there? For the very good reason that countries do take trade agreements seriously. As Michael Hart, one of Canada's leading experts on trade, recently wrote, "The WTO...provides the most advanced set of rules capable of being enforced among the community of nations."

The WTO's Article 16 compels all signatory governments to comply with the agreement. It does so by obligating governments to ensure that domestic law is consistent with WTO "laws, regulation and administrative procedures." To date, over one hundred countries have signed on to the WTO and its obligations. If member states can take on obligations to ensure that the interests of corporations are internationally protected, then they owe it to those who work for those corporations to provide them with comparable protection. When commercial rights have an impact on human rights, as they most often do, then human rights should receive equal concern.

Implementation of a social clause must be impartial. It could be done in the following way: When an alleged violation of core rights is cited, a committee established by the International Labour Organization (ILO) and WTO would investigate and make a report. If a violation is confirmed, this committee could recommend technical assistance to a government of good faith. If such help is refused, then an instruction to meet human rights obligations over a specified period of time could be issued. Failure to comply with this last step should result in multilaterally imposed commercial sanctions. The fundamental objective of this process, as with the law in any country, is to ensure compliance by the vast majority—not to punish, *ex post facto,* the violators.

Let me deal briefly with an argument made frequently by governments which seek to avoid their rights obligations when they apply to workers' or, for that matter, many other rights. Such governments normally invoke a variant of "cultural difference"—just as representatives of the *ancien régime* in 18th-century France did about so-called English principles of responsible government. Present at the APEC meeting were some of the strongest opponents of democracy and of the principle of the universality of human rights. I note in particular the governments of China, Singapore, Malaysia and the then government of Indonesia. Such opponents have said that Asian values are not only different from those of the so-called West but have priority when there is a conflict between such values and international human rights.

The truth is that these governments, as members of the United Nations, are obligated to the "promotion of universal respect for and observance of human rights and fundamental freedoms" (Preamble to the Universal Declaration of Human Rights). In addition, they are obligated as governments to implement the UN's Vienna Declaration on Rights adopted in 1993. Asian NGOs and human rights organizations repeatedly reject arguments based on "Asian values" as self-serving propaganda by those autocratic governments in their region who want to continue to deny their own citizens basic rights. These organizations, not their governments, repeatedly reaffirm the principles of universality and indivisibility of rights, arguing that when a cultural tradition, whether in Asia or anywhere else, clashes with such a right (e.g., freedom of association), it is the cultural tradition and not the right which must yield.

While it is clear that those states which openly and systematically deny the rights of their citizens are in violation of their international commitments, it is equally clear that democratic states have an obligation to pursue a rights-based agenda as an integrated part of their foreign and trade policies. Canada, for example, should at minimum live up to its general obligation to promote human rights as found in the preamble to the Universal Declaration and the two covenants covering civil, political, economic, social and cultural rights.

In addition, the Universal Declaration's preamble includes a requirement that states and any organizations within society meet their human rights obligations. The wording is quite specific: "Every individual and every organ of society, keeping this Declaration constantly in mind, shall strive...by progressive measures, national and international, to secure their universal and effective recognition and observance." If these words mean anything, they mean that democratic governments must stop compartmentalizing their agendas. It is time to put an end to debating human rights matters only in Geneva and at the same time signing trade agreements as if these human rights obligations were nonexistent. As for transnational corporations, as "organ(s) of society," they too must cut out the pretence that they have obligations only to their shareholders. Respect for their workers' fundamental human rights is also an obligation.

■ Conclusion

As citizens in a democracy in a world that is being transformed by the new trade rules of globalization, we have a job to do. The cliché is true: We are no longer only citizens of our cities, provinces and countries. We Canadians are now citizens of the world. But so are the working men and women I met a few years ago in Thailand, Indonesia and China—as well as those from Burma, Malaysia and Bangladesh, whom I met in 1997 in Vancouver during the People's Summit at APEC. As global citizens we must make sure that the governments we elect and the corporations we buy from live up to basic democratic requirements. When it comes to rights, a young woman in Bangkok deserves no less than her sister in Vancouver. When it comes to democratic governments, they must stop making trade agreements with only commercial rights. They should stop the complicit reinforcement of the inequality suffered by the millions whose labour is the essential foundation for all such trade in the first place. The world is indeed becoming, in one sense, one big economy. It's time we started writing international rules to protect rights that have the same force of implementation as those that protect property.

REFERENCES

Hart, Michael, "A Question of Fairness," Occasional Papers, Centre for Trading Policy and Law, Carleton University, December 1996. In the same paper, Mr. Hart, once a strong opponent of making a link between trade and rights, indicates he has changed his mind.

The Case of International Trade Agreements

Protecting Refugees from Persecution

THE RIGHT TO SANCTUARY

LOUIS KUOL AROP

I Am a Refugee

Louis Kuol Arop was born in the town of Abyei in
southern Sudan. He was educated in Sudan and
Europe before joining Sudan's Central Ministry of
Culture and Information in the mid-1970s. He was
involved in the founding of the Khartoum-based
English-language monthly *Sudanow* and has been a
vocal supporter of human rights. Since the mid-1960s
his home region has been at the centre of the long-
running civil war between Sudan's Arab north and the
Christian and African south. He now lives in
Edmonton, Canada.

WE ARE CELEBRATING THE FIFTIETH ANNIVERSARY of the Universal
Declaration of Human Rights. In fifty years we have seen a lot of changes and
much of the progress we have made is due to the Declaration. Yet we still have a
long way to go, especially where I come from. We don't have this kind of liberty
and freedom that you have gained after fifty years.

In the Third World we have speeches from individuals, from government,
but the people know nothing about what they are talking about because they
don't live it. They don't experience the Universal Declaration of Human Rights. I
am called a human rights activist. It is not quite so. If I was born here in Canada
and lived here and then wept for the human rights, for those who are denied
their rights, I would call myself an activist.

But I was born and raised in a country where there is no respect for the
human being. We grew up knowing that. That is why I wouldn't say I was an
activist. I am not talking in a legal sense, like a lawyer citing the Article 14. We
don't have Article 14. Maybe the government of Sudan knows it but it is not
practised. At this conference we have said we are working for "a blueprint for
peace and justice." That is quite true, but in the Western world only.

Since 1965 my country has been at war. When we talk about refugees,
refugees come about for various reasons—war, natural disasters and so on.
There is a movement of people all over the world. I am one of those people. I am
a refugee, uprooted from my own home, from my own people and from my own

life that I had started but was interrupted. This is the experience of each and every individual that we call a refugee.

The protection of refugees can only come about through what we are celebrating today. The world community should think about the Third World and think about how it can be brought to the level of rights that we here in Canada are enjoying today. I haven't lived freedom. I have seen freedom only when I was in Europe and when I came to Canada. We have experienced individual freedom and liberty here. Refugees could be anyone of you. I know I am one. They are all the so-called immigrants in this country. They are all refugees because for one reason or another they have moved to take sanctuary in Canada.

As others have said, even here in Canada we are still struggling with how to protect refugees, especially those who just present themselves at the border. There are laws about whether to accept them or send them back, to deport them, that need to be changed. But this is nothing compared to what happens to refugees who are in camps in countries neighbouring their own. It is not the same. Even if a refugee claimant is put behind bars here, his rights are protected. It is not like being thrown in jail in my country or anywhere else in the Third World. So there is a difference here.

But what I am saying is the refugees who are in camps or, in my country's case—refugees within their own borders—their treatment is indescribable. They are under a tree with nothing and no one to help them. Here in Canada we only know refugees like myself, refugees who have been lucky enough to be brought here by the government. Unless you have travelled around the world and gone to refugee camps, you can't understand what it means to be a refugee. I am the only kind of refugee you know. I speak English. I am educated. Most of the world's refugees are not like me and they will never know the freedom I am now enjoying.

I am sharing these experiences because I have lived them. One of the first articles of the Declaration of Human Rights is that men and women are born free. The refugee does not have this right. We live in a world full of contradictions. If the world was not full of contradictions, we wouldn't need these declarations. Many of us are not born free, nor do we live freely. But I believe that individuals can change the lives of millions. We saw how this happened in World War I and World War II. And because the changes brought the world to its knees, some very distinguished individuals like John Humphrey sat down and wrote the Universal Declaration of Human Rights. And so there has been another kind of change.

My appeal to you in the West and particularly in Canada, because this is where I now live, is that we have to read between the lines whenever we read about anything coming from the Third World. Maybe some of you know that Sudan, my country, has been in a civil war for the last almost forty years. My appeal to you is to let the government of Sudan know that those refugees in their own home, the ones beneath the trees, that something must be done to help them, to give them their rights.

By pressuring the government in Khartoum, maybe something will be done about it. I have freed myself by coming to Canada but I wouldn't say that I am free. Half of me is still in Sudan. I am unable to bring my family here because there are certain laws that one has to follow. My mother, my sister—I am divided from them. So even if I am enjoying freedom in Canada, there is something inside of me, eating away at me. There are millions of others like me.

I have a personal gratitude to the Canadian government because when I came here I was treated as a human being, right from when I met the officers at the Canadian embassy. I was welcomed. I was treated like a human being. This is a kind of treatment that I could not get from my own country.

In 1970, in my home town of Abyei in southern Sudan, seven of my cousins were shot and killed in cold blood by government soldiers. Ten years later, two of my brothers were also targeted by the army. One was killed and the other survived but was paralyzed. If I had been there with them I would have been shot too. But I myself could not return to my home village. I stopped trying to return because the army would arrest any of us who were educated whenever we tried to come home. And this is only my own family. There are hundreds more who have been affected in only my home village, tens of thousands more in my home province of Bahr el Ghazal and millions in my home region of southern Sudan.

Here we talk about the dignity of men and women. In Sudan we don't have that dignity. And when you can no longer accept the way you are treated, you either become a rebel to fight against it or you get killed. I rebelled against it but I did not become a fighter. I went into exile. Some people were not so lucky.

Sudan is labelled as one of the poorest countries in the world, but it is a rich country. We have natural resources. We have a good culture. We have oil. We have gold. We have everything that makes a country rich, but we cannot utilize our riches because we are at war. We are fighting ourselves. It is not another country fighting us. But Sudan is bordered by nine African countries and when this house in the middle catches fire, everything around it is on fire too.

This is what is happening today in east Africa. In Sudan, in Ethiopia and Eritrea, in Somalia, in northern Uganda and the Congo—our houses are on fire. And when you hear of countries fighting, you know there are refugees. Every one of us must ask ourselves what we can do to prevent still another generation of Sudanese from becoming either the victims or the perpetrators of genocide and war. And not only for my country, but for all countries of the world, we must ask ourselves this question.

MARY JO LEDDY

Refugees and the Sanctuary Movement

Mary Jo Leddy is the director of Romero House
Community for Refugees. She is an adjunct professor at
Regis College, University of Toronto. She is also a
member of the Ontario Sanctuary Coalition and the
editorial board of *Catholic New Times*. She received
the Order of Canada in 1996.

THE UNIVERSAL DECLARATION ON HUMAN RIGHTS was born out of the agony of World War II. It is a magnificent and important achievement. However, two things should be noted. The Declaration included bold statements about the rights of man and the constitution of nations. Nevertheless, as the great 20th-century political thinker Hannah Arendt pointed out, the rights of man remained an enfeebled concept in Europe in the period between the two great wars because it lacked the necessary legal and political mechanisms to enforce that ideal.[1]

It is also important to remember that there was a shadowy side to Canada's enlightened decision to resist the threat which the Nazis had posed to humanity. While Canadian men and women were fighting Nazis in Europe, Canada's immigration officials were quietly but surely refusing to accept Jewish refugees into Canada. The story has been irrefutably documented in Irving Abella's ground-breaking book, *None is Too Many*. In addition, the Canadian government completely suspended the human rights of Japanese Canadians and forced them into internment camps.

These sobering thoughts may give us an insight into some of the operative policies regarding human rights in Canada today. In Canada, as elsewhere in the Western world, the rights of human beings are dependent on legal and political guarantees and on having the status of citizenship. Those who are most vulnerable are those who do not have the status of citizens. Those who are most at risk in this country are refugees.

In the 1940s as now, there are two sides to Canada. On the one hand we are a tolerant and generous country, a country which is seen internationally as a defender of human rights. On the other hand, we can be extremely intolerant and racist. Justice Thomas Berger of British Columbia, in his book *Fragile*

Freedoms, has argued that Canada has all too easily suspended its commitment to human rights in times of social and economic stress.

The fine line between these two sides runs through the middle of this country, through the middle of each of us. Thus, we tend to think that we are more than gracious in welcoming refugees. The reality, however, is quite different. I remember meeting Rabbi Gunther Plaut in Costa Rica in the 1980s, at a time when refugees from many surrounding countries were finding refuge there. The Rabbi noted that this little country, hardly the size of Toronto, had welcomed four times the number of refugees as Canada had that year.

In times of social stress we have suspended the rights of Jehovah's Witnesses, the Dukhabors and the aboriginal peoples. We have invoked the War Measures Act easily and quickly. Today we do not simply suspend the rights of refugees in this country. Immigration officials act as if refugees do not even have such rights until an officer grants them.

For the last eight years I have been living with and working with refugees. They are my neighbours and I have told their story in my book, *At the Border Called Hope*.[2] These refugees are not government-sponsored. They are refugee claimants, those who have had to make their way here on their own, usually because there were no Canadian immigration officials to be seen within the conflict which had engulfed them. I have gone with them to appointments at Immigration Canada. More often than I care to remember, I have heard an officer make it abundantly clear to an anxious refugee, "You don't have any rights until we give them to you."

I have been forced to conclude that there are two sets of human rights in Canada: the rights of those who are citizens, and the tentative and merely theoretical rights of those who are not citizens or landed immigrants. The only rights they have are those which are determined by Immigration Canada.

In 1995, Tom Clarke of the Interchurch Committee on Refugees described the situation of refugees in this country as that of those who live in "a state-within-a-state." This apartheid-like situation is not usually visible and most Canadians would probably be horrified to know of its existence. Yet it is there and exists most clearly in various immigration detention centres in Canada. In these centres, such as Celebrity Inn in Toronto, you see the raw dynamics of power and powerlessness fuelled by blatant racism.

Families are thrown into these places, women and children, sometimes by mistake and may stay there for months without access to legal representation. The guards who work in these detention centres operate with little accountability as they are hired by private security firms who have been contracted by the government. This state-within-a-state called Immigration Canada has its own private police force and security agents. There is no political or civilian oversight committee to monitor their activities. It is quite doubtful whether they see themselves as accountable to either the minister of immigration or to other elected officials.

In this state-within-a-state, the human rights of refugees are routinely violated. They may be picked up arbitrarily, detained arbitrarily and they have no right to access to counsel. Within this system, the employees of the same agency act as prosecutor, judge, jury and enforcer.

The detention centre is a concrete example of the lack of what has been called "a culture of human rights" in Immigration Canada. Human rights are crushed by the sheer weight of paper. Documents are lost and the lives of people are filed away. One doubts that such sheer inefficiency would ever be tolerated in Revenue Canada.

For many, life within this state-within-a-state can become a permanent form of existence, a state of living in limbo. Thousands of refugees who have had their claims accepted remain waiting for their landed immigrant documents. Without those documents they usually cannot get work or enrol in any significant job training program or educational courses. Most importantly, they cannot sponsor the members of their immediate family.

Just recently I have been involved in the efforts of four young people, a sister and three brothers from Eritrea, to get their landed documents. All four had been accepted by universities and all four had the same identity documents. Their entrance into university depended on getting the landed immigrant document so they could get student loans. The sister was accepted by one officer, but the three boys were rejected by other officers. This leads me to conclude that a pretty black girl has more rights than a young black man.

I am reminded of the poem by Langston Hughes in which he writes: "What happens to a dream deferred? Life is a broken winged bird that cannot fly." Sometimes there are refugees who are at risk of being broken completely. There are times when a refugee with a serious and legitimate claim is refused and is at risk of being returned to a country where he or she will be in danger of torture, detention or death. The reasons for being rejected are varied: a culturally insensitive panel member on the Refugee Board, the fact that the information about a repressive situation may not have arrived before the refugee (unfortunately for some refugees, the most repressive regimes are also the ones where censorship is the most effective), or the refugee's case may have been jeopardized by corrupt or negligent refugee lawyers.

If a genuine refugee is refused, it is difficult for him or her to know where to turn for help. There is virtually no viable way to appeal this decision based on the merits of the case. One would have hoped that the United Nations High Commission for Refugees (UNHCR) would intervene in such a situation but, as Amnesty International has pointed out, the UNHCR in Canada remains relatively ineffectual in this regard.

Because of this there have been desperate refugees who have turned to the churches and church persons for protection. A spontaneous sanctuary movement has developed across this country from that need. It is not an organized movement but has arisen in places like Montréal, Vancouver and the Maritimes as desperate people have come to the church to ask that their rights be respected and protected. The Christians who have responded are not left-wing radicals but rather modest people who have never done anything illegal in their lives. They simply don't want to see someone sent to their death.

For the past six years I have been part of the Southern Ontario Sanctuary Coalition based at the Church of the Holy Trinity in Toronto. Our little group has hidden refugees while we attempted to obtain some safe status for them from the government. We worked quietly and diligently and we were able to help some people. We are now convinced, however, that such quiet diplomacy is not effective. We are looking for a church in which we will declare public sanctuary for refugees who need protection. We will declare the right to sanctuary in a massive and public way. When the state will not give the protection which it has promised (through the signing of international conventions), then citizens and Christians must step in to do what the state has refused to do.

We know the consequences of our actions—jail terms and large fines. But we also know the consequences of not protecting human rights. We see the faces of these terrified people. They are human beings—not problems, not objects of derision or even of politically correct concern.

The philosopher Emmanuel Levinas has described the beginning of the ethical response as the moment when you are "faced" by another. In that moment you are commanded, at that moment you are faced with the imperative "Thou shalt not kill." At that moment you know that you cannot take the life of another for granted and then you want to act as a guarantor for the life of another.

REFERENCES

1. Arendt, Hannah. *The Origins of Totalitarianism.* San Diego: Harcourt Brace Jovanovich (1973).
2. Leddy, Mary Jo. *At the Border Called Hope: Where Refugees are Neighbours.* Toronto: HarperCollins (1997).

Refugees and the Sanctuary Movement

DAVID MATAS

The Universal Declaration of Human Rights

Fifty Years Later

David Matas is vice president of the International
Commission of Jurists, Canadian Section, and the
League for Human Rights, B'nai Brith Canada. He is an
author and the recipient of the Dr. Percy Barsky
Humanitarian Award, the Centennial Community
Service Award from the National Council of Jewish
Women and the Outstanding Achievement Award from
the Manitoba Association of Rights and Liberties.

FIFTY YEARS AFTER THE UNIVERSAL DECLARATION OF HUMAN RIGHTS,
what should we think of it? For a person to reach fifty years is an achievement.
For a document to reach fifty years is an inevitability. The mere longevity of the
Declaration does not justify recognizing its anniversary. Like any fifty-year-old,
some parts have fared better than others. Some of the articles in the Declaration
have flourished while others have withered. The right to democracy, the right of
everyone to take part in the government of his country directly or through freely
chosen representatives, has become the ideology of the end of the 20th century.[1]
A myriad of states that once touted the nondemocratic ideologies of communism, apartheid or the national security state have become democracy adherents.
The Internet has given the right to freedom of expression a scope and breadth
unimaginable in 1948.[2]

The Universal Declaration has grown internationally and nationally while
the international system has developed standards detailing specific parts of the
Declaration and mechanisms to implement those standards. Take for instance
the right to be free from torture.[3] There is now a Convention Against Torture, a
UN committee against torture and an individual complaints mechanism. Many
states have legislation criminalizing torture. A myriad of political and civil
rights in the Universal Declaration of Human Rights, such as the right to life,
liberty and security of the person can be found in the International Covenant on

Civil and Political Rights.[4] A UN human rights committee oversees the implementation of this covenant and an optional individual petition mechanism provides a remedy for violations.

The economic, social and cultural rights in the Declaration, for example, the right to education, have been strengthened and amplified by the International Covenant on Economic Social and Cultural Rights.[5] Again, there is a committee established to oversee the implementation of this covenant. The Universal Declaration of Human Rights has been an inspiration for national legislation and national constitutions. Many clauses in the Canadian Bill of Rights, the Canadian Charter of Rights and Freedoms, the Canadian Human Rights Act and provincial human rights legislation are drawn directly from the Universal Declaration of Human Rights. The Universal Declaration of Human Rights has become a key tool when interpreting the Charter. Mr. Justice Dickson wrote, in a 1987 case, "The content of international human rights standards is, in my view, an important indicator of the meaning of the full benefit of the Charter's protection."[6]

The Universal Declaration of Human Rights has spoken to individuals as much as to governments. Human rights organizations use the Declaration to hold governments to account, to rally support for human rights. The Declaration has given hope, has held out a promise to the people of the world. It has penetrated and sensitized the consciousness of humanity throughout the globe. All the same, I believe that the Universal Declaration of Human Rights was partner to a great mistake. The year 1998 is the fiftieth anniversary not only of the Declaration but also of the end of the prosecution of Nazi war criminals.

On 13 July 1948 the British government issued a secret cable to the seven Dominions of the Commonwealth directing that "as many as possible of [Nazi war criminal] cases which are still awaiting trial should be disposed of by 31st August, 1948." It also stated, "no fresh trials should be started after 31st August, 1948 ... In our view, punishment of war criminals is more a matter of discouraging future generations than of meting out retribution to every guilty individual."[7]

One might well ask, how was it possible to discourage future generations without punishing the guilty? The answer the global community gave at the time was the Universal Declaration of Human Rights. This is acknowledged in the preamble to the Declaration, which states: "Whereas disregard and contempt for human rights have resulted in barbarous acts which have outraged the conscience of mankind." The global community proposed to prevent human rights violations by proclaiming human rights standards in the Universal Declaration of Human Rights.

Although the Universal Declaration has thirty articles and asserts a myriad of rights, it can be summed up in two words—"Never again." The Declaration was an outgrowth of the Holocaust and a direct reaction to it. In the words of Mr.

Justice Dickson in the *Keegstra* case: "Following the Second World War and revelation of the Holocaust, in Canada and throughout the world a desire grew to protect human rights, and especially to guard against discrimination. Internationally, this desire led to the landmark Universal Declaration of Human Rights in 1948."[8]

Of course, it would have made no sense after terminating the Nuremberg prosecutions to create an international criminal court which could resume those very prosecutions. The United Kingdom, which led the charge to dismantle the Nuremberg prosecutions prematurely in the early 1950s, also led the opposition to the creation of an international criminal court.[9] The British government's argument was that there was no point in setting up a permanent tribunal for war crimes since war itself is not permanent. *Ad hoc* methods of adjudication used in the past were reasonably adequate, it argued. A permanent court might not be set up by victors in a war, but it would be activated by them. The charge of one-sidedness, if there was a permanent court, would remain.

For crimes against humanity, the UK argued that no government that was complicit in crimes against humanity would surrender its nationals for trial before an international criminal court. The only time outside of war and defeat where criminals against humanity would be tried is after a revolutionary change of government. But, so said the UK, that rarely happened. Few people out of power are international criminals. It is hard to take these British arguments at face value. In light of what we know now about British efforts to stop all war crimes prosecutions after 1948, the UK interventions in the early days of the international criminal court debate have a decidedly disingenuous air about them.

If a permanent court of international criminal justice had been established after World War II, it could have taken up the unfinished business of prosecuting Nazi war criminals that the British had themselves abandoned and encouraged others to abandon. The UK arguments against such a court now read like camouflage, an attempt to forestall the Nazi war crimes prosecutions through this court (if established) that the British had succeeded in blocking off in other ways. With the benefit of hindsight we can see what a tragic mistake it was to disband the Nuremberg prosecutions before they were complete, to thwart the establishment of an international criminal court, and to rely only on the Universal Declaration of Human Rights to prevent future wrongs.

Though the spirit of the Universal Declaration of Human Rights can be captured in the words "never again," in fact, since 1948, genocide has happened again and again: in Uganda, in Cambodia, in Rwanda, in Somalia, in Bosnia and I could go on. In the last fifty years, the global community has lived in a regime of international lawlessness where the worst perpetrators have gone free. It is eminently predictable that when the perpetrators of the worst crimes go free, the crimes will continue to be perpetrated. The death of millions can be laid at the feet of those who decided to dismantle Nuremberg and thwart the establishment of an international criminal court.

It is going too far to say that the international human rights system had no enforcement mechanism without an international criminal court. Nongovernmental organizations sprang up to fill the void, to provide an enforcement mechanism that governments had not, to report on violations and to publicize them, to mobilize public support for the respect of human rights, to shame and to blame. The nongovernmental publicity about violations and mass mobilization around them prompted governments to set matters right. The trouble with this sort of remedy was that it was helpless against the worst violators, those who killed shamelessly. Against the likes of Idi Amin, Pol Pot or Radovan Karadzic, the Universal Declaration of Human Rights was defenceless.

In 1998 the global community finally admitted the mistake made fifty years before, that relying on the Universal Declaration of Human Rights was not enough. On 17 July 1998 in Rome the global community agreed to the establishment of an international criminal court. A gaping hole in the institutional structure of the international system is in the process of being filled. But it is not yet filled. The court will not come into being until sixty states have ratified it. So far sixty-one states have signed the treaty indicating an intention to ratify. Canada has yet to sign but is expected to sign shortly.

Before ratification each state has to ensure that its legislation complies with the treaty. Canada will have to amend both its Extradition Act and its Criminal Code. It is regrettable that the government of Canada is not taking advantage of amendments to the Extradition Act going through Parliament in Bill C-40 to bring its legislation up to the mark, and that the Extradition Act will have to be amended once again before Canada can ratify the treaty establishing the international criminal court. Ratification of the statute by every state in the global community has to be a priority for anyone concerned with realization of the rights set out in the Universal Declaration of Human Rights. For the Universal Declaration of Human Rights promise of "never again" to be kept, the planet must not only establish an international criminal court. We must also remember and respect those rights that are essential to prevent the tragedies of the past from occurring again.

The rights in the Universal Declaration of Human Rights may not be universally respected, but at least they are widely accepted. There are some who argue against the universality of rights, who argue that the Universal Declaration is a Western cultural imposition on the rest of the world. There are others who argue that economic and social rights are not really rights, but just aspirations. These points of view are not widely shared, however, and are uniformly rejected by those sensitized to the meaning of human rights. Nonetheless, there are two rights in the Universal Declaration of Human Rights whose very existence is contested, not only outside, but inside the rights-seeking community.[10] For other rights, the battle to assert their value has been won, though the battle to ensure compliance remains to be fought. For these two rights, the battle is more basic, more fundamental. Even fifty years after the Universal Declaration of Human Rights, we still have to convince the human rights community of the importance of these two rights. I am referring of the right to be free from incitement to discrimination and the right to seek asylum. Both these rights are in the Universal Declaration of Human Rights yet both are hotly contested today.

The Universal Declaration of Human Rights does not rank rights and quite properly so. In a sense, the Universal Declaration does not assert many rights, but just one right with many facets—the right to dignity, self realization and self worth of the individual. The Universal Declaration, in its preamble, refers to the inherent dignity of all members of the human family. For the inherent dignity of the individual to be respected, all rights must be respected. Nonetheless, ranking of rights occurs.

At the conference in Edmonton commemorating the fiftieth anniversary of the Universal Declaration of Human Rights, William Thorsell, the editor of the *Globe and Mail*, spoke on the importance of the right to freedom of expression. He said, "I hold that freedom of expression is not equal in weight with other fundamental human rights. Freedom of expression is the superior or core human right among the many others that are listed in its presence....Freedom of expression is a seminal, germinal, essential, necessary, prior right in the pantheon of rights."

Now, it may seem churlish to argue with someone about his favourite right. In some ways it is like arguing with people about their favourite food or favourite colour. One can expect a newspaper editor to have a special liking for freedom of expression. I assume teachers are inclined towards the right to education and doctors probably favour the right to medical care.[11] As a lawyer, I have a weakness for the right to counsel.[12]

If a mere indication of favouritism were all that was at stake, I would be happy to pass over without comment anyone's choice of a favourite right. However, those who puff up freedom of expression go on to deny another right in the Universal Declaration of Human Rights, the right to be free from incitement to discrimination. William Thorsell stated in Edmonton, in elaboration of his penchant for freedom of expression, "I do not support all the legal limits on free speech that exist in Canada—our criminal hate laws, for example."

Objectively, if we have to rank rights, which I am loathe to do, I would suggest that the right that stands head and shoulders above all others is the right to life. If you are dead, the right to freedom of expression is meaningless. The greatest crimes of this century are not crimes of censorship. They are genocide: the Holocaust, the Armenian massacre, the Bosnian ethnic cleansing, the Cambodian killing fields and other mass killings. If we go beyond the right to life and ask which human rights violations led to these mass killings, surely the answer must be the violations of the right to be free from incitement to discrimination. In the words of Mr. Justice Dickson in the *Keegstra* case, "The experience of Germany represents an awful nadir in the history of racism, and demonstrates the extent to which flawed and brutal ideas can capture the acceptance of a significant number of people."

The Holocaust did not begin with censorship. It began with hate speech. What strange logic could possibly lead any human rights advocate to deny the very right, the right to be free from hate speech, whose violation led first to the *Shoah* and then to the Universal Declaration of Human Rights? The argument Thorsell used to arrive at his quixotic position was that "almost every other human right is dependent for its achievement and defence on freedom of expression." He said: "It should be obvious that the very life-blood of democratic politics is the right to free expression."

Because human rights are an interconnected whole it is easy to link one right to another. Free expression is important to other rights, as other rights are important to respect for freedom of expression. Take any thread out of the quilt of rights and the quilt unravels. To choose only one thread and proclaim that this is the thread that counts is arbitrary. It can just as easily be said that tolerance is the life-blood of democracy. Without tolerance, neither democracy nor freedom of expression can survive. Incitement to hate speech is an assault on that very tolerance which is essential to the respect for so many other rights.

We do not have to go abroad to find a direct link between incitement to hatred and the worst violations of human rights. While the ranking of human rights violations, like the ranking of human rights, is invidious, the internment and deportation of Japanese Canadians and the steadfast Canadian refusal to grant asylum to Jews fleeing the Holocaust are among the most shameful episodes of recent Canadian history. Neither of these events can be traced to censorship. Both are the direct consequences of the then untrammelled incitement to hatred against ethnic Japanese and Jews.

The second right I mentioned in the Universal Declaration of Human Rights that remains contested today is the right to seek asylum. The right to enjoy asylum, also in the Declaration, is reflected in the United Nations Convention and Protocol on the Protection of Refugees. The office of the United Nations High Commissioner for Refugees works actively to promote this right to enjoy asylum. The realization of this right is far from perfect. Many refugees get asylum without enjoying asylum because of the enforced misery which accompanies the granting of asylum. Nonetheless, there is at least a partial realization of the promise of the Declaration of the right to enjoy asylum in UN institutions. The same cannot be said of the right to seek asylum. Everywhere around the world, the principle seems to be that an asylum seeker has a right not to be returned to danger once the person has arrived at a safe destination, but there is no right to get to that safe destination.

The Universal Declaration of Human Rights asserts the right of everyone to leave any country, including his own.[13] The right to leave is meaningless without the right to enter another country. Yet for refugees the right to enter is everywhere denied. Again, there is a total disconnect between the Holocaust, which led to the Universal Declaration of Human Rights, and the implementation of the Declaration. The need to respect the right to seek asylum was a lesson learned from the gas chambers of World War II. Jews attempted to flee Nazi prewar Germany but had nowhere to go. In March 1938, the Jewish refugee problem was compounded when Hitler invaded Austria and Austrian Jews attempted to flee. At a conference in Evian, France, in 1938, the governments of thirty-two nations got together to decide what to do about Jewish refugees fleeing Nazi Germany and Austria and decided to do nothing. The Evian conference, by showing that the world was not prepared to provide a haven to Jewish refugees, justified Nazi Germany's policy against Jews and sealed their fate for the Holocaust to come.

Today, for the right to seek asylum, it is as if the failure at Evian never happened. Canada is as good example as any of the universal denial of the right to seek asylum. Canada recognizes the right to enjoy asylum, perhaps more consistently than most states. Yet, Canadian policy is to deny the right to seek asylum not in some cases but in every case. Every effort is made to prevent refugees from arriving in Canada. The Canadian house of asylum has a door with many bolts. The first bolt is the Canadian Immigration Act's universal visa requirement. According to the act, everyone from every country needs a visa issued from a Canadian visa post abroad before coming to Canada. The Act allows the cabinet to designate countries which are exceptions to the general rule. If we look at the list of exceptions and the history of the granting and removal of exceptions, we see that refugee-producing countries are invariably visa-requirement countries. A person fleeing a country where there is generalized persecution will need a visa issued at a Canadian visa post abroad to come to Canada.

The second bolt on the door locked against those seeking asylum is the criterion for granting visas. A person will be granted a visitor's visa only if the person is coming to Canada for a temporary purpose. Claiming refugee status in Canada is not considered a temporary purpose. Refugee claimants are considered to be people who want to stay, rather than people who want to visit. The result is that no person who goes to a Canadian visa post abroad and says that he or she wants to come to Canada to claim refugee status will be given a visitor's visa.

Canada has an immigration program at visa posts abroad that allots permanent resident visas to a set number of those at risk whom visa officers consider likely to become successfully established in Canada. However, a person who wants to come to Canada to claim refugee status either has to obtain a visitor's visa by concealing his or her true intentions in wanting to come, or has to try to come to Canada with no visa at all. The third bolt on the door against refugees is carrier sanctions. Before 1 February 1993, carriers—whether using ships, trains, planes, or buses—were penalized for bringing undocumented passengers to Canada. A person from a visa-requirement country without a visa is considered undocumented. Carriers who brought undocumented passengers to Canada were prosecuted in criminal court.

Since 1 February 1993, this criminal system has turned into a civil system. Now carriers are assessed a fee for any passenger who arrives in Canada and is subject to an immigration inquiry.[14] A person from a visa-requirement country without a visa is subject to inquiry. The question of whether the fee should be imposed never goes to court. The system is entirely administrative. Before 1 February 1993, carriers could plead a number of defences. They could argue due diligence, that they had tried their best to prevent the person coming to Canada but failed. They could ask for the same immunity refugee claimants and refugees get. Neither refugees nor refugee claimants whose cases have yet to be determined can be convicted for entry to Canada with improper documents.[15]

If the carrier could establish due diligence, if it could establish that the passenger was a refugee claimant or was recognized as a refugee, the carrier would not be penalized. Since 1 February 1993, those defences have disappeared with the disappearance of criminal proceedings. Now the liability of the carriers is absolute.

The Department of Citizenship and Immigration employs immigration control officers abroad in an interdiction program which helps airlines prevent undocumented persons coming to Canada. The government has spent millions of dollars on this interdiction program. On a couple of occasions, immigration control officers have engaged in Operation Shortstop. They have stationed themselves at airports abroad to prevent arrival of the undocumented to Canada. Mostly, what these officers do is to train airline staff at airports or private security agents the airlines have hired. They are trained to do Canadian immigration control work. Much of this control work consists of denying transportation to those persons who are from visa-requirement countries but who do not have visas. Airlines willingly cooperate with Canadian officials in order to avoid the carrier sanctions or administrative assessments that are imposed on them for bringing the undocumented to Canada.

This interconnected system of bolts is working. The number of claimants arriving in Canada has gone down from 1992 to 1993, when the new law came into effect with its enhanced carrier sanctions and the increase in the immigration control program overseas, from 30,000 to 21,000. Right now the system does not prevent every claimant from coming to Canada. But that is the scheme of the Act and its intended effect. Those who do arrive represent the failure of the system now in place.

The denial of the right to seek asylum is global, not just Canadian. Canada is far from being alone in frustrating attempts of those fleeing persecution to leave their countries. Many countries generating refugees are faced with global visa requirements. For the unfortunate attempting to escape from these countries, there is no destination to which they might flee without first seeking and obtaining a visa from the government of the destination country. The inevitable consequence of these global visa requirements and the denial of the right to seek asylum is that those internally displaced far exceed those who have managed to escape. For 1995, for instance, there were fifteen million refugees in the world and twenty-seven million internally displaced persons.[16]

What is Canada's proper role in all this? What are its responsibilities? I suggest that Canada should be a leader in the promotion of the Universal Declaration of Human Rights. We have the wealth, the population and the institutions to do it. Canada is a humane, tolerant, diverse nation, with a stable democracy, an entrenched constitutional Charter of Rights and Freedoms, human rights commissions, an independent judiciary and ombudsman institutions. If any country can set an example of respect for the Universal Declaration of Human Rights, Canada can.

Canada has the human and material resources to make human rights work. In Canada we should be able to show that it can be done, that respect for human rights can be an everyday practical reality. By that standard, Canada falls short in its failure to prosecute international fugitive mass murderers, to prohibit hate speech and to respect the right to seek asylum. Today in Canada, international fugitive mass murderers are unlikely to be prosecuted. Hate promoters are unlikely to be deterred from their incitement and refugees have difficulty getting access to Canada's protection.

Parliament legislated war crimes and crimes against humanity as Criminal Code offences, but only in 1987, over forty years after the Holocaust. In 1994 the Supreme Court of Canada made that legislation unworkable by its decision in the case of Imre Finta, a man against whom there was overwhelming evidence of his complicity in shipping the Jews of Szeged, Hungary, to Auschwitz. The government of Canada promised amending legislation to overcome that Supreme Court decision. Four years later that legislation has yet to see the light of day.

The judgement about incitement to hatred is as grim. The Supreme Court of Canada, in the *Keegstra* and *John Ross Taylor* cases, did the legal work for us, showing how freedom of expression and the prohibition of hate speech can live together conceptually, respecting both.[17] However, the practical work of legislation and enforcement has yet to be done. The government of Canada attempted to prosecute Ernst Zundel for Holocaust denial. The prosecutors succeeded in getting a conviction and Zundel was sentenced to jail, but the Supreme Court of Canada in 1992 threw out the conviction on the ground that the legislative provision under which he was convicted was drafted too broadly. The court suggested that a more narrowly drafted provision might well survive constitutional challenge, but the government of Canada has yet to accept that suggestion and propose a specific ban on Holocaust denial in the Criminal Code. Zundel, in the meantime, carries on with his Holocaust denial activities.

For refugees too, Canada has fallen short of the mark set by the Universal Declaration. The refugee determination procedure in Canada is by and large fair, but only for those who can access it. But getting access to the system is difficult indeed. Government officials, though they have set up a system that is motivated by the principle of no access, are realistic enough to acknowledge that denying everyone access is impossible. No system works perfectly, including immigration control. The system should generate a number of refugees that is commensurate with Canada's fair share of the world's displaced population. Beyond that, it should distinguish, before arrival, between those truly in need of protection and those who are not.

For the Universal Declaration of Human Rights to work, we must remember that it goes hand in glove with effective prosecution of the worst violators of human rights standards. We must not only appeal to the good in humanity. We must also guard against evil. Fifty years after the Universal Declaration of Human Rights, its promise has yet to be kept. For at least two of its provisions—the right to be free from incitement to discrimination and the right to seek asylum—the promise has yet to be wholeheartedly made. If we are to fulfil the promise of the Universal Declaration of Human Rights, we must respect not just some of its provisions but all of its provisions, including the right to be free from incitement to discrimination and the right to seek asylum.

REFERENCES

1. Article 21(1).
2. Article 19.
3. Article 5.
4. Article 3.
5. Article 26.
6. Reference Re: Public Service Employees Relations Act of Alberta (1987) 1 S.C.R. 313: 349.
7. Matas, David with Susan Charendoff. *Justice Delayed: Nazi War Criminals in Canada.* Toronto: Summerhill Press (1987): 68.
8. *R. v. Keegstra* (1990) 3 S.C.R. 697.
9. Matas, David. "Nazi War Criminals in Canada: Five Years After." B'nai Brith Canada (1992): 81.
10. Articles 7 and 14.
11. Article 25.
12. Article 11(1).
13. Article 13(2).

14. Immigration Act Section 91.1(1)(a).
15. Immigration Act Section 95.1.
16. UNCHR Refworld CD-ROM, July 1996.
17. *Canadian Human Rights Commission v. Taylor* (1990) 3 S.C.R.

ANNE F. BAYEFSKY

Protecting Those
Who Flee Abuse

Anne F. Bayefsky is director of the Centre for Refugee
Studies at York University in Toronto, Canada. She
served on the first External Research Advisory Council
to the United Nations High Commissioner for Refugees.
In 1992 she was awarded the Bora Laskin National
Fellowship in Human Rights Research and in 1995–96
received a MacArthur Foundation award for research
and writing.

THE OCCASION OF THE FIFTIETH ANNIVERSARY of the Universal Declaration
is an opportunity to highlight and to probe the relationship between the protection of the world's fifty million refugees and internally displaced persons and
the protection of human rights. The two regimes are closely connected, and
their alliance is supported by both the United Nations High Commission
for Refugees (UNHCR), the world's leading refugee agency, and Amnesty
International, the world's most prominent nongovernmental human rights
organization.

In 1998 the UNHCR Note on International Protection stated that "a comprehensive approach to refugee protection comprises ... respect for all human
rights."[1] Mrs. Sadako Ogata, the UN High Commissioner for Refugees, told the
UN Commission on Human Rights in March of 1998 that "the whole refugee
experience—from forcible displacement, provision of asylum and the search for
solutions—is related to the protection of human rights."[2] Dennis McNamara, the
director of UNHCR's Division of International Protection, stated in August of
this year: "While not all human rights issues concern refugees, all refugee issues
have some connection to human rights. The refugee cycle is entwined with the
deprivation and the restoration of fundamental human rights."[3] Furthermore,
"We must recognize that refugee law is born of and forms part of human rights
law, which remains relevant at all stages of refugee displacement."[4]

In 1997 Amnesty International launched a refugee campaign. Its campaign
literature explained Amnesty's involvement this way: "People become refugees
because they are fleeing human rights abuses;" "Human rights and refugees are
not separate issues. If governments protected human rights there would be no
refugees;" "The rights of refugees and basic human rights are inextricably linked

...today's human rights abuses are tomorrow's refugee movements."[5, 6, 7] In the conclusions and recommendations of the campaign's report, Amnesty again points out: "If respect for human rights was universal, no one would be forced to flee their home in search of protection abroad."[8]

These general principles are supported by the legal framework. The Universal Declaration of Human Rights itself sets out the cornerstone of refugee protection. Article 14 of the Declaration states that "everyone has the right to seek and enjoy in other countries, asylum from persecution." Other basic rights which underpin refugee protection are also outlined in the Universal Declaration: the right to life, liberty and security of the person; the right not to be subjected to cruel, inhuman and degrading treatment or punishment; the right to freedom of movement and the right to leave and return to one's own country; the right not to be subjected to arbitrary arrest, detention or exile; the right to a nationality; the right to an adequate standard of living, to education and to family unity.[9]

Human rights standards are thus the source of existing refugee protection principles and structures. Subsequently, the 1951 Refugee Convention transcribed the ideals of the Universal Declaration into legally binding obligations. The convention, together with the 1967 Protocol, now ratified by 136 governments, comprises a bill of refugee rights which elaborates on the specific entitlements of the vulnerable group identified by the Declaration.

The interdependence between the protection of human rights and refugees explains the conceptualization of the work of UNHCR as articulated in 1998. Mrs. Ogata told the UN Human Rights Commission that year: "It is important to mainstream human rights in all our work."[10] The UNHCR mission statement formulated in 1998 commits the body to "seek...to reduce situations of forced displacement by encouraging states and other institutions to create conditions which are conducive to the protection of human rights and the peaceful resolution of disputes."[11] In October 1998 the states which oversee UNHCR's work through its Executive Committee recognized that "the refugee experience, in all its stages, is closely linked to the degree of respect by States for human rights and fundamental freedoms..."[12] and "[e]ncourage[d] UNHCR to strengthen further its collaboration with the Office of the High Commissioner for Human Rights and with relevant human rights bodies and mechanisms."[13]

On a practical level, in the past couple of years UNHCR has produced training modules on human rights and refugee protection which start with the premise that UNHCR is the world's largest operational UN human rights agency.[14] Manuals and subsequent papers seek to draw out the consequences of this claim and a framework of human rights protection.

On the one side, international human rights law can assist in protecting refugees. It can reinforce existing refugee law. Many refugee protection standards are set out in nonbinding conclusions of the Executive Committee. While states should follow Executive Committee conclusions, they are not legally obligated to do so. But similar standards are set out in international human rights treaties, which do create legal obligations. For example, parts of an Executive Committee conclusion on protection of asylum seekers in situations of large-scale influx can be matched by specific parts of human rights treaties. References "not to be subjected to restrictions on their movements" can be found in the Covenant on Civil and Political Rights and the Convention on the Elimination of Racial Discrimination. This complementarity is also evident in the contents of the Convention on the Rights of the Child. "The Convention on the Rights of the Child is important to refugee children because it sets comprehensive standards...UNHCR...applies the Convention to its work by using the rights as guiding principles."[15] In fact, UNHCR policy on refugee children states that the Convention constitutes a normative frame of reference for UNHCR's actions.

International human rights law can supplement or bridge gaps in existing refugee law. This point is made both by Amnesty International and UNHCR. Amnesty pointed out in its refugee campaign that it is important "to ensure that the full framework provided by human rights law is applied to the protection of refugees."[16] UNHCR said in July 1998 that "'non-refoulement'...has found a parallel meaning and expression in broader human rights instruments...this complementary development...is adding a new avenue of protection for persons either erroneously rejected for refugee status or with clear protection needs whose circumstances are nevertheless not directly addressed by the 1951 Convention."[17]

For instance, there is no provision in the 1951 Convention regarding the rights of detained refugees. The Covenant on Civil and Political Rights grants essential rights to all detained persons, including refugees, such as the right to an independent review of the legality of the detention. To take another example, persons wrongly rejected from refugee status or who have protection needs not covered by the 1951 Convention in some circumstances can turn to the UN Convention Against Torture, which prohibits absolutely the expulsion of any person to a country where he or she may face torture. In Europe, under Article 3 of the European Convention on Human Rights, "no one shall be subjected to torture or to inhuman or degrading treatment or punishment," and an asylum seeker may be able to resist expulsion using a broad interpretation of this provision. Unlike the Refugee Convention, a person fearing such return does not have to prove that he or she risks persecution for one of the Refugee Convention reasons, the latter failing to include, for example, gender.

Many international human rights provisions are more widely applicable than the 1951 Convention. One hundred and thirty-six states are parties to the

1951 Convention together with the 1967 protocol, but the Convention on the Rights of the Child has 191 ratifications, and the Convention on the Elimination of Discrimination Against Women has been ratified by 154 states.

International human rights law is associated in some cases with quasijudicial implementing bodies, while the implementation of refugee law is primarily up to states. When there is a serious question about the implementation of refugee law standards, the issue cannot be effectively submitted to international adjudication. Three of the international human rights treaties, by contrast, provide for a system of individual complaints. For example, an asylum seeker whose case has been rejected but fears that he or she would be subjected to torture if returned could address a communication to the Committee Against Torture. There have already been decisions under the individual complaint procedure of this Committee related to asylum seekers.

In one case a Zairian was threatened with deportation from Switzerland, but following the rejection of his asylum application and appeal, the case was taken to the Torture Committee. After examining the case, the committee told Switzerland that returning the individual to Zaire would constitute a violation of the convention, and the Swiss government subsequently annulled the deportation order. A detained refugee or asylum seeker could also petition the Human Rights Committee established under the Covenant on Civil and Political Rights alleging that his or her detention was "arbitrary." While these committees do not have the power to order compliance, they publish their "views" on the merits of a case, and these have proven to carry a great deal of weight with state parties. The European human rights protection system also offers a judicial remedy and hence leaves the "interpretation of the human rights provisions of the Convention ...less to politics than to jurisprudence."[18]

In addition to a quasijudicial function, all six of the international human rights treaty bodies supervise the implementation of the treaties through state reports on compliance. These state reports are considered at regular intervals. During the consideration of state reports, state parties send government representatives to open meetings in which state compliance is discussed with treaty body members. Following the dialogue with the state party, the treaty bodies adopt concluding observations. For example, the Human Rights Committee adopted a concluding observation concerning Gabon and reported in its 1997 annual report as a principal subject of concern the following: "With regard to the rights of non-Gabonese citizens and refugees living in Gabon, the Committee is concerned about legal impediments to their freedom of movement within the country...the requirement of an exit visa for foreign workers...[and] the appalling conditions prevailing in refugee camps."[19] The committee made specific recommendations on the treatment of refugees in its conclusions. The 1997 annual report also raises refugee and displaced persons issues with respect to the states party reports from Peru, Germany, France and India.[20, 21, 22, 23] Hence, the state reporting process under the human rights treaties can serve as a forum for discussion, attention and commentary on refugee issues.

UNHCR should and does bring problems affecting the protection of refugees in a particular country to the attention of treaty bodies prior to their consideration of a state report. They are particularly well placed to do so. UNHCR protection officers regularly gather human rights information relevant to refugee protection issues as part of their reporting activities. Since 1994, and as part of the annual protection reporting exercise, UNHCR field offices are required to report on the treatment and protection of refugee women and children and to specific questions concerning aspects of respect for human rights within the country of origin, including any factors which could be considered as indicators for early warning.

As UNHCR papers attest, "[a]s a consequence of our extensive field presence, humanitarian objectives, and ability to gain access to refugees and other displaced persons, UNHCR is fully capable of gathering first-hand and front-line human rights information relevant to refugee protection....[T]he potential value of the information which UNHCR collects should not be underestimated."

The relationship between international human rights mechanisms and refugee protection agencies is not unidirectional. On the other side, human rights principles are also implemented through the actions of UNHCR. This occurs through a number of avenues. For one, UNHCR prevention activities involve initiatives designed to safeguard the security and well-being of people within their homeland, thereby removing or mitigating the causes of flight. UNHCR Executive Committee documents justify the interest in internal events this way: "Refugee movements and internal displacements frequently have the same causes, and it therefore makes little sense to deal only with the crossborder aspects of the problem. It is also clearly preferable to obviate the need for people to flee from their own country in order to find safety and to meet their basic needs."[24]

On the basis of specific requests from a secretary general, or the competent principal organs of the UN, and with the consent of states concerned, UNHCR therefore provides assistance and protection to internally displaced persons.[25] UNHCR is currently involved with some six million of an estimated twenty-five million internally displaced persons worldwide.[26] These are one-quarter of the people currently of concern to UNHCR.[27]

Secondly, at the field level UNHCR is increasingly involved in operations which incorporate a human rights component. A prime example of this is in the context of voluntary repatriation. Voluntary repatriation cannot take place in a human rights vacuum. The very basis for successful voluntary repatriation rests on fundamental changes in the countries of origin leading to the elimination of the root causes of flight, including the human rights situation. The UNHCR guidelines on voluntary repatriation refer to "return in conditions of safety and dignity," which entail certain human rights conditions.[28] In UNHCR's words: "Human rights standards help define the conditions for the safe and dignified return and reintegration of refugees to their country of origin. If returnees are to reintegrate successfully...they must have a place...to live...to be able to work, to educate their children, to participate in the political and cultural life of the community, and to be free from discrimination in exercising these rights."[29] Similarly, the criticism levelled at UNHCR for its involvement in repatriation exercises is rooted in the perceived failure to affirm and insist upon the maintenance of such human rights standards prior to encouraging repatriation.

Thirdly, the success of reintegration often depends on the rehabilitation and development of societies devastated by conflict, which in many cases goes beyond traditional assistance provided by development agencies. The creation or support of national legal, judicial and administrative capacity is frequently necessary to address the causes of refugee movements and to promote sustainable return. UNHCR therefore stresses the linkage of an effective human rights regime, including institutions which sustain the rule of law, justice and accountability to the ability to reintegrate refugees. Consequently, they have become increasingly involved in national legal and judicial capacity-building.[30]

All these initiatives mean that at the field level, human rights principles are implemented through the actions of UNHCR field officers who, according to the high commissioner, "are expected not only to observe human rights violations and report, but to act upon the information by seeking remedial action from the concerned authorities."[31] This approach is said by the high commissioner to comprise UNHCR's "operational conception of protection."[32]

In sum, the unique operational capacity of UNHCR can frequently make an important contribution to the implementation of international human rights standards. It will often be the case that UNHCR gathers human rights information from a much broader range of countries than is mandated by political UN bodies, such as the Commission on Human Rights. Furthermore, the UN human rights fora, as evidenced by the limited number of special rapporteurs or the field missions emanating from the Office of the High Commissioner of Human Rights or the treaty bodies, do not have the field operations capacity of UNHCR.

Still, this jurisdictional blurring of capacities between refugee and human rights protection agencies has its limits. The restricted scope of the UN's formal human rights agencies is a consequence of deliberate political reticence, which is only checked in the context of UNHCR because its role and the context is carefully circumscribed. While the "implementation" of human rights standards is viewed with suspicion by UN member states, UNHCR's "operationalizing" human rights protection is given operating room. This gives UNHCR a manoeuvrability which it is anxious to retain. UNHCR officials stress the impartial and nonpolitical nature of their work and their differences from the Office of the High Commissioner for Human Rights.

In the words of UNHCR's legal director: "The Office of the High Commissioner for Human Rights must, at times, be judgemental and perform investigatory and persecutory activities as it monitors human rights standards, particularly in field operations. But the impartiality of humanitarian action, the broad environment within which UNHCR functions, is a *sine qua non* of its effectiveness. Our nonpolitical approach allows us access to all victims on all sides of conflicts....To best protect [uprooted] populations...humanitarian action and human rights advocacy must remain distinctive but mutually supportive."[33] Similarly, the 1998 UNHCR Note on International Protection cautions: "UNHCR has been guided by its clear awareness of the complementarity but difference between the refugee specific mandate of UNHCR and the broader human rights mandate of other concerned organs....The need to maintain the mutually supportive but separate character of respective mandates is particularly clear in the area of monitoring. While human rights monitoring missions must investigate and encourage prosecution of human rights violations, action in support of refugees and returnees is essentially humanitarian, involving confidence-building and creation of conditions conducive to peace and reconciliation."[34]

The Executive Committee is also concerned. In October 1998 it encouraged UNHCR "to strengthen further its collaboration with the Office of the High Commissioner for Human Rights and with relevant human rights bodies and mechanisms...keeping in mind the need to...preserve the distinct character of the respective mandates."[35] Thus, while willing to cooperate and assist the high commissioner for human rights, UNHCR urges the mobilizing of "more operational human rights machinery as a necessary complement to its own protection efforts."[36] They advocate "human rights monitoring in some countries of refuge, and a whole range of human rights activities in many countries of return, from monitoring and reporting to rebuilding the central elements of law-based societies."

But they note, "Who exactly will undertake these difficult (and often unpopular) activities on behalf of the UN needs further definition. If UNHCR is to avoid 'overextending' itself on behalf of returned refugees—whether in providing basic shelter or monitoring their legal rights—other organizations and agencies need to be much more engaged in these areas. This is not humanitarian relief, but rather capacity building/human rights programming/essential postconflict reconstruction."[37]

In other words, however clear the importance of an integrated or comprehensive approach to the prevention and solution of forced displacement which is grounded in human rights norms, the requirements of operationalizing human rights in the context of forced displacement necessitate a division of labour as well as collaboration. Those requirements include monitoring, reporting and verifying human rights conditions; introducing mechanisms of international accountability of human rights violators; ensuring effective local law enforcement capabilities; and identifying and securing a range of local capacity-building requirements. Such an array of activities points to the challenge for the immediate future: a much clearer understanding among the actors in the field—UN human rights mechanisms, NGOs, relief agencies and national institutions—in terms of expectation, mandates and responsibility.

In summary, there are some facts which are widely accepted. Violations of human rights are a major cause of forced displacement. Human rights considerations are central across the spectrum of the refugee problem, from departure, through refuge, to solutions, including successful repatriation. Invoking the language of human rights and available international remedies for human rights violations can help the victim of forced displacement. There is a growing understanding that refugee protection issues should no longer remain on the fringes of the international human rights machinery and the interests of human rights organizations. At the same time, the work of relief agencies including UNHCR is, and should be, premised on human rights principles. Human rights bodies increasingly understand that effective implementation of human rights requires a field presence and because of this recognize the imperative of operationally oriented strategies.

Relief agencies, with the information at hand, recognize the potential benefits from alliances with human rights organs and their networks. Overall, there is a convergence of interests today among human rights actors which suggests new opportunities for meeting the challenges of forced displacement.

REFERENCES

1. A/AC.96/898, 3 July 1998, para.2; "In the last analysis, the entire refugee experience, from forcible displacement, through the search for asylum, to the securing of a durable solution, is an important indication of the respect accorded to basic human rights principles worldwide." A/AC.96/898, 3 July 1998, para. 3.
2. Statement to the United Nations High Commission on Human Rights, 19 March 1998: 1.
3. McNamara, Dennis. Director, Division of International Protection, UNHCR. Summer Course on Refugees and Human Rights. Universidad Complutense, Madrid, 24 August 1998: 1.
4. McNamara, Dennis. "The Law and the Protection of Refugees: The Way Ahead." 1998 Conference of the International Association of Refugee Law Judges, Ottawa, 16 October 1998: 4.
5. "Learning More About...Refugees and Human Rights." Amnesty International, 1997: 1.
6. "Refugees: Human Rights Have No Borders." Amnesty International Publications, 1997: 15.
7. Ibid.: 29.
8. Ibid.: 107.
9. McNamara, Dennis. "Human Rights and Refugees." Universidad Complutense, Madrid, 24 August 1998: 2, 3.
10. Statement by Mrs. Ogata, United Nations High Commission on Human Rights, 19 March 1998: 1.
11. A/AC.96/900, p. 18, para. 19, Overview of UNHCR Activities, UNHCR Mission Statement.
12. Report of the Forty-ninth Session of the Executive Committee of the High Commissioner's Programme, A/AC.96/911, 12 October 1998, p. 7, para. 21(g).

13. Ibid.: 7, para 21(i).

14. Human Rights and Refugee Protection, Part I, Training Module, RLD5, October 1995.

15. "Refugee Children: Guidelines on Protection and Care." Convention on the Rights of the Child, 1989.

16. "Refugees: Human Rights Have No Borders," Amnesty International Publications, 1997: 108.

17. A/AC.96/898, 3 July 1998, Note on International Protection, para. 11, p. 3.

18. McNamara, Dennis. "Human Rights and Refugees." Universidad Complutense, Madrid, 24 August 1998: 6.

19. Human Rights Committee Annual Report, A/52/40, Vol. I (1997), paras. 132, 142.

20. Ibid.: para. 151.

21. Ibid.: paras. 180, 181.

22. Ibid.: paras. 407, 408.

23. Ibid.: para. 445.

24. EC/46/SC/CRP.33, 28 May 1996, paras. 3, 12.

25. A/AC.96/865: 15.

26. E/CN.4/1998/53, 11 February 1998, para. 1, Report on Internally Displaced Persons.

27. Six million persons of the 22.4 million people currently of concern to UNHCR, A/AC.96/900, p. 240, Annex 1A, Overview of UNHCR Activities.

28. UNHCR has also developed operational guidelines on detention of asylum seekers, community services, evaluation and care of victims of trauma and violence, refugee women, refugee children, unaccompanied minors, preventing and responding to sexual violence against refugees and emergency response.

29. McNamara, Dennis. "Linkages Between Basic Human Rights Values and Refugees." Symposium Commemorating Fiftieth Anniversary of Universal Declaration of Human Rights, Bangkok, 25 May 1998: 4.

30. EC/46/SC/CRP.31, 28 May 1996, Standing Committee of ExCom: "I would like to recall...that activities in support of returnees, and of their reintegration, have been endorsed by this Executive Committee as an essential aspect of our responsibility for return—an inherent part of UNHCR's mandate." Opening Statement by the United Nations High Commissioner for Refugees at the Forty-ninth Session of the Executive Committee of the High Commissioner's Programme, A/AC.96/911, p. 25, Annex II, 5 October 1998: "UNHCR has over the past year intensified its...involvement...including support for national human rights institutions to strengthen local capacity to protect human rights; assistance in training the judiciary and government officials in refugee and related human rights concepts." A/AC.96/898, 3 July 1998, Note on International Protection, p. 12, para. 46. Furthermore, the international community is increasingly according greater priority to addressing the causes of population displacement and on measures to prevent their reoccurence. There is also a growing recognition that lasting solutions will require a concerted effort to promote good governance which respects human rights. Both in the context of working towards prevention and solutions UNHCR activities have a clear human rights dimension.

31. Statement of Mrs. Ogata to the UN High Commission on Human Rights, 1995.

32. Ibid.

33. McNamara, Dennis. "Linkages Between Basic Human Rights Values and Refugees." Symposium Commemorating Fiftieth Anniversary of Universal Declaration of Human Rights, 25 May 1998, Bangkok: 5.

34. A/AC.96/898, 3 July 1998, Note on International Protection, p. 12, para. 47.

35. A/AC.96/911, p. 7, para. 21(I), Report on the Forty-ninth Session of the Executive Committee of the High Commissioner's Programme, 12 October 1998.

36. A/AC.96/898, Note on International Protection, 3 July 1998, p. 12, para. 47.

37. McNamara, Dennis. "The Future of Protection." Conference on the Protection Mandate of UNHCR, The Hague, 18 September 1998.

The Economy, the Environment and Human Rights

CROSS CURRENTS OR PARALLEL STREAMS?

CINDY KENNY GILDAY

A Village of Widows

Cindy Kenny Gilday is a member of the Deline Dene
tribe, Treaty 11, in the Northwest Territories, Canada.
She received the 1994 Aboriginal Achievement Award
in recognition of her international work on environmental issues and aboriginal rights. She served as the
first indigenous representative at the World
Conservation Union, the first chair of the IUCN World
Conservation Union Task Force for Indigenous Peoples
and moderator for the first United Nations Conference
on Aboriginal Peoples and the Environment.

There can be no peace or harmony without justice.
—Report of the Royal Commission on Aboriginal Peoples, Canada, 1996.

The contempt for and the indifference towards Indians which countenanced the
savagery of the conquistadors has persisted: the conquistadors' legacy is our
refusal in our own time to take Indian culture seriously, our disregard for Indian
assertions of their rights as peoples, our view that we have an absolute right to
appropriate their wealth.
—*A Long and Terrible Shadow* by Thomas R. Berger, 1991.

O N 27 O CTOBER 1998 the Treaty chiefs of Canada met in Yellowknife to hear
the long-awaited United Nations report on treaty rights and aboriginal peoples.
It appears that for the first time the voice of the aboriginal peoples regarding
their version of the treaties instead of the written Western version is being given
some credibility. The majority of evidence regarding the aboriginal side of the
story of treaties in Canada is passed on through oral tradition. In 1997 the
Supreme Court of Canada recognized the legitimacy of aboriginal oral tradition
for the first time through the *Delgamuukw* case. Had it not been for these two
events, I would not have told the following story based on the Dene oral tradition with confidence that it would be taken as the truth. This is the Dene oral
history of the impact of development and transportation of radium and

uranium from Port Radium on Great Bear Lake in the Northwest Territories (NWT) to Fort McMurray in northern Alberta. This was the uranium used to develop the first atomic bomb dropped by the Americans on Hiroshima in 1945. It is the Dene ore carriers' tragedy. The case is self-evident in speaking to human rights issues, the environment and the economy in Canada's North.

Every day, spring, summer, winter or fall, unless he is sick, I see him walking slowly on the old trail in the village. He carries a traditional canvas pack and a .22-calibre gun. He is on his way to check snares for rabbits, shoot a few ptarmigan and check his net on the little lake for loche. He is too old to go on big hunts or on traplines but he is continuing a way of life on the land, a subsistence economy that his father before him and his father's father before him had done for thousands of years on these lands and waters. As Chief Kodakin once told the government people, "Great Bear Lake is our freezer. Without the food it provides for us to eat, we will starve."

The old man on the trail is one of the few remaining old men in the village. He does not speak a word of English. He is not only engaging in a cultural pursuit but is providing the necessary food for his family in the only way he knows how. They say it was his father, Beyonnie, who first found the money rock at Port Radium. Beyonnie gave it to the white man, for which he received a bag of flour, baking powder and lard about four times.

In the days before the European descendants (white people, as the Dene call them) came down the Mackenzie River, the Bear River to Great Bear Lake, and before Treaty 11 was signed with the government of Canada in Tulita, NWT, in 1921, and Treaty 8 further south earlier in northern Alberta and northern Saskatchewan, and before the establishment of communities along the river, the Great Bear Lake Indians—Sahtugot'tine—lived a nomadic lifestyle. They moved on a seasonal and rotational basis around the lake, following the migration of caribou, the cycles of the fur-bearing animals they trapped and the seasons of different species of fish. They followed the culture of caring for the earth.

Dene believe if you care for the earth and life forms, she can provide for your life and your people. They had a subsistence economy based on a clean environment that sustained all forms of life. Small groups of families lived and travelled together through the trapping, fishing and hunting seasons and the tribe would meet once a year in the summer in and around what is now called Tulita and Deline for clan gatherings. This type of lifestyle and culture was similar among the Dene from Great Bear Lake down Bear River and the Mackenzie River, across Slave Lake and down Slave River to Fort McMurray, Alberta—the route of the transportation of radium and uranium ore.

One of the few surviving elders in Deline, who was an ore carrier for only a short time but who was a traditional chief in Tulita for many years, tells the story in vivid detail. The story of the Treaty in 1921 was etched in his memory. The Dene came from their winter camps all over the land and lakes to gather in

Tulita for two months in the summer. The government came and asked the people to sign a treaty so that white people coming from the south and the Dene could life in peace together. Like many Dene witnesses of the signing of the treaties along the river, the elder insists the Dene were adamant and clear that this was not a land transaction deal. The government of Canada promised the Dene that if they would each accept five dollars a year, then the government would look after the Dene for "as long as the sun rises and does not go backwards, the Mackenzie River flows and does not go backwards and the grass grows."

To the Dene, as a people who lived and died by their words according to oral tradition, this government promise was a formal agreement that took place in public and was taken to heart to last forever. The Dene even consulted the Catholic Bishop. On the Bishop's assurance, the Dene accepted the government's promise with confidence. In later years, as the Indian Brotherhood (now Dene Nation) was established by all the chiefs along the Mackenzie River in the NWT, the story was the same all along the river for the Dene.

To a people who lived by the seasons, calendar and dates had very little significance. They remember events by the daily drama of living off the land. The few surviving ore carriers from the community of Deline on Great Bear Lake and the surviving members of families from Yellowknife and the Dogrib region concurred on the following story of the discovery of the money rock (what they called radium and uranium). It is also a story my father and his friends told many times over the years. I first wrote about this issue in the early 1980s for the *Dene Nation Newsletter*.

It was a few years after the signing of Treaty 11 in Tulita in 1921. There was a white trapper who lived with a group of families on the east side of Great Bear Lake in their traditional trapping territory, in and around the area on what was later to become Port Radium. Nobody could remember his name. It was during that winter that Beyonnie found the unusual rocks that he showed to the white trapper. That spring and summer the white trapper left the camp with the rocks, travelling in a boat across the lake and down the river. It was a year later, in the summer, that he came back by boat with more white people and it was at that time Beyonnie received flour, baking power and lard four times for the rocks he gave to the white people.

It was around this time, the story goes, that an important medicine man of the Dene had a very powerful dream and warned his people. It is said he sang through the night and his people came to him in the morning to inquire about what he had seen. To the Dene, dreams have as much impact on daily life as the cycle of caribou migration. It is said he dreamt that a deadly material would come from around the rock outcrop of what was to become Port Radium. This material was put into a big stick and then onto what looked like a metal bird. This bird dropped this big stick on many people living far away and it burned them all. These people looked just like us. The truth of this dream was brought back to the people of Deline only in 1998, with their visit to Hiroshima.

A few years later the Labine brothers came to Great Bear Lake and started digging rocks out of the ground. More white people came and started to live around Cameron Bay. Through these early years the Dene provided caribou, moose and fish in exchange for trade goods. As the elders say, "They were strangers living among us on our land so we took care of them." Because nobody understood English, the Dene were never told by anybody, including the government of Canada, what was happening on their land. The families whose traditional territory was this area of Great Bear Lake continued their pattern of life on the land. Nobody asked their permission or even acknowledged their existence. Some started to live on the periphery of the mining camp, cutting logs to sell to the miners and doing labour jobs. Their specific harvesting areas on the land and water around Port Radium were affected and life for the Dene on Great Bear Lake was changed irreversibly. Starting in the 1930s, it also affected the Dene in general along the transportation route for radium and uranium.

The few surviving members of the Dene families who lived around Port Radium recall their observations of changes. There were families from the Dogrib region as well as Yellowknife. The mine people (white people) set up some structures with the logs the Dene provided, right over the place where they were digging up the rocks. Out of these structures on the edge of the lake, into the water, were dumped what looked like mud, sand and pebbles: leftovers from the money rocks the miners extracted. In this area, across the bay from where the Dene families lived in tents, many dead fish would float to the top of the water and these were offered to the Dene for use. One elder recalls that at one point there was so much debris coming out of the mine that it covered a large enough area to become a bridge to one of the islands offshore. The dust from the mine made the snow and ice in the bay melt faster than that on the rest of the lake.

The miners left for a few years but came back in bigger numbers in the early 1940s. This time they dredged up the material they had dumped in the lake the first time, as well as from a bigger underground operation. The Dene continued their way of life on the land around the mine, selling meat, fish and logs. As before, only white people were hired to work in the mine. But this time around the mine had to do the work faster and provide a greater volume of radium to transport. This time they hired all able-bodied young Dene men to carry the ninety- to one-hundred-pound bags of uranium ore on and off boats, barges and trucks, along the transportation corridor of the historic route of radium and uranium to Fort McMurray.

The Dene ore carriers' experiences along the transportation route of radium and uranium were similar. Most of the stories came from my relatives, my time at the Dene National Office and from other Dene men along the Mackenzie River, the Dogrib region and most recently from the surviving Dene elders in

Deline and Tulita. Coming from the background of making a living off the land and providing for their families, most of the Dene men were physically very strong and used to hard work. Most of their grandfathers lived to be in their nineties or older. Coming from a patrilineal society, they were responsible for the survival of their tribe. By this time the Dene had become accustomed to trade goods so most of the men came off the land in the summertime to work as labourers, and very often their families went with them to live in nearby tent communities on the periphery of transportation and storage and docking facilities that dotted the river route and around Port Radium. The women continued the traditional way of making a living from the land and waters.

From very early in the morning to very late at night the men would load and unload those ninety- to one-hundred-pound bags of uranium ore at transfer points along the river. The men slept and ate on the bags during the long trips. Dust from uranium ore bags was part of everything. At the beginning the gunny sacks contained rocks with a brown-black, fine dust which was later replaced by a yellow material with yellow dust. The women often talked of their husbands coming home late with dust in their hair, on their skin and clothing. The men explained that aside from carrying ore bags on their backs all day, the bags would break and they would have to clean up the mess manually. They also had to sweep the entire huge barges which were full of dust from the bags. They did this for three dollars a day for four months every year, some for only a couple of seasons, but most for the duration of the uranium mining at Port Radium.

The ore carriers divided into crews to cover different transfer points along the route. It started in Port Radium where the first crew loaded from the mill to the barges that were attached to boats like the *Radium Gilbert*. The crew would travel with the load on the barges, sleeping on the bags for 250 kilometres across Great Bear Lake and docking at the mouth of Bear River at Franklin Landing, five kilometres from what is now the village of Deline. Franklin Landing is where there is open water all year round and was traditionally relied on by the Dene for fish all of the year. Here they were joined by another crew to unload the barges onto small river boats to go down the Bear River to a docking area just above Saint Charles Rapids.

At the docks before the rapids another crew of Dene men from Deline and Tulita unloaded the barges onto trucks. They travelled on the loads eighteen kilometres over a gravel road to Bennet Fields. This field was at one time a spiritual gathering ground where some of their ancient ancestors were buried. In the Bennet Fields the bags were either stored or loaded onto the next boat to Tulita, another Dene community at the confluence of the Bear River and the Mackenzie River. Many families from Deline and Tulita lived at the Bennet Fields all summer while the men were working. In Tulita, on the banks in front of the village, the uranium ore bags were again either stored or loaded onto barges. From there they travelled down the Mackenzie River, across Great Slave Lake,

111

CINDY KENNY GILDAY

then down the Slave River to Bell Rock and Fort Fitzgerald. The Dene men from this area did the same type of work to load and unload the boats at Bell Rock and Fort Fitzgerald. From there on the journey continued to Fort McMurray where again the same work was done. One surviving ore carrier estimates the time period to be from about the 1930s to 1950.

It was in the 1970s that the ore carriers and members from families who lived around Port Radium started to die from many forms of cancer. The elders said it was the first time they had heard of this type of disease. Because radium and uranium mining was the only industrial activity on Great Bear Lake and the river route that connects the ore carriers, the people suspected it was this that was causing the horrible deaths. The chiefs, from community meetings to the Dene National Assembly, called on the government of Canada to investigate the situation. After years of oral tradition appeals were ignored by the government of Canada, the chiefs of the Mackenzie Valley started to write resolutions in the 1980s.

The widows of the ore carriers tell their story. Most of their men were considered to be in their prime when they died horrible deaths from cancer. The men were grandfathers, fathers and uncles—the people responsible for the survival of the tribe. The widows are traditional women who learned their roles in the ways of the land. They are skilled in tanning hides, drying fish and caribou and sewing clothing for their families. Most of them speak only their aboriginal language. Like most Dene families along the river, they had many children. The family is most important to the Dene, therefore the women and children went with the men to make a living. When the men died these proud women of the land, with many small children to care for, were without providers and were plunged into desperate poverty. Unlike families of uranium miners from the south, there was no compensation package for ore carriers' families. They were reduced to depending on handouts from other families who still had males who could hunt, trap and fish. With shame they accepted handouts from the "ration" or government welfare office. They supplemented donations of food by selling handicrafts when possible to anyone who would buy them for small amounts of money.

The hardest times came with seasonal changes. They would see and hear families with surviving fathers, grandfathers or uncles go with boats, dog teams and snowmobiles to roam and taste the freedom of living on the land. An acute sense of longing would descend on these widows to visit the ancestral graves of traditional family territory. It had been part of their identity since time immemorial to roam with husband and family. Economic conditions made it difficult to even retain a sense of dignity and the identity that comes with fulfilling one's ancestral obligations.

The daughter of a widow from Deline, while visiting the community, said, "Every day as I got up in the morning, I saw the *Radium Gilbert* sitting out in the bay in front of the village, a cruel reminder to all the widows whose husbands worked on that boat carrying ore on their backs for three dollars a day. That must be the reason that they died early and horrible deaths, bringing so much suffering to our families and the community. They say the government sold the boat to the community for one dollar. In the past the children played on the boat. The people of Deline have been asking the government to remove it for years but still it sits in the bay as a reminder of the ore carriers' tragedy.

The tears which never go away start afresh when the question arises: Who is going to teach my son the ways of the land and the ways of my people so he can take his responsibility for the survival of the tribe? Without the grandfather to pass down spiritual teachings and values, without the uncles to correct the behaviour of a nephew and without a father to train his sons to assume obligations and responsibility for the survival of the tribe, hope dies quickly. What will become of these sons and the people in these confusing times? Many young men of the village are dysfunctional because they have no one to answer to for their behaviour and actions. However, to give up on them would be to give up on the tribe.

Some recent events regarding radium and uranium contamination have made the few surviving ore carriers and widows question if the government of Canada has any humanitarian values. In recent years government officials and other scientists reported that the Bennet Fields, Sawmill Bay and many spots along the river route were contaminated and radioactive. The people from Tulita and Deline have since abandoned the Bennet Fields as a spiritual gathering ground. Some scientists said that the water, soil and fish are contaminated around the Port Radium area. They also said that caribou pass over contaminated soil around Port Radium in their migration. But the government officials keep telling the Dene that it is not dangerous. Other scientists, including those from the Navajos, warn of extreme dangers to human health from uranium exposure. It is harmful if touched, inhaled or digested. In the meantime, more and more people are dying of cancer and now the widows are starting to die the same deaths as their husbands. The people are now concerned for their health and living in fear of their food source and their land and waters.

They heard stories that the material that killed the Japanese civilians came from their land and a monument still stands at Port Radium glorifying that fact but, until 1998, the people of Sahtu were not told. One of the widows who died with cancer in October 1998 sent a message to the Japanese people to say, "We Dene are a kind people. We did not know that the material that came from our land killed and makes your people suffer today. We are very sorry about that. We want to heal our suffering too."

We have a sixty-year legacy of a toxic environment. The Dene have been appealing to the government of Canada with the following questions: Did radium and uranium mining at Port Radium and transportation of the ores down the river bring about the contamination of our lands, water and traditional foods? What has caused the increasing rate of cancer among our people and why have so many Dene ore carriers died horrible cancer deaths? Even up to the time of the Dene Assembly in Hay River in the summer of 1997 when the issue was raised again by the chiefs, the government of Canada claimed it was not sure who is the responsible party for this situation. To date no one answers the Dene's cry for help.

Robert Bothwell's book *Eldorado: Canada's National Uranium Company* (1984) reflects the written Western view. The author clearly did not consult the Dene or the workers from Port Radium. It is a glorification of Canada's involvement in the nuclear industry and the development of the first A-bomb for World War II. On the other hand, Andrew Nikiforuk of the *Calgary Herald* wrote an article called "Echoes of the Atomic Age" (April 1998) in which he used independent current sources, including oral tradition. He looked more realistically at what actually took place. Independent research and other expert opinions confirm the following events from written sources:

1921 Treaty 11 was signed by the Federal Crown of Canada and the Dene of the Mackenzie Valley in the villages along the river route, including Tulita, NWT, at the confluence of the Mackenzie and Bear rivers.

1930 Gilbert Labine discovered pitchblends on the east shore of Great Bear Lake, an important ore of radium and uranium.

1931 Port Radium began production and the price of radium was $70,000 per gram. Radium was extracted, tonnes of uranium tailings were dumped on land and into the lake, and crude sorting and bagging by hand was done for shipment. Mines Canada issued health warnings on radon gas and radioactive dust and required precautions for the miners and lab workers. Exposure to uranium dust was lethal. The Dene were never warned or told of the dangers of the ore they were carrying on their backs and they unknowingly endangered the health of their families as well.

1936 Labine Brothers purchased Northern Waterways and renamed it Northern Transportation (NT), a subsidiary of Eldorado Mining and Refining Ltd. NT was the shipping line that transported the ore.

1939 Canadian ore was used in the first atomic chain reaction experiment.

1932–1940 The mine complex remained in operation but was temporarily shut down due to the lower price of radium and market conditions in Europe.

1941 Port Radium reopened for the war effort. It was the first uranium mine in the world. Dene ore carriers were recruited to transport uranium ore. Tonnes of uranium ore were transported along the river route from Port Radium to Fort McMurray, on its way to Port Hope in Ontario.

1942 The United States government ordered 60 tonnes of uranium, followed by 350 tonnes in July and 500 tonnes in December. Large sums of money changed hands. The Canadian government secretly began to buy out the mine.

1944 The government of Canada completed the incremental transaction of buying the Port Radium mine (Order in Council P.C. 535, January 1944). Crown Corporation Eldorado was established along with NTCL, the subsidiary. The federal government was involved right from the beginning of the reopening of Port Radium to the extraction of uranium to sell to the US.

1945 The Americans dropped A-bombs on Hiroshima and Nagasaki.

1949 US officials raised health concerns about Port Radium miners.

1953 The first Port Radium miner died of cancer. The US government secretly began health studies on US uranium miners. The US developed the Radiation Exposure Victims Act largely due to the efforts of Navajo uranium miners. This compensation act is being revisited now to address justice for all uranium workers, labourers above ground, truckers and their families.

1956 The value of Canadian uranium production hit $1-billion. The Port Radium mine, which produced uranium, operated from 1942 to 1960. In 1976, Eldorado was reopened by Echo Bay Mines and silver was mined until 1982.

1960 The Port Radium uranium mine closed and the first Dene man whose family lived around Port Radium died of cancer.

1972 A federal fisheries officer expressed concern over fish and water contamination around the Port Radium area.

1979 The first cancer death study on Port Radium miners was carried out. The concerns of the Dene were ignored and continue to be ignored. There were no studies carried out on Dene exposure to uranium dust, Dene exposure to radioactive lands and waters and traditional foods, and the linkage to human health and increasing cancer deaths. No studies on the Dene ore carriers have been done.

1982 A Low-Level Waste Management Office (LLWMO) was established in Port Hope, Ontario, and was operated by Atomic Energy of Canada. A 1992–93 report showed they spent almost $3 million on southern communities from Fort McMurray to Port Hope in Ontario to consult, identify and clean up radioactive and contaminated soil in those places. Recently, Port Hope got another $150 million to address its concerns.

1993 The Federal Crown of Canada signed a land claims deal with the Sahtu Dene and Metis. Documents confirmed that 1.7 million tonnes of radioactive tailings were dumped in Great Bear Lake and the surrounding land. Bennet Fields, the hard-won Dene spiritual gathering grounds, was not listed in the documents as being contaminated.

1994 Senes Consulting report for LLWMO: Production from Eldorado and Echo Bay Mines included 37 million ounces of silver, 10.5 million pounds of copper and 13.7 million pounds of uranium ore. They also identified "hot spots" from ore spills at transfer points along the transportation route. These included Port Radium, Sawmill Bay, Bennet Fields, Tulita and Fort Fitzgerald to Fort McMurray. This report was delivered to the Dene Assembly in Tulita in 1996. It is a technical and economic analysis of radioactive soil spillage along the transportation route and does not answer any questions about Dene health concerns. Nor was the report ever made understandable to the average person who has no scientific background. Consultation was minimal and did not include the necessary aboriginal language translations required in all Dene communities.

1997 There was a controversial clean-up of radioactive "hot spots" at Sawmill Bay, land which was given to the Dene in the land claims deal of 1993. Ten young Dene men and two women from Dene sent to clean up claimed inadequate conditions and exposure to radioactive dust. They were told by LLWMO officials that the soil was not dangerous.

"Canada was the first country to mine uranium. The world's first uranium mine was at Port Radium, NWT, on the shore of Great Bear Lake. Canada was also the first country to refine uranium on an industrial scale. Uranium for the WWII Atomic Bomb Project was processed in secrecy at Port Hope, Ontario." So wrote Gordon Edwards from the Canadian Coalition for Nuclear Responsibility. "Canadian uranium miners have died from lung cancer at a rate many times higher than nonminers. Ottawa knew of the health dangers of uranium and radium as early as 1932, but did not inform workers or compensate their widows until 1973." The Dene were never informed or recognized as victims and the ore carriers' widows and families were never compensated. Someone was quoted in the media as saying, "We just left them to die." One has to ask what Canada's responsibilities are.

Perhaps one of the most poignant moments in my work with the Dene of Deline on the uranium issue was at a public meeting where their lawyers delivered a year's worth of research from the archives in Ottawa on this issue. In a packed community hall, from elders to young people, the senior lawyer informed them, "In the mountain of papers we dug up in Ottawa this year on this issue, there is not one mention of the Dene, your people." The hall went completely silent. The elders had incredulous looks on their faces, a combination of sadness and anger. One of them could only say, "How could that be? We helped them." The young people immediately expressed anger, saying, "We are people. We are not dogs."

For the old man on the old trail in the village, for the widows, for a small tribe on Great Bear Lake, for the Dene along the river struggling to survive and for the Navajos in New Mexico, the environment and the economy are one and the same—one cannot be without the other. They now live in fear of the land, water and traditional foods on which their very communities depend to survive as a people. They are rightfully concerned for the health of their children. The Japanese experience in health matters regarding radiation illnesses gives the Dene every reason to be concerned about their children. Their patrilineal society is hanging by a threat. But the broader issue is that, like most Native Americans, their culture, spirit and their very beings are intimately linked with the well-being of Mother Earth. It is this that has been compromised by uranium mining contamination in the North by Canada's crown corporation, Eldorado, mining that contributed to the first nuclear weapon used to destroy life on earth.

"The right to the environment will unquestionably be one of the major human rights of the 21st century, since the most fundamental human right, the right of existence, is under threat," wrote K. E. Mahoney and P. Mahoney in *Human Rights in the Twenty-First Century: A Global Challenge*. Perhaps more than anyone else, because of their immediate reliance on their environment for their sustenance, the Dene of the north know the truth of this statement. If their environment is compromised, their lives are compromised.

This story speaks volumes about human rights violations as identified in the 1948 Universal Declaration of Human Rights and the 1966 International Covenant on Economic, Social and Cultural Rights. Whether it is deliberate or by negligence, the government of Canada participated in this issue in a major way. If Canada's signature is to mean anything on the Universal Declaration of Human Rights, then the government must redress this historic and outstanding injustice to the Dene and the Village of Widows. If the Canadian government fails to take responsibility for this legacy of a toxic environment, the result of activities which filled its coffers at the expense of the people for whom they had fiduciary obligations, and if it fails its obligation to protect the environment for all Canadians, then the government of Canada has failed us all. The United Nations must not assume that there are no serious human rights problems in a privileged country like Canada. The United Nations, as the champion of human rights at the global level, must seriously consider helping the Dene of the North in their struggle to survive as a culture in their own environment. For the families and the widows of the Dene ore carriers, there will be no peace without justice and redress. They carry wounds of World War II that have yet to be addressed.

REFERENCES

Oral tradition of the Dene of the Mackenzie Valley.

Alt, P. and S. McCormick. "Lethal Impact, Environmental Racism Targets Native Americans." *Briarpatch* (Nov. 1998).

Bothwell, R. *Eldorado: Canada's National Uranium Company*. Toronto: University of Toronto Press (1984).

Environmental Sciences Group. "An Environmental Assessment of Sawmill Bay, NWT." Royal
   Military College, 1997.

Falk, M. R. "Preliminary Investigations into Pollution Potential of Tailing Discharge into Great Bear
   Lake by Echo Bay Mines Ltd." Fisheries Services, Department of Environment, 1972.

Edwards, Gordon and R. Del Tredici. Nuclear Map of Canada, 1997.

Harris, Phil. Uranium Radiation Victims Committee (Navajo), Presentation of Radiation Victims
   Compensation Act and Congressional Intervention, 1998.

Hatfield Consultants Ltd. "An Evaluation of Environmental Conditions Associated with Abandoned
   Uranium Mines at Rayrock and Echo Bay." Science Institute of NWT, 1985.

Kalin, M. "Port Radium NT: An Evaluation of Environmental Effects of Uranium and Silver
   Tailings." Toronto Institute for Environmental Studies, University of Toronto, 1984.

Lockhart, W. L. Head Arctic Contaminants Research Station, Letter to G. Bayha, Levels of
   Contaminants in Fish and Sediments in Great Bear Lake, 1997.

Low-Level Radioactive Waste Management Office. 1992–93 Annual Report, Port Hope, Ont. Canada
   (31 March 1993).

Mahoney, K. E. and P. Mahoney. *Human Rights in the Twenty-First Century: A Global Challenge.*
   Dordrecht, Boston: Martinus Nyhoff Pub. (1992).

Mandell, Louise. Analysis *of Delgamuukw vs. BC.* Banff Lectures, 1998.

Morris, Margaret W. "Great Bear Lake Indians: A Historical Demography and Human Ecology."
   Master of Arts Thesis, University of Saskatchewan, 1969.

National Film Board of Canada. *Uranium: A Discussion Guide*, 1991.

Nikiforuk, Andrew. "Echoes of the Atomic Age." *Calgary Herald*, April 1998.

Norecon Ltd. (for the economic planning section of Resource, Wildlife and Economic Development
   for Government of Northwest Territories), NWT Economic Review and Outlook, 1997.

Senes Consultants Ltd. Phase I, II, III Investigations into the Historic Northern Uranium
   Transportation Network in the Northwest Territories and Northern Alberta, 1994.

Swanson, S. M. Report on Port Radium Analytical Report, second draft prepared for Department of
   Indian Affairs and Northern Development, 1995.

UN Committee on Elimination of Racial Discrimination Concerning Indigenous Peoples, General
   Recommendation XXII(51) (August 1997).

UN General Assembly Res. 2200/XX/ on 16 December 1966, Human Rights International
   Convention on Civil and Political Rights.

UN General Assembly Res. 2200/XX/ on 16 December 1966, International Covenant on Economic,
   Social and Cultural Rights.

D.W. SCHINDLER

The Ecological Rights of Humans

David Schindler is Killam Memorial Professor of
Ecology at the University of Alberta in Edmonton,
Canada. He has headed the International Joint
Commission's Expert Committee on Ecology and
Geochemistry and the US Academy of Sciences'
Committee on the Atmosphere and the Biosphere. He is
a recipient of the Stockholm Water Prize and the Volvo
Environment Prize.

N O ONE WILL ARGUE that the basic rights of humans must include freedom
from personal or cultural oppression, clean water, uncontaminated and
adequate food, and a pleasant, healthy and productive environment in which to
live a happy and fruitful life. We have made great strides in the first of these.
While dictators and racists still exist, none are safe from global scrutiny and
most are ousted before very long. Similarly, overt cultural oppression is widely
censored.

But we are clearly losing the battle for water, adequate and clean food, for
pleasant and productive environments. In some cases, cultures are being oppressed unwittingly, most notably those small cultures that require large
pristine areas to exploit for food or for cultural context, such as aboriginal
peoples. If we allow the deterioration in these environmental elements to
continue, there will be great human suffering and social strife to a degree that
will make us forget all but the most inhumane dictators of the past. To prevent
this from happening we must begin now, making some decisions that will be
unpleasant and controversial but not so unpalatable as the disasters that we can
prevent.

Water, Food and Ecosystem Preservation

Most ecologists are very concerned about the global state of water (Naiman et al.
1998). In some areas it is already impossible to ensure that drinking water is
sufficient in quantity, safe and palatable (Gleick 1998), let alone to consider
needs for agriculture or to maintain the biodiversity of the ecosystems which
have been a fundamental part of human cultural development. If global populations continue to grow we will not be able to feed them. If agricultural advances

do not limit us first, the amount of water and its distribution on the planet will do so within the next quarter century. We simply will not have enough water to grow sufficient food. The situation is nicely summarized by Postel (1998). Most water-impoverished countries already must import much of their food because they simply don't have enough water to grow it (Table 1). Postel estimates that even if global distribution problems are ignored, we would have to double the amount of irrigation to keep pace with demand. There is not enough available water to do this easily. Unless we take action to prevent it, there will be increasing human conflict over water supplies.

But the green revolution is also in question. Global grain production, which increased two to two-and-a-half per cent per year from 1950–1990 as the result of the "green revolution," declined to about one per cent per year in the 1990s (Brown 1997; Daily et al. 1998). Economic conditions in Asia will probably aggravate the decline. Perhaps the green revolution has peaked. It would be unrealistic to expect it to continue forever, but the turning point is difficult to predict with accuracy. The big increases in crop production have been in developed countries, using methods that are very expensive, both in energy and in currency. Contamination of watercourses with nitrogen and pesticides has resulted (Vitousek et al. 1997; Pimentel 1978). As we have seen with relief efforts in several famine-stricken countries in the past decade, distribution of large quantities of food to sites half-way around the world remains a problem. Even the most modern transportation systems are not up to the task, regardless of funds and energy available.

Demotechnic Dilemmas

Ecologists, who deal with populations of animals and plants on a day-to-day basis, have long viewed the exploding human population with concern. The number of people on the planet is triple the number that lived here when I was born. All of us believe that growth must halt. The debate is about when and how. I am sure that other presentations at this conference will emphasize that educating women will bring down the birth rate, that there are humane methods of contraception, and other discussions that are widely acceptable in the global society. All of this is wonderful, but it is my view that change will not be fast enough to prevent severe ecosystem degradation, shortage of food and water and resulting conflict.

A second dilemma is that much of the world is striving to obtain a lifestyle similar to that of western Europe and North America. This cannot happen because we simply do not have the global resources. As Vitousek et al. (1986) have demonstrated, we already use a high percentage of the photosynthetic energy reaching the earth's surface each year. Several scientists have calculated the distribution of resource use. I will use the demotechnic index (Mata et al. 1994) to make my point.

The demotechnic index is simply the ratio of technological energy consumption, in gigajoules per capita year, to the energy required for physiological subsistence alone, which is estimated to be 3.57 gigajoules per capita year. Canadians and Americans have huge demotechnic indices, 118 and 91 respectively (Table 2), meaning that each North American uses about one hundred times more energy than required for subsistence alone. European countries tend to have indices between twenty-five and seventy-five. Most other countries are much lower. In some cases values are four or less. If we multiply populations by these indices to get consumption-adjusted populations (Mata et al. op. cit.), the numbers are enormous. We are already supporting the subsistence equivalent of 104 billion people. The richest twenty-nine countries account for eighty-six per cent of this energy use. Obviously, if we double the population and allow energy consumption of all countries to reach North American values, several additional planets will be required. We must have more realistic expectations.

There are three things that we can do to prevent our demotechnic demands from exceeding global supplies. We can act more rapidly to decrease populations. This needs to be done most urgently in countries that already greatly exceed local food supplies because their costs of transporting food add to the demotechnic dilemma. It should be the goal of each country to reduce its population to levels where energy requirements can be met locally. We can still trade with each other to obtain variety but we will be secure in knowing that if all else fails we can control our own basic needs and protect our local environments.

How to reduce population rapidly and humanely is an enormous question. Science can estimate only how far and how fast we must move. Executing the necessary changes require changes in ethics, religions, politics and medical practices. All these sectors must participate and be prepared to bend somewhat if global disaster is to be prevented. We can also reduce our demotechnic demands. What sort of energy consumption is required for humans to live healthy, happy lives? It is certainly not one hundred, perhaps not even twenty-five. I suspect that it could be much lower.

I have lived through much of the demotechnic revolution. When I was a child we still heated with wood. It was cut by hand or with simple mechanical saws. We had one small tractor but much of our fieldwork was still done by horses. We had a car but anything over thirty kilometres was regarded as a long trip. We had oil lamps, a few books, a radio and a wind-up phonograph. We raised a big garden, canned our own vegetables for winter use, raised and ate our own chickens, hogs and cows. Water was pumped from a well. We did not have indoor plumbing. I can well remember trips to the outhouse on frosty winter nights. My guess is that our demotechnic demands were around ten. All of that changed rapidly after the end of World War II. Within a few years we had electricity and electrical appliances, several tractors, cars and trucks. We first had an oil stove, then a furnace with an electric blower. But it has always struck me as curious that these energy-consuming devices brought us no additional happiness. So perhaps there is a demotechnic level that will ensure that humans have what they need to live comfortable and productive lives without extravagant wastes of energy.

We should agree on some acceptable global ranges for national demotechnic demands. Some countries would have to decrease their energy consumption to meet their objectives and to allow others to increase. Individual countries could choose to have small populations with larger demotechnic indices or larger populations with lower energy demands. I estimate that, with its current demotechnic index, a human population in Canada that would allow us to sustain energy, food, water and native species of animals and plants for the indefinite future is probably less than ten million people. Much of our abundant water is in the north while the land suitable for agriculture and comfortable for most people is a narrow band in the south. Make no mistake, these will be hard choices. But they are choices that we must make if we do not want to precipitate one of the greatest convulsions in the history of our fauna and flora.

■■■ The Special Problem of Small Cultures

As national and world populations grow, small groups suffer. It is a very simple problem. Democracy is regarded as one vote per human. When a decision involves conflict between a larger and a smaller cultural group, the smaller loses—even if it is not overtly oppressed—for the smaller group simply has fewer votes. Larger, richer societies also are better able to invade, if not with armies then by radio, television and movies. The result is homogenization of cultures. Small cultures get deeply buried by the mainstream.

An example is that of northern native people in this country. Even today, most of them live much as I lived as a child, not sharing in much of the country's lavish energy consumption. Many still burn wood and rely on country food to a large degree. Snowmobiles and outboard motors provide transportation but satellites have allowed American culture to invade the north. Fortunately, we have ceased forcing our religions and educational systems on northern people. These caused tragedies which were not realized at the time.

But there are other, less visible problems. The bodies of aboriginal northerners have been found to contain peculiarly large concentrations of PCBs, mercury and other contaminants (Jensen et al. 1997; AMAP 1998; Table 3). Scientists have discovered that these contaminants are carried in the atmosphere from distant sites, some on the other side of the earth. They have entered ecosystems and been biomagnified as they are passed up the food chain. The biomagnification can be thousands or millions of times, as the ratio of the concentration in organisms to that in the water which pollutants first contaminate shows. This ratio is known as a bioaccumulation factor or BAF. The ratios can be very high, hundreds of thousands or even millions of times. The US Environmental Protection Agency's (EPA) BAF for mercury at the fourth step in an aquatic food chain is 6.8 million!

There is an ongoing debate as to whether people should limit their consumption of contaminated foods. In general it is believed that the health benefits outweigh the risks from pollutants. But many native people are mistrustful of these recommendations. Who can blame them after the history of mission schools and the story that Cindy Kenny Gilday relates in this chapter? Some regard their traditional foods as contaminated and do not eat them any longer.

For these people it is not simply a matter of switching grocery stores. Alternative foods of equivalent nutrition are expensive because they must be flown in from the south. There is a tendency to substitute southern junk food which is of doubtful nutritional benefit. Obesity, diabetes and other southern ailments are increasing. But hunting, fishing and gathering of food are more than subsistence to native people. These activities are part of the cultural and spiritual fabric of their society. Contaminating their food will rend this social fabric just as surely as sending their children to mission schools did in past decades.

There are some real dilemmas here. Some of the pesticides probably originate in tropical countries where they are important in controlling the insects that carry malaria and other serious human diseases. Must we poison northern natives to protect tropical peoples from disease? Should the decision be based only on numbers of deaths or population sizes? Again, this is no longer the realm of science except for the possibility of producing pesticides that are less persistent and less amenable to long-range transport in the atmosphere.

In some cases the answer to these questions is clear and heavily based on science. We know that demotechnic activities have released mercury to the atmosphere, causing increased mercury deposition in northern regions by from two- to several-fold. We know that the increase in mercury is reflected as methyl mercury in food chains so that it biomagnifies. We know that it is a powerful neurotoxin that produces abnormalities in the neurological functioning of fetuses and newborns at very low doses. We know the major sources. Medical and ecological scientists agree that mercury emissions to the atmosphere must be reduced. We know the major sources.

All who value human rights should be asking their regulators and politicians why the control of mercury emissions to the atmosphere has been delayed for long. This problem can be addressed today. Here we can see the sorts of cultural biases that I argue above. The costs of controlling mercury release are resisted by a large, powerful society because the dangerous effects are predominantly focused on a small, poor one. Just as surely as ecology must protect ecosystems to ensure the survival of species, we must protect cultures that depend on sparse populations and large land areas from being oppressed by those who refuse to curb their reproduction or lavish energy use. In summary, in order for all people to have the prospect of enjoying human rights, there are some urgent, complicated and important decisions that must be made. The decisions must engage sectors of society because they go well beyond the realm of science. I cannot predict where the debates will take us, but they must begin now.

REFERENCES

AMAP, Arctic Monitoring and Assessment Program, Assessment Report: Arctic Pollution Issues. Oslo, Norway (1998).

Ayotte, P., É. Dewailly, S. Bruneau, H. Careau and A. Vézina. "Arctic Air Pollution and Human Health: What Effects Should Be Expected?" *Sci. Tot. Environ.* 529–537 (1995): 160, 161.

Brown, L. R. *The Agricultural Link: How Environmental Deterioration Could Disrupt Economic Progress.* Washington (DC): Worldwatch Institute (1997).

Daily, G., P. Dasgupta, B. Bolin, P. Crosson, J. du Guerny, P. Ehrlich, C. Folke, A. M. Jansson, B. -O. Jansson, N. Kautsky, A. Kinzig, S. Levin, K. -G. Mäleer, P. Pinstrup-Andersen, D. Siniscalco and B. Walker. "Food Production, Population Growth, and the Environment." *Science* 1291–1292 (1998): 281.

Gleick, P. H. "Water in Crisis: Paths to Sustainable Water Use." *Ecol. Appl.* 8 (1998): 571–579.

Jensen, J., K. Adare and R. Shearer (eds.). Canadian Arctic Contaminants Assessment Report. Indian and Northern Affairs Canada, Ottawa, 1997.

Mata, F. J., L. J. Onisto and J. R. Vallentyne. "Consumption: The Other Side of Population for Development". Paper prepared for the International Conference on Population and Development, Cairo, 13–14 September 1994. Earth Council: Apartado 2323 - 1002 San José, Costa Rica.

Naiman, R. J., J. J. Magnuson and P. L. Firth. "Integrating Cultural, Economic and Environmental Requirements for Fresh Water." *Ecol. Appl.* 8 (1998): 569–570.

Pimentel, D., J. Krummel, D. Gallahan, J. Hough, A. Merrill, I. Schreiner, P. Vittum, F. Koziol, E. Back, D. Yen and S. Fiance. "Benefits and Costs of Pesticide Use in US Food Production." *BioScience* 28 (1978): 772–784.

Postel, S. L. "Water for Food Production: Will There Be Enough in 2025?" *BioScience* 48 (1998): 629–637.

Schindler, D. W., K. A. Kidd, D. Muir and L. Lockhart. "The Effects of Ecosystem Characteristics on Contaminant Distribution in Northern Freshwater Lakes." *Sci. Tot. Environ.* 160/161 (1995): 1–17.

Vitousek, P. M., J. D. Aber, R. W. Howarth, G. E. Likens, P. A. Matson, D. W. Schindler, W. H. Schlesinger and D. Tilman. "Human Alteration of the Global Nitrogen Cycle: Causes and Consequences." *Ecol. Appl.* 7 (1997): 737–750.

Vitousek, P. M., P. R. Ehrlich, A. H. Ehrlich and P. A. Matson. "Human Appropriation of the Products of Photosynthesis." *BioScience* 36 (1986): 368–373.

▇▇▇ Table 1

Grain import dependence of African, Asian and Middle Eastern countries with per capita runoff of less than 1700m³/yr[a]. From Postel (1998).

Country	Internal runoff per capita, 1995 (m³/y)[b]m	Net grain imports as share of consumption (%)[c]
Kuwait	0	100
United Arab Emirates	158	100
Singapore	200	100
Djibouti	500	100
Oman	909	100
Lebanon	1,297	95
Jordan	249	91
Israel	309	87
Libya	115	85
South Korea	1,473	77
Algeria	489	70
Yemen	189	66
Armenia	1,673	60
Mauritania	174	58
Cape Verde	750	55
Tunisia	393	55
Saudi Arabia	119	50
Uzbekistan	418	42
Egypt	29	40
Azerbaijan	1,066	34
Turkmenistan	251	27
Morocco	1,027	26
Somalia	645	26
Rwanda	808	20
Iraq	1,650	19
Kenya	714	15
Sudan	1,246	4
Burkina Faso	1,683	2
Burundi	563	2
Zimbabwe	1,248	2
Niger	380	1
South Africa	1,030	-3
Syria	517	-4
Eritrea	800	Not available

[a]From WRI (1994), FAO (1995) and USDA (1997a).
[b]Runoff figures do not include river inflow from other countries, in part to avoid double-counting. Only Armenia, Azerbaijan, Djibouti, Iraq, Mauritania, Sudan, Turkmenistan and Uzbekistan would have more than 1,700m³ per capita in 1995 and 2025 if current inflow from other countries were included.
[c]Ratio of annual net grain imports to grain consumption averaged over the period 1994–1996.

■ Table 2

Populations and demotechnic indices for selected countries.
For a complete listing see Mata et al. (1994).

Country	D-index	Populations (000)	Consumption Adjusted Population
Canada	118.11	26,521	3,158,916
German Dem Rep	64.50	16,249	1,064,310
India	3.58	853,094	3,907,171
Japan	37.75	123,460	4,784,075
Kenya	5.25	24,031	150,194
Mexico	15.25	88,598	1,439,718
Spain	24.36	39,187	993,782
Sweden	78.55	8,444	671,720
United Kingdom	44.36	57,237	2,596,270
United States	91.26	249,224	22,993,406
U.S.S.R.	57.31	288,595	16,827,974

■ Table 3

Mean concentration of various organochlorines in milk fat from Inuit women of northern Québec and Caucasian women from southern Québec (ng/g lipids).
From Ayotte et al. (1995).

Organochlorine compound	Inuit women ($N = 107$) n^b	Mean^c ± C.I.	Caucasian women ($N = 50$) n^b	Mean^c ± C.I.
DDE	107	1212 ± 170	50	336 ± 18
Hexachlorobenzene	107	136 ± 19	48	28 ± 3
Dieldrin	102	37 ± 5	46	11 ± 1
Mirex	90	16 ± 4	3	1.6 ± 0.3
Helptachlor epoxide	45	13 ± 2	29	8 ± 1
trans-Chlordane	18	3.7 ± 0.4	0	< 6
Endrin	1	< 8	0	< 6

[b] n, number of milk samples with concentration above the detection limit.
[c] Arithmetic mean and ninety-five per cent confidence interval.

ERIC P. NEWELL

Achieving the Right Balance

Economic, Environmental and Human Development in Syncrude's World

Eric P. Newell is the chair and chief executive officer of Syncrude Canada Ltd. He is also chair of the 2000 Governor General's Canadian Study Conference and the University of Alberta Board of Governors, and a member of the Aboriginal Human Resource Development Council.

IN A DISCUSSION OF THE RELATIONSHIPS between the economy, the environment and human rights, I take the position that the three can and should be balanced each against the other. We can, in my experience and based on my objectives, strike an acceptable balance between economic and environmental sustainability, and respect and protect human rights both of those people who comprise a part of our day-to-day world, as well as those people of the larger global community whom we will never meet.

But beyond business and the expression of points of view on specific issues, I do want to pay brief tribute to the overall purpose of this conference and the significant milestones that we are marking here in Edmonton. I do not think we celebrate fifty years of human rights universally applied throughout our world with this event. It wouldn't be much of a celebration. Rather, we can celebrate the lasting vision of the noble ideals expressed in the UN Declaration soon after one of the greatest conflicts ever experienced in the history of humankind, and since reaffirmed in Canada by the establishment of federal and provincial bodies with similar aims and ideals. We mark and learn from the successes and failures of the last half century. Whether achieving a better balance between economic and environmental goals or ensuring the dignity and rights of women in our societies, we must acknowledge that there is more yet to do, that challenges do remain. Shaping the very nature of our existence—these are fundamental issues which affect us all, wherever we live, whatever our walks in life.

I do not have definitive answers for global challenges. But, perhaps using Syncrude as a singular model of a progressive company that has and is taking steps to both create and protect opportunity, I can contribute an idea or two that will help sustain the human rights vision as we move forward. Syncrude Canada produces oil from oil sands. We currently supply about twelve per cent of Canada's crude oil requirements and are the country's largest single source of oil. That's not something we accomplished overnight. We didn't explore. We didn't discover the resource, not really. Instead, along with other members of our industry, with academia and with the scientific community, over many decades, we invented the technologies and processes that allowed us to extract the resource efficiently and economically.

We've known it was there for a long time, centuries. Generally, it has been put to use in a manner that tends to reflect the pace of human advancement over those centuries. Aboriginals and early explorers used the bitumen to patch their birch-bark canoes, for example. Later, it was used as a roofing and road-paving material and today, as a high-quality fuel used to power and move a good part of this nation.

Covering an area of about 77,000 square kilometres, which is roughly the size of Taiwan, and spread over four deposits in northeast and north-central Alberta, the resource itself is huge by any standards. It has been estimated that the bitumen in place amounts to 1.7 trillion barrels, an amount greater than the reserves of the entire Middle East. With current technology there are recoverable reserves of over 300 billion barrels, which is sufficient to supply Canada's oil needs for well over the next two hundred years.

Headquartered in the city of Fort McMurray, Syncrude is located in the midst of the largest of the deposits, the Athabasca oil sands. The company was established in 1964, produced its first barrel of oil in 1978, put its one billionth barrel into the pipeline in 1998 and currently has new investment plans on the books valued at $6 billion. It is part of an industry-wide expansion plan valued at about $25 billion, an expansion that is expected to create thousands of new jobs, billions of dollars in new revenues to government, economic growth and energy security for this and future generations of Canadians.

Now that's just an overview of our past, present and future. Frankly, to me, it is a story of human potential and achievement and I am not the only one to look at it that way. For example, Peter C. Newman, a noted Canadian journalist and writer, has called Syncrude an accomplishment of ingenuity and doggedness, the toast of corporate Canada's resource sector, a Canadian success story. On an economic and business basis alone, it is difficult not to agree with his assessment.

I am often called upon to frame that success more broadly, to place it in the context of the impact of our operation beyond economics, its impact on people, communities and the environment. Are we a success in that context as well? These are legitimate and important issues. Years ago, as petroleum became more and more of a staple product in the global economy, the oil sands resource started to get attention. That's when efforts to conquer the challenge of separating the oil from the sand intensified. That's just the way it works, after all. In a free market economy, if the demand is there, human ingenuity will be applied to develop the ways and means to satisfy that demand and to earn a living or a profit doing it. That is, to me, a basic, acceptable and vital motivation for conducting business. Of course the pursuit of profit is not always considered a particularly noble or admirable motivation, especially when it is juxtaposed with other objectives such as preservation of the environment and protection of human rights. Some even look at profit as simply being the pursuit of a self-interest rather than a social benefit.

While I would argue that the profit motive has served us well, that does not mean I support unbridled greed. Unbridled greed or ignorance and the societal costs that come with them are certainly not foreign to the human experience. Yes, there was a time, in my view, when economic advancement crossed currents with environmental preservation. But if we are not now running in parallel streams, I believe we are headed in that direction.

Syncrude entered the industry because it recognized a business opportunity, an opportunity to conquer a challenge, to satisfy a market demand and to earn a profit. But we also recognized a number of other things. We knew, for example, that whatever shape our operations took, they would be massive. The opportunity would not be ours alone but would have to be shared, shared through the employment opportunities we would create both locally and further afield, shared through the wealth we would generate through taxation and business spin-offs, and shared through all of the other benefits that went along with the domestic production of such a vital strategic resource. We also knew we would have an impact on the environment. And we knew that we had arrived relatively late, that other communities and cultures had established themselves in the region long before we got there.

Indifference to all of this would have been the outcome of greed or ignorance on our part. But instead, we were "green" before it became popular or necessary to be green, at a time when it was still only a colour. For example, we established our environmental department fully a decade before site construction began and we made a point of getting to know and understand the communities we were becoming a part of.

We did make progress in those early years and I could speak at some length of how that was achieved. But for now, I will limit my point to the proposition that respect for people and the environment was as important a part of our corporate culture as any other right from the very beginning. Yes, we pursued profit. We could not have survived otherwise. It is the political nature and relative privilege of our particular society that we were allowed to do so.

But it was not profit at any cost. Rather, economic opportunity that could be and, indeed, was shared with the people of our region which includes, not incidentally, a relatively high proportion of aboriginal people; opportunity that could be seized not at the expense of the environment, but in keeping with our responsibility to help preserve or restore it. I believe that we have, throughout our corporate history, been very progressive in those respects as well.

Let me give you a few indications of what we have managed to achieve on the environmental and human rights sides of the equation. In twenty years of operation we have never had a major environmental incident on our site. Nor have we ever been fined or issued a control order for noncompliance with environmental regulations. We invest about $30 million every year in research and development, much of which is devoted to improving our environmental performance. Of that $6 billion I mentioned earlier, some $1.6 billion, or one dollar out of every four, will be invested in new technologies and processes that improve our environmental performance.

Syncrude also has a long record of continuously reducing all emissions per unit of production, whether particulates, sulphur dioxide or carbon dioxide. One of the ways we do that is through our participation in the Canadian government's Climate Change Voluntary Challenge Program; we are committed to reducing the uneconomic consumption of energy in our operations and, relatedly, our emissions of greenhouse gases. Our CO_2 emissions per barrel of production will drop by sixteen per cent between 1990 and 2000 and by thirty per cent by 2007. Our SO_2 emissions have dropped by thirty-one per cent per barrel over the last decade and by 2007 they will have declined by seventy per cent compared to 1990.

We also observe and practice responsible and effective corporate policies with respect to water quality, land reclamation and tailings management. As a few brief examples, we've reclaimed more than 2,200 hectares of mining land, planted nearly two million tree and shrub seedlings, and, in partnership with a local aboriginal community, established a unique wood bison habitat on reclaimed land. Currently, we have about two hundred head.

We have an aboriginal development program in place and, like our environmental department, it can be traced back to long before the first barrel of oil was produced. Since our earliest beginnings we have recognized that local aboriginal people have a significant stake in the responsible and successful development of the oil sands. We have respected the community's needs, built bridges between cultures, helped educate the community and learned from it ourselves. Today we are Canada's largest industrial employer of aboriginal people, with over seven hundred working on our site in highly skilled, high-paying jobs. Overall, we provide safe and healthy working conditions while continuously working to eliminate incidents and to reduce the risk of harm to people, the environment and to our operations. Incorporated into our loss management policy, it is simply the way we do business.

I have told you a little of the Syncrude story to demonstrate that it is possible to move forward on all fronts. Our story and those of other responsible companies are examples of how we can continue to create economic opportunity without sacrificing human life, human dignity or human rights. I have devoted the bulk of my remarks to Syncrude because my experience lies primarily there. A great majority of my time is devoted to helping ensure that the balance is maintained in what I must call my "small corner" of the world.

I say my "small corner" because as big as Syncrude is, I acknowledge that the global issues we are dealing with here today extend far beyond the scope of my influence. For example, I have the power to influence hiring policy at Syncrude but I cannot demand that a company somewhere else establish nondiscriminatory practices, safe working conditions or pay a fair wage. I can dedicate some Syncrude resources to community and employee programs and to research and development designed to improve our environmental performance. But I cannot demand the same of all businesses the world over.

To me, the best I can do is act within my sphere of influence: to build a company, not a world, that will offer future generations the chance to earn a decent living and the right to live in a decent world. To those who say that we are now at a crossroads in human development, a crossroads where one path requires fundamental changes in human behaviour and will yield, in return, a pristine environment, clean air and healthy flora and fauna, and another path, involving no change and leading to some kind of industrial oblivion—to those people—I have to say, no, it's not that clear. You haven't factored companies like Syncrude into the equation. There is a middle path. In other words, environmental improvement and economic growth need not be at cross currents—they can be parallel streams.

When I quoted Peter C. Newman a moment ago, I left out a phrase. He actually called Syncrude the Canadian success story that no one knew about. In effect, he politely chastized Canadians for not glorifying their own economic accomplishments, as though, perhaps, economic success didn't have the appeal of, say, a Canadian winning a gold medal at the Olympics. Yet lack of economic opportunity has been known to topple governments. When it's not there, we hear about it.

Economic opportunity for a country or an employment opportunity for a single person is, to me, a fundamental human right in any society. I could frame that in the context of discriminatory and nondiscriminatory human rights. But I'm thinking more in terms of the availability of employment. It often seems to me that those who think in terms of the economy and environment flowing as cross currents to one another would quite arbitrarily restrict or restructure the activities and potential of industry and, in doing so, limit the availability of employment.

If you do look at it that way, if you believe that industry is destroying the planet, then understandably it would seem quite cold for someone to put their interests before the common good. But on a global scale, certainly as we struggle to address environmental challenges, we also struggle to address crippling issues of poverty throughout the world. According to a recent UN report, for example, well over a billion people are today deprived of their basic consumption needs. This while twenty per cent of the world's richest people account for eighty-six per cent of total private consumption, whether it's food, energy, transportation or communications equipment.

If we attempt to address environmental challenges in this country by restricting industry's ability to be innovative by deliberately or unwittingly limiting the availability of employment—the very source of its innovation—then we are making ourselves poorer rather than working to share the benefits and opportunity of our knowledge more widely.

In addressing global issues and challenges, am I contradicting what I said earlier about not speaking outside my sphere of influence? No, I don't think so. My world, again, for the most part is the city of Fort McMurray and its environs. In truth, the region is not a heavily populated area but it is diverse. All manner of people, young and old, educated and not, from all walks of life, live there. It is not a microcosm of the world but as close to it as I am ever likely to come.

We, along with other oil sands industry companies, are the major employers in the region and the region's economic fortunes tend to mirror ours. There are, no doubt, disparities. But I believe that our average income is among the highest in the country. Our quality of life is high and we are free to pursue our own adventures, whether it's raising a family, getting an education, attending patients in the hospital, driving one of the biggest trucks in the world, tending a herd of wood bison or walking the trapline. As I've said, the land, the air and the water are all intact and we aim to keep it that way as we grow.

We are not guaranteed economic opportunity and we are not guaranteed employment. Ideally, we earn those things and work to maintain them. But the opportunities are there and, if things go as planned, they will be there for some time to come. I do believe that in my corner of the world we have achieved a balance. We are not perfect. We don't have all of the answers, but we do need to reach out beyond our small corner of the world to be part of the solution.

Businesses like mine can and have banded together to serve as models for others and espouse values and principles that have been proven to work. Syncrude is not generally active in other countries but that does not preclude us from taking an active interest in working to ensure adherence to responsible and respectful business policies and procedures where we can. For example, the North American Committee, a private sector network of senior business, labour and academic leaders from Canada, the United States and Mexico, issued a set of principles in 1997 for socially responsible business practices. At the time the principles were aimed specifically at Cuba. But they serve as beacons for more widespread adherence to universal standards of human rights anywhere and ring true with me. They include providing a safe and healthy workplace; employing fair employment practices; working to gain the right to recruit, contract and pay workers directly; respecting employees' right to organize freely in the workplace; maintaining a corporate culture that respects free expression; and supporting the strengthening of legal procedures.

Some of these may sound pretty basic from the perspective of developed countries. But there are some indications that many companies operating outside their home bases in developing countries have not adopted codes of conduct which promote the protection of international human rights and sustainable development. Compared with economic sanctions, the North American Committee believes that the widespread adoption of a code of socially responsible business practices would positively affect the long-term development of civil society, democratic principles and basic human rights. I tend to agree. I am speaking primarily from the perspective of a producer and attempting to demonstrate that we do balance economic, environmental and human objectives and considerations in the way we operate our business. But I have not devoted a great deal of attention to the consumption side of the equation.

I suppose part of the reason for that is that ours is a market-driven company; in other words, we supply a product at a price we do not set to satisfy a demand we cannot really influence other than by the quality of our product, which would include its environmental attributes, its sulphur content, for example. If Syncrude or the oil sands did not exist I am not at all convinced that demand would diminish in equal proportion to the lost supply. There are other sources of crude oil and other forms of energy so people would simply get it from somewhere else. Energy is a product crucial to human and economic development. The wise use of our energy is very much impacted by consumption patterns and behaviours.

The UN report I referred to earlier did, however, make a distinction between necessary consumption and conspicuous or excessive consumption. This kind of excess or waste can arise from irresponsible or self-centred human behaviours that do not have a beneficial impact on quality of life in well-to-do countries. These human behaviours, if modified, could go some way to improving the way we share our resources and, more importantly perhaps, our know-how with the less well-off. With only ten per cent of the world's population accounting for eighty-six per cent of the consumption, there is a lot of scope for improvement here.

Individual modifications to the way we behave, whether as people or as businesses, if applied collectively by a society as a whole will produce the kinds of national and global outcomes that I think we all seek—a balance between economic opportunity and environmental responsibility and a common standard of achievement for all peoples and all nations, a world where peace, justice and freedom can be enjoyed by all.

Crimes Against Humanity and Their Punishment

Crimes Against Humanity and the Law

Leslie C. Green is honourary professor of law and
professor emeritus at the University of Alberta. From
1996–98 he was the Charles H. Stockton Professor of
International Law at the US Naval War College. He is a
recipient of the John Read Medal in International Law
and the University of Helsinki Rector's Medal. He is also
a Member of the Order of Canada.

THERE IS A VIRTUALLY UNIVERSAL ASSUMPTION that the concept of crimes
against humanity had its origin in discussions leading up to the creation of the
International Military Tribunal at Nuremberg at the end of World War II.
Responding to the Holocaust and the Nazi occupation of Europe, it is believed
that the first expression of such crimes came in the charter which governed the
tribunal's jurisdiction.[2] This is far from correct.

Peter of Hagenbach had been installed by Charles, Duke of Burgundy as
governor of territories in the Upper Rhine. These territories had been pledged to
Charles—Charles the Terrible or Charles the Bold, depending on one's alle-
giance—by their sovereign, the Archduke of Austria. Acting in accordance with
instructions from Charles, Peter instituted a policy of taxation, accompanied by
rape, murder, looting and attacks on Swiss merchants. This was aimed at
subduing the local population.

After Hagenbach's German mercenaries revolted at Breisach, Hagenbach was
captured and in 1474 put on trial before an *ad hoc* tribunal of twenty-eight
judges. Eight of the judges were nominated by citizens of Breisach and two by
each of the Hanseatic towns, together with a representative of Berne and
Solothurn, a Berne ally, and with Austria as sovereign of Breisach providing the
presiding judge.

Hagenbach put forward as his defence that he was merely carrying out the
orders of his lord and master, the Duke of Burgundy. This defence was rejected
on the ground that he had "trampled underfoot the laws of God and man" and he
was sentenced to death. He was also deprived of his knighthood as he was guilty

137

of the crimes knights were obliged to prevent.[3] If one applies this case to the present understanding of what is meant by crimes against humanity, it is not difficult to conclude that Hagenbach was clearly guilty of the same.

Some four and a half centuries later, in 1915, the governments of France, Great Britain and Russia issued a declaration denouncing as "crimes against humanity and civilization," the atrocities committed by the Ottoman Empire against its Armenian minority.[4] This led the 1919 Commission on Responsibilities for the Outbreak of World War I to propose for insertion in the peace treaties: "Article 1. The Enemy Government admits even after the conclusion of peace, every Allied and Associated State may exercise, in respect of any enemy or former enemy, the right which it would have had during the war to try and punish any enemy...who had been guilty of a violation of the law of nations as these result from the usages established among civilized peoples, from the laws of humanity and from the dictates of public conscience."[5]

Article 226 of the Treaty of Sèvres, drawn up between the Allied powers and Turkey, called for the surrender for trial of those "accused of having committed an act in violation of the laws and customs of war." Clearly confined to victims who were Allied nationals, Article 230, specifying no particular system of law which had been breached, provided:[6] "The Turkish Government undertakes to hand over to the Allied Powers the persons whose surrender may be required by the latter as being responsible for the massacres committed during the continuance of the state of war on territory which formed part of the Turkish Empire on 1 August 1914."

This could only refer to nationals of Turkey who would not be protected by the laws and customs of war. Moreover, the Article, almost foretelling what was done in 1945, proceeded: "In the event of the League of Nations having created in sufficient time a tribunal competent to deal with the said massacres, the Allied Powers reserve to themselves the right to bring the accused persons mentioned above before such a tribunal, and the Turkish Government undertakes equally to recognize such tribunal." Turkey refused to ratify Sèvres which was replaced by the Treaty of Lausanne in which there is no reference to any crimes against the laws of wars, the massacres or humanity.[7]

The penal clauses of all the other treaties terminating World War I only refer to crimes against the laws and customs of war directed against Allied nationals.[8] It was only when an attempt was made to indict Wilhem II, former emperor of Germany, that anything like recognition of any principle of humanity was introduced. The Treaty of Versailles, Article 228, providing for the trial of accused Germans, in common with the others is confined to "acts in violation of the laws and customs of war."[9] Article 227, however, arraigned the Kaiser "for a supreme offence against international morality" and instructed the tribunal to be established for his trial to "be guided by the highest motives of international policy, with a view to vindicating...the validity of international morality"—whatever that may mean.

While there were allegations that the Italian forces had used gas or committed atrocities against the civilian population during their aggression against Abyssinia, there was never any suggestion that Mussolini or any of his military or political advisers should be tried for war crimes or crimes against humanity. It was only in the light of Nazi activities, particularly in occupied Europe and especially against non-German civilians, that the issue of prosecuting those guilty of offences not falling within the traditional concept of war crimes came into prominence.

However, it may be argued that to a great extent, in so far as non-German civilians in occupied territories were concerned, this introduction of a new offence was probably unnecessary. Many of the acts directed against them would have fallen within the purview of restrictions imposed upon an occupant in accordance with the regulations annexed to Hague Convention IV, 1907, regarding the laws and customs of warfare on land.[10] Where this would not have been the case, they would clearly be covered by the terms of the Martens Clause, part of the preamble to the Convention: "[I]n cases not included in the Regulations, ...the inhabitants and the belligerents remain under the protection and the rule of the principles of the law of nations, as they result from the usages established among civilized peoples, from the laws of humanity and the dictates of the public conscience."

A cursory glance at the history of the law relating to armed conflict would indicate that most of the offences committed against these persons had been condemned in ancient times, during the feudal era and by all the "fathers" of international law who were often more concerned with writing of the law of war than one of peace.

However, the law of armed conflict, both customary and treaty, only applied as between the belligerents and had no effect in so far as the treatment of its own civilian population by a belligerent was concerned. Knowledge of the Holocaust and of other Nazi activities directed against a variety of German minority groups, together with the sentiment that occupation policy was so outrageous as to warrant direct condemnation, resulted in the adoption of a new type of offence. But, as drafted in the Charter establishing the Nuremberg Tribunal, any hope that this would be the case proved futile.

Article 6(c) of the Charter defines crimes against humanity as "murder, extermination, enslavement, deportation and other *inhumane acts committed against any civilian population*, before or during the war, or persecution on political, racial or religious grounds *in execution of or in connection with any crime within the jurisdiction of the Tribunal*, whether or not in violation of the domestic law of the country where perpetrated."[11]

Prima facie, this language would appear to embrace any of the acts listed when committed by the accused against their nationals and whether those acts had been perpetrated in Germany or elsewhere. However, as was made clear in the Tribunal's judgement,[12] which took a rather literal and restricted interpretation of its jurisdiction: "With regard to crimes against humanity, there is no doubt whatever that political opponents were murdered in Germany before the war, and that many of them were kept in concentration camps in circumstances of great horror and cruelty. The policy of terror was carried out on a vast scale, and in many cases was organized and systematic. The policy of persecution, repression and murder of civilians in Germany before the war of 1939, who were likely to be hostile to the Government, was most ruthlessly carried out. The persecution of Jews during the same period is established beyond all doubt. *To constitute crimes against humanity, the acts relied on before the outbreak of war must have been in execution of, or in connection with, any crime within the jurisdiction of the Tribunal.*

"The Tribunal is of the opinion that revolting and horrible as many of these crimes were, it has not been satisfactorily proved that they were done in execution of, or in connection with, any such crimes. The Tribunal therefore cannot make a general declaration that the acts before 1939 were crimes against humanity within the meaning of the Charter but—insofar as the inhumane acts charged in the Indictment, and committed after the beginning of the war, did not constitute war crimes—they were all committed in execution of, or in connection with, the aggressive war [declared criminal by Article 6(a) of the Charter], *and therefore constituted crimes against humanity."*[13]

Since non-German Jews only came within the range of the Holocaust as a result of Germany's aggression, it was this last caveat that enabled the Tribunal, insofar as the persecution of Germany Jews was concerned, to accept the prosecution's contention that:[14] "[C]ertain aspects of this anti-Semitic policy were connected with the plans for aggressive war. The violent measures taken against the Jews in November, 1938, were nominally in retaliation for the killing of an official of the German Embassy in Paris.[15] But the decision to seize Austria and Czechoslovakia had been made a year before. The imposition of a fine of one billion marks was made, and the confiscation of the financial holdings of the Jews was decreed, at a time when German armament expenditure had put the German treasury in difficulties, and when the reduction of expenditure on armaments was being considered. These steps were taken, moreover, with the approval of the defendant Goering, who had been given responsibility for economic matters of this kind, and who was the strongest advocate of an extensive rearmament program notwithstanding the financial difficulties."

This restrictive interpretation of the concept of crimes against humanity has led one of the earliest commentators on the subject to point out that[16] "all the crimes formulated in Article 6(c) are crimes against humanity only if they are committed in execution of or in connection with a crime against peace or a war crime. The scope of the phrase 'before or during the war' is therefore considerably narrowed as a consequence of the view that, although the time when a crime was committed is not alone decisive, the connexion with the war must be established in order to bring a certain set of facts under the notion of a crime against humanity within the meaning of Article 6(c).... Although in theory it remains irrelevant whether a crime against humanity was committed before or during the war, in practice it is difficult to establish a connexion between what is alleged to be a crime against humanity and a crime within the jurisdiction of the Tribunal, if the act was committed before the war.

"On the other hand, if the commission of an inhumane act...took place during the war, its connexion with the war was presumed.... [A]n act, in order to come within the notion of a crime against humanity...must [therefore] be closely connected either with a crime against peace or a war crime in the narrower sense.... The restrictive interpretation placed on the term 'crimes against peace' was not so strictly applied by the Tribunal in the case of victims of other than German nationality.... [T]he Tribunal treats the notion of crimes against humanity as a kind of subsidiary provision to be applied whenever any particular area where a crime was committed was not covered by the Hague Rules of Land Warfare. Germanization is,[17] therefore, considered as criminal under Article 6(b) [defining war crimes] in the areas covered by the Hague Regulations and as a crime under Article 6(c) as to all others.

"*The crime against humanity, as defined in the London Charter, is not, therefore, the cornerstone of a system of international criminal law applicable in times of war and of peace, protecting the human rights of inhabitants of all countries, 'of any civilian population,' against anybody, including their own states and governments....* It is, as it were, a kind of by-product of war, applicable only in time of war or in connexion with war and destined primarily, if not exclusively, to protect the inhabitants of foreign countries against crimes committed, in connexion with an aggressive war, by the authorities and organs of the aggressor state.... As defined in the Nuremberg Judgement, the crime against humanity is an 'accompanying' or an 'accessory' crime to either crimes against peace or violations of the laws and customs of war."

That this was not the isolated view of a single scholar is confirmed in the International Law Commission's statement of Principles of International Law Recognized in the Charter of the Nuremberg Tribunal and in the Judgement of the Tribunal,[18] and which are to be regarded as statements of positive international law for the future. Principle 6(c) affirms that to constitute crimes against humanity, "the acts are done or persecutions are carried out in execution of or in connexion with any crime against peace or any war crime." In other words, the Nuremberg Judgement has, despite all assertions to the contrary in the fifty years that have elapsed since then, made little real or substantial contribution to the concept of crimes against humanity outside of war and when directed against one's own nationals.

Some advance appeared to have been made with the adoption in 1948 of the Universal Declaration of Human Rights[19] and the Genocide Convention.[20] While the former appears to confirm the existence of rights in peace and war, it is not a treaty, but a non-obligatory and unenforceable resolution of the General Assembly, and imposes no obligation upon any state to respect those "rights." Nor does it suggest in any way that disregard thereof would give a right to the victim or constitute a crime. Equally, neither the International Covenant on Civil and Political Rights nor that on economic, social and cultural rights really makes any substantive advance.[21] Even the European Convention on Human Rights, which to some extent appears to raise the Declaration to statutory level, and in its amended form gives the individual victim the right of direct access to the European Court of Human Rights, contains no provision suggesting that any breach however serious constitutes a crime or may be subject to any criminal sanction.[22]

As to the Genocide Convention, substantial steps forward appear to have been made. While the definition of genocide is specialized and, from the point of view of what tends to be regarded as a crime against humanity, somewhat narrow, although the destruction of "a national, ethnical, racial or religious group as such" clearly constitutes a serious crime against humanity, it specifically declares that "genocide, whether committed in time of peace or in time of war, is a crime under international law," which the parties undertake "to prevent and punish." Genocide, of necessity, is not a crime likely to be committed by an individual offender as a matter of "private enterprise." It is essentially an offence based on policy and is committed either at the instigation of an authority, or with the authority's connivance, complicity, tolerance or collusion as may be seen in the policies of "ethnic cleansing" which have been conducted in the former Yugoslavia or Rwanda. Unfortunately, Article 6 of the Convention, the penal provision, virtually destroys the very basis of the Convention, for "persons charged [with genocide] shall be tried by a competent tribunal of the State in the territory of which the act was committed, or by such international penal tribunal as may have jurisdiction with respect to those Contracting Parties which shall have accepted its jurisdiction."

Until the establishment of the *ad hoc* tribunals for the former Yugoslavia and Rwanda, there was no such tribunal. Trial and punishment, therefore, depended on the goodwill of the authority in whose territory the genocide had been committed. Since, as has been suggested, this is an offence that requires complicity of an authority, it would seem that those committing genocide would only be offenders who had committed either war crimes in the normal sense of that term when the Convention would be unnecessary, or had been involved in a noninternational conflict and been captured by their opponents, either government or rebel, as has been the case in Rwanda. Otherwise, it is submitted that Article 6 is no more than a "paper tiger," especially as the Statutes of the two tribunals,[23] and also of the proposed International Criminal Court,[24] expressly confer jurisdiction over genocide, which is specifically defined, even though the definition is taken from the Convention.

In view of the fact that the Statute of the International Criminal Court gives jurisdiction over crimes against humanity, there is no need to discuss the various attempts made by the International Law Commission to draft codes of international criminal law or to examine its draft statute for such a court. Before looking at the court, however, it is advisable to pay some attention to the work of the two *ad hoc* tribunals to which reference has just been made since they exist, possess such jurisdiction and are functioning.

Both tribunals are granted jurisdiction over genocide, thus constituting the international tribunal envisaged by the Convention, as well as over crimes against humanity. It is enlightening to look at the way in which the concept of crimes against humanity was construed as having developed since Nuremberg. The two tribunals were established as a result of reports rendered to the secretary general of the United Nations by commissions established to examine the "atrocities" alleged to have been committed during the conflicts in the former Yugoslavia as well as in Rwanda. The Commission on Rwanda stated:[25] "[T]he normative content of 'crimes against humanity'—originally employed by the Nuremberg Tribunal for its own specific purposes in connection with the Second World War[26]—has undergone substantial evolution since the Second World War.

"First, even the Nuremberg Tribunal itself had established that 'crimes against humanity' covered certain acts perpetrated against civilians, including those with the same nationality as the perpetrator [although as to these the acts had also to amount to constituents of crimes against peace or war crimes]. Indeed, 'crimes against humanity' as a normative concept finds its very origins in 'principles of humanity' first invoked in the 1800s by a State to denounce another State's human rights violations of its own citizens [normally when the victims had the same religious beliefs as the protester].[27] Thus, 'crimes against humanity' as a judicial category was conceived early on to apply to individuals regardless as to whether or not the criminal act was perpetrated during an armed conflict and regardless of the nationality of the perpetrator or victim.

"Secondly, the content and legal status of the norm since Nuremberg has been broadened and expanded through certain international human rights instruments adopted by the United Nations since 1945.[28] In particular, the Genocide Convention of 1948 affirms the legal validity of some of the normative content of 'crimes against humanity,' as conceived in Article 6(c) of the Nuremberg Charter, but does not overtake it....

"Thirdly, the Commission of Experts on the former Yugoslavia...has stated that it considered crimes against humanity to be: 'gross violations of fundamental rules of humanitarian and human rights law committed by persons demonstrably linked to a party to the conflict as part of an official policy based on discrimination against an identifiable group of persons, irrespective of war and the nationality of the victims.' This view finds support in the writing of publicists and is accepted by the Rwanda Commission."[29]

Perhaps all that need be said of this definition is that, by speaking of 'discrimination against an identifiable group of persons,' it comes perilously close to analogizing 'crimes against humanity' with 'genocide.' In fact, the trial chamber of the Yugoslav Tribunal has held that genocide is itself a crime against humanity, suggesting that there is no longer any need to charge this offence separately if a charge of crimes against humanity has been lodged, since the latter may be considered the totality under the penumbra of which genocide is merely an instance falling within the *res gestae*.[30]

To all intents and purposes the statutes of the two tribunals define crimes against humanity in the same terms[31]—murder, extermination, enslavement, deportation, imprisonment, torture, rape, persecution on political, racial and religious grounds. They differ, however, as to the situations affected, reflective of the fact that the Yugoslav Tribunal was to deal with issues arising in both international (e.g., Bosnia v. Serbia) and non-international (e.g., Bosnian Serbs v. Bosnia) conflicts, while the situation in Rwanda was purely non-international in character.

Thus, the former had jurisdiction over "persons responsible for the [named] crimes when committed in armed conflict, *whether international or internal in character*, and directed against any civilian population," while the latter was restricted to "crimes...committed as part of a widespread or systematic attack against any civilian population on national, political, ethnic, racial or religious grounds," again coming very close to the definition of genocide. There is certainly no obvious reason for restricting the concept in this way, for it stands to reason that crimes against humanity as defined in the Statute need not be directed at the named groups—what of a linguistic group?—and why must they be "part of a widespread or systematic attack," especially when no such restrictions apply in the case of the Yugoslav tribunal?

The Yugoslav Tribunal in its first judgement, that concerning Erdemovic, stated:[32] "Crimes against humanity are serious acts of violence which harm human beings by striking what is most essential to them: their life, liberty, physical welfare, health and dignity. They are inhumane acts that by their extent and gravity go beyond the limits tolerable to the international community, which must perforce demand their punishment. But crimes against humanity also transcend the individual because when the individual is assaulted, humanity comes under attack and is negated. It is therefore the concept of humanity as victim which essentially characterizes crimes against humanity.... There is a general principle of law common to all nations whereby the severest penalties apply for crimes against humanity in national systems. [The Trial Chamber] thus concludes there exists in international law a standard according to which a crime against humanity is one of extreme gravity demanding the most severe penalties, when no mitigating circumstances are present.

"It might be argued that the determination of penalties for a crime against humanity must derive from the penalties applicable to the underlying crime. In the present indictment, the underlying crime is murder. The Trial Chamber rejects such an analysis. Identifying the penalty applicable for a crime against humanity...cannot be based on penalties provided for the punishment of a distinct crime not involving the need to establish an assault on humanity."

Two comments may be made concerning this statement. In the first place, the use of the phrase "serious act of violence which harms an individual" suggests that any act resulting in grievous harm to the individual, especially destroying his life, brings "humanity under attack." Moreover, the assertion that punishment does not depend on the "underlying crime" but on an "assault on humanity" raises an interesting question since neither tribunal has the power to impose the death penalty, which may well, as in Rwanda, be the penalty which would be imposed by a tribunal proceeding in accordance with the local law.

Since the purpose for which both tribunals was established is identical, namely the vindication of the law and punishment of those committing outrageous acts during conflict, and since one appellate tribunal serves both, it may be presumed that the jurisprudence of the one will be more or less in line with that of the other. It is not necessary, therefore, to examine any further decisions of the Yugoslav Tribunal, or comment for our purpose on any of those rendered by the Rwanda Tribunal.

The two tribunals are *ad hoc* and will presumably eventually become *functus officio*. However, if the judgements are well reasoned and prove consistent and receive general approval, the law, particularly concerning crimes against humanity, that they develop should prove of precedential value.[33] Coming from two "objective" international tribunals as distinct from one established by victors or by particular states, the judgements may well amount to a veritable *vade mecum* on the law concerning this topic. They may also make a major contribution to the laws on war crimes and genocide.

When the International Criminal Court eventually comes into existence it should no longer be necessary for *ad hoc* tribunals like those for the former Yugoslavia and Rwanda to be instituted. The jurisdiction of this new court is not wide enough to embrace everything that has during the last thirty years or so come to be generally regarded as constituting international criminal law. For example, terrorism, the taking of hostages and even drug trafficking would be outside its scope. Rather, the court's jurisdiction is limited to genocide, crimes against humanity, war crimes and aggression, most of which are likely to be committed in times of conflict, although crimes against humanity may occur at any time, as may be seen for example in Argentina, Chile or Greece during military regimes.

For our purpose it is only necessary to refer to Article 7 of the Statute: "'[C]rime against humanity' means any of the following acts when committed as part of a widespread or systematic attack directed against any civilian population, with knowledge of the attack: (a) Murder; (b) Extermination; (c) Enslavement; (d) Deportation or forcible transfer of population; (e) Imprisonment or other severe deprivation of physical liberty in violation of fundamental rules of international law; (f) Torture; (g) Rape, sexual slavery, enforced prostitution, forced pregnancy, enforced sterilization or any other form of sexual violence of comparable gravity; (h) Persecution against any identifiable group or collectivity on political, racial, national, ethnic, cultural, religious, gender, or other grounds that are universally recognized as impermissible under international law, in connection with any act referred to in this paragraph or any crime within the jurisdiction of the Court; (i) Enforced disappearance of persons; (j) The crime of apartheid; (k) Other inhumane acts of a similar character intentionally causing great suffering or serious injury to body or to mental or physical health."

A number of queries arise with regard to this definition. In the first place, does the restriction to "any civilian population" mean that crimes against humanity cannot be committed against military personnel even by their own governing authority in suppressing a mutiny or by a civilian mob? If committed by an adverse party, presumably they would amount to war crimes. Then one would have thought that "extermination" and certain forms of "forced sterilization" would have amounted to genocide. Does a policy of population restriction involving forced sterilization or directed at births by mothers of unsound minds also amount to a crime against humanity? Does the reference to "imprisonment...in violation of fundamental rules of international law" extend to the conditions of imprisonment or is it confined to an arbitrary act?

Problems also arise in respect of the definition of torture: "'Torture' means the intentional infliction of severe pain or suffering, whether physical or mental, upon a person in the custody or under the control of the accused; *except that torture shall not include pain or suffering arising only from, inherent in or incidental to, lawful sanctions.*"[34]

This raises again the problem of the extent to which national policies would fall within this rubric, particularly since many countries still apply capital punishment by a variety of means often considered inhumane at least by Western standards, as well as amputation of limbs and severe floggings. It is also interesting to note that the crime of "persecution" does not include linguistic communities among the groups that would be affected.

Finally in this connection, the definition of "apartheid" possibly would not have extended to the conditions in pre-majority-ruled South Africa, which formed the basis of the convention definition.[35] According to the court's statute:

"'The crime of apartheid' means inhumane acts of a character similar to those referred to in paragraph 1 [listing the crimes], committed in the context of an institutionalized regime of systematic oppression and domination by one racial group or groups and committed with the intention of maintaining that regime." It would seem, therefore, that a policy based on denial of political and civil rights including the right to vote, ghettoization and the criminalization of miscegenation without the accompanying violence would not amount to a crime against humanity.

Unlike the position established for the two ad hoc tribunals whose jurisdiction takes priority over that of national tribunals, the court will lack jurisdiction if "the case is being investigated or prosecuted by a State which has jurisdiction over it, unless the State is unwilling or unable genuinely to carry out the investigation or prosecution; [or] the case has been investigated by a State which has jurisdiction over it and the State has decided not to prosecute the person concerned, unless the decision resulted from the unwillingness or inability of the State genuinely to prosecute."

If the Security Council adopted a resolution under Chapter VII of the Charter asking the court not to proceed, jurisdiction may not be exercised for a period of twelve months thereafter, although the council may renew the request thus producing a further delay. In this way, powers possessing the right of veto can prevent any case coming to court if it might embarrass it or one of its allies or satellites. In the same way, if a national court decides to proceed, the court will be unable to do so until such time as it becomes clear that the national process is a farce.

The court only possesses jurisdiction if a case has been referred to the prosecutor by the Security Council or a state party to the statute, provided it is the state on whose territory the crime was committed or of which the accused is a national, thus precluding the possibility of an "objective" accusation by a third state or even the state of which the victim is a national, although the prosecutor has the right to instigate an investigation *proprio motu.*

The statutes of the two *ad hoc* tribunals as well as of the International Criminal Court, reflecting the Nuremberg Charter, reject compliance with orders as a defence, recognize command responsibility and denies immunity arising from the status of the accused. In addition, while there is no period of limitation, the court will only have jurisdiction over crimes committed after it has come into existence so that any allegation lodged by relatives of the "disappeared" in Latin America would not fall within its compass. The principles *nullum crimen sine lege* and *nulla poena sine lege* are narrowly defined:

Article 22.1. A person shall not be criminally responsible under this Statute unless the conduct in question constitutes, at the time it takes place, a crime within the jurisdiction of the Court.

2. The definition of a crime shall be strictly construed and shall not be extended by analogy. In case of ambiguity, the definition shall be interpreted in favour of the person being investigated, prosecuted or convicted.

3. This article shall not affect the characterization of any conduct as criminal under international law independently of this Statute.

This means that general views that a particular line of conduct constitutes a crime against humanity will not be amenable to the court's jurisdiction unless it falls narrowly within the definitions already embodied in the court's statute. Equally, any attempt by a further treaty to condemn such action as a crime against humanity will require the establishment of another tribunal for its enforcement.

Article 23 states that a person convicted by the court may be punished "only in accordance with this Statute" and the court cannot impose a death sentence. As has been pointed out, if a national court recognized as being independent and abiding by the rule of law is seized of a case, the court would be denied jurisdiction while those possessing competence to refer a matter to the court are narrowly defined. This would not, of course, prevent any national court with legislative authority to try crimes against humanity from doing so, regardless of the nationality of the accused or the victim or the location of the offence and the normal rules with regard to extradition would apply. In this connection, it should be noted that genocide, aggression and crimes against humanity as defined in the court's statute are being increasingly regarded as subject to universal jurisdiction and tend to be perpetrated almost exclusively as a matter of policy.

It is important, therefore, to remember that modern extradition treaties have tended to limit the "political offence" defence almost to disappearance.[36] It has been held in some jurisdictions that offences of a criminal character which are ordered by a government as a matter of policy and are not directed against that government can never be regarded as political offences.[37] Moreover, extradition treaties do not always operate *in futuro*, so that an offender's return may be requested in respect of an offence committed before the treaty becomes effective. After all, the purpose of extradition is more procedural than substantive, seeking to provide a forum for what is already a criminal offence.

Such a case arose in the United Kingdom in 1998 with regards to General Pinochet, former dictator of Chile, during whose regime there were allegations of extensive crimes against humanity involving torture, murder, rape and disappearances, with the victims not only Chileans but also foreign nationals or persons possessing both Chilean and some other nationality. Pinochet was admitted to England for surgery and while he was in hospital, Spain, acting in accordance with the 1989 extradition treaty with the United Kingdom, requested his extradition for trial relating to victims of his government's policies who were dual Spanish-Chilean nationals, the crimes concerned being regarded as crimes against humanity.

Regardless of the Convention Against Torture,[38] to which Britain is a party and which clearly provides: "No exceptional circumstances whatsoever, whether a state of war or a threat of war, internal political instability or any other public emergency, may be invoked as a justification of torture [and even the European Convention on Human Rights, which has just come into force as part of English municipal law, asserts that the ban on torture is non-derogable in time of emergency].[39] An Order from a superior officer or a public authority may not be invoked as a justification of torture."

The current trend in anti-terrorism and similar treaties dealing with criminal offences, together with the statutes of the Nuremberg Tribunal, the two *ad hoc* tribunals and the International Criminal Court, is to deny immunity to those ordering their perpetration regardless of status. This may well have developed into a rule of international customary law. Britain's Lord Chief Justice in the Divisional Court rejected the Spanish application.

The arguments submitted by Pinochet and the government of Chile was that he was exempt from jurisdiction since he was in possession of a diplomatic passport. But this argument was of no avail since Pinochet was not accredited to the United Kingdom, nor was he in transit to take up a diplomatic post, as provided for in the Vienna Convention of Diplomatic Relations.[40] However, the court held that all offences in which he is alleged to be involved had occurred while he was head of state and as issues of state policy, and so were exempt from jurisdiction under the State Immunity Act, 1978.[41]

By what is submitted to be a misunderstanding of the rules concerning act of state and the immunity of a head of state—for he no longer held that position—the court held that as the acts had been committed while he was head of state, no English tribunal possessed jurisdiction over him. This implied that any head of state accused of a crime against humanity would, in fact, enjoy impunity in England even though he was now a private citizen, regardless of any honorific status he might enjoy in his own country. By taking such a line the court ignored the fact that an ex-diplomat visiting England would not be able to argue that he possessed diplomatic immunity even for an offence committed while he held a diplomatic post in England.[42]

Perhaps it is unfortunate that the Chief Justice overlooked or paid insufficient attention to the decision of the Court of Appeal of Ghana in the *Schumann* case:[43] "Merely carrying out wicked orders [or ordering them to be carried out] or plans of a governing political party by State agents against the persons or properties of individuals or groups of individuals who manifestly do not demonstrate any organized violent resistance to the execution of those plans would not stamp the offences committed in such a situation with political character so as to afford the perpetrators an excuse from due prosecution. It is absolutely absurd to me to hold that what is clearly murder in one territory in response to the superior orders of a ruling offender [should not be] extradited because it was done in obedience to superior orders of a governing political party.... The offence of murder...is no more of a political character than the offence of, say, robbery with violence or burglary committed by a political party activist in a desperate bid to seek means of replenishing the dwindling coffers of his political party."

While these words were directed at those obeying orders, they apply with perhaps even greater force to those issuing such illegal commands. If the jurisprudence of the two *ad hoc* tribunals and the International Criminal Court are to mean anything and if municipal courts recognize that the denial of impunity extends to a head of state as much as to anyone else, we may yet see a world in which those tempted to commit crimes against humanity will realize that forums exist before which they can be brought to justice and that they can no longer find asylum anywhere.

The House of Lords, by a majority of three to two, reversed the decision of the Lord Chief Justice. They held that Pinochet was, from the point of view of English law, neither a diplomat nor a head of state and therefore had no claim to immunity from the local jurisdiction, thus confirming his amenity to the extradition process. Moreover, as Lord Nicholls dealing with the issue of act of state pointed out in the course of his judgement, the Vienna Convention and the English statute "confer immunity in respect of acts performed in the exercise of functions which international law recognizes as functions of a head of state, irrespective of the terms of his domestic constitution. This formulation, and the test for determining what are the functions of a head of a state for this purpose, are sound in principle.... International law does not require the grant of any wider immunity. And it hardly needs saying that torture of his own subjects, or of aliens, would not be regarded by international law as a function of a head of state.

"Similarly, the taking of hostages, as much as torture, has been outlawed by the international community as an offence.... [I]nternational law has made plain that certain types of conduct, including torture and hostage taking, are not acceptable conduct on the part of anyone. This applies as much to heads or state, or even more so, as it does to everyone else; the contrary conclusion would make a mockery of international law.... Acts of torture and hostage taking, outlawed as they are by international law, cannot be attributed to the state to the exclusion of person liability.... It cannot be stated too plainly that the acts of torture and hostage taking with which Senator Pinochet is charged are offences under United Kingdom statute law. This country has taken extraterritorial jurisdiction for these crimes.

"The sole question...is whether, by reason of his status as a former head of state, Senator Pinochet is immune from the criminal processes of this country, of which extradition forms a part. Arguments about the effect on this country's diplomatic relations with Chile if extradition were allowed to proceed, or with Spain if refused, are not matters for the court. These are, *par excellence*, political matters for consideration by the Secretary of State in the exercise of his discretion under section 12 of the Extradition Act," which gives him the power to disregard a ruling in support of extradition.

In some ways, Lord Steyn's comments were even more significant. He stated: "Municipal law cannot be decisive as at where the line [between legitimate and illegitimate state acts] is to be drawn. If it were the determining fact, the most abhorrent municipal laws might be said to enlarge the functions of a head of State. But...it is conceded on behalf of General Pinochet that the distinction between official acts performed in the exercise of functions as a Head of State and acts not satisfying these requirements must depend on the rules of international law.... Negatively, the development of international law since the Second World War justifies the conclusion that by the time of the 1973 *coup d'état* [in Chile which brought Pinochet to power], and certainly ever since, international law condemned genocide, torture, hostage taking and crimes against humanity (during an armed conflict or in peacetime) as international crimes deserving of punishment.

"Given this state of international law, it seems...difficult to maintain that the commission of such high crimes may amount to acts performed in the exercise of the functions of a Head of State. The essential fragility of the claim to immunity is underlined by the insistence on behalf of General Pinochet that it is not alleged that he 'personally' committed any of the crimes. That means that he did not commit the crimes by his own hand. It is apparently conceded that if he personally tortured victims the position would be different. This distinction flies in the fact of an elementary principle of law, shared by all civilized legal systems, that there is no distinction to be drawn between the man who strikes, and a man who orders another to strike....

"Qualitatively, what he is alleged to have done is no more to be categorized as acts undertaken in the exercise of the functions of a Head of State than...of a Head of State murdering his gardener or arranging the torture of his opponents for the sheer spectacle of it. It follows that...General Pinochet has no statutory immunity.... [T]he issue of act of state must be approached on the basis that the intent of Parliament was not to give statutory immunity to a former Head of State in respect of the systematic torture and killing of his fellow citizens.

"The ground of this conclusion is that such high crimes are not official acts committed in the exercise of the functions of a Head of State.... [T]he Spanish authorities have relied on crimes of genocide,[44] torture, hostage-taking and crimes against humanity. It has in my view been clearly established that by 1973 such acts were already condemned as high crimes by customary international law. In these circumstances it would be wrong for the English courts now to extend the act of the state doctrine in a way which runs counter to the state of customary international law as it existed in 1973.

"Since the act of state doctrine depends on public policy as perceived by the courts in the forum at the time of the suit, the developments since 1973 are also relevant and serve to reinforce my view. I would endorse the observation in the Third Restatement of *The Foreign Relations Law of the United States*, published in 1986 by the American Law Institute, Vol. 1, at 370, to the effect that: 'A claim arising out of an alleged violation of fundamental human rights—for instance a claim on behalf of a victim of torture or genocide—would (if otherwise sustainable) probably not be defeated by the act of state doctrine, since the accepted international law of human rights is well established and contemplates external scrutiny of such acts.' But in adopting this formulation I would remove the word 'probably' and substitute 'generally'."

There is, of course, unfortunately, no guarantee that a similar finding would be reached by a court in another state. Nor does it follow that a serving head of state or diplomat would not be entitled to claim the immunities flowing from customary law or the Vienna Convention. However, in view of the increasing numbers of treaties which deny immunity to heads or state committing or ordering particular international crimes, and especially those amounting to crimes against humanity, as well as the number of states in addition to Italy, namely, France, Germany, Switzerland and Belgium, that had also applied for Pinochet's extradition, it may well be that there has developed, at least in so far as Europe is concerned, a new rule of customary law in this matter replacing the former rules concerning immunity and applicable even as regards states which have not become parties to the various treaties denying such impunity.

At the same time, it is submitted that since it has been held that genocide is but an example, even though it may be the most grievous one, of crimes against humanity, while the more serious war crimes among those directed at human beings, both military and civilian, may equally be considered as coming within that category, there may develop a practice whereby—and this would at least reduce the multiplicity of charges which have become common in the indictments issued by the two *ad hoc* tribunals—all such offences are treated as crimes against humanity and charged as such, with genocide or specific war crimes cited as instances of this more serious concept.

Regarding the eighty-two-year-old General Pinochet, his fate has not yet been determined. Even if the courts hold that he is extraditable, the ultimate decision does not rest with the court. It rests with the government. Whether he will be allowed to stay in the UK, whether they will send him back to Chile, then begin the extradition proceedings of Germany, France, Switzerland, Belgium and the rest of them, it is going to be a long process. But if the authorities carry out what the House of Lords ruled, we are at last on the march towards dealing with crimes against humanity, regardless who orders these crimes or who commits them.

▄▄▄▄ Postscript

The initial decision of the House of Lords concerning Pinochet was declared invalid when it was ascertained that Lord Hoffman, who had not delivered a separate judgement but concurred in that of Lord Nicholls, thus creating a majority in favour of extraditability, was a senior adviser of Amnesty International, which had intervened in the case. A new hearing with an enlarged bench was decided upon.

On this occasion, in early April 1999, the Lords decided that Pinochet did not possess immunity as a former head of state in respect of acts which amounted to crimes under international law. For extradition to be possible, the act alleged must be criminal under the law of both the requesting and the requested state. In this case, Lord Browne-Wilkinson presiding held that the charges of torture could only be relevant if they concerned acts committed after 1988 when Britain ratified the Torture Convention and made torture a crime under English law.

He stated: "The *jus cogens* [overriding and unquestionable rules of law] nature of torture justifies states in taking jurisdiction over torture wherever committed. International law provides that offences *jus cogens* may be punished by any state because the offenders are 'common enemies of all mankind [*hostes humani geners*] and all nations have an interest in their apprehension and prosecution.'...[L]ong before the Torture Convention of 1984 state torture was an international crime in the highest sense.... The Torture Convention was agreed not in order to create an international crime which had not previously existed but to provide an international system under which the international criminal could find no safe haven.... Can it be said that the commission of a crime which is an international crime against humanity and *jus cogens* is an act done in an official capacity on behalf of the state [to which immunity would attach]? I believe there to be strong ground for saying that the implementation of torture as defined by the Torture Convention cannot be a state function.... How can it be for international purposes an official function to do something which international law itself prohibits and criminalizes?... [I]f the former head of state has immunity, the man most responsible will escape liability while his inferiors [the chiefs of police, junior army officers] who carried out his orders will be liable. I find it impossible to accept that this was the intention.... [T]he notion of continued immunity for ex-heads of state is inconsistent with the provisions of the Torture Convention."

While denying immunity in respect of torture, Lord Browne-Wilkinson upheld the immunity of an ex-head of state in respect of the charges of murder. As a result, he considered that only three of the thirty-one charges were extraditable and suggested that the home secretary might even reconsider his view that Pinochet was amenable to extradition. The remaining Law Lords, with only one dissentient, were of similar view. Nevertheless, unless the home secretary intervenes, Pinochet will become subject to normal extradition proceedings. Even if it be held, consequent to a prolonged appellate procedure, that Pinochet was extraditable to Spain to stand trial for torture, it would remain open to the home secretary—as it would to the minister of justice in Canada—to exercise his jurisdiction and extend asylum, which would be done for political or humanitarian reasons. Should Pinochet be not extradited, even though this be for purely political reasons, it remains true that the judicial reasoning to be found in the two House of Lords judgements constitutes a historic precedent contributing to the universality of criminal jurisdiction for crimes against humanity, regardless of the status of the offenders.

REFERENCES

1. C.M., L.L.B., L.L.D, F.R.S.C., Stockton Professor of International Law, US Naval War College; University Professor Emeritus, Honorary Professor of Law, University of Alberta.
2. Schindler and Toman. *The Laws of Armed Conflicts*. 1988, 911, Art. 6(c).
3. For an account of the trial and the background history, see Schwarzenberger, *International Law*, Vol. 2, *The Law of Armed Conflict*, 1968, ch. 39.
4. UNWCC, *History of the United Nations War Crimes Commission and the Development of the Laws of War*, 1948, 35.
5. Ibid., 1948, 41.
6. 1920, Israel, 3 *Major Peace Treaties of Modern History 1648–1967*, 2055.
7. 1923, 4 ibid., 2301.
8. Neuilly with Bulgaria, Arts. 118–120; St. Germain with Austria, Arts. 173–176; Trianon with Hungary, Arts. 157–160, ibid., 1727, 1535, 1863, resp.
9. 1919, 2 ibid., 1265.
10. Schlinder and Toman, op. cit., 63.
11. Italics added.
12. H.M.S.O., Cmd. 6964 (1946); 41 *Am. J. Int'l Law* (1947) 172.
13. At 65,247, resp.
14. At 61,244, resp. (italics added).
15. The so-called *Kristallnacht*.
16. Schwelb, Crimes Against Humanity, 23 *Brit. Y. B. Int'l Law* (1946), 178, 204–207.
17. This was the term applied by the German government to the policy of extermination regardless of the group affected.
18. 1950, Schindler and Toman, op. cit. 923.
19. Gen. Ass. Res. 217A(III).
20. Res. 260(III)A.
21. 1966, 6 I.L.M. 360, 368.
22. 1950, 213 UNTS 222.
23. 1991, 32 I.L.M. 1192; 1994, 33 I.L.M. 1598.
24. 1998, 37 I.L.M. 999.
25. UN DOC/S/1994/1125, paras. 114–117.

26. In fact, the Nuremberg Tribunal had no discretion in the matter since, as has been seen, the restrictive meaning of 'crimes against humanity' was set in its constituent Charter.

27. Green, "International Law and the Control of Barbarism," in Macdonald, et al., *The International Law and Policy of Human Welfare*, 1978, 239; 'The Role of Law in Establishing Norms of International Behaviour,' 17 *Israel Y B. Human Rights*, 1987, 149.

28. Dinstein, "Crimes Against Humanity," in Makarczyk, *Theory of International Law at the Threshold of the 21st Century*, 1997, 891.

29. The quotation from the Yugoslav Commission's Report must have come from the Interim Report, since in the wording cited it does not appear in that Commission's Final Report, UN DOC/S/1994/674, although it forms a summary of paras. 84–86 of the Final Report.

30. *Prosecutor v. Dusko Tadic*, Case No. IT-94-1-T, 14 July 1997, para 8.

31. Yugoslavia, Art. 5; Rwanda, Art. 3.

32. *Prosecutor v. Drazen Erdemovic*, Sentencing Judgement, Case No. IT-96-22-T. 29 November 1996, paras 28, 31–32.

33. Kelsen, "Will the Judgement in the Nuremberg Trial Constitute a Precedent in International Law?", 1 I.L.Q. 1947, 453.

34. Italics added.

35. International Convention on the Suppression and Punishment of the Crime of Apartheid, 1998, 13 I.L.M. 50.

36. Green, "The Nature of Political Offences," 3 *The Solicitor Quarterly* 1964, 213; Van Den Wijngaert, *The Political Offence Defence in Extradition*, 1980.

37. *State v. Ghana (Director of Prisons), ex p. Schumann* (1966) 39 I.L.R. 433, commenting on Nazi Germany's euthanasia policy.

38. Convention Against Torture and Other Cruel, Inhuman or Degrading Treatment or Punishment, 1984, 23 I.L.M. 1027, Art. 2.

39. Green, "Derogation of Human Rights in Time of Emergency," 16 *Can. Y. B. Int'l Law* 1978, 982.

40. 1961, 500 UNTS 95, Arts. 29, 31, 40.

41. 1978, c. 33.

42. *Ghosh v. D'Rozario* [1963] 1 W.B. 106.

43. See n. 34 above.

44. It should be noted that the Genocide Convention does not include political groups or opponents among those specified as potential victims of genocide.

JULES DESCHÊNES

Justice and Crimes Against Humanity

Jules Deschênes served as a judge on the International Criminal Tribunal for the former Yugoslavia and chaired the Commission of Enquiry on War Criminals in Canada. He also served as chief justice of the Superior Court of Québec and justice of the Québec Court of Appeal. He is a Companion of the Order of Canada.

THE TITLE OF THIS PAPER HAS REMINDED ME of the celebrated novel by Dostoevsky, *Crime and Punishment*. He was writing about his hero Raskolnikov and, in a line and a half towards the end of the novel, he painted the picture of his hero. I quote from an English translation: "Tears and agonies would at least have been life. But he didn't repent of his crime."

About ten years ago, during my inquiry on war criminals in Canada, that was the feeling which I found deeply ingrained in the minds and hearts of the suspects who were summoned before me. None of them ever uttered a single word of regret or compassion. None of them ever begged for forgiveness from the victims. I even saw the Iron Cross being held in support of a lament that the fortunes of war should not have turned otherwise.

Half a century after the proclamation of the United Nations Declaration of Human Rights we are still facing cynical violations of its lofty ideal, possibly the worst of which is genocide—the "crime of crimes" in the words of the International Criminal Tribunal for Rwanda.[1] But we are not concerned with genocide today. Not far behind are looming crimes against humanity. In recent years, the definition of such crimes has gone through a critical evolution.

Pursuant to the 1993 Report of the UN Secretary General to the Security Council, the latter body created, on 25 May 1993, the International Criminal Tribunal for the former Yugoslavia and adopted the statute which would govern its work. Article 1 of the statute establishes the general competence of the tribunal

157

over "persons responsible for serious violations of international humanitarian law."

The statute then goes into particulars of the violations. Article 5 is entitled "crimes against humanity" and defines them as follows: "crimes when committed in armed conflict, whether international or internal in character, and directed against any civilian population."

On 2 October 1995, in its first decision in the matter of Dusko Tadic, the appeals chamber of the Yugoslavia Tribunal, of which I was a member, affirmed the tribunal's jurisdiction to try the particular issue and subtly criticized the above-quoted provision in Article 5: "141. It is by now a settled rule of customary international law that crimes against humanity do not require a connection to international armed conflict. Indeed, as the prosecutor points out, customary international law may not require a connection between crimes against humanity and any conflict at all. Thus, by requiring that crimes against humanity be committed in either internal or international armed conflict, the Security Council may have defined the crime in Article 5 more narrowly than necessary under customary international law."

Indeed, already in 1949, the International Court of Justice had recognized that "elementary consideration of humanity (can be) even more exacting in peace than in war."[2] The evolution of minds was confirmed at the Rome Conference in July 1997, when the Statute on the Establishment of an International Criminal Court was adopted by a vote of 120 in favour, seven against and twenty-one abstentions.[3] I am aware that the court will not come into actual operation before there are sixty ratifications from as many governmental authorities around the world. Nevertheless, the first big step was taken through the vote in favour of the creation and establishment of that first International Criminal Court in the history of the world. Our generation should be considerably proud of having been able to reach that agreement in spite of the negative votes of the United States of America, Israel, China and four other countries.

Article 7 of the statute creating the court says this: "For the purpose of this Statute, 'crime against humanity' means any of the following acts (list of eleven) when committed as part of a widespread or systematic attack directed against any civilian population, with knowledge of the attack." One immediately notices the difference between the 1993 and the 1998 definitions. The reference to an armed conflict has been dropped while the concept of a "widespread or systematic attack" has been introduced. Now those definitions are very dry. Let us see how they have been applied in three recent cases—one in Yugoslavia, the other two in Rwanda.

Before the Yugoslavia Tribunal, one Erdemovic was charged in 1996 with a count of a crime against humanity or, alternatively, a count of a war crime for his participation in the execution of about 1,200 unarmed civilian Muslim men in the aftermath of the fall of the UN "safe area" of Srebenica in July 1995. He was then a twenty-three-year-old private.

Upon his appearance before the tribunal, Erdemovic pleaded guilty to the charge of crime against humanity, but explained that he had acted under duress, i.e., threat of death for himself and fear of the same fate for his wife and nine-month-old son. Erdemovic was convicted on the strength of his guilty plea, but the trial chamber felt that duress had not been proven. After consideration of some mitigating circumstances, Erdemovic was finally sentenced to ten years in jail. Erdemovic appealed. The chamber of five judges was divided on more than one issue but in a final analysis allowed the appeal on 7 October 1997.

Unanimously, the five judges found that the accused's guilty plea had been voluntary. On the question of duress, they split three to two. The minority would have found that duress afforded a complete defence to the accused. The majority, however, refused to go that far, at least in such a case as involved the killing of innocent human beings. For the majority, duress could only be invoked as a mitigating factor. A majority of four to one, however, found that the guilty plea had not been well informed. That is where the case is of special interest to us today.

The indictment was framed in the alternative, on the basis of the same facts: that Erdemovic had committed either a crime against humanity or a war crime. He pleaded guilty to the first branch of the alternative. Now the trial chamber and the majority in the appeals chamber held that a crime against humanity is a more serious offence than a war crime. As the appeals chamber stated (para. 20): "All things being equal, a punishable offence, if charged and proven as a crime against humanity, is more serious and should ordinarily entail a heavier penalty than if it were proceeded upon on the basis that it were a war crime. (Underlined in the original.)"

Hence, of course, the importance that the accused, before registering a guilty plea, thoroughly understand the nature and weight of the charge against him. Now here was, in the words of the appeals chamber, what had transpired (para. 19, pp. 16–17): "With respect, the difference between a crime against humanity and a war crime was not adequately explained to the Appellant by the Trial Chamber at the initial hearing nor was there any attempt to explain the difference to him at any later occasion when the Appellant reaffirmed his plea. The Presiding Judge appears to assume that the Appellant had been advised by his counsel as to the distinction between the charges and that the Prosecution 'will make things very clear'. From the passage of the transcript previously quoted, it is apparent that defence counsel himself did not appreciate either the true nature of the offences at international law or the true legal distinction between them. It is also clear on the record that the difference between the charges was never made clear by either the Prosecution or by the Presiding Judge.

"We have, accordingly, no doubt that the misapprehension regarding the true distinction between the two alternative charges led the Appellant to plead guilty to the more serious of the two charges, that is, the charge alleging the crime against humanity."

The appeals chamber had, therefore, no choice, in spite of Judge Li's dissenting opinion, but to quash the sentence and remit the case to another trial chamber for further process. You will not be surprised that, upon appearing anew, the accused changed his plea—not guilty anymore of a crime against humanity, but guilty of a war crime. The prosecutor withdrew the charge of crime against humanity. The question then was: The accused having been previously sentenced to ten years in jail on a more serious charge, what would be the appropriate sentence now?

There were a number of mitigating circumstances: age, family, lack of previous record, duress, cooperation with the prosecutor. Let us add, to be fair, that Erdemovic was no Raskolnikov. He has shown remorse in spite of the duress which he had to undergo. A complicating factor was injected into the matter through the filing of an agreement following some plea bargaining between prosecution and defence. They agreed that a sentence of seven years would be appropriate. They also acknowledged that such an agreement could not bind the tribunal.

The three judges of the second trial chamber were unanimous in imposing on Erdemovic, on 5 March 1998, a sentence of five years imprisonment, from which could be deducted the two years he had already spent in jail. No specific reasons were given for the choice of the figure, outside of the "family difficulties" which were cursorily referred to. The separate opinion of Judge Shahabuddeen, though concurring with his two colleagues, shows the ambiguity of the situation but throws no particular light on the solution adopted vis-à-vis Erdemovic.

To sum up, we have in this case a given set of facts which can be qualified equally as crime against humanity or war crime. Depending upon which qualification is retained at the end of the day, the crime may be deemed more or less serious and entail an appropriately graded penalty. But it will take more than this single case to clarify all the issues.

The two other cases are even more recent and come from the Rwanda Tribunal. They are straightforward and need but a few words of exposition.

In the first one, the former prime minister of Rwanda, Jean Kambanda, pleaded guilty to six counts: four relative to genocide and two to crimes against humanity, being murder and extermination. The accused signed with his counsel a detailed plea of guilty including twelve paragraphs covering all six counts of the charge. The tribunal, in a detailed judgement, considered all relevant circumstances as well as the plea of the accused's counsel that his client was only a puppet of military authorities, and concluded (page 16): "[T]he

Chamber is of the opinion that the aggravating circumstances surrounding the crimes committed by Jean Kambanda negate the mitigating circumstances, especially since Jean Kambanda occupied a high ministerial post at the time he committed the same crimes." On 4 September 1998 the tribunal lumped together all charges and sentenced Kambanda to a single penalty of life imprisonment. The accused has appealed.

The other relevant case involved one Jean-Paul Akayesu. At the time of the events in 1994, Akayesu was mayor of Taba, a small town in Rwanda. The accused pleaded not guilty but on 2 September 1998, after a lengthy trial, he was finally found guilty of nine counts of genocide and crimes against humanity involving extermination, murder, torture, rape and other inhumane acts.

On 2 October 1998 the tribunal imposed on Akayesu the following sentences: life imprisonment for genocide, incitement to genocide and extermination; fifteen years for murder and rape; ten years for torture and other inhumane acts; finally merging all sentences into one of life imprisonment. The accused has lodged an appeal.

It does not belong to me to comment on the guilt or innocence of the accused Akayesu. But assuming for purposes of discussion the correctness of the conviction, the penalty would appear amply justified from the point of view of a Canadian observer.

It is of course much too early to foresee what attitude the future permanent International Criminal Court will take towards those cases of crimes against humanity. In the meantime, other cases which are progressing before the two *ad hoc* international tribunals should help to fashion a better understanding and a clearer disposition of that issue.

Both tribunals have expressed interesting views in their sentencing decisions. Let me conclude by quoting from the sentence meted out by the Rwanda Tribunal in the *Kambanda* case (para. 28): "It is clear that the penalties imposed on accused persons found guilty by the Tribunal must be directed, on the one hand, at retribution of the said accused, who must see their crimes punished, and over and above that, on the other hand, at deterrence, namely dissuading for good those who will attempt in future to perpetrate such atrocities by showing them that the international community was not ready to tolerate the serious violations of international humanitarian law and human rights."

Retribution and deterrence—those should indeed be the controlling elements. Which one of the two, if any, should be accorded precedence is a matter for future jurisprudence.

REFERENCES

1. Conviction and sentence of Jean Kambanda, 4 September 1998, para. 16.
2. The Corfu Channel Case, I.C.J. Reports 1949: 22.
3. 17 July 1998.

Military Sexual Slavery

Crimes Against Humanity

Indai Lourdes Sajor is executive director of the Asian
Centre for Women's Human Rights and a member of the
International Council of the International Human Rights
Law Group. She organized the International
Conference on Violence against Women in War and
Armed Conflict held in Tokyo in November 1997.

ON 9 OCTOBER 1998 the Tokyo District Court dismissed the claims for
compensation and reparations filed against the Japanese government by
Filipino comfort women forced into sexual slavery by the Japanese Imperial
Army during World War II. The presiding judge refused to accept and examine
the case despite six years of court hearings and testimony; legal experts were of
the opinion that there was no legal basis for the claims of the victims, even
under international humanitarian law.

The forty-six plaintiffs had pursued the case to the Tokyo High Court. As we
shift gears for a fresh round of battle, as well as assist another group of Filipino
women survivors of systematic rape during World War II in filing their own
case, we draw support from the women and men who are fighting to eradicate
violence against women in war and armed conflict situations.

On Military Sexual Slavery

Most of the wars in world history have integrated rapes, prostitution, sexual
slavery and sexual violence of all kinds in the conduct of war. But the case of the
Asian comfort women kept by the Japanese Imperial Army during World War II
is unparalleled. The government itself systematically planned, ordered,
conscripted, established and controlled the army brothels. Using the resources
of the entire army, women from occupied territories and countries were forcibly
abducted. The abduction, detention and mass rape of a large number of women
in Asia during World War II should be understood as part of military strategy to
defeat the enemy by demoralizing and terrorizing the population.

163

When the Japanese Imperial Army invaded the continent of Asia at the beginning of the 1930s, it immediately started to build army brothels. After the Japanese invasion of China in 1937 this practice was systematically and officially implemented in almost all garrisons, including northeast China (which the Japanese called Manchuria), other parts of China, the Philippines, Korea, the South Sea Islands and Dutch East Indies (Indonesia), Malaysia, Indochina and even in Japan itself. The tragedy of this action is that most of these women were young girls between eleven and twenty years old when they were forcibly detained and repeatedly raped. Many of these women were kidnapped while washing clothes at the river, working in the fields or walking to the market. Others were induced into slavery by officials of the colonial government who promised good pay for work in factories. All these young women left home without imagining that they would become *jug ianfu* or comfort women for the Japanese Imperial Army.

Many of these girls were so young that they did not even know the meaning of sex. Many of them were raped on their way to the brothels. In the brothels the comfort women usually had to service ten to forty soldiers a day and generally more on weekends. Many who were infected by venereal diseases were treated with large doses of harmful drugs and others had to undergo forced abortions. Most of the women who were injured in the process of torture and rape were never given any medical treatment and such abuses resulted in the death of a considerable number of them. It is estimated that some 200,000 women from all over Asia were officially conscripted as sex slaves for the Japanese Imperial Army. Eighty per cent of them were from Korea. Historians estimate that, at the close of the war, fewer than thirty per cent had survived their ordeal.

After the war, the Japanese soldiers abandoned the comfort women. In some military outfits, the comfort women were summarily executed. Others were ordered to commit suicide along with the Japanese soldiers. In other countries they were killed in trenches. Many of them were abandoned by the Imperial Army and had to return home by themselves with great difficulty. Upon returning home many of these comfort women carried the burden of shame. Because of their traumatic experiences, many could not marry or failed in their marriages because of the sense of guilt, sickness or the isolation they suffered in their own community or society. For those women who came from poor and deprived backgrounds, the conditions they returned to were even harder because they had been comfort women.

After World War II, the Allied Western nations did not force Japan to pay full and comprehensive reparations for the damages incurred during the war. Nor did they punish all the Japanese war criminals (some of them became members of parliament after the war), as strictly as they had punished war criminals in Germany. One of the reasons for this is that the nations in Asia were former

colonies of the Allied nations and were too weak to demand full war reparations, including the prosecution of the war criminals. There is much speculation
regarding the silence of the Allied nations regarding the information in its
archives on these atrocities. Most of the documents which detail the existence of
the comfort stations and the conditions suffered by the comfort women were
taken by historians and researchers to the Washington War Archives. Some
historians believe that the West treated the issue as an "Asian" matter; secondly,
that women as a whole are a low priority, even when subjected to such inhumane treatment and gross human rights violation.

In addition, the West, in its guilt for the Nagasaki and Hiroshima bombings,
wanted to rehabilitate Japan as quickly as possible. Whatever the actual reasons,
it is distressing to know that the Allied nations did nothing for the comfort
women even though they clearly knew of their existence. The stories of the
comfort women speak of Allied forces rounding up the women from the army
brothels to be released after the war.

▆▆▆ Why Women Victims of Armed Conflict Should be Compensated

Based on the testimonies given by the Asian comfort women, it is evident that
more than one crime has been committed against every woman. Evidence
points to crimes of rape, murder, abduction, forced labour, kidnapping, sexual
slavery, torture, racial discrimination, forced sterilization, massacre and genocide. Never before in Asian history have so many crimes been systematically
perpetrated against individual women on such a massive scale and with
impunity.

On 6 December 1991 a class action suit was filed against the Japanese government by Korean comfort women belonging to the Association of Pacific War
Victims and Bereaved Families. A second class action suit was filed on 2 April
1993, by Filipino comfort women of the Task Force for Filipina Victims of
Military Sexual Slavery by Japan. Both suits, filed at the Tokyo District Court,
demand post-war responsibility, compensation and reparations for the crimes
against humanity committed during World War II.

In August 1993 the Japanese government admitted for the first time that "the
then Japanese military was directly or indirectly involved in the establishment
and management of the comfort stations and the transfer of comfort women."
The government also admitted that the recruitment and transportation of the
women were carried out against the women's will by deceit and pressure and
that the military personnel directly took part in the recruitments. Since then
two former members of the Japanese Imperial Forces have come out to speak of
their participation and knowledge of the running of the comfort stations.

The Japanese government also stated that "it is apparent that there existed a
great number of comfort women" and that life at the comfort stations was

INDAI LOURDES SAJOR

miserable. The Japanese government has recognized that "this was an act that severely injured the honour and dignity of many women" and it apologized to all these women.

Each of the class action suits, filed by the Filipino and Korean comfort women, has a different legal basis. Korea had been a colony of Japan for more than thirty years when Japan invaded other Asian countries, while the Philippines was a colony of the United States when Japan invaded that country. The cases have different legal grounds because of the different historical perspectives of the two countries, but the demands are the same.

■ The Hague Convention: War Crimes

The Hague Convention of 1907, which provides specific regulations to protect civilians in occupied territories, was ratified by Japan in 1912 with the signature of Aimaro Sato. The convention provides a general prohibition of torture and other atrocities against combatants and civilians. For example, it provides that prisoners of war "must be treated humanely." (See The Hague Convention; Regulations, Article IV.) Article 46 of the Hague Convention stipulates respect for the lives of the person and rights of the family. This regulation prohibits violation of the basic rights of an individual or of his or her body. Thus it is obvious that rapes and sexual abuse of women are a breach of this provision.

The Hague Convention also contains the famous Martens clause, which provides: "Until a more complete code of laws of war has been issued,...in cases not included in the Regulations...the inhabitants and belligerents remain under the protection and the rule of the principles of the law of nations, as they result from the usages established among civilized peoples, from the laws of humanity and the dictates of the public conscience." (See The Hague Convention of 1907, 8th Preamble.)

The significance of regulations set out in the Article 46 has been reiterated and developed in the later international laws. It was further articulated in Article 27–2 of the Geneva Convention on the Protection of Civilians of 1949. It refers to obligations with regards to protection of women from violation, particularly from rapes, forced prostitution and all kinds of obscene acts. The International Committee of the Red Cross acknowledges, in its commentary on the Geneva Convention, that this provision articulated the concept of the Hague Convention. A protocol of the 1977 Geneva Convention of Protection of Civilians includes more detailed provisions on the protection of women's dignity.

The violations of the Hague Convention by the Japanese Imperial Army were partly judged at the International Military Tribunal for the Far East (1948), when the members of the Japanese Imperial Army were found guilty of breach of war regulations by ordering, conferring the competence and permitting war crimes to be committed. Although rapes and forced prostitution are duly applicable to the said violations, the fact is, the cases handled focused on the abuses of prisoners of war, while the damages incurred by civilians have not yet been fully uncovered. A penalty is imposed for any breach of the Hague Convention. Article 3 reads: "A belligerent party which violates the provisions of the said regulations shall, if the case demands, be liable to pay compensation. It shall be responsible for all acts committed by persons forming part of its armed forces." According to these provisions, the Japanese government is liable to pay compensation for murder and rape cases committed by the Japanese Imperial Army in the occupied territories.

■■■ Crimes Against Humanity

The term "crime against humanity" refers to acts that are so atrocious that all of humanity suffers the damage and demands redress. The concept of crimes against humanity was first employed at the Paris Peace Conference in 1919. At that time, the concept was not yet distinguished from crimes against peace: namely, crimes of waging war. After the World War II, war crimes were divided into categories, giving crimes against humanity a technical definition.

As one of the major counts of war crimes, crimes against humanity are defined in Article 6 of the Charter of the International Military Tribunal for the Far East (IMTFE) or Tokyo Tribunal. Punishment for conspiracy to commit such crimes is also mentioned in this document. This charter enumerates murders, annihilations, slavery, abuses, deportations and other nonhumanitarian acts committed before or during the war. However, there was little reference to crimes against humanity in the judgements given at the (IMTFE) Tokyo Tribunals. The concept of crimes against humanity is repeatedly adopted thereafter in such international laws as the Convention on Genocide of 1948 and the Convention on Apartheid.

The IMTFE had the authority to punish such war crimes and crimes against humanity committed by the Japanese Imperial Forces and government. Documents have shown that the IMTFE did not address any case of sexual slavery, despite the testimony of Ester Garcia Moras, a Filipina, and other women who testified in the Tokyo Tribunal about their experience as sex slaves. No other military tribunal punished any perpetrator of these crimes against Asian women victims. The one exception was the punishment by a Dutch Military Tribunal established in Indonesia and referred to as the Batavia trial. The trial saw charges against ten Japanese officers who committed war crimes against thirty-five Dutch women who were sex slaves in the Dutch East Indies (Indonesia). The trial concerned the forcible taking of the Dutch women only, despite the existence of evidence that Indonesian women had also been taken against their will to be abused in the comfort stations established in Indonesia. Despite the demands of the Asian people, the Japanese courts have never punished any war criminal since the end of the World War II.

As long ago as the 1950s, relevant UN bodies such as the Commission on the Status of Women adopted resolutions that led to the adoption by the Economic and Social Council of Resolution 353 (XII) (19 March 1951). In that resolution, the council formally appealed to the competent German authorities to consider making the fullest possible reparations for injuries suffered under the Nazi regime by persons subjected to human experiments. To date the UN has made no formal recommendation for reparations to Asian victims of sexual slavery.

International Law and Individuals

A new concept of war reparation was introduced by the Paris Peace Treaty which ended World War I. Unlike traditional reparations, Germany became liable to damages inflicted upon individuals, in addition to those of a state (see Article 231 and 232 of the Versailles Peace Treaty). The treaty also refers to redressing damages to civilian victims and allowed that an individual could receive compensation through the judgement of a mixed arbitration court. Traditionally, reparations had been regarded as being performed between countries in which a state represents collective claims. The Paris Peace Treaty separated and articulated the individual's right to apply to a state for personal damages.

After World War II, subjectivity (or the right to claim) of an individual in international law has been substantiated in accordance with the increased awareness and practice of human rights protection. With regard to war reparations, efforts have been made to acknowledge the right of individual victims to make claims for damages. The concept of diplomatic protection has also changed in regards to claiming reparations for individual damages. Many opinions now support the view that diplomatic protection is no longer a mere discretion of a state. It is an obligation of the state as an entrustee to protect the welfare of its citizens. The above-mentioned views and practices lead to the point that, in principle, an individual right to make a claim against a state should not be affected even when a state does not recognize diplomatic protection or abandons claims through reparations.

UN Mechanisms

When the women slowly started to come out and tell their horrifying stories from World War II, several women's nongovernmental organizations and human rights groups took the issue to the United Nations. They looked to the United Nations as the world body which could ensure that justice would be done for the women victims of war. International pressure from the UN to the governments which perpetrated these crimes would be a major step towards a negotiated settlement. There is now worldwide concern for these victims and a number of international nongovernmental organizations have invited the victims and their representatives to participate in the sessions of the UN

Commission on Human Rights, its subcommission on the Prevention of Discrimination and Protection of Minorities and the subcommission's Working Group on Contemporary Forms of Slavery.

The International Commission of Jurists (ICJ) in Geneva launched a fact-finding mission to Asia in 1994 and a product of that mission is a report of the ICJ by Ustinia Dolgopol and Snehal Paranjapein. The Secretary General of ICJ, Adama Dieng, stated: "It is imperative that the government of Japan take immediate steps to provide full rehabilitation and restitution to the victims. The ICJ sincerely hopes that this report will make a contribution to provide immediate relief to the victims and to ensure that they do not remain forgotten forever."

The ICJ recommended that Japan expeditiously provide and set up an administrative forum where the claims of the victims can be heard and disposed of within a time frame of six months or so. Alternatively, Japan should enact appropriate legislation enabling an expeditious disposal of the pending law suits and waive preliminary technical objections of jurisdiction and limitation. In the event of Japan's refusal to rehabilitate the women, a tribunal or an arbitration panel consisting of international law experts from countries not directly concerned with this issue should be formed as soon as possible. NGOs and individuals should also be permitted to appear in their own right as parties. All must agree in advance to abide by and accept the opinion of the tribunal or panel.

Several NGO forums on these issues have been held at the United Nations Centre for Human Rights—in August 1992, February 1993, August 1993 and March 1994. The NGOs also made interventions at the Asia Pacific Conference on Human Rights in Bangkok on 30 March 1993 and at the World Conference on Human Rights, Fourth Preparatory Committee Meeting in Geneva on 20 April 1993. NGOs participated in the World Conference on Human Rights in June 1993 in Vienna, demanding government accountability for all war crimes committed during the war and armed conflict situations. In 1994, at the International Conference of Population and Development in Cairo, women's organizations organized workshops to bring out the issues of forced impregnation during war as a war crime.

The United Nations and the international community have also begun to address the issues raised by the women. At the commission and subcommission sessions in 1992 and 1993, governments joined the NGOs in making statements on these issues during the debates. For example, in the 1992 session of the Working Group on Contemporary Forms of Slavery, the Working Group "request(ed) the secretary general to submit to the Special Rapporteur information received by the Working Group regarding the situation of women forced to engage in prostitution during war time...on the right to restitution, compensation and rehabilitation." (See UN Doc. E/CN.4/ Sub.2/ 1993/ 8 at p. 12.) It is one issue on which the governments of the Republic of Korea and the People's Democratic Republic of Korea are united.

In August 1993 the UN Subcommission on Prevention of Discrimination and Protection of Minorities adopted a resolution (E/CN.4/Sub.2/ 1993/ L.12/ Rev.1) to appoint a special rapporteur to undertake an in-depth study on systematic rape, sexual slavery and slavery-like practices during war time, including internal conflict. This is very important since the special rapporteur will look into the current situation of abuses of women in internal conflict as well as the slavery and slavery-like practices during World War II and study recommendations for the solution of past and present situations of victims, including human rights abuses against women in the former Yugoslavia.

The final report on the right to reparation submitted by special rapporteur Theo Van Boven to the forty-fifth session of the Subcommission states: "The issue of violence against women has become a matter of urgent and widespread concern and is highly relevant in the context of the present study about the right to reparation for the victims. In the draft Declaration on the Elimination of Violence Against Women, prepared and adopted in March 1993 by the Commission on the Status of Women and submitted for adoption by the General Assembly, states are called upon to pursue by all appropriate means and without delay a policy of eliminating violence against women. The draft Declaration describes "violence against women" as "any act of gender-based violence that results in, or is likely to result in, physical, sexual or psychological harm or suffering to women, including threats of such acts, coercion or arbitrary deprivations of liberty, whether occurring in public or private life" (Art. 1). (See UN Doc. E/CN.4/ Sub.2/1993/8 p. 10.) It is very clear in this Declaration, adopted by the Commission on the Status of Women, that the states are called upon to recognize a responsibility for eliminating violence against women. Unfortunately, many of these states are the perpetrators of violence against women in situations of armed conflict.

The principle confirmed by Prof. Theo van Boven states that individual victims of gross violations of human rights, including those of sexual slavery, must have the right to claim state compensation. He further stressed in his final report of August 1993 that the UN should work to address the demands of the sexual slavery victims by the Japanese Imperial Forces.

At the World Conference on Women in Beijing in September 1995, the Platform for Action addressed specific issues concerning the situation of women in wartime and recommended that international bodies should: "uphold and reinforce standards set out in international humanitarian law and international human rights instruments to prevent all acts of violence against women in situation of armed and other conflicts; undertake a full investigation of all acts of violence against women committed during war, including rape, in particular systematic rape, forced prostitution and other forms of indecent assault and sexual slavery; prosecute all criminals responsible for war crimes against women and provide full redress to women victims" (para. 145[e]).

In the April 1996 Radhika Coomaraswamy, the special rapporteur on violence against women to the UN Commission on Human Rights, reported on her mission to Asia to investigate military sexual slavery by Japan. The UN rapporteur urged the government of Japan to acknowledge that the system of comfort stations was a "violation of its obligation under international law; to pay compensation to the victims of sexual slavery; to make sincere public apology to the victims; to ensure disclosure of all war documents and materials; to amend educational curriculum in Japan to include the history of comfort women; and to identify and punish the perpetrators of the war crime" (UN Doc. E/CN.4/1996/53/Add. 1., paras.137–140).

The report clearly condemned Japan's systematic recruitment of sexual slaves, which clearly constituted a crime against humanity and identified Japan's violations of international humanitarian law. It stated that the government of Japan has both a legal and a moral responsibility towards the women who were held in military sexual slavery during World War II. Ms. Coomaraswamy found that the conduct against Asian women victims by the Japanese Imperial Forces violated customary international law. Her report stated that Japan is legally responsible not only for compensation to the victims but also for punishing the perpetrators. Her report further recommended that the victimized countries consider requesting the International Court of Justice to help resolve the legal issues concerning Japanese responsibility and payment of compensation for the former comfort women.

The Japanese government challenged Coomaraswamy's report and raised a number of legal arguments, which included (1) that acts of rape were not prohibited by either the Regulations annexed to the Hague Convention No. IV of 1907 or by applicable customary norms of international law in force at the time of the Second World War; (2) that, with regard to claims for legal compensation, individual "comfort women" have no right to such compensation; and (3) that, alternatively, any individual claims that these women may have had for compensation were fully satisfied by peace treaties and international agreements between Japan and other Asian States following the end of World War II.

The final report on the systematic rape, sexual slavery and slavery-like practices during armed conflict (E/CN.4/Sub.2/1998/13) was submitted to the UN by Gay McDougall, an American alternate member of the UN Subcommission on Prevention of Discrimination and Protection of Minorities. The report, released on 12 August 1998, examined not only the above-mentioned points but also all other major legal arguments raised by Japan. Her conclusion, essentially the same as that of Ms. Coomaraswamy, was that Japan had committed serious crimes against many women, mainly Asian, and has the legal duty to punish those responsible and to pay compensation to the victims. Her recommendations included a call for mechanisms to ensure criminal prosecutions; mechanisms to provide legal compensation; that compensation be adequate; and that reporting requirements be defined.

She concluded her report as follows:

> The present report concludes that the Japanese government remains liable for grave violations of human rights and humanitarian law, violations that amount in their totality to crimes against humanity. The Japanese government's arguments to the contrary, including arguments that seek to attack the underlying humanitarian law prohibition of enslavement and rape, remain as unpersuasive today as they were when they were first raised before the Nuremberg war crimes tribunal more than fifty years ago. In addition, the Japanese government's argument that Japan has already settled all claims from the Second World War through peace treaties and reparations agreements following the war remains equally unpersuasive. This is due, in large part, to the failure until very recently of the Japanese government to admit the extent of the Japanese military's direct involvement in the establishment and maintenance of these rape centres. The Japanese government's silence on this point during the period in which peace and reparations agreements between Japan and other Asian governments were being negotiated following the end of the war must, as a matter of law and justice, preclude Japan from relying today on these peace treaties to extinguish liability in these cases.
>
> The failure to settle these claims more than half a century after the cessation of hostilities is a testament to the degree to which the lives of women continue to be undervalued. Sadly, this failure to address crimes of a sexual nature committed on a massive scale during the Second World War has added to the level of impunity with which similar crimes are committed today. The government of Japan has taken some steps to apologize and atone for the rape and enslavement of over 200,000 women and girls who were brutalized in "comfort stations" during the Second World War. However, anything less than full and unqualified acceptance by the government of Japan of legal liability and the consequences that flow from such liability is wholly inadequate. It must now fall to the government of Japan to take the necessary final steps to provide adequate redress.

The Japanese government responded that it "cannot agree with the legal interpretations expressed in the appendix to this report nor can we accept its conclusion and recommendations which request the Japanese government to take steps to provide redress rather than that which we are already undertaking."

McDougall's report was, however, overwhelmingly welcomed by not only NGOs but also many governments. The report has been lauded for its legal definitions of sexual slavery as a war crime under international law. The McDougall report has drawn the attention of not only NGOs but also politicians in the concerned countries. President Kim, Dea-Jung of the Republic of Korea, (ROK), cited it in an interview with chief editor of a Japanese journal (*Sekai*, October 1998. p. 61). Citing it, House resolution No. 378 was submitted to the Philippines' House of Representatives by Hon. Romeo D. C. Candazo on 30 September 1998.

■■■ Japan's Failure: The Asian Women's Fund Policy

The Japanese government has not given up the policy of the Asian Women's Fund that symbolizes three aspects of the Japanese government's attitude as pointed out by Mr. Koki Abe, a Japanese teacher of international law: racism, colonialism and state-ism, namely state-oriented-undemocratic-philosophy. These were particularly dominant in pre-war Japan. I will not go into this in detail, but one may confirm the historical fact that Japanese governments after World War II have never officially recognized the past war crimes during the fifteen-year war or the illegal colonization of the Asian nations such as Korea. All these were committed by the Japanese Emperor's governments and military on the basis that the Japanese people, namely the subjects of the divine emperors, were superior to other Asian peoples.

The acts of "advancement" in Asia by Japan were claimed as actions of self-defence against the West and in protection of the Asian peoples. Therefore, there was no "invasion" of Asia according to their interpretation. There existed no drastic change in the attitude of the Japanese people at the "end" (not defeat) of the war. These thoughts held by the Japanese governments and majority of the Japanese people have survived until today.

There is a reason why the Japanese governments have failed to acknowledge the "invasion" of Asia. Historically the Litton Report, made by the League of Nations in 1932, found that the conduct of the Japanese Army in Manchuria in 1931 had been aggression. Japan never accepted this report and the subsequent actions taken by the League of Nations. Japan protested against and withdrew from the League of Nations and continued its military aggression against China and other Asian nations until the Allied nations defeated it in 1945.

The movement for war reparations in Japan has developed greatly in the past years. The turning point was in 1992 when the former comfort women issue came out to the world. No other issue has ever brought the Japanese government so much challenge and shame as that of the comfort women. To this day the issue is still being fought in halls of the United Nations and in the rooms of the Tokyo District Court. The comfort women issue has become a diplomatic irritant in the relationship of Japan with its neighbouring Asian countries, including the Philippines.

But Totsuka notes some healthy and undeniable developments in Japan: "There emerged, in recent years, an increasing number of citizens, historians, lawyers, journalists, politicians and others, who are aware of the facts; who are willing to accept the historical facts as war crimes committed by the Japanese; and who are working in letting the state of Japan take its state responsibilities. This is a hope for new Japan. Although it will take some time for them to become majority, they are becoming a formidable power and willing to cooperate with and fight for the victims and peoples in Asia."

■ Japanese Courts

In April 1998, the Shimonoseki branch of the Yamaguchi Prefectural Court ordered Defendant Japan to pay compensation to the ex-"comfort women" plaintiff for Defendant National Diet Members' failure to carry out the constitutional duty to enact an appropriate compensation law. The judgement recognizes that the Diet members have a duty to enact the law to compensate the victims and that they have failed to do so. Since it took a clear stance against the legislature, it is politically important and will help the lobbying activities. In contrast to the recommendations from the United Nations or the Japan Federation of Bar Associations (JFBA), which were helpful but did not impose any legal duty, this judgement will force the Japanese government to act as it orders if it is put into effect. This judgement was made possible by the courage of the plaintiff, by the widening support in domestic as well as international arenas such as the United Nations and International Labour Organization (ILO), and by the strong efforts of the support group members and concerned lawyers.

The judgement touches the heart of the "comfort woman" issues. First, in reference to finding the truth about the matter, the court considered to be true not only the unchallenged claims but the claims based on the personal experiences of the plaintiffs. The latter may lack objectiveness. Nevertheless, the court stated, "These testimonies should be believed to be true given the personal nature of the content" and "[the court] considered all of them to be sound evidence." The judgement stated: "[T]he court recognizes the fact that the 'comfort women' plaintiff were forcefully taken to the comfort stations without knowing they would have to serve as a 'comfort woman'; that they were raped and forcefully turned into 'comfort women'; that the comfort stations were deeply related with the Imperial Japanese Military and until the end of war in August of 1945, they were forced to have sexual intercourse primarily with Japanese imperial soldiers; and that they had had to hide their past as comfort women until the instituting of this case."

This recognition will have a major impact on the textbook issues as well. For the legal interpretations that directly concerns the "comfort women" issues, in light of making the legislation possible, there are following important points:

"There [was] no interaction other than sex. The soldiers [came to the comfort station] purely for sex. The comfort women [were] simply the necessity for the comfort station. This institution was designed for just sex and the release of sexual desire. Given the purpose and day-to-day reality of the comfort station as described above, the comfort women were sex slaves. The comfort woman system could have been a violation of the International Convention for the Suppression of the Traffic in Women and Children (1921) or the Forced Labour convention (1930)....[T]he comfort woman system was extremely inhuman and horrifying even [in] the standard of the civilized state in the middle of the 20th century...since Japan had known the facts about the comfort women for such a long time, by refusing to provide the measures for many years since the enact-ment of the Japanese Constitution, it doubled the plaintiffs' suffering. In other words, the failure to legislate the necessary law caused another violation of the personhood of the comfort women. Germany, the United States and Canada had already enacted certain laws to apologize and compensate the foreign victims whose rights were violated by the state (Separate Sheet 1 and 2; both parties are in agreement).

"Given these facts and the notion that the comfort women system stands side by side with the Nazi war crimes in its scope of human rights violations, the failure to legislate the law for the official apology and compensation further violates the human rights of the victims. At latest, soon after Cabinet Secretariat's comment on August 4, 5th year of Heisei (1993), enactment of such a law became the constitutional duty of the government. By the end of August, 8th year of Heisei (1996), three years after the comment, there has been reason-able time for the legislation. At this point of time, the failure to enact the law became illegal according to the State Tort Liability Act."

Needless to say, these statements were given by a national institution, namely the court. They were put forth in order to write a judgement. However, we should all remember that in addition to the recognition of the facts, the court judgement itself restores the honour of the victims.

The biggest problem is that the government of Japan did not accept this judgement and appealed to the Yamaguchi High Court. Few observers expect it will be upheld by the higher courts including the Supreme Court.

As was mentioned, on 9 October 1998, the victims and supporters were saddened by the judgement by the Tokyo District Court that rejected the claims made by Philippines' sexual slavery victims. The court not only ruled that there was no customary international law which gave individuals the right to compensation against the state of Japan without being represented by their home state, but also turned down all of the legal arguments raised by the lawyers for plaintiff.

Japanese National Diet

Responding to the recommendations made by the 1995 Subcommission, an attempt for a solution through legislative measures in accordance with the UN recommendations was made by some Diet Members and supporters of the victims. The UN suggested that Japan might establish an administrative tribunal to settle the military sexual slavery victims' claims or to settle the case through international arbitration procedures such as that of the Permanent Court of Arbitration. As a result, Mr. S. Motooka and twenty-five members of the House of Councillors submitted a "Bill for establishment of fact-finding committee on the issue of the victims of sexual coercion during wartime" to the House in June 1996. This was aborted with no debate. Further movements for legislative measures are continuing.

The Filipino Comfort Women

On 9 October 1998 the victims and supporters were saddened by the judgement by the Tokyo District Court that rejected the claims made by Philippines' sexual slavery victims. The court ruled that there was no customary international law, which gave individuals the right to compensation against the state of Japan without being represented by their home state. The judgement also turned down a number of other legal arguments raised by the lawyers for plaintiff. Very few Japanese observers expect that this judgement may be overturned by higher courts. One thing sure is that many of the surviving elderly women victims cannot see the consequences of this long judicial process in Japan. Therefore, there seems to be no effective domestic remedies for the victims from the Philippines in Japan.

The victims then wish to be assisted by the international human rights machinery such as the UN Commission on Human Rights. As mentioned above, however, the Japanese government's treaty defence will be the most problematic barrier against them under international law. It is remarkable, however, that Art. 148 and Art. 7 (1) must break the Japanese government's most important defence at the UN against the victims from the Philippines, namely the claim that the 1951 San Francisco Peace Treaty and other bilateral treaties relinquished the rights to compensation of the individual victims. It is true that the text of its Article 14 (b) of the 1951 San Francisco Peace Treaty stipulates as follows: "Except otherwise provided in the present Treaty, the Allied Powers waive all reparations claims of the Allied Powers, other claims of the Allied Powers and their nationals arising out of any actions taken by Japan and its nationals in the course of the prosecution of the war, and claims of the Allied Powers for direct military costs of occupation". One must be very careful in assessing the Japanese government claims, as there is a vital dead angle, which has not been considered by observers.

Military Sexual Slavery

■ The Philippines and Japan in Relation to the San Francisco Treaty

In the San Francisco Peace Treaty no negotiations were made, however, on the issue of military sexual slavery and Japan paid no compensation for the victims of military sexual slavery. Although the Philippines was invited to the San Francisco Peace Conference, it was not satisfied with the treaty and did not ratify it for several years. Then, the reparation agreement between the Philippines and Japan was signed on 9 May 1956. It was at this point on July 16 of that year that the Philippines ratified the 1951 Treaty of San Francisco. Again, no negotiations took place between the Philippines and Japan on the issue of military sexual slavery towards this agreement and Japan paid no compensation for the victims of military sexual slavery.

By this time of 1956, Japan became bound by Art. 148 and Art. 7 (1) of the IV Geneva Convention. Japan acceded to it on 21 October 1953 and the Philippines had been an original Contracting Party to it since its adoption on 12 August 1949. On the other hand, Art. 3 of the 1907 Hague Convention was customary international law and Japan was bound by it, as Kalshoven clarified. Therefore, at the time of the ratification made by the Philippines in 1956 of the San Francisco Peace Treaty, it was already prohibited by Art. 148 and Art. 7 (1) of the IV Geneva Convention for Japan and the Philippines to relinquish the right to compensation of the victims guaranteed under Art. 3 of the 1907 Hague Convention and customary international law. As a result, even if the Philippines agreed to relinquish the right of individual Philippines victims to compensation against Japan in 1956, that agreement and the ratification of that part must be regarded as null and void in violation of Art. 148 and Art. 7 (1) of the IV Geneva Convention. It is also to interpret the ratification made by the Philippines of the San Francisco Peace Treaty did not include the relinquishment of the right of the victims of military sexual slavery or any rights possessed by the victims of war crimes in the grave crime category. (In passing, it can be also argued in another way, as the ROK government is asserting. As the crimes of military sexual slavery had been officially denied by the Japanese governments towards January 1992, it was impossible for the Philippines and Japanese governments to conclude any treaty or agreement, in which the issue with no official existence was possibly dealt with.)

This argument mentioned above has not been asserted by any NGO. It was probably because many observers assumed that the 1949 Geneva Convention could not be applied to this case, as Japan was not a party to it at the time of the 1951 San Francisco Peace Treaty. The fact that the date of the ratification of the Philippines of it was later than the date when Japan was bound by the IV Geneva Convention must have been neglected.

It is clear that the victims and the government of the Philippines have a legitimate right against Japan to demand compensation to the individual victims of military sexual slavery despite the Japan's Treaty defence based on Art. 14(b) of the San Francisco Peace Treaty. The civil and women groups in many concerned countries and NGOs are advised to demand the Japanese government to withdraw its treaty defence at the UN and the ILO at least in relation to the Philippines and Chinese victims, as the current Japanese government's treaty defence against them is wrong. There seems to be no other conclusion than Japan has mislead the United Nations and the ILO.

A government cannot and must not relinquish the rights of victims under Articles 148 and 7(1). The true nature and extent of the harms suffered by women who were raped, sexually violated and enslaved by parties to an armed conflict must be exposed. The veil of silence that surrounds this violence must be lifted through prosecutions and other forms of redress including compensation. Justice must be done, dignity must be restored and future violations must be prevented.

When it comes to war time responsibilities, the Japanese government has lost face in the international community. It refuses to adhere to the recent developments of international law and, more importantly, it denies the fundamental rights of the people. As long as Japan's justice system continues to be backward and authoritarian, people's rights will not exist and justice will only be for the powerful.

It is ironic that such a highly modernized society and economic world power still has a justice system that belongs to the days of the emperor. Japan refuses to adhere to the international norms and standards of international law and uses its traditional system as a cover for its ineptness to face its legal responsibility for the war crimes it committed fifty years ago.

Justice will always be the cry of the women in Asia who suffered during World War II and history will be written by the cries of these women. Unless the Japanese government takes the necessary steps to provide adequate redress, Japan will be condemned for its inability to face up to its responsibilities.

REFERENCES

1. Report of the Working Group on Contemporary Forms of Slavery, UN Doc. E/CN.4/Sub.2/1992/34.
2. Statement of the Republic of Korea UN Commission on Human Rights, UN Doc. E/CN.4/1993/SR.27.
3. Convention on Non-applicability of Statutory Limitations to War Crimes and Crimes Against Humanity in Force, 11 November 1970, 754 UNTS 73.
4. Historical Understanding on the "Military Comfort Women" Issue by Yoshimi Yoshiaki, Professor of History, Chuo University, Tokyo. 1992.
5. War Crimes on Asian Women: Military Sexual Slavery by Japan During World War II; The Case of the Filipino Comfort Women, published by the Task Force for Filipina Victims of Military Sexual by Japan and Asian Women's Human Rights Council—Philippine Section, Manila 1993.
6. Rape of Women in War, Report of the Ecumenical Women's Team Visit Zagreb (December 1992), World Council of Churches, Geneva. 1992.

7. War, Victimization and Japan: International Public Hearing Report, Toho Shuppan Inc., Osaka 1993.

8. The Issue of Korean Human Rights During and After the Pacific War, published by the Association of Pacific War Victims and Bereaved Families, March 1993, Seoul.

9. Philippines Comfort Women Compensation Suit, published by the Task Force for Filipina Victims of Military Sexual Slavery by Japan and the Japanese Committee for the Filipino Comfort Women, Tokyo, June 1993.

10. Comfort Women: The Unfinished Ordeal, Preliminary Report of a Mission by the International Commission of Jurists, Geneva 1993.

11. Compensation for Japan's World War II Victims, by Karen Parker, attorney at law, International Educational Development, San Francisco 1992.

12. Study concerning the right to restitution, compensation and rehabilitation for victims of gross violations of human rights and fundamental freedom. Final Report submitted by Mr. Theo Van Boven, Special Rapporteur, UN Doc. E/CN.4/Sub.2/1993/8.

13. Message by Indai Lourdes Sajor, Executive Director of the Asian Centre for Women's Human Rights (ASCENT)—Malaya Lolas On the Report by Gay J. McDougall, Special Rapporteur on Systematic Rape, Sexual Slavery and Slavery-like Practices during Armed Conflict, 1998.

14. Women in Armed Conflict Situations, Indai Lourdes Sajor, delivered at the Expert Group Meeting on Measures to Eradicate Violence Against Women sponsored by the United Nations Division for the Advancement of Women, DPCSD, Rutgers University, New Brunswick, N.J. USA, October 1993.

15. Systematic Rape, Sexual Slavery and Slavery Like Practices during armed conflict Report Submitted by UN Special Rapporteur Gay J. McDougall at the UN Subcommission on Prevention of Discrimination and Protection of Minorities Session, August 1998.

16. International Justice and Redress Issues: Did the Treaties Settle All of Japan's Issues in Relation to War?, Etsuro Totsuka, Bengoshi (Japan), Visiting Scholar, University of Washington for GA of Global Alliance for Preserving the History of WWII in Asia, 16–18 October 1998, in Toronto.

17. Comfort Women and Sexual Slavery: Achievements in the UN and further Challenges, Etsuro Totsuka, Bengoshi (Japan), Visiting Scholar, University of Washington for GA of Global Alliance for Preserving the History of WWII in Asia, 16–18 October 1998, in Toronto.

18. Dolgopol, Ustinia and Snehal Paranjape, Report of a Mission: Comfort Women an Unfinished Ordeal, International Commission of Jurists, Geneva, November 1994.

19. Hicks, George. *Japan's War Memories: Amnesia or Concealment.* Ashgate Publishing Limited, England (1997).

Are We Our Brothers' and Sisters' Keepers?

From Witness
to Advocate

Nathaniel Bimba was born and raised in the town of
Foya, Lofa County, in northern Liberia. He worked as a
teacher and administrator in Monrovia after studying
religious education at the Liberia Baptist Theological
Seminary. When the Liberian civil war broke out in
1990, he fled to neighbouring Sierra Leone but was
forced to seek refuge in another African country after
Liberian rebels began making incursions into Sierra
Leone. In 1997 he emigrated to Canada where he now
works for the Mennonite Central Committee in
Edmonton as a refugee assistance coordinator.

I WANT TO SHARE MY STORY FROM LIBERIA. The International Centre for
Human Rights and Democratic Development, in collaboration with the
Canadian Council of Refugees, has embarked on a project to mark the fiftieth
anniversary of the Universal Declaration of Human Rights. This project is called
From Witness to Advocate. It is an effort to bring to life the words and reality of
the Declaration to the Canadian people. This will bring home the fact that
someone in their neighbourhood may have experienced a violation of his or her
rights and that this is not just a media story or something that is remote. I am
one of those neighbours.

For those of us working on this project, our effort is to testify to the real-life
experiences that have desecrated our human rights as enshrined in the
Declaration.

As you may recall, the Declaration of Human Rights was drawn up just after
World War II. It is one of the greatest accomplishments of human history. Call it
human sanity at its best. The spirit of this document was to deter the waste of life,
as it were, and serve as a wake-up call for the respect of human rights at all levels.

Fifty years ago the world had just witnessed some of the grossest violations
of human rights. To not allow such occurrences again, the world was, and I hope
is, determined to live up to the principles of the Declaration. This document is
the basic international pronouncement on the fundamental rights of all members

of the human family. It consists of a preamble and thirty articles that set out fundamental rights that all of humanity should be entitled to.

The first two articles emphasize that all human beings are born free and equal in dignity and rights, and then set out basic principles of equality and nondiscrimination. The next nineteen articles are concerned with the civil, economic, social, cultural and political rights which all people are entitled to. Under Article 28, everyone is entitled to a social and international order in which the rights and freedoms set forth in the Declaration can be fully realized.

Article 29 is concerned with the exercise of these rights. Article 30 states that nothing in the Declaration may be interpreted as implying that there is a right to do anything that destroys the rights and freedoms set out in the Declaration.

In agreement and solidarity with this illustrious document, it is my fervent desire and wish that what happened to me should never happen again to anybody.

For example, Article 5 states: "No one shall be subjected to torture or to cruel, inhuman or degrading treatment or punishment." Article 15 says that I have the right to be treated as a citizen of my country. It also asserts that I have the right to a fair and public hearing if I am accused of breaking the law.

This was not true for me. My experience in Liberia in 1991 is just one of many instances. These fundamental principles and values were not respected or adhered to when two other Liberian friends and I decided to take food, medicine and relief items to Liberia in September 1991. Compelled by the desire to help our people, relatives and friends, we travelled to Liberia through the northern border of Sierra Leone. We took with us food donated by the Feed the Hungry Organization, an American charity group.

While distributing the food, rebels of the National Patriotic Forces of Liberia arrested us and accused us of reconnaissance and spying for the Americans, a crime punishable by death. The rebels used torture, physical and psychological abuse to interrogate and collect information from enemies and any suspicious persons. This is what we were to them.

The rebels, during the interrogations, held us at gunpoint or used their infamous form of torture referred to as *tapai*. This is when a person's hands are pulled from behind and tied around the elbows. What inflicts the most excruciating pain is the pressure of the ropes on the elbows and the upper arms. As the arms meet at the back, the chest is badly stretched. In no time, the blood stops flowing to the hands and fingers and the strain is felt literally in the heart.

This is so terrible that once a person is released he or she faints. The hands go numb and may become paralyzed. The torture and detention went on for six weeks. Many others were not as lucky as some of us. They were executed by methods not decent to describe. Several church groups and international organizations lobbied for our freedom. We finally got released and returned to Sierra Leone.

To risk our lives to provide food to suffering and hungry Liberians does not pose a threat to anybody. At the time, all relief agencies had to evacuate because of the danger and threat to life. What we did was not harmful to anybody. We were not accused of supplying weapons or anything detrimental to life. Our gesture was done in good faith.

But I guess this is what happens when human rights are ignored and disrespected. Since my ordeal I have asked myself these questions a million times: Why was my good intention perceived as evil? What did I do wrong to be treated worse than a human being? And many more whys and whats.

And I still wonder why, in spite of technological and human advancement, there are serious human rights violations. Is it because of the ready availability of arms and ammunitions, where mass destruction is easily possible? What if guns were not sold by greedy profit-makers to selfish warmongers who negotiate with verbal promises? Since 1945 there have been over two hundred wars resulting in the destruction of over thirty million lives and, worst of all, two-thirds of these are helpless and harmless women, children and civilians. This figure increases even as I write.

What can we do to avert this insanity that besets the progress of our generation and civilization? As Canadians you must be challenged by the fact that you have a very significant role to play in contributing to the greater realization of a world where human rights are respected.

Thanks to John Humphrey, a Canadian and a professor at McGill University in Montréal, who helped draft the document. I also acknowledge with high esteem the position of Canada on the human rights map.

In 1956, when Britain, France and Israel tried to prevent Egypt from seizing control of the Suez Canal, Canada proposed the first UN peacekeeping force to "secure and supervise the cessation of hostilities." Canada has undertaken similar initiatives and missions to resolve other crises of our times.

In 1996 Canada posed a challenge to the world to ban land mines. This has made a resounding sound around the globe. Note also that the human rights path on which this nation is travelling includes the elimination of racial discrimination and the introduction of the resolution on integrating women's rights into the UN human rights system. I must also mention the Convention on the Rights of the Child and the specific goals and actions focusing on child health, nutrition, education and protection which Canada respects.

The point is this: What can you do to be a player on the field of human rights? My guess is that the worst anyone can do is not to do anything at all. The issues of human rights range from what one might consider simple or common, to big and complex. That is to say that whoever chooses to do something has a place and a room on board.

The place to start is at home, in one's school, college, neighbourhood and community. Read the Universal Declaration. Canadians, as part of the human rights solution, can continue to influence human rights policies that business and corporations should follow. In this regard, you might want to know about the health and safety standards at workplaces or in factories, be sensitive to environmental concerns, and support education. I believe that education is pivotal in alleviating ignorance, poverty and disease. Education is the highway on which democracy strides.

It is about time that you checked the business relations Canada has with the despotic governments of China, Nigeria, Burma and, probably the most undemocratic, the Republic of Congo. Check labels on products that come from overseas to see if these products are from corporations that are being nourished by the labour of boys and girls who should be in school but are used as cheap labour. Can you afford to brag about a healthy and growing economy if it is built on the gross background of hidden truth and realities? You can make a difference in making the dream of the Universal Declaration of Human Rights come true.

Fight against ignorance, poverty and disease by helping underprivileged children get an education. Make contributions towards basic health needs through nongovernmental organizations. Remember that refugees and immigrants are part and parcel of the Universal Declaration of Human Rights. They need the protection of their lives and rights. Work for peace, conflict resolution and reconciliation. Remember that justice must be restorative rather than a means of revenge.

ROGER CLARK

Human Rights Defenders in the Global Village

Roger Clark is secretary general of the Canadian Section of Amnesty International. He has led research missions to Cambodia, Ethiopia, Tanzania, Guatemala and Liberia. In 1995 he travelled to Rwanda and Zaire to investigate human rights violations following the Rwandan genocide.

THIS ESSAY IS DEDICATED to the memory of Jean-Paul Simbizi, medical doctor and human rights activist from Kisangani, in the former Zaire. After narrowly escaping death at the hands of the military, he went through immense hardships to reach safety in Canada at the end of 1996. Earlier this year he returned to try to bring his wife and family to safety. Sadly, he became ill and died in Kinshasa before he could accomplish this mission. Jean-Paul Simbizi was a true human rights defender.

If there is any substance to the notion of the global village, it may be that today we have a stronger and clearer sense of world community. I want to take a look at some of the challenges of this new-found neighbourhood and suggest where they lead in terms of responsibility for ourselves and for others. As with any neighbourhood, we have to come to terms with both good and bad, dealing with difficult realities that are occasionally too close for comfort and exploring the dreams that are part of our common heritage.

None of this is particularly new. John Donne's caution against insularity goes back three hundred years and there were philosophers and theologians from the earliest times who, understanding the interdependence of humankind, designed their systems accordingly. It is largely the 20th century, however, that has experienced at firsthand the realities of our small planet, whether through the upheaval of two world wars, the perils of global warming, the creation of the World Trade Organization or the perspective of earth seen from outer space. It is the 20th century which has been obliged to come to terms with its own inhumanity, driven by the spectres of genocide, the Holocaust and massive human rights violations in all corners of the world.

While the fiftieth anniversary of the Universal Declaration of Human Rights is less a celebration than a realization of the short distance we have travelled since its creation, it is still unique in its expression of global values and standards. That we are continually found wanting is a sad commentary on human nature rather than a reflection of the inadequacies of those principles adopted by the nations of the world in 1948. I would like to consider three phenomena which have emerged largely as a result of the adoption of the Universal Declaration of Human Rights. How we deal with each of them may ultimately determine our success or failure in dealing with each other as neighbours in this global village. These are the meaning of international community, the emergence of the human rights movement and the importance of human rights defenders.

▰▰▰ The International Community

Who, or what, then is the international community? We talk glibly of the need for the international community to intervene in one crisis after another, or we refer to the responsibility of the international community in regard to a major catastrophe, but if we stop and attempt a precise definition things are not so clear. The international community is certainly more than a simple conglomeration of states meeting with questionable effectiveness in Geneva or New York. It is also more than the sum total of the various other bodies which have emerged at regional and subregional levels to deal with issues ranging from free trade and economic advantage to military or political alliance.

The 1990s have spawned a flurry of international conferences covering the environment, development, the rights of women and human rights, among other challenges. Innumerable meetings and events designed to mark the survival of the Universal Declaration of Human Rights have been held in 1998. The preamble to that Declaration provides a helpful clue to the identity of the international community when it speaks of the duty of "every individual and every organ of society [to] strive by teaching and education to promote respect for these rights and freedoms and by progressive measures, national and international, to secure their universal and effective recognition and observance." There are two vital messages which derive from this statement. The first is the universality of responsibility for human rights. The second is the clear assignment of that responsibility to every individual and every organ of society. In both, the key word is responsibility and I conclude that the international community is in fact a community of shared responsibility which extends to all people everywhere.

However frustrating the unceasing struggle for human rights, it is a source of some satisfaction that the Universal Declaration of Human Rights has produced (and continues to produce) a wealth of conventions, covenants, declarations and treaties, all designed to give shape to an acknowledged body of international responsibility. The 1998 agreement in Rome to finally proceed with the creation of an International Criminal Court (ICC) marks a significant elaboration of global jurisdiction. Our enthusiasm is properly tempered when we wonder aloud just how effective such a court will prove, although such doubts and cynicism are all too familiar to those of us who are practitioners in the field of human rights. What is most disturbing, and conducive of a certain pessimism, is the spectacle of the United States refusing to join its signature to those of the vast majority of nations which supported the establishment of the ICC. As if that were not shameful enough, we are now witnesses to the reprehensible lobbying by the US to prevent the ratification of the Rome Treaty and the subsequent entry into force of the ICC. This should not be so much of a surprise. The history of the US as a partner within the international community is one of pathetic disrespect and consistent non-cooperation, except in those instances when self-serving goals may be achieved. We may be forgiven for questioning the reality of the international community when confronted by such examples.

The ICC is in a sense the conclusion of a process which began in Nuremberg. A vital test of the capacity of the international community to assume its responsibilities lies in the ability of the nations of the world to co-operate in bringing to justice those who carry the heaviest burden in the commission of human rights violations and crimes against humanity. The very notion of a crime against humanity is a reflection of the authenticity of an international community characterized in terms of its own rights and responsibilities. Until there is a genuinely universal jurisdiction and a universal rejection of impunity we must conclude that we are still far from that shared community of responsibility.

The issue of responsibility within the international community has assumed some fascinating dimensions in the case of Augusto Pinochet and his arrest in the UK. His case takes us to the heart of the tension between universal jurisdiction and national sovereignty. The initial ruling of the British courts to refuse extradition was both a denial of international responsibility and a rejection of the concept of international community. It is to be hoped that the international treatment of Pinochet will ultimately become a positive demonstration, not only of the legitimacy of the international community of responsibility but above all its political will to achieve justice for the countless victims of human rights violations.

Another critical example of the challenge of universal responsibility lies within the world of international business. Over recent years, countries of the West have engaged in internal debate over trade and human rights, as though the two were somehow in opposition to each other or mutually exclusive. The debate continues to flourish in spite of increasing evidence that a refusal by the corporate world to pay attention to human rights is both counter-productive and short-sighted. Ironically, those countries such as China or Malaysia which argue that human rights violations are an internal matter unrelated to trade and therefore of no concern to the international community, do not hesitate to threaten reduced trade opportunities to those states that dare to raise human rights concerns.

The business sector, particularly at the transnational level, is one of the most powerful agencies for change and a key player in the international community. It is one of the organs of society referred to in the Universal Declaration of Human Rights and yet it still remains largely divorced from the community of responsibility. Until the business sector assumes its responsibilities to the fullest extent, whether in respect of its own record or in terms of its public interventions on human rights issues, the international community will be judged as falling short. The welcome focus on human rights issues around the recent Asia Pacific Economic Conference (APEC) summit in Kuala Lumpur may be something of a breakthrough, not only in the raising of concerns in a forum where such things have been generally considered taboo, but because it may ultimately legitimize consideration of the human and social dimension within APEC itself. The nervousness of offending states and their paranoid refusal to contemplate any human rights agenda is a clear measure of the urgency for that very consideration to take place.

■■■ The Human Rights Movement

The human rights movement embodies the energy and dynamics of a widespread popular demand for respect for human rights. It is the driving force which holds the international community to account and demands that the world make provision for the proper protection of human rights and the prevention of human rights violations.

In May 1961, when Peter Benenson wrote his article "Forgotten Prisoners" for the London *Observer*, he little suspected that he had responded to a need felt by thousands of ordinary people to react and respond to fundamental human rights concerns wherever they may occur. That was the beginning of Amnesty International, and within a matter of months the organization had been established in half a dozen countries in Europe and North America. Today there are over one million members in 150 countries and although the mandate and working methods have evolved over time, the basic premise remains the same: that publicity and pressure generated by individuals around the world can result in improved human rights situations. That is not to say that Amnesty International is always successful or even that it is effective when confronted by some of the situations of mass human rights violations such as those in Rwanda or Kosovo. On the other hand, this expression of public concern made possible by the nongovernmental sector is a vital part of the process of advocacy and change in the domain of human rights.

Since those early days of the post-war human rights movement, there has been an explosion of popular, nongovernmental organizations throughout the world. In some cases, they have been instrumental in triggering dramatic and radical change, as in the former Soviet Union, the Philippines or even Indonesia. The concept of a "Peoples Forum," whether as an adjunct to meetings of the G7 or parallel to the APEC summit, is an established and legitimate channel for expression of fundamental demands for human rights. They are meeting places for neighbours in the global village and an opportunity to advance shared concerns which lie beyond national boundaries or differences of language and culture.

It may be wise and timely, however, to give ourselves a word of caution. An article in the current issue of the *Inter Pares Bulletin* (November 1998) reminds us that the world is not a single community and that "there is incredible and wondrous diversity within and among the communities of the world, a diversity to be cherished and protected." The writer points out that "the global village is a gated city inhabited by the affluent few. For most people, alienation and inequity have increased, and these new technologies have deepened the margin-alization of those without access to this new future." As we witness the widening gaps between rich and poor, between the North and South, we do well to consider those who are most vulnerable and who find themselves on the outer limits of our communities. It is ironic that it has been the world's indigenous peoples, often among the most marginalized, who have perhaps been first to understand the potential strength and purpose of the international dimensions of community.

The human rights movement addresses an extraordinary variety of issues: the rights of indigenous peoples, the disabled, children in armed conflict, poverty, migrant workers, refugees, freedom of expression and association, language, religion, female genital mutilation, the environment, disarmament, child labour and so many more, all worthy but far too numerous to mention. What is striking about such a list is both the universality of the issues and the shared concerns which find common expression in a myriad of international organizations. While there will always be exceptions, what is vital is the serious-ness of purpose and dedication to shared working methods to be found throughout the community of nongovernmental organizations in general. The net result is an increasingly irresistible power of public advocacy which counts amongst its participants and allies those in faith communities, in trade unions and within the academic world who share similar aspirations and hopes for the future.

It may be a little premature to conclude that the communications revolution of the past decade has been a key factor in the fostering of the human rights move-ment. It is certainly true that the instant availability of information, the capacity to share that information with broad networks of like-minded activists and the greater access to those in power which such communication offers, have all contributed to the creation of a genuinely international human rights movement.

We have yet to fully realize the potential of these changes in information sharing for the work of human rights in today's world. They have already contributed to new dimensions of action and solidarity which are powerful forces for change.

Human Rights Defenders

I referred earlier to Peter Benenson and the beginnings of Amnesty International. There is a story which is now legend that the incident which inspired all of this was news received in London of two Portuguese students who were sentenced to several years in prison for drinking a toast to freedom. The point, of course, is that there exists a profound and intensely human impulse which impels many of us to seek new ways of supporting those who are the victims of human rights violations, to say nothing of those who are caught up in natural disasters around the world. Increasingly, I am of the belief that this is driven less by well-intentioned altruism than by an increasingly strong sense of self-interest. I attribute some of this to the growth of the international community and a conviction that the protection of rights is itself an example of the interdependence of human values which we seek to promote.

One of the most remarkable developments in the field of human rights work has been the recent recognition of human rights defenders. The definition of a human rights defender must be broad and inclusive. Essentially, the term refers to any person who acts alone, in a group or in an association, to promote, implement and apply the fundamental rights guaranteed under the Universal Declaration of Human Rights. In a general way it applies to all men and women throughout the world who are struggling to preserve their dignity, feed their children and live decent lives. In some countries, the actions of these human rights defenders working on the front-line make them actual or potential victims of reprisals, threats, harassment, arbitrary arrest, torture, murder, sudden disappearance or forced exile.

Are we our brothers' and sisters' keepers? As part of the international community and as part of the human rights movement, we can be nothing less than the defenders of each other's human rights. That we may sometimes fail should be a cause for renewed endeavour. That we sometimes succeed is reason to feel strengthened in our shared purpose. The Welsh poet Dylan Thomas described the death of another as like a thread being torn from the tapestry of humanity. The work of human rights defenders is part of the weaving, the repair, of that same tapestry.

ANNE McGRATH

Basic Human Rights
—It's Time

Anne McGrath is the Canadian program officer for
OXFAM Canada, a former executive member of the
National Action Committee on the Status of Women
and has served on the boards of the Elizabeth Fry
Society and Women Looking Forward.

IN THE PAST FIFTY YEARS a global consensus has emerged on basic human rights. A range of international and regional agreements and conventions has affirmed the rights of people to have enough to eat, clean water, a home, health care, an education, a livelihood, a safe environment, protection from violence, equality of opportunity and a say in the future. The three main international agreements are the UN Declaration of Human Rights (1948), the International Covenant on Civil and Political Rights (1966) and the International Covenant on Economic, Social and Cultural Rights (1966). By signing these agreements, governments have committed themselves to these basic human rights.

The preamble of the Universal Declaration of Human Rights reads:

Whereas recognition of the inherent dignity and of the equal and inalienable rights of all members of the human family is the foundation of freedom, justice and peace in the world,

Whereas disregard and contempt for human rights have resulted in barbarous acts which have outraged the conscience of humankind, and the advent of a world in which human beings shall enjoy freedom of speech and belief and freedom from fear and want has been proclaimed as the highest aspiration of the common people . . .

The declaration outlines economic, social, cultural and political rights for all humanity. Other key United Nations agreements include the 1965 International Convention on the Elimination of all Forms of Racial Discrimination and the 1979 International Convention on the Elimination of all Forms of Discrimination Against Women. In 1995 a new key covenant was agreed to in Beijing, namely the Platform of Action on Gender Equity.

The OXFAM Canada Campaign for Basic Human Rights aims to persuade governments that signed these UN human rights agreements to turn their words into action. We are demanding that social and economic rights be accorded the same importance as civil and political rights. We are also demanding compliance from other economic powers such as transnational corporations. OXFAM aims to increase public awareness that people everywhere have basic rights, that these rights should be protected, respected and made a reality for all, so that people can take control of their lives and poverty can be defeated. As United Nations Special Advisor Richard Jolly has said: "Poverty is no longer inevitable. The world has the material and natural resources, the know-how and the people to make a poverty-free world a reality" (United Nations Development Programme (UNDP), 1997).

In 1993, heads of government attending the Vienna World Conference on Human Rights reaffirmed the principle of the indivisibility and interdependence of human rights. Despite this declaration, different views about the relative priority of categories of rights continue to prevail. In the West, we tend to priorize civil and political rights over economic, social and cultural rights. The OXFAM Basic Human Rights Campaign seeks to reaffirm that economic, social and cultural rights are of equal importance to civil and political rights. Many treaties have been signed at the United Nations that focus on human rights issues. These include the 1951 International Convention and the 1967 Protocol on the Status of Refugees, 1965 International Convention on the Elimination of all Forms of Racial Discrimination, 1979 International Convention on the Elimination of all Forms of Discrimination Against Women, 1984 Convention Against Torture and Other Cruel, Inhuman or Degrading Treatment or Punishment, 1989 Convention on the Rights of the Child and the 1995 Platform of Action on Gender Equity.

These treaties establish international legal obligations for signatory governments to promote and protect universally recognized human rights and fundamental freedoms for all their citizens. Human rights are inalienable, universal and indivisible. Basic human rights are integral to the human condition and cannot be taken away. They apply to everyone regardless of nationality, gender, race or sexual orientation. Basic human rights are a package, with no rights having priority over others. The OXFAM Basic Human Rights Campaign wants the words in these international agreements acted upon. With the OXFAM campaign, we are issuing a challenge to world leaders: It is time to honour your commitment to basic human rights. It is time basic human rights were respected, protected and fulfilled.

Some remarkable changes have occurred in the five decades since the formation of the United Nations in 1945. Global economic wealth has increased seven-fold, average incomes have tripled, people are living longer, fewer children are dying and more children are attending school. The UNDP has estimated that by the end of this century "some three to four billion of the world's total population of 5.7 billion will have experienced substantial improvements in their standards of living, and about four to five billion will have access to basic education and health."

The problem is, despite the improvements and projections, over 1.5 billion people will continue to be denied access to basic health and education. It is projected that these 1.5 billion people—the poorest of the poor—are unlikely to experience any substantial improvements in their standard of living. Poverty violates one's basic rights. Poverty occurs when basic rights do not form the foundation of policies and practices of governments, corporations, international bodies and local institutions. Other factors also increase people's vulnerability and deepen their poverty. These factors include discrimination, exploitation, the lack of access to resources like land and water, environmental degradation, conflict and natural disasters, unfair trade, unpayable debt and inappropriate aid.

According to the UNDP, we have the resources and knowledge that would allow us to banish extreme poverty by early next century. Eliminating mass poverty, it would appear, has less to do with economic well-being and more to do with political will. Does the will exist to rid the world of mass poverty? Are those with the wealth willing to share it? All the evidence points to the contrary. The 1997 UNDP Human Development Report states that "to provide universal access to basic social services and transfers to alleviate income poverty would cost roughly $80 billion—less than the combined net worth of the seven richest men in the world" (UNDP, 1997). In fact the problem of global poverty does not appear to be a major issue for our current world leaders. A case in point is the foreign aid budgets of the northern or developed countries.

The 1997 Progress of Nations Report from UNICEF shows that aid from the industrialized countries is currently at its lowest level in forty-five years. Development aid has slumped to a global average of just a quarter of a per cent of GDP. This is less than half of 0.7 per cent, the target agreed to by the United Nations over twenty-five years ago. Only Norway, Denmark, Sweden and the Netherlands currently meet this aid target. Canada has long prided itself on being one of the globe's leading humanitarian countries. A recent Angus Reid poll found that most Canadians assume we are generous in providing foreign aid. Apparently most Canadians are not aware of today's reality. Canada is currently spending one-third less on aid than it did five years ago. No other federal program has been cut more in recent years than Official Development Assistance (ODA). Canada's foreign aid commitment is at its lowest level in thirty years. In 1988 Canada's ODA budget was $2.9 billion; today it is $1.9 billion with more cuts planned. And while it remains government policy for the ODA/GDP to reach 0.7 per cent, this ratio has fallen every year since 1992. It is projected that this ratio will decline to 0.24 per cent.

Like many other countries, Canada spends proportionately more on defence than it does on foreign aid. Canada currently spends over five times as much on defence ($10 billion) as it does on overseas development support. Most nongovernmental aid agencies have long contended it is time some defence funds were reallocated to overseas development assistance. Obviously, reduced aid budgets alone cannot explain why extreme poverty grows apace with the population. To fully understand this problem, we must look at the role global trade and investment rules play in both the economics and politics of today's world. Most economic power rests in the North: it lies with northern governments; with big companies based in the North; and with international institutions like the United Nations, the International Monetary Fund and the World Bank, all of which are dominated by Northern governments and Northern interests.

It has been these same Northern interests that have set the agenda for a new globalized agenda, the defining features of which are a sharply reduced role for governments in shaping economic and social policy and increased legal protection for foreign investors. Globalization is about establishing a new set of rights—corporate rights. In comparison with basic human rights, corporate rights are assigned greater legal protection and they have sharp teeth in the form of economic sanctions.

If globalization is the end result sought by foreign investors and their adherents, then the establishment of the North American Free Trade Agreement (NAFTA) and the establishment of the World Trade Organization (WTO) must be recognized as the means to that end. The intention to create the Multilateral Agreement on Investment (MAI) currently under negotiation by the world's wealthiest countries, is but another. And lest it be forgotten, these trade agreements take precedence over UN agreements.

Powerful foreign investors are demanding a world where they can freely move their money in and out of countries. And more and more countries are ready to oblige. New trade rules are designed to protect corporate rights and to restrict the scope and ability of individual governments as they attempt to implement domestic policies that deal with the social consequences of rising unemployment, higher poverty rates and the need for improved social and health infrastructure. Any domestic social or environmental policy that interferes with free trade can now be subjected to legal challenges.

Advocates of globalization like to point to the growth in global wealth over the past fifty years as reason enough for support. The question is, are all benefiting from this growth? According to the 1997 UN Human Development Report, the main beneficiaries of globalization are its promoters—the rich and powerful nations, transnational corporations and other wealthy investors. Furthermore, globalization has been found to be hurting both poor countries and poor people, South and North.

The distribution of economic power has certainly shifted in recent years. Fifty per cent of the world's largest one hundred economies are now megacorporations, whose only responsibility is profit generation and satisfying their shareholders. The one hundred largest transnationals now control over one-third of all foreign investment. And forty per cent of world trade occurs within transnationals. Can we force these corporations to be more socially responsible? As UNDP has suggested, "An incentive system should be put in place to encourage multinational corporations to contribute to poverty reduction and to be publicly accountable and socially responsible." Others contend that voluntary codes of conduct are the answer. However, few corporations adopt them and fewer still respect them. All trade and investment treaties should contain legally binding clauses with enforceable penalties that force corporations to respect, protect and fulfil basic human rights for all. This will only occur if there is enough increased public awareness and citizen pressure.

Globalization advocates cannot ignore the growing global poverty gap, for to do so is to ignore a possible day of reckoning. At the September 1997 World Bank meetings in Hong Kong, Bank President James Wolfensohn acknowledged the widening gap between the rich and the poor and warned, "We are living in a time bomb and, unless we take action now, it could explode in our children's faces." The World Bank, the International Monetary Fund and bilateral creditors, can take action to defuse this "time bomb" by quickly moving on its debt reduction plan—the Highly Indebted Poor Countries (HIPC) initiative. In many developing regions the situation is the same—countries like Uganda, Ethiopia, Mozambique, Bolivia and Nicaragua, are forced to spend more on repaying foreign creditors than they are able to spend on health and education programs.

According to the World Bank there are approximately forty counties that are heavily indebted, that is they have debt payments that are at least twice as big as what these countries earn from their exports. The debt problem is often presented as a purely financial problem but let us not forget that the debt crisis wears a human face. The debt crisis is the face of a young girl denied an opportunity for the education which could lift her out of poverty because some northern governments regard national debt repayment as a higher priority than her schooling. It is the face of a child whose mind and body are not growing properly because of recurrent infectious diseases—diseases which could be prevented by transferring a fraction of what is spent on debt to primary health care.

Poor Country Debt Relief: False Dawn or New Hope?

The Highly Indebted Poor Countries initiative was intended to begin a process for redressing such wrongs. This initiative was adopted by both the World Bank and International Monetary Fund boards in September 1996. Despite some flaws in the time-frame for implementation, many recognized its potential for achieving debt sustainability and enabling some of the world's poorest countries, like Uganda and Bolivia, to begin implementing major poverty eradication programs. OXFAM International estimated that over a five-year period, the Ugandan program would save the lives of almost four hundred thousand children, prevent the deaths of thirteen thousand women who will otherwise die in childbirth and provide a full primary education for all of Uganda's children.

James Wolfensohn proclaimed that the new HIPC initiative brought "good news for the world's poor." For all the "good news" rhetoric, however, little of substance has yet to occur. Yet the poor can wait no longer. To slow down implementation of the debt relief plan is to condemn more people to a life of hardship and misery. The World Bank knows the seriousness and urgency of the matter. The time for action is now. "The shocking fact is that a child born in Sub-Saharan Africa today is still more likely to be malnourished than to go to primary school and is as likely to die before the age of five as to enter secondary school" (Poverty Reduction and the World Bank, Executive Summary, 1996).

It is time people everywhere were guaranteed their basic human rights—like the right to health care and to an education. It is time for the governments and those people with the power to do so, including the World Bank, the International Monetary Fund and the world's largest corporations, to secure basic human rights for all. The Basic Human Rights campaign is closely linked to the fiftieth anniversary of both the United Nations and the Universal Declaration of Human Rights. Half a century later, the rights contained in both the UN Charter and the Declaration continue to be violated on a massive scale. OXFAM wants to see basic rights respected and fulfilled so that people can overcome poverty. We want to see policy changes at the national and international levels that will enable people to fulfil their basic rights and we want these policies implemented. OXFAM is demanding that Canada's military expenditures be reduced and the subsequent savings be reallocated to improve the foreign aid budget, that more be done to reduce the unpayable debt burden of poor countries, that Southern producers be given fair returns for their labour and products and greater access to Northern markets, and that corporations respect the right of workers to a decent wage and safe and healthy working conditions.

As James Gustave Speth, administrator of the United Nations Development Programme, has said: "Poverty is not to be suffered in silence by the poor. Nor can it be tolerated by those with power to change it. The challenge is to mobilize action state by state, corporation by corporation, individual by individual."

DARREN E. LUND

Young People Mobilizing on Human Rights Issues

Darren E. Lund is a PhD candidate at the Centre for the Study of Curriculum and Instruction, University of British Columbia, Vancouver, BC. He is a teacher at Lindsay Thurber Comprehensive High School in Red Deer, Alberta.

THE ADAGE "YOUTH IS WASTED ON THE YOUNG" was just plain wrong. I admit that I am always a bit dismayed at the response I get from some adults when I tell them that I teach high school. A polite smile quickly turns to a grimace as they envision locking themselves in a room full of adolescents for two hundred days a year. Wait a minute, now that I reflect on it, this is indeed a strange profession I have gotten myself into. But what a rewarding adventure it has turned out to be. I have been most fortunate to have spent over a decade advising a student action group.

199

Young people are in a unique and problematic position in contemporary society, particularly in Western cultures. Poised in that void between childhood and adulthood, they are unable to express political power as votes, yet are too often offered up as sacrificial lambs on the altar of conservative panic over declining values and standards in education. When high school students manage to attract public attention it is often for breaking norms, providing yet more fuel for their critics. As one of my professors at the University of BC (UBC), Leslie Roman, has said, "Youths have become the subject of consternation, outrage, concern, explanation, and, not inconsequentially, commodification and appropriation. Whether vilified or applauded, philanthropized or harassed, jailed or held out as the hope for the future, they are exerting the only real power they have in a public debate which simultaneously makes them visible as spectacle and inaudible as voice" (Roman, 1996: p. 21).

I recognize the accuracy in this analysis of the unflattering public stereotyping of youth as a category synonymous with "social problem." But I flatly reject the notion that such sensational characterizations are the "only real power" young people have. My own experience working alongside students in human rights activism reveals that young activists have a tremendous energy that would put most adult social action projects to shame.

Those young people who choose to shoulder the social responsibility of protecting human rights share a crucial characteristic: they are idealists. I do not refer to them as unrealistic dreamers who seek some untenable panacea for social injustices. I am speaking about a genuine belief that there can be something better and that their actions will make a positive difference toward that change. This predisposition toward idealism is at the core of what makes progressive social change possible, and what gives young people their tremendous potential to mobilize on human rights and other issues of fairness.

I will share with you an example of a mobilization for social justice that began innocently one afternoon about twelve years ago in one of my classes. This is just one case among several others (e.g., Berlin and Alladin, 1996; Cogan and Ramsankar, 1994; Rivera and Poplin, 1995; SooHoo, 1995; Walsh, 1996). It is my hope that from these experiences you may recognize similarities and relevance to your own educational or community contexts.

▄▄▄ Spontaneous Social Action

What began as a spontaneous classroom interchange on discrimination has become an ongoing program called Students and Teachers Opposing Prejudice (STOP). The program has been nationally recognized as an innovative model for social justice programming (Lund, 1993; 1998). I was a young rookie just starting out but already understood that very little was expected from this particular class at Lindsay Thurber Comprehensive High, a school of approximately 1,800 students in the city of Red Deer, an hour's drive south of Edmonton. Several of the twenty-seven boisterous students were repeating this remedial English literature course for the second or third time. All but three of the students were boys. As a group they projected a collective attitude that didn't exactly radiate enthusiasm for my Friday afternoon poetry lesson.

To my wonder, a poem I had written for the class on the subject of racism led to a lively exchange. By the end of the period, students had opened discussion on a wealth of social issues for examination, including the unfair stereotyping of youth and the obligation to act on important social issues like human rights. "We should form a group like those neo-Nazis do, but ours would be the opposite," suggested a student called John. Several others voiced their support. These supposedly unmotivated students wanted to take control of their education. Who was I to hold them back?

I was caught off-guard the following Monday morning, however, by a telephone call from the local radio station. "So, what can you tell me about this student action group that formed in your class last week?" an announcer asked.

"Your group spokesperson called me this morning and was very articulate." One of the students, Wade, had taken on the duty of media relations, initiating a public response we had never expected.

In the past decade's conservative political climate, any student or teacher activism around human rights issues has sounded downright revolutionary. Despite the risk of being seen as too political, of ruffling the feathers of narrow-minded community members, of rocking the status quo boat, human rights need defending by young activists. In our case, school administrators were initially hesitant. I remember one telling me, "I'm pleased for your program. But if the whole thing blows up in your face, I knew nothing about it."

From the beginning, student enthusiasm has been the cornerstone of STOP. The first school-wide STOP meeting attracted almost two hundred students, along with local newspaper and television reporters. Within a week the group had been featured in a story on a national television news broadcast! The students and I sensed we had stumbled onto something of profound social urgency. Our program's exposure began a symbolic healing for a community that has long been in the national spotlight because of incidents of racist extremism.

■■■ Countering a Regional Extremist Image

We understood that much of the media interest in our STOP project had to do with the presence of several highly publicized hate-mongers in central Alberta. Right-wing extremists had already etched the city of Red Deer into the minds of Canadians. The Red Deer dateline adorned articles about Terry Long, Canadian leader of the Aryan Nations movement, then running a "white power" training camp at a nearby town. Long had also run a classified advertisement in the local newspaper promoting a pre-recorded "hate line" for over a year. (Long was eventually convicted of promoting hatred against an identifiable group.) Red Deer also hosted the trial of school teacher James Keegstra, an unrepentant Holocaust denier convicted in 1985 for promoting hatred in his high school social studies classes. Now the media had a story with a new angle—local young people were actively opposing anti-Semitism and other forms of bigotry.

Instead of ignoring contentious issues or engaging in fruitless confrontations with extremists, the youth in STOP understood that they could take proactive steps to begin rebuilding within our community. They had begun to hear echoes of their own voices in unexpected places and it seemed to fuel their determination and enthusiasm. These "nonacademic," streamed students who admitted they had often found school assignments lacked relevance to their lives had become active agents in their own education. Now they were eager to share their growing awareness with others.

The students knew they needed to begin some planning and research and began to shape the direction and moral foundations of STOP. A key principle was to use education to promote the belief that all individuals, regardless of ethnic origin, skin colour, age, gender, sexual orientation, religion, disability or any other physical traits, deserve to be respected based on their own merits. Rather than pointing fingers or seeking scapegoats, we have sought to address our own biases. For me, this has meant an ongoing process of overcoming my own upbringing with a racist father and my past use of racist and hurtful remarks.

My view of student involvement respects student autonomy and agency with teachers as partners in a common project for social justice. I have sought to limit my role to one of facilitator or advisor, tapping students' energy and ideas without appropriating their intentions for the group. Students began planning and rehearsing talks, writing letters, conducting interviews, researching diversity and human rights issues in the library (where we learned, for example, that the Ku Klux Klan had a chapter in our area in the 1930s), and booking videos and guest speakers for our class.

An amusing incident happened one day when one of the more gregarious class members requested class time to speak at his former junior high school. I consented and helped him make the arrangements. The class worked in small groups to aid in planning similar presentations. The day came for his scheduled talk and, while Trent was waiting in the hallway outside the classroom where he was to talk on behalf of the STOP group, the school principal rounded the corner, approached him with suspicion and abruptly asked, "What the hell are you doing here?" The young man replied, "Relax man, I'm the guest speaker!"

Within the first few months STOP organized a province-wide art and writing contest that attracted hundreds of entries. In the past twelve years it has attracted thousands of entries and distributed thousands of dollars in prizes. The following fall a student nomination led to my being honoured with the first ever Alberta Human Rights Award from the Alberta Human Rights Commission.

At the request of several students, STOP became a regular part of the school's extra-curricular program and continues to hold regular weekly meetings attracting dozens of students. With no attendance policy or formal rules, students are free to drop in to the program any time during the school year. There isn't a typical student who is attracted to our group, but members share an idealistic desire to make their world a fairer place. Through an egalitarian consensus model, we discuss and debate issues, brainstorm new ideas for activism, and maintain our annual commitments along the way. Despite the seriousness of the issues of racism, sexism, homophobia, hatred and others we deal with, students report that it is actually a lot of fun.

During the second year of STOP, drama students from the local college volunteered to direct our first elementary drama presentation on discrimination. Our all-amateur troupe performed it at several schools around the city and, in the years to come, took a similar drama production on the road to dozens of primary schools in a hundred-mile radius. The performances were unapologetically uneven and always unpredictable, but the message we shared must have gotten through. Some of the local children who had seen our performances became members of STOP years later when they reached high school.

▆▆▆ Facing Hatred and Resistance With Activism

Often local and international news items might stimulate interest that leads to mobilizing on a certain pressing issue. In our case, when a town about an hour away from Red Deer encountered its own extremist activity in the form of a publicized cross-burning at a hate rally, STOP members arranged their own transportation and volunteered a weekend of their time to work with students there. Together they shared ideas and resources in a collective effort to counter hate groups. As part of a Human Rights Awareness Week a few years ago, STOP arranged noon forums featuring anti-racist skinheads from SHARP (Skinheads Against Racial Prejudice), the president of the World Sikh Organization, a former Iranian university professor (then a caretaker at our school) and the chair of the Alberta Human Rights Commission.

Occasionally, and quite predictably, the group will confront serious resistance to its efforts. We have to be realistic in our acknowledgement of the risks involved in this kind of work. When the national head of the Simon Wiesenthal Centre in Toronto travelled to Red Deer in 1989 to present STOP with a Courage to Remember award, the response from the extremist fringe was immediate. Aryan Nations leader Terry Long made the front page of the local newspaper decrying the Holocaust as a hoax while a blurb on our national award was buried in the local section. Meanwhile, numerous cars in the school parking lot were littered with KKK brochures, and STOP received revisionist "historical" material and pseudo-scientific studies in the mail.

We responded by laminating the Holocaust posters we had received as part of the award and donating them to the school district. Burgeoning student interest in exploring this dark period in human history led STOP to organize an annual Holocaust Awareness Symposium. For the past four years, survivors of Nazi concentration camps have spoken to hundreds of spellbound city high school seniors. One student, Joshua, whose grandparents were killed at Auschwitz, was especially moved and said, "These living sources of history have so much to tell us about ourselves and the terrible results of hatred."

STOP's mandate is to educate rather than confront, yet it seems counter-educational to ignore hatred and shy away from hot local issues. For example, when a Sikh man was denied entry into a local Royal Canadian Legion meeting room because he was wearing unauthorized "headgear" (his turban), the students of STOP took action. Rather than staging a boycott or public protest, they wrote letters to the parties involved and to the media. STOP also invited the victim, Ram Chahal, to address a group of about three hundred fellow students at the school to share his perspective and shine light on Sikh faith.

As you have likely learned, Alberta is one of just two provinces in Canada that does not include sexual orientation as grounds for discrimination in its human rights legislation. Just last spring, the Alberta government was finally forced by the federal Court of Appeals to extend rights protection to all of its citizens. When local politicians garnered media attention with homophobic comments on gays and lesbians, STOP decided to address stereotyping and discrimination in our community with a public forum on the topic. We invited homosexual people to share their experiences and encountered resistance from staff and community alike, some of whom feared we were "promoting a lifestyle choice." This only confirmed our commitment to increased public awareness on diversity.

■■■ Getting Political

Students have sought national and international avenues for working toward social justice. For example, the group supports Amnesty International, sending hundreds of letters each year to government leaders around the world. Locally, STOP members have drafted two official proclamations, both signed by Red Deer's mayor at council meetings. One declared December 10 as International Human Rights Day and the other denoted March 21 as the International Day to Eliminate Racism and Discrimination. Though largely symbolic, the events represented the students' collective desire for political engagement with the adult community. In addition, STOP student members study government policies and agencies that relate to our group's interests.

The political climate in Canada, as elsewhere, has undergone a dramatic shift to the right in the past decade. STOP members have responded by lobbying politicians for changes to existing human rights legislation. In 1997 the group engaged in a public debate, later aired on national radio, with the provincial minister of social services on this province's continuing and shameful refusal to ratify Canada's signing of the United Nations Convention on the Rights of the Child. In 1994 the STOP group submitted a written brief to a public human rights review panel.

A few years back our province's top politician, then Premier Don Getty, made inflammatory statements against Canada's official bilingualism and multiculturalism policies. When Red Deer's own government representative, Stockwell Day, supported Getty's stand, STOP members penned letters to their offices and newspapers. Day judiciously arranged a visit to a STOP meeting, during which he presented his views to the group. STOP also responded to a series of public statements from another elected official. Dianne Mirosh caused controversy with attacks on gays, non-English speaking immigrants, and the very existence of a Human Rights Commission. Students in our group sought dialogue with her and when she failed to respond, wrote to newly elected Premier Ralph Klein and various media.

STOP publicly supports Canada's federal and provincial multicultural policies which were drafted to help eliminate the barriers faced by some people. Our collaborative efforts with the Alberta Multiculturalism Commission over the years have been rewarding. In 1992 we secured a $17,000 grant to coordinate an ambitious province-wide youth conference to foster student leadership in social justice.

███ Engaging With the World Beyond Our Community

Over the years STOP members have arranged for school visits from experts on issues such as mental health, native issues, world development, human rights legislation, women and poverty, discrimination based on sexual orientation, torture and human rights violations, refugee and immigration issues, world peace, public health, and physical and mental disabilities. Guest speakers have been diverse, coming from the ranks of government representatives, community volunteers, torture victims, people with disabilities, exchange students and political activists.

STOP has received national recognition for its efforts, including a 1998 Race Relations Award from the Federation of Canadian Municipalities, two Together We're Better awards from the Canadian government, a 1993 Canadian Youth Human Rights Achievement Award from the Human Rights League of B'nai Brith Canada and a 1989 Multicultural Leadership Award from the Canadian Association for Multicultural and Intercultural Education. I am very pleased to report that additional chapters of STOP have formed in other schools, and other student activist groups have been modelled on this program. These young people are among a growing number of students who refute the belief that youth are apathetic or destructive. Given a legitimate forum for activism, they are leaders in the ongoing struggle for social justice.

REFERENCES

Berlin, M. L., and M. I. Alladin. "The Kipling Collegiate Institute Story: Towards Positive Race Relations in the School." In M. I. Alladin (ed.). *Racism in Canadian Schools*. Toronto: Harcourt Brace (1996): 131–146.

Cogan, K. and S. Ramsankar. *Alex Taylor Community School: A Quarter Century of Programs and Promises*. Edmonton, AB: Alex Taylor School, 1994.

Lund, D. E. The Evolution of STOP: Students and Teachers Opposing Prejudice. In K. A. McLeod (Ed.), Multicultural Education: The State of the Art National Study, Report #1. Winnipeg: Canadian Association of Second Language Teachers (1993): 50–58.

Lund, D. E. Social Justice Activism in a Conservative Climate: Students and Teachers Challenging Discrimination in Alberta. *Our Schools/Our Selves*, 9 4 (1998): 24–38.

Rivera, J. and M. Poplin. "Multicultural, Critical, Feminine and Constructive Pedagogies Seen Through the Lives of Youth: Toward a Pedagogy for the Next Century." In C. E. Sleeter and P. L.

McLaren (eds.). *Multicultural Education, Critical Pedagogy, and the Politics of Difference*. Albany, NY: SUNY (1995): 221–244.

Roman, L. G. Spectacle in the Dark: Youth as Transgression, Display and Repression. *Educational Theory*. 46 (1996): 1–22.

SooHoo, S. Emerging Student and Teacher Voices: A Syncopated Rhythm in Public Education. In B. Kanpol and P. McLaren (eds.). *Critical Multiculturalism: Uncommon Voices in a Common Struggle*. Westport, CT: Bergin & Garvey (1995): 217–234.

Walsh, C. E. (ed.). *Education Reform and Social Change: Multicultural Voices, Struggles and Visions*. Mahwah, NJ: Lawrence Erlbaum Associates, 1996.

HUGUETTE LABELLE

A Question of
Caring and Sharing

Huguette Labelle is president of the Canadian International Development Agency (CIDA). She is also chancellor of the University of Ottawa and vice chair of the World Health Organization's Working Group on Health and Development Policies. She was made an Officer of the Order of Canada in 1990.

ARE WE OUR BROTHERS' AND SISTERS' KEEPERS? We are, in the general sense of the brotherhood of humankind. Humanity knows no borders and makes no hemispheric distinctions. It is universal, just as human rights are. As keepers of humanity, we are responsible for protecting all human rights and for considering poverty a violation of the political, civil, economic, social and cultural rights of every human being. In accepting these responsibilities, we not only protect others, we protect our own societies, our own values of peace and security.

From a rights point of view, there is no difference between poor people in the North and poor people in the South, between children who are denied access to education and women who die in labour for lack of basic health care. They are all human beings denied the full exercise of their human rights.

No one, no single organization or type of organization has supreme responsibility for the fight against human rights violations. The duty to protect human rights is ours collectively: countries, international bodies, nongovernmental organizations, individuals. The views and means of each group of players are complementary.

When John Humphrey and Eleanor Roosevelt sat down to discuss the first draft of the Universal Declaration of Human Rights, they were convinced the issue of human rights was not only a matter of being able to vote, or being ruled by fair laws. It was about having food on the table, assuming you do have a table. It was about getting an education in order to express yourself through work and culture. In their view then, these and many more were all part of universal human rights, as they are in our view today.

Throughout the years, governments around the world have reiterated their commitment to human rights by ratifying both the International Covenant on Civil and Political Rights and the International Covenant on Economic, Social and Cultural Rights, as well as numerous other conventions. But if we have ratified all these conventions, then why is it that today there is still so much wanting? Why is it that the current situation of humanity is not what all of us feel it should be?

We all recognize that a lot of progress has been made, and on many fronts. We have to build on that. We also know that progress can regress; we have seen this happening in countries around the world in more recent times, be it because of financial crisis, natural disasters or civil conflicts.

We know we cannot be complacent because, as we speak, we know there are children scavenging in garbage dumps for scraps of probably rotten food. We know there are millions of children who are parentless, meaning that not only are they without a father and mother, but without older brothers and sisters, and without aunts and uncles because of these disasters, these conflicts, and because of AIDS, particularly in a number of countries in Africa.

In all of our countries, there is also a huge segment of our society called youth, the people between the age of fifteen and thirty years, who have been marginalized because of lack of employment, lack of sustainable occupation. As a result, we now have a few generations where thirty to fifty or sixty per cent of our youth have not had the opportunity to contribute to our societies, to fulfil themselves, to learn how to make a living. In addition, we must not forget the well over 130 million children around the world, two-thirds of them girls, who do not have access to school.

The great culprit is poverty. We do hear the figures and we do repeat them...about the 1.3 billion people living on less than a dollar a day, and the three billion living on less than two dollars a day. Even those figures mask unbelievably worse situations, where people struggle on less than thirty to fifty dollars a year.

Is it a question of a lack of resources? Of course not. There are tremendous resources around the world. There is capacity to provide clean water to all the people of the world. There is capacity to provide sanitation, to provide shelter, to support the development of sustainable occupations. There is a possibility also to ensure that wealth is created and that wealth is equally distributed in countries.

There are plenty of resources to go around. It can be seen in military expenditures, which total over $700 billion a year. It can be seen in the fact that two of the world's largest automotive companies have aggregate revenues of more than the total GNP of forty-seven of the poorest countries of the world. Of course, there are plenty of other examples. Clearly, there is a lot of wealth.

We have to stop measuring success and failure or measuring progress in terms of markets and changes in gross domestic product. We have to look at a much broader picture of human well-being than just an economic pointer.

In the last few years there has been a renewed sense of urgency to see governments fulfil their role with respect to equity and equilibrium. Some countries have been able to fulfil such a role in the past and, hopefully, some still have that ability to a great extent, today. We have seen that the equilibrium between the creation of wealth through markets and ensuring a fair distribution of that wealth rests on ensuring that there are rules that make it possible for people to thrive. Markets do contribute by creating wealth, but equity does not come from trickle-down economics. Government have an essential role to play, today more than ever.

Having spoken of national governments, we need to look beyond their sphere of action to discuss international governance. It has arisen as an important question in light of the need for international rules to ensure the game is played fairly. It is important to ensure countries don't see themselves stripped of a tremendous amount of their wealth overnight, which leaves people in very vulnerable situations.

But just as it is individuals who ultimately suffer, individuals can initially take action. This, to me, is where it all starts. It starts with parents bringing their children along when they do volunteer work. It starts with parents from wealthier countries expecting their children to set aside some of their allowance money to share with those less fortunate in their community or their world community. It does start at home.

Individuals who come together to form organizations also take an active role, as a collective conscience, within our societies. They report on abuses, foster opportunities for grassroots initiatives and put forward concrete proposals for international action. We think of people in cities and villages in all parts of the world who are conscious of their rights and mobilize their communities to ensure they are respected. We think of people everywhere who recognize the responsibilities that come with these rights, and who lend their voice and support to both local and global efforts to help the underprivileged get ahead and live with dignity.

Coming back to the fundamental question, "Are we our brothers' and sisters' keepers?", the answer must be a resounding, "Yes, we all are." We are accountable and responsible for contributing to making our communities, our cities, our countries and our world a place where we can all live in dignity. It is not acceptable for any person, anywhere, to be deprived of his or her rights, because when the rights of one person are diminished, the rights of all are diminished. We must take our "stewardship" role to heart and take action as governments, organizations and individuals, at home and abroad. What matters are that we complement each others' efforts to reduce poverty and to help the poor of the world to fully claim their human rights, in order to contribute to a safer, more prosperous and more equitable world. It is a question of caring and sharing.

Human Rights and Indigenous People

A GLOBAL SEARCH FOR JUSTICE

JUAN LEÓN

Recognizing the Rights of Indigenous Peoples

Juan León is a member and founder of the National
Front of Human Rights Organizations of Guatemala. He
is also a consultant for the Danish government on the
Human Rights Program of Central America for the
Documentation and Political Participation of
Indigenous Peoples. He was a member of the Working
Group on Indigenous Peoples at the United Nations in
Geneva and participated in deliberations by the United
Nations on the Draft Declaration of the Rights of
Indigenous Peoples.

213

I T HAS BEEN DEMONSTRATED that the struggle for human rights in any part of the world carries high risks. In my country of Guatemala, thousands upon thousands of indigenous people and poor Ladinos have been assassinated for demanding rights for their people. Even today there are various governments in the world, some civil, some military, which still do not understand that their role is to be at the service of their people.

For this reason I offer my words in honour and in remembrance of all those people, known and unknown, women, men, young, old, who have defended the dignity and the rights of ourselves and others. I invoke the memory of the thousands of people who have been made to disappear, who have been killed, tortured and jailed and aren't here with us.

Much of what we enjoy right now in Guatemala and other parts of this world has been thanks to the blood that they shed. The fiftieth anniversary of the Universal Declaration of Human Rights has meant great advancements in humanity. This has allowed for the development of new relationships between states and also between individuals. We are now just beginning through various international forums to understand and acknowledge the collective rights of various indigenous peoples.

In many countries of the world our people are still ignored and treated as slaves or servants of a minority. But as our elders have taught us, there will once again come a time when our cosmic vision, our knowledge, our values and our morals as a people will come together to help build a new world. We have shared this idea in many places throughout the world, including the United Nations. We have put forward our philosophy, the essential basis of which is the search for and creation of a harmony of political balance as well as a balance in the economy, society and environment.

We seek to counter a vision that is exclusionary and imposed by a very small percentage of humanity. Our vision not only calls us to work together for humanity, but also to start to prevent the slow death of Mother Nature. For example, there exists an accumulation of capital, of material wealth, held in the hands of only a few people. Free market commerce has been established and economic blocks have been established by the large countries. Economic globalization continues its course, imposing itself on the weakest, and the consequences today are a greater violation of human rights which affects mainly the indigenous peoples, minorities and women throughout the world. The profound values and principles of sensitivity and respect of life in all of its magnitude, of working to benefit others and of thinking of other people, have disappeared.

What exists now is an uncontrollable anxiety. There is material wealth but an emotional and spiritual poverty. This is creating a great economic, political, social and cultural imbalance in humanity. Because of this, after many years of intense labour, especially in the areas of sensitization, education, and negotiation by indigenous peoples and their representatives with governments and states, we recognize that there has been some advancement in the understanding and the existence of our peoples. But it is not enough when we consider that many countries are still practising internal colonialism and discrimination. They put our people in a secondary status and subjugate them through national legislation.

We also understand that combating discrimination is not something new. We need to change the structures of norms and laws. We also have to change our thoughts and actions because even involuntarily we continue to commit acts of discrimination. This is a very large challenge for indigenous peoples, particularly in our work in the United Nations, where we have to work against the political will of various governments to not only accept and implement the Draft Declaration on the Rights of Indigenous Peoples but also to find ways to begin to implement these rights. But we cannot do this work alone. We need the help of all agencies, governments and organizations which work to promote human rights.

In Guatemala, seventy per cent of the total population of eleven million is Mayan, Garifuna and Xinka. These three groups form the indigenous population. The rest of the population is made up by the Ladino people. In the last almost five hundred years the state of Guatemala has been built on the basis of internal colonization and domination over seventy per cent of the population. This has produced exclusion and secular domination.

Many are familiar with the way the voices of the poor and marginalized in our country have been silenced—by systematic repression, human rights violations and violation of international instruments ratified by the state. As a consequence, there have been divisions, confrontation and greater poverty in our beloved land, leading to an internal war that lasted more than thirty-six years. There were thousands and thousands of assassinations and 440 indigenous communities were destroyed and disappeared.

With the end of the internal armed conflict on 29 December 1996, we are now opening up new possibilities for political change. Despite the genocide suffered by our people, there have also been advances that we must stress. The peace process generated agreements between the guerrillas and the government that have made small steps towards the creation or a state and a nation without exclusions, without racism or discrimination of any kind.

We still have many more problems to solve, but we greatly appreciate the absence of armed conflicts which justified the presence of the military and the government oppression of our people. And now we have the accord on the rights of indigenous people. This accord contains provisions which could insure the participation of indigenous people at all levels in society—political, social and economic.

Over the last two years (1997, 1998) we have been in intense negotiations with the government and its agencies to put forward proposals for new political and judicial structures. In this way, on 14 October 1998, we ended one more important stage of constitutional reform in our country. Among these reforms we have established the acknowledgement of the existence of the Mayan, Garifuna and Xinka peoples, as well as the requirement that indigenous peoples be consulted every time political and administrative actions are taken. It establishes the official recognition of all indigenous languages. There are also other reforms which increase our power in civil society and reduce that of the army.

But as I said earlier, we still face many challenges to our human rights and the development of our peoples. One of these is the lack of clarification on the assassination of Monsignor Juan Juardi Calanara, a Catholic archbishop. People who work for human rights still face threats and intimidation.

In the struggle of indigenous peoples throughout the world, it is important that we all contribute ideas and resources to make these rights a reality. This is the moment that we, the aboriginal people, must realize that we have scientific, technical and spiritual knowledge that can be used to develop new models of rule around the world. This is the moment when we must work together to find new paths of development and new rights for our benefit and for the benefit of the generations that follow us.

OLGA HAVNEN

Indigenous Internationalism Today

Olga Havnen[1] is an executive officer of the National Indigenous Working Group on Native Title and director of Indigenous Development Programs with the Fred Hollows Foundation. She is an advocate for indigenous rights in Australia and internationally and has participated in deliberations by the United Nations on the Draft Declaration of the Rights of Indigenous Peoples.

MANY PEOPLE SAY that Australia and Canada have little to teach other. Surely January temperatures of minus forty and plus forty in central and northern Australia and western and northern Canada are more similar than dissimilar. Both extremes confronted European settlers who came from more temperate lands and who found buffalo or bilby, kangaroo or caribou, strange and exotic creatures which would be replaced by herds of European cattle.[2] I hope I can show that the two countries, and others, have much to share. I will use the Australia–Canada experience to illustrate wider points about indigenous internationalism.

Some Australians try to defend an isolationist and exceptionalist view of indigenous history and policy by saying that Canada has old and unique legal frameworks while Australia has none. This view overlooks the fact that until very recently the Canadian courts and governments ignored or forgot much of that legal and constitutional framework, such as common law rights, crown fiduciary responsibilities, treaties and even the Royal Proclamation of 1763. In other words, both Canada and Australia have developed their separate national approaches in light of shared factors in the post-World War II era.

Among these shared factors are renewed confidence of indigenous peoples in relations with whites through war service, urbanization, better indigenous education and the reach of mass media; changing social attitudes among European peoples, including Canadians and Australians, towards social and racial equality in the wake of the Depression and the wars with Hitler and Japan; images and press reports of de-colonization of countries and islands large and small around the world, by Britain in particular, but also the Dutch, Portuguese, French and others in the post-war period; the TV impact of the American civil rights and black power movements; and the impact of post-war United Nations ideals and instruments opposing racism.[3]

One may wonder how much other factors have impacted in each of our situations. Canada has had successful indigenous self-government and claims movements on its borders in Alaska and Greenland, as well as the example of tribal government in the US's Lower 48. Australia has the experience of its own three populated island territories, each with a tailor-made regional constitution.[4] Then there is the case of New Zealand whose social and political relations with Maori are far in advance of our own, and the home-rule island territories of New Zealand, Niue and the Cook Islands, as well as de-colonization of many parts of Melanesia and Polynesia. It seems that Canadians may have been more open to such influences than Australians.

All these factors have assisted the rewriting of indigenous–white relations. With both Australia and Canada having British-derived political culture, a federal structure with states or provinces and federal territories in which white settlers and indigenous peoples have been struggling for autonomy, it should be obvious that each has much to share with the other. The big difference between them is that in Canada the highest level of government is responsible for indigenous affairs, however minimal the exercise of such power at various times. In Australia, the states had exclusive power in indigenous affairs until a national referendum in 1967 gave the federal government a paramount role if it chose to exercise it. Aborigines and many other Australians since then have been disappointed by federal timidity in a field where the states have failed utterly—or succeeded too well, depending on your viewpoint.[5]

They have displaced and dispossessed Aborigines in many areas, leaving them marginalized, sick and poor. There has been much soul-searching among concerned publics in Australia in recent years at the failure of Australian health and social services to turn around the grim statistics concerning indigenous peoples, a problem heightened by awareness of the greater relative success in Canada, New Zealand, the US and especially Scandinavia. For five years a federal ombudsman, the aboriginal social justice commissioner, hammered away at such problems in his annual reports. The government has followed up its usual failure to act on his recommendations with the quiet abolition of his position.[6]

■ Moving Forward or Moving Back?

It had seemed as if Australia was at last joining the First World in indigenous policy progress. In a speech in late 1992 to launch the international UN indigenous year, Prime Minister Keating spoke movingly about the wrongs of the past and needs of the present in Sydney's urban aboriginal district of Redfern. The

speech electrified Australia. The following year Prime Minister Keating personally led the complex negotiations resulting in the Native Title Act which set up
the machinery and guidelines for resolving land disputes.

But aborigines and Torres Strait Islanders have been dealt a major shock in
recent years. Having finally achieved recognition of native title rights in principle in the High Court's *Mabo* (1992) and *Wik* (1996) decisions, our national
politics have been dominated for the past two years by the determination of
federal and state governments simply to roll back or extinguish in all but name
any rights we have. This is being done through federal and complementary state
legislation. As the coordinator of the National Indigenous Working Group
(NIWG) on Native Title, I have been in the thick of this battle.

The biggest impact of *Mabo* had been the end of a sort of moral *terra nullius*
in which many Australians and their governments took the denial of rights as
an imperative for social policy, too. Now we have seen this view returning to
quasirespectability in some circles. However, public debate has also had encouraging aspects. After some years in which indigenous policy was a dialogue
between indigenous organizations and governments, with the usual rednecks
(notably grazing and mining industry associations) chipping in, the battle over
native title brought many other Australians from both sides of politics into
the fray.[7]

These people, including many liberals who do not support the prime
minister's archaic social and cultural views, have swung national opinion
behind a more cooperative and harmonious approach. One may hope that some
positive developments will occur in time to make Australia's centenary of federation in January 2001 a less divisive time than the bicentenary of white
settlement in 1988. After years of playing a constructive role in international
UN work on indigenous rights, Australia has served notice that it will back-pedal
there, too.[8]

What may be most disturbing is that this decision to further water down the
UN Draft Declaration on the Rights of Indigenous Peoples follows the vehement
demands of the populist politician Pauline Hanson on June 2 in Parliament for
just such an approach. The speech caused a national furore and Prime Minister
Howard said the next day it "verges on the deranged" and was "fanning racist
sentiment." Now her views are good enough to become national policy, it seems.
A particular issue has been the Stolen Children. This refers to the generations of
indigenous children taken from their families for permanent removal to the
nonindigenous world. The purpose according to official documents was to
hasten the assimilation or extinction of the aboriginal race into the European
Australian gene pool. The formal inquiry generated much painful news
coverage and more painful memories for indigenous peoples. It even prompted
indigenous suicides. At length the report "Bringing Them Home" appeared at
the end of May 1997.[9]

With the country's attention focused at the time on the Australian Reconciliation Convention in Melbourne, the prime minister had an opportunity to say something. However, he and his government publicly challenged the human issues involved, even arguing that Aborigines removed had benefited— a view demolished by the detailed studies undertaken by the inquiry. Needless to say, Aborigines and many other Australians were interested and impressed by the Canadian government's apology and healing package announced earlier this year.

The Australian government has waged a war on the Aboriginal and Torres Strait Islander Commission (ATSIC) since the 1996 election campaign. ATSIC, the former federal Aboriginal Affairs Department, has an elected indigenous commission at its head and elected regional councils across the country. In other words, unlike Canadian indigenous self-government where funds and decision-making are moving to local First Nations, Australia has advisory bodies elected to influence or direct the spending of a central agency.[10]

The movement for genuine self-government sometimes runs up against opposition from ATSIC regions no less than from senior governments.[11] Meanwhile, by constantly calling for special audits and feeding the redneck view that blacks should have no money or are unfit to manage it—so-called wedge politics, usually hidden behind a veneer of national unity bombast—the government plays to public fears and prejudice. ATSIC's principled resistance on many issues in recent years has won it admiration and respect within the aboriginal community and erased many doubts about its credibility as an authentic indigenous body.

Wedge politics are an old tradition in parts of Australia, especially the North, as I will show in a moment. However, at the national level they had been repudiated in matters of race, whether aboriginal or South Sea Islander or Asian, by both sides of politics since the 1960s. Long gone is the day when a national immigration minister could say that "two Wongs don't make a white" and expect a positive audience reaction. Wedge politics have proven a dangerous strategy since used by the Coalition to win the 1996 election. Pauline Hanson's One Nation now lurks in the Coalition's shadow and any number of extreme right fringe groups, in turn, in One Nation's shadow.[12]

One Nation's indigenous policy appears to be derived from one such group which affects to believe that Prince Philip has been using the late great Australian, Dr. H. C. Coombs, plus a Canadian who worked with the Inuit, to break up the country. They say this has already happened in Canada thanks to Nunavut, and that self-government and land claims are a device for the British royal family to siphon off resource revenue from gullible indigenous people![13] Meanwhile, the prime minister has repeatedly said that the policy balance had swung too far towards Aborigines under Labour and that he is now bringing it back to centre. In fact, Aborigines had a fractious relationship with Labour during its thirteen years in power but, as in Canada with the fifteen-year Trudeau government, over time it became possible to make various advances.

Most worrying may be the prime minister's view that recognition, rights and indigenous leadership are politically correct nonsense, a passing Labour fad. His view is that basic services in health, education and employment are the only answer. Of course, we Aborigines would love to have the quality of services available to other citizens of all modern countries, including Australia. However, the return to paternalism and the pretence that this is somehow a new approach which deserves respect is hard to fathom. Canada and other countries abandoned that approach precisely because it did not work and moved to a rights and self-government based policy which has transformed the relations between indigenous peoples and government. Such an approach—rights and recognition —was proposed by the extraordinary indigenous social justice exercise of 1994–95.[14]

In this effort the National Council for Aboriginal Reconciliation, ATSIC and the Aboriginal Social Justice Commission combined to hold two national rounds of community hearings and expert workshops as well as intense multi-day discussion groups to arrive at a consensus for policy directions. The social justice package had been promised by the prime minister as an accompaniment to native title clarification. It was an amazing indigenous-run effort to write a national policy and may prove a starting-point for resumed work when the political climate is more promising.[15]

Meanwhile the Sydney Olympics, the centenary of federation and turn-of-the-millennium are occurring in a one-year period. This convergence has made many Australians long for a symbolic and actual renewal, to shake off our brutal colonial history and assert our proud new nationhood in the world. The end of monarchy and an Australian head of state are an item on this agenda for many people. Even at the largely hand-picked and conservative national Constitutional Convention in 1998, it was evident that aboriginal voices had moral standing if they could get into the room. The final report of the 1998 Constitutional Convention in Canberra made proposals for aboriginal content in future constitutional reform.[16] In other words, Aborigines and Torres Strait Islanders are engaged in many political issues on rights and other strivings which are familiar to Canada's indigenous peoples.

Trees and Tories

Canadians I know tend to refer to the Northwest Territories, while Australians talk about the Northern Terri-tree. There are other differences between the NT and NWT. Like Canada's Northwest Territories, Australia's Northern Territory is seen in the national capital as a piece of the country left over from the early colony-building period.[17] Like Northern Canada, what whites see as a frontier, indigenous peoples see as their homeland. The NT is a patchwork of traditional regions and peoples, of town camps and urbanized indigenous communities. The white administrative and resource towns owe much more to the aboriginal economy then they admit. Like many hinterlands, the whole NT is heavily underwritten by national subsidies.[18] The population proportions are about one-quarter aboriginal and three-quarters non-aboriginal in a total population of 180,000. Anyone who wants to get a sense of the background to contemporary black–white relations can read Xavier Herbert's *Capricornia*, one of Australia's classic novels.

The NT has two main population centres: Darwin, the capital, on the Timor Sea, and Alice Springs at the heart of the continent. The NT's non-aboriginal population is highly transient. Many or most people are not around long enough to be counted in the five-yearly national census. Aboriginal communities have been dated to fifty thousand years, on the other hand, and the rock art galleries all over the NT tell us much about the preoccupations, beliefs and extinct species of the distant past. Australia has not been ice-covered like Canada in times of human settlement. However, the global Ice Ages made for extreme changes of climate and sea level and forced tremendous adaptation on Aborigines. In Australia today one can see pockets of landscape left over from earlier eras, the more important to protect because they are genuinely irreplaceable, e.g., the huge ancient Antarctic beech trees.

The early history of white incursion into the NT was extremely brutal.[19] Massacres of Aborigines were all too common. In many areas a sort of *modus vivendi* was achieved, however, and as in the rest of the hinterland, cheap or unpaid aboriginal labour was the key to the success of the cattle industry.[20] Today the NT and adjacent parts of several states are like Northern Canada: a few largely white towns with a visible aboriginal underclass as well as other successfully urbanized Aborigines, and a largely aboriginal hinterland of seasonal or more permanent camps and villages. Thanks to the Land Rights Act conceived by Whitlam Labour and enacted by Fraser Coalition governments in the 1970s, almost half of the NT is now aboriginal-owned land.

Since the NT gained self-government and virtual statehood in many respects in 1978, one party, the Country Liberal Party (CLP), a right-wing populist and strongly pro-development group, has held power strongly and without interruption. The CLP are masters at wedge politics, using white fears of Aborigines to launch every federal and territory election campaign.[21] While redneck hinterland groupings in other countries are kept in their place by national authorities or party machines, in Australia we have seen the reverse. National and state politicians have made pilgrimages to Darwin to find out how the CLP deals with blacks. The coalition government drew on this background for its 1996 election campaign.

Since 1985 there has been a persistent NT statehood push centred on an NT Legislative Assembly committee. The trouble is that this approach is based on the late 19th-century approach to state and national constitutions of Australia, a system which not only excluded Aborigines but saw them decimated. However, whatever the deficiencies of that process, it was too progressive for the NT chief minister (premier) who pushed it aside and insisted on his own more aggressive approach over the past two years. He and his hand-picked delegates swept aside aboriginal claims and culture, of course. In a joint pre-election press conference on 11 August 1998 with the chief minister, the prime minister said that statehood would commence on 1 January 2001 to celebrate the centenary of federation. He unwisely added that this move "will be applauded by all but the mean in spirit and narrow of vision." Polls showed NT support running at eighty per cent for statehood so the referendum to be held on federal election day, October 3, seemed a foregone conclusion. But the chief minister's manner of bulldozing this issue through, and a strong campaign of principle led by Aborigines against statehood on such terms, saw the statehood option defeated. This has given the NT another chance.

The NT statehood push, like that of white elites in the Yukon, Northwest Territories and Alaska in the recent past, is all about facilitating access to aboriginal lands and resources, of course. The NT government has a fantasy that if only they could take over our lands they would be wealthy, they could make the desert bloom and Darwin would quickly have a million people. The indigenous nations who now occupy much of the land have rather different aspirations. Soon after the NT's Legislative Assembly statehood push began in 1985, national discussion of a 21st-century constitution which would take a whole new approach, i.e., to Aborigines through recognition of rights and inclusion, began.

That new viewpoint has developed steadily, but has had little impact in the NT. The Australian Constitution requires (Section 121) that federal Parliament set the terms and conditions for any new state, a clause which negates the view of the NT government that it should simply be identical in all respects to the existing states. In August 1998 a constitutional conference of Central Australian Aborigines was held at Kalkaringi, with a statement of constitutional principle resulting.[22] The key item is the second general principle: that we will withhold our consent until there are good faith negotiations between the Northern Territory government and the freely chosen representatives of the aboriginal peoples of the Northern Territory leading to a Constitution based upon equality, coexistence and mutual respect.

As we are meeting here in Edmonton, delegates are arriving at Batchelor (south of Darwin) for a five-day aboriginal constitutional convention which will begin with the Kalkaringi statement. Many materials will be provided as resources, including information drawing on the transformation of Canada's northern territories by indigenous political movements. In the NT we are trying to start a negotiation with federal and NT governments, neither of which has seemed open to recognition of our claims for participation. Australia would be self-righteous and critical about another countries which attempted to transfer lands and peoples from one government to another against their will, of course. The issue of the future of the Northern Territory is a fundamental one for Australians and for the world. If the rights and status of indigenous peoples are going to be unilaterally dismissed by Thatcherite governments at whim, then international law and world opinion are meaningless. The Northern Territory is a test for us all.

▇▇▇ International Connections

The present Australian prime minister has attacked international visits and speaking tours by Aborigines as "stunts." Of course his friends in the mining industry busily share their secrets of how to deal with local indigenous peoples and indigenous land and water rights. What is more, his own government collects information on indigenous issues and has done so for many years, especially here in Canada but in other countries too. Australian federal and state ministers and senior officials have been visiting Canada for decades to speak with indigenous and non-indigenous people about politics and experience in self-government; land, sea and resource rights; and many other indigenous-related issues from alcohol to zinc mining.

Indeed, some Australians have become positively neurotic about all the Canadian information reaching us. The populist politician Pauline Hanson has used speeches to rail against the Inuit Nunavut project which she claims is the source of Australia's aboriginal land rights movement. This is a strange assertion for an ultranationalist politician. Doesn't she know that land and sea rights are old news? Captain Cook was taken to task for taking turtles in aboriginal waters off North Queensland, an event fully recorded and useful in a recent court case. Since the 1960s Australia has had a strong minority of non-aboriginal people across the country and across the political spectrum supporting aboriginal rights. Many more take a sort of national pride and interest in aboriginal culture. Whatever we may say about Australian racism, the fact is that many aged pensioners drive across the continent to view ancient aboriginal rock art galleries in northern and central Australia, and to walk with aboriginal guides in heat often in the range of thirty-five to forty-five degreess Celsius to learn about traditional resource use, oral culture and ceremonies.

Nevertheless, the Australian political system has only engaged briefly with indigenous rights and other world currents applicable to indigenous needs— under both Labour and Coalition governments in the second half of the 1970s and under Labour prime ministers in the 1990s. It is a widespread Australian perception that membership in the world is optional and selective. A premier may be a clever diversity-embracing fellow on visits to Asian capitals and then return to brutish obscurantism towards blacks at home. We may campaign in the world to sell mangoes or university student places, but pull down the shutters when our more embarrassing prejudices are exposed.

A mistake we have often made in Australia is to think of indigenous internationalism too narrowly, in terms of the annual trek to Geneva. Our literature on practical international work is limited.[23] However, there has been growing contact between Australian and overseas indigenous rights lawyers, and valuable comparative social science studies.[24] What is needed is much more interaction between indigenous political practitioners and organizations. For instance, there has been great interest in Australia in recent years in Canada's northern land claims settlements. In Australia we call these regional agreements.[25]

However, much of the work done by academics has focused on narrow reading of documents without a proper understanding that each of those documents is merely one item in a long-running ethnopolitical, self-determination movement's history. Context and dynamics are lost. Canadian indigenous visitors have come out of meetings with Australian officials amazed that those people seem to imagine one can simply fit a pre-determined document over a problem and all will be well. The sense of evolution and renewal in political relations is missing. We need to get together people from different continents to discuss many key issues: sea rights and coastal management, management regimes for resources and environment, local and regional self-government, territory constitutions, national constitutions and permanent networks for indigenous information exchange.

◼◼◼ Final Remarks

Indigenous peoples in all countries have no greater weakness than their lack of political information and resources. Governments have great strength in these matters. If we are to even up the odds a little we must take some of that oral knowledge and experience from different indigenous groups negotiating claims or establishing self-government and find ways to share it with other peoples. Along the way we must also lose one unfortunate habit. Often when representatives of one or other people travel abroad they use speeches to heap scorn or ridicule on other indigenous groups at home. We don't need to know about old squabbles and one-upmanship. All of us in all countries are seeking very similar goals. People in Australia do not need to hear putdowns of others in need. What we need are options, hope, precedents. All of us can learn from each other if we will only listen to each other.

This intangible world of indigenous political science needs to be made more concrete, useable and accessible. In the long run it will prove every bit as important as the search for formal international standards in human rights. Meanwhile, we in Australia—indigenous peoples, governments, media, academics and the general public—have much to learn from Canada and other countries. What Australia's national political class needs to learn most urgently is that the rights and recognition of indigenous peoples are a worldwide current of civilized progress, not an expendable item to be trivialized by blaming it on a single former political leader or party.

We believe Canada and other countries have things to learn from us, too. And we may especially hope that some of your Canadian experience is transferable. For instance, if a premier of British Columbia in 1998 can centre his re-election campaign on the social justice of the Nisga'a self-government and land claims settlement—despite that province's difficult history of indigenous–white relations—then surely there is hope for Queensland, Western Australia and the Northern Territory.[26]

REFERENCES

1. ohavnen@hollows.com.au
2. A good contemporary survey of Australian history focuses on aboriginal–European relations: *Claiming a Continent: A New History of Australia.* Sydney: Angus & Robertson (HarperCollins), 1997. For Northern Territory see Downing, J. *Ngurra Walytja: Country of My Spirit.* Darwin: Australian National University North Australia Research Unit, 1988. For black–white relations on the expanding frontier see the books of historian Henry Reynolds, books which have transformed Australians' sense of themselves and their history, but also provoked some persons including the prime minister to denounce such a "black armband view of history." For such people history is supposed to be a litany of triumphs.
3. Ball, D. (ed). *Aborigines in the Defence of Australia.* Sydney: Australian National University Press, 1991.
4. Fletcher, C. "The Australian Territories: Diversity in Governing." *Australian Journal of Political Science* 27 (1992): 159–176. Also, House of Representatives. Islands in the Sun: The Legal Regimes of Australia's External Territories and the Jervis Bay Territory, Report of the House of Representatives Standing Committee on Legal and Constitutional Affairs, Parliament of the Commonwealth of Australia, AGPS, March 1991.
5. A recent breakthrough history of state indigenous policy in Queensland reveals the full horrors of public policy and outcomes: Kidd, R. *The Way We Civilize: Aboriginal Affairs—The Untold Story.* Brisbane: University of Queensland Press, 1997. See also Brennan, F. *Land Rights Queensland Style: The Struggle for Aboriginal Self-Management.* Brisbane: University of Queensland Press, 1992.
6. First Report, 1993, to Fifth Report, 1997, are available in libraries or from the Human Rights and Equal Opportunity Commission, Sydney. The former ombudsman, Mick Dodson, will be familiar to many in Canada from his speaking tours and annual attendance at UN meetings.
7. Australian national politics is a struggle between two sides: the Australian Labour Party on the one hand, and the Coalition (of Liberal and National parties) on the other. However, the elected federal Senate sees the Democrats and Greens also making a showing and playing helpful roles on indigenous issues. The new party, Pauline Hanson's One Nation, however, is largely centred on anti-aboriginal rhetoric (see Canada's *Maclean's* magazine, 14 Sept 1998 issue). The small parties also play a role in the states' elected upper houses, only Queensland and the Northern Territory being single-chamber legislatures.
8. Dodson, M. and S. Pritchard. "Recent Developments in Indigenous Policy: The Abandonment of Self-Determination?" *Indigenous Law Bulletin* 4 15 (October 1998): 4–6.
9. Wilson R. et al. "Bringing Them Home: Report of the National Inquiry into the Separation of Aboriginal and Torres Strait Islander Children from Their Families, Human Rights and Equal

Opportunity Commission." Sydney: Commonwealth of Australia, 1997. A more affordable and available abridgement with other useful material is Bird, C. (ed.). *The Stolen Children: Their Stories*. Melbourne: Random House, 1998.

10. A full discussion of ATSIC in theory and practice is Sullivan, P. *Shooting the Banker: Essays on ATSIC and Self-Determination*. Darwin: Australian National University North Australia Research Unit, 1996. See especially the editor's useful final essay, "All Things to All People: ATSIC and Australia's International Obligation to Uphold Indigenous Self-determination," p. 105–129. ATSIC is also on-line: http://www.atsic.gov.au/ http://www.atsic.gov.au/

11. Work proceeding does include reference to Canadian and other experience, however, e.g., Crough, G. Indigenous Organizations, Funding and Accountability: Comparative Reforms in Canada and Australia, Report Series No. 2. Darwin: Australian National University North Australia Research Unit, 1997; and Jull, P. "The political future of Torres Strait." *Indigenous Law Bulletin* 4 7 (November 1997): 4–9.

12. In the 1998 federal election the Coalition's vote fell eight per cent and Pauline Hanson's new party's share was eight-and-a-half per cent.

13. See Pauline Hanson's speeches in federal Parliament 1 October 1997 and 2 June 1998, and her campaign speech in Longreach, 11 September 1998, all on-line at her party site. The conspiracy theory is found in various texts, notably *The New Citizen* 3 11, February–March 1995, Melbourne, an organ of the Lyndon Larouche movement.

14. Dodson, M. Indigenous Social Justice, Vol. 1, Strategies and Recommendations, Submission to the Parliament of the Commonwealth of Australia on the Social Justice Package by Michael Dodson, Aboriginal and Torres Strait Islander Social Justice Commissioner, Human Rights and Equal Opportunity Commission, Canberra, 1995. The other two reports in this exercise are Recognition, Rights and Reform: A Report to Government on Native Title Social Justice Measures, Native Title Social Justice Advisory Committee, Aboriginal and Torres Strait Islander Commission (ATSIC), Canberra, 1995; and Going Forward: Social Justice for the First Australians, A Submission to the Commonwealth Government from the Council for Aboriginal Reconciliation, Canberra.

15. "Australia" sections of *The Indigenous World*, 1994–95, and, 1995–96. Copenhagen: International Work Group for Indigenous Affairs.

16. The communique notes that the Constitutional Convention of 2–13 February resolved that a preamble should include among other things "acknowledgement of the original occupancy and custodianship of Australia by aboriginal peoples and Torres Strait Islanders" and "affirmation of respect for our unique land and the environment." It adds that it was resolved that "The following matters be considered for inclusion in the preamble: [two items with the third and last being] Recognition that Aboriginal people and Torres Strait islanders have continuing rights by virtue of their status as Australia's indigenous peoples." Finally the convention called for "a further Constitutional Convention" some years after institution of a republic on whose agenda various items would be, including "constitutional aspects of indigenous reconciliation."

17. The standard and rather Eurocentric history is Powell, A. *Far Country: A Short History of the Northern Territory*. Carlton, Victoria: Melbourne University Press, 1982.

18. Crough, G. et al. Aboriginal Economic Development in Central Australia, Report for the Combined Aboriginal Organizations of Alice Springs, NT, 1989; and Crough, G. Visible and Invisible: Aboriginal People in the Economy of Northern Australia. Darwin: Australian National University North Australia Research Unit, 1993.

19. Downing, J. *Ngurra Walytia: Country of My Spirit*. Darwin: Australian National University North Australia Research Unit, 1988.

20. Peterson, N. "Capitalism, Culture and Land Rights," *Social Analysis* 18 (December 1985): 85–101.

21. Williams, P. *The Victory: The Inside Story of the Takeover of Australia*. Sydney: Allen & Unwin, 1997.

OLGA HAVNEN

22. Pritchard, S. "Constitutional Developments in the Northern Territory: The Kalkaringi Convention." *Indigenous Law Bulletin* 4 15 (October 1998): 12–13; followed by "The Kalkaringi Statement, Constitutional Convention of the Combined Aboriginal Nations of Central Australia," 14–15.

23. Pritchard, S. (ed.). *Indigenous Peoples, the United Nations and Human Rights*. Sydney: Zed Books, London & Federation Press, 1998; Dodson, M. "International Perspectives." Second Report, Aboriginal and Torres Strait Islander Social Justice Commissioner, Human Rights and Equal Opportunities Commission. Sydney: Commonwealth of Australia (1994): 203–219; Dodson, M. "International Connections." *Indigenous Social Justice* Vol. 1, Strategies and Recommendations (see note 13) (1995): 41–48; and two related pieces by Jull, P. "First World Indigenous Internationalism After Twenty-five Years." *Indigenous Law Bulletin* 4 9 (February 1998): 8–11; and "Indigenous 'Stunts' Abroad." *Arena Magazine* 33 (February-March 1998): 37–38.

24. One recent study compares Northern Australia and Northern Canada, Young, E. *Third World in the First: Development and Indigenous Peoples*. London & New York: Routledge, 1995. See also Jull, P. and S. Roberts (eds). *The Challenge of Northern Regions*. Darwin: Australian National University North Australia Research Unit, 1991.

25. Richardson, B. J., D. Craig and B. Boer. *Regional Agreements for Indigenous Lands and Cultures in Canada*, Darwin: Australian National University North Australia Research Unit, 1995; Jull, P. and D. Craig. "Reflections on Regional Agreements: Yesterday, Today and Tomorrow." *Australian Indigenous Law Reporter* 2 4 (1997): 475–493; and Edmunds, M. (ed). Regional Agreements: Key Issues in Australia, Volume 1, Summaries, Native Title Research Unit. Canberra: Australian Institute of Aboriginal and Torres Strait Islander Studies, 1998.

26. Tennant, P., *Aboriginal Peoples and Politics: The Indian Land Question in British Columbia, 1849–1989*. Vancouver: University of British Columbia Press, 1990.

A Global Search
for Justice

Doreen Spence is the founder and executive director of
the Canadian Indigenous Women's Resource Institute.
She is also a representative to the United Nations
Working Group on Indigenous Populations and a
member of the International Spiritual Elders Council of
New Zealand. She is the recipient of several awards,
including the Chief David Crowchild Award and the
Alberta Human Rights Award.

THE ISSUES SURROUNDING INDIGENOUS PEOPLES are so overwhelming
when compared to other cultural groups in the mosaic of the international
community. It is impossible to address the complexities of these issues and do
full justice to the people. Firstly, I wish to give thanks to the old ones who left
their sacred teachings behind through oral traditions. I wish to acknowledge
above all our elders who have guided us and shared their wisdom, encouraging
us along the way. I also wish to thank those who so tenaciously ploughed the
way to the United Nations Working Group on Indigenous Peoples and the representatives of indigenous organizations who came to the United Nations to make
the working group a strong international voice for indigenous issues and
concerns.

There are four issues that are critical to the indigenous peoples in terms of
human rights and a global search for justice: the Decade of the World's
Indigenous Peoples, the Draft Declaration on the Rights of Indigenous Peoples,
the need for a permanent forum for indigenous peoples and Martinez Cobo's
report on the study of treaties. In 1982 the United Nations Human Rights
Commission and the Economic and Social Council approved the establishment
of the UN Working Group on Indigenous Populations. The working group is an
organ of the Subcommission on the Prevention of Discrimination and Protection
of Minorities. The working group is an important platform for the dissemination of information and exchange of views among indigenous peoples,
governments, NGOs and others.

■ The Decade

Following a recommendation by the World Conference on Human Rights, the General Assembly proclaimed the International Decade of the World's Indigenous Peoples (1995–2004). It was launched on 9 December 1994 and proclaimed by the General Assembly in its resolution 48/1630 on 21 December 1993 under the theme Indigenous People: Partners In Action. My interpretation of "Partners In Action" is two groups of people working in mutual respect for the benefit of all.

The main goal of the decade is the strengthening of international cooperation for the solution of problems faced by indigenous people in such areas as human rights, the environment, development, health, culture and education. Indigenous people have expressed grave concern that exploitation has taken place upon their indigenous lands without the enjoyment of huge profits made by corporations. Indigenous peoples continue to live in substandard living conditions. This gives the international community the opportunity to take up the challenge of alleviating the deplorable situation of the indigenous peoples. It would also intensify efforts to respond to the legitimate demands and needs of the indigenous peoples.

This has been highlighted in the Royal Commission on Aboriginal Peoples in Canada and should be adopted along with the Draft Declaration on Aboriginal Peoples. In this respect, it is important to achieve the following goals: raise international awareness; promote and protect the rights over autonomy; empowerment to retain cultural identity and social identity and giving full respect to their cultural values, languages, traditions and social organization; educate the indigenous and nonindigenous communities on these same rights; consult and cooperate with indigenous people and take part in the decisions that affect their daily lives; acknowledge the value of diversity and culture in the social organization of the world's indigenous people; train and provide technical assistance to indigenous peoples, as well as supporting their initiatives; and improve the socioeconomic conditions of indigenous populations and their political participation in international decision-making.

The decade offers an opportunity to further strengthen the partnership established between the indigenous peoples and the international community and between states and indigenous peoples. The decade is an opportunity for the international community to redress the legacy of colonization and marginalization. Major accomplishments of the International Decade would be the adoption of the Draft Declaration by the United Nations General Assembly Resolution 50/157 for the establishment of a permanent forum for indigenous people within the United Nations.

This recommendation was made in the Vienna Declaration and Programme of Action and adopted at the World Conference on Human Rights in June 1993. Discussions are still under way to determine the mandate of the permanent forum, its membership, structure and funding. The purpose of the forum would be to create a permanent arena where indigenous peoples could raise and discuss with government matters of interest to them. Governments, intergovernmental and nongovernmental organizations and other interested parties should plan activities to raise awareness of the issues of concern to indigenous people. The Working Group on Indigenous People has become one of the largest UN forums in the field of human rights. In 1998 nearly one thousand indigenous people attended the working group. The Working Group On Indigenous Peoples appointed Mr. Miguel Alfonso Martinez to develop a study on treaties, agreements and other constructive arrangement between states and indigenous populations.

▆▆▆ The Draft Declaration

The working group began preparing a Draft Declaration on the Rights of Indigenous Peoples in 1985 and submitted it to the Commission on Human Rights for consideration. The draft is now being discussed in an open-ended intersessional working group, set up by the Commission on Human Rights Resolution 1995/32 of 3 March 1995. The Draft Declaration on the Rights of Indigenous Peoples represents one of the most important developments in the promotion and protection of the basic rights and fundamental freedoms of indigenous peoples.

Since the adoption of the Universal Declaration of Human Rights, and despite all the achievements by the United Nations in the field of human rights, much remains to be done to address human rights violations that are still taking place around the world. For the survival of indigenous peoples, it is imperative that the declaration be adopted. The declaration covers the preservation and development of ethnic characteristics and distinct identities and protection against ethnocide and genocide.

The Draft Declaration would provide indigenous peoples with the right to be as free and equal in dignity and rights as all other peoples under the Universal Declaration of Human Rights; the right to self-determination and to freely determine their political status and freely pursue their economic, social and cultural development; the right to practise and revitalize their cultural tradition and customs, and also the right to develop and teach their spiritual and religious traditions; the right to establish and control their education systems and institutions providing education in their own languages; the right to participate fully at all levels of decision-making in matters which may effect their rights, lives and destinies; and the right of indigenous people to their lands, territories and resources.

Under the Draft Declaration (E/CN.4/1995/2 pg. 114 VII Article 36), indigenous peoples have the right to the recognition, observance and enforcement of treaties, agreements and other constructive arrangements concluded with states or their successors, according to their original spirit and intent, and to have states honour and respect such treaties, agreements and other constructive arrangements. Conflicts and disputes which cannot otherwise be settled should be submitted to competent international bodies agreed to by all parties concerned. The draft further states in VIII Article 37, that states shall take effective and appropriate measures, in consultation with the indigenous peoples concerned, to give full effect to the provisions of this Declaration. The rights recognized herein shall be adopted and included in national legislation in such a manner that indigenous peoples can avail themselves of such rights in practice.

Under Article 40, the organs and specialized agencies of the United Nations system and other intergovernmental organizations shall contribute to the full realization of the provisions of this Declaration through the mobilization, *inter alia,* of financial cooperation and technical assistance. Ways and means of ensuring participation of indigenous people on issues affecting them shall be established. The Royal Commission on Aboriginal Peoples repeatedly reinforced the need for ongoing dialogue and full participation of indigenous peoples.

◼ Permanent Forum

In 1995 a workshop was held in Copenhagen following the recommendations by the World Conference on Human Rights that the General Assembly considered the establishment of a Permanent Forum for the Indigenous Peoples in the United Nations. The need for a Permanent Forum for Indigenous Peoples at the highest level of the United Nations body is imperative. This was voiced by the majority at this Working Group on Indigenous Peoples. The indigenous people still have many grievances to be addressed. Locally there has been absolutely no information regarding the Decade of Indigenous Peoples. While the Canadian government prides itself in being a leader in human rights, from an indigenous perspective this often difficult to accept. Most indigenous communities have found that their governments do not deal effectively with many of their concerns.

The United Nations is a safe place and the only political forum that attempts to address indigenous issues. Clearly, the Declaration on Indigenous Peoples must be given the utmost attention and be accepted and passed without any changes before the end of this decade. The United Nations must accept this declaration. Senior officials at the United Nations must ensure that this declaration is given the highest priority and accept this as a legal document in its present form. The United Nations' mandate is the promotion of fundamental freedoms and rights for all populations. Indigenous peoples make up a large percentage of the total international population, yet their freedoms and rights continue to be under-represented.

■■■■ Martinez Cobo's Final Report on the Study of Treaties

In July 1998 Miguel Alfonso Martinez, special rapporteur to the Working Group on Indigenous Peoples, released his final report (unedited version) on the study of treaties, agreements and other constructive arrangements between states and indigenous populations. The report addresses many of the indigenous peoples interpretations, stating:

> Article 256. General conclusion concerns the issue of recognition of indigenous peoples' right to their lands and their resources and to continue engaging, unmolested, in their traditional economic activities on those lands. This is the paramount problem to be addressed in any effort to establish a more solid, equitable and durable relationship between the indigenous and nonindigenous sectors in multinational societies. Due to their special relationship—spiritual and material—with their lands, the special rapporteur believes that very little or no progress can be made in this regard without tackling, solving and redressing in a way acceptable to the indigenous peoples' the question of the uninterrupted dispossession of this unique resource which is vital to their lives and survival.

Further, Article 264 states, as recognized in the United Nations Draft Declaration on the Rights of Indigenous Peoples submitted by the working group to the sub-commission and adopted by the latter, that all the human rights and freedoms recognized in international instruments—either legally binding norms or nonbinding standards—accepted by the state in which they now live, are applicable to indigenous peoples and individuals now living within their borders. This also applies to all rights and freedoms recognized in the domestic legislation of the state concerned, for all individuals and social groups under its jurisdiction. In the view of the special rapporteur this is so, provided that the manner in which said rights and freedoms are recognized in said instruments is, in fact, consistent with indigenous customs, societal institutions and legal traditions.

It also states in Article 286 that it should be taken into account that indigenous practices of treaty-making were totally oral in nature and written documents were absent from this process. In addition, it was extremely difficult to fully follow all aspects of the negotiation through translators (who, most likely, were not always completely accurate), not to mention the fine print in the written version submitted to them in an alien language by the nonindigenous negotiators. Further, it was impossible for them, in most instances, to produce a written copy with their understanding of the rights and obligations established in said instruments.

Article 36 of the draft establishes that "Indigenous peoples have the right to the recognition, observance and enforcement of treaties, agreements and other constructive arrangements concluded with States or their successors, according to their original spirit and intent, and to have States honour and respect such treaties, agreements and other constructive arrangements."

In conclusion, the text of "Human Rights: The Rights of Indigenous Peoples" states that there must be ways to promote human rights in relation to the specific circumstances of individuals and groups properly identified as indigenous, in particular to ensure protection against exploitation by nonindigenous structures. This forum is another step to achieve human rights and assist indigenous peoples in their global search for justice. It is evident that we have a long way to go when it comes to the issues of human rights and indigenous peoples. I believe these four issues pertaining to indigenous peoples and a global search for justice are positive steps forward to achieve these goals.

Bioethics and Biotechnology

BUILDING A HUMAN RIGHTS FRAMEWORK

RICHARD J. SOBSEY

Human Rights, Bioethics and Disability

Richard J. Sobsey is a professor of educational psychology at the University of Alberta, a director with the J.P. Das Developmental Disabilities Centre and the principal investigator of the Violence and Disability Project. He was recently elected a fellow of the American Association of Mental Retardation.

PEOPLE WITH DISABILITIES have been and continue to be frequent victims of discriminatory concepts and practices, including gross violations of human rights. Rather than helping to affirm the human rights of people with disabilities, many bioethicists and much that is written in the name of bioethics have contributed to the denial of the human rights of people with disabilities. This is not to negate the fact that bioethics as a field and many specific bioethicists have made positive contributions to furthering the rights of people with disabilities. What is needed is a new bioethics which is based on a human rights agenda.

The violations of human rights experienced by people with disabilities are many, too many to attempt to list here. Therefore, I will present only a relatively small number of examples. Although most of the examples are related to people with developmental disabilities, most apply to a people with a wide range of disabilities.

Life, Liberty and Equal Protection

In many parts of the world, violence is a reality for people with disabilities. The University of Alberta's Violence and Disability Project is currently analyzing 730 cases of homicide resulting in the death of more than 1,200 people with developmental disabilities. These cases take many forms. For example, in the area of South Africa previously known as Venda, ritual killings have been frequently reported. According to one report in the *San Jose Mercury News* (Lyman, 1992), "The most infamous aspect of this village spiritualism is the use of human body parts for medicine. The victims are usually mentally or physically handicapped or illegitimate, thus deemed to be a small loss to the community" (P. 2A). Ironically, there has been much less public outrage and

237

media attention given to this slaughter of people with disabilities to make potions than to the corresponding poaching of wildlife for the same purpose.

According to a report from Human Rights Watch Asia (1996), more than one thousand children died because of maltreatment in the Shanghai Children's Welfare Institute and other similar Chinese facilities between 1986 and 1992. While these children are described as "orphans," they are more typically abandoned disabled children who are viewed as poor candidates for adoption because of their disabilities. Many of these children were sent to "dying rooms" where they were tied to their beds and systematically deprived of the necessities of life until they died of starvation, exposure or the lack of required medicines. According to the report, the mortality rate was 22.2 per cent although Chinese authorities argued that it was only about nineteen per cent. Death rates at other similar facilities, the report found, were even worse: "[The Henan Provincial] orphanage, which in 1989 had a stated capacity of thirty beds, began the year with a population of twenty-three infants and children. During the year, seventy-two orphans were admitted to the institution, four left the orphanage alive and sixty-two died, leaving the year-end population at twenty-five" (Human Rights Watch, 1996).

In addition to these deaths, the report detailed physical and sexual abuse of children and embezzlement of funds. China responded to the issue in several ways. First, they denied the charges and allowed press and representatives to tour the facility, but only after a long delay that allowed the facility to be substantially changed largely through the transfer of residents and abusive practices to other institutions (Human Rights Watch, 1996). Second, they denied the charges while making attempts to prosecute Zhang Shuyuan, the physician who had supplied most of the evidence of the abuses to human rights agencies. Finally, the *People's Daily* published an extensive report of abuse of children in American institutions suggesting that China was unfairly singled out for political reasons.

This final defence that the US and other wealthy nations have their own share of abuses of human rights of people with disabilities clearly has some basis in fact, although the universality of such abuses does not make them more acceptable. For example, during almost the same period as the one used to record the deaths of Chinese children, Wall and Partridge (1997) published a study of deaths in the intensive care nursery at a California hospital. According to the report, eighty-three per cent of children who died did so because treatment was withheld or withdrawn. Only seventeen per cent died in spite of continued treatment. While the most frequent reason for withholding or withdrawing treatment was the belief that further treatment would have been futile, twenty-three per cent of those whose treatment was withdrawn could likely have been saved, but were allowed to die only because of "quality of life issues."

In most of these cases, the reason was someone's judgement that living with a severe disability would be worse than death. Equally disturbing was that for an additional twenty-eight per cent of children who died from the withholding or withdrawing of care, quality of life was presented as a reason along with futility. How much the judgement that treatment was futile was influenced by the belief that the child's life was not worth saving is impossible to determine, but many practical examples in my own and others experience suggest this kind of influence is frequent and substantial. Furthermore, in some cases, health care providers create conditions of futility and use those conditions as a reason for allowing a patient to die. Since this study was based on a single hospital during a particular time period, it is difficult to know how typical these figures are, but numerous other studies have suggested that similar patterns have been long-established trends (e.g., Duff & Campbell, 1973).

▮▮▮▮ The Role of Bioethics

Many bioethicists have supported or justified these death-making practices by using philosophical reasoning. In fact, many have advanced a variety of arguments in favour of legitimizing the killing of people with disabilities. Popular bioethicists, Joseph Fletcher and Peter Singer, for example, have advanced arguments that people with severe disabilities are not persons and therefore have no human rights and can be killed with impunity. In Singer's view, "Killing a defective infant is not morally equivalent to killing a person" (1979, p. 138). More recently, Singer has elaborated this view by suggesting that some animals such as gorillas and chimpanzees should have human rights, while some humans with severe disabilities should be denied these rights (Singer, 1994). David Larson, co-director of the Centre for Christian Ethics at Loma Linda University, provides a clearer statement of the implications of this view, suggesting that it is ethically appropriate "to transplant [a heart] from a [severely mentally handicapped] child to save the life of a healthy baboon or chimpanzee" (quoted in Shapiro, 1993, p. 273). A particularly interesting distortion in this statement is the notion that a baboon is considered healthy in spite of a critical heart problem while a mentally handicapped child who may be viable and robust is not.

While Singer is unclear about exactly where we should draw the line between those protected by law and those who are not, Fletcher is more precise, suggesting that IQ scores should be used to decide who is and who is not a person. Kluge (1994), suggests that once we give competent people the right to choose their own deaths, it would be discriminatory not to allow some other decision-makers to choose death for those whose disabilities do not allow them to make their own choices. Testifying before the same Canadian Senate Committee, several other bioethicists argued that we should first agree in principle to the legalization of assisted suicide and euthanasia and only later work out how we will prevent abuses and mistakes that result in killing people who do not really want to die.

Even where safeguards against wrongful deaths have been proposed, they tend to be substantially less than those used in the notorious Nazi euthanasia program that killed 275,000 Germans with disabilities during the 1930s and 1940s. Those procedures required the approval of two doctors and an appeals process. This is not to say that the Nazi safeguards were effective, but rather to question the protection of lesser safeguards. More importantly, currently proposed safeguards are largely categorical rather than procedural. They restrict who can be killed to those with terminal diseases and chronic disabilities. Yet if suicide can be a rational and autonomous decision, why should it be assisted and encouraged for those who choose to die because of disease or disability while it is being prevented or discouraged for thoose who chose it for other reasons?

Why is it more acceptable to kill someone who faces a lifetime of disability than someone who faces a lifetime of disgrace and imprisonment? Do we believe that disability and nothing else is worse than death? A police officer who kills a criminal to prevent the suffering of disgrace and prison is not more or less compassionate than a physician who kills a patient to prevent the suffering of disability. Furthermore, there is no reason to doubt a police officer who claims such compassionate motives while believing the physician who makes the same claim.

All these justifications for denial of personhood are outrageous. They trivialize and endanger the lives of many thousands of people with disabilities. While the reasons for my own view (and that of many others) of these arguments as abhorrent and potentially catastrophic are many, the point that I wish to make here is that these bioethical arguments are devoid of any human rights perspective. The logic behind the arguments is sometimes sound. But the values and assumptions that they are based on are fundamentally flawed and the antithesis of the most fundamental principle of human rights—the principle of equality, the belief that all human beings have rights. The same logic and assumptions that are accepted in the bubble universe of bioethics would be untenable in anything but the most repressive dictatorship.

History provides too many examples of the denial of personhood and basic human rights to various groups on the basis of religion, race, gender, sexual preference, poverty, disability and a variety of other characteristics. The human rights movement cannot reject such violations of fundamental rights based on any of these characteristics while it passively ignores and accepts violations based on others. Here in Canada, for instance, in the early years of this century, some advocates of women's rights argued that an effective balance could be achieved by giving voting rights to woman and at the same time taking them away from Catholics and immigrants from Eastern Europe. Clearly, any legitimate view of human rights must be all-inclusive. Those who consider themselves advocates for human rights must fight the injustices faced by people with disabilities with the same vigour as they fight for other marginalized groups.

The artificial separation between bioethics and human rights has allowed bioethicists to function in an artificial environment where their arguments and the ramifications of them are restricted to a medical setting. The denial of the personhood of people with disabilities cannot be restricted to medical purposes. When the equality rights of any child or adult are denied in a hospital—when he or she is declared a nonperson—those rights are equally deniable in every other setting. The arguments of Singer, Kluge, Fletcher, Larson and others cannot be isolated from other aspects of life. If it is a lesser crime to take the heart of a child with a disability, it is also a lesser crime to rape or beat that child. If it is acceptable that a child with a disability can be "sacrificed" for body parts for transplantation to a more valued individual, it will be acceptable that that child can be slaughtered for body parts for making potions or for food. If it is a lesser crime to kill a person because his or her quality of life is judged to be poor because of disability, it is also a lesser crime to kill a person whose quality of life is judged as poor because of homelessness, grief, poverty, addiction or even discrimination.

Perhaps not surprisingly, people with disabilities are already among the most frequent victims of crime. They are victims of violence two to four times as often as others are (Sobsey, 1994). More disturbingly, crimes committed against people with disabilities appear to be less frequently investigated or prosecuted. Most disturbingly, even when convictions occur, there appears to be a pattern of lighter sentences for crimes committed against people with disabilities. The notions that people with disabilities provoke the crimes against them or are better off dead anyway are rampant in our society.

These bioethical arguments of worthlessness are extended to the most unlikely of circumstances. Among the homicides we are currently studying, all of these trends are clear. Of those sentenced for these homicides, fifty per cent were sentenced to prison terms of less than five years. One young woman was burned to death by adoptive parents who bought a $100,000 life insurance policy on her, spread gasoline around the garage, locked her in and set it afire. They were allowed to plead guilty to insurance fraud with no further charges. According to the arguments of Singer and Fletcher, she might not be a person, and thus the only crime committed was against the insurance agency. According to Kluge's argument, as substitute decision-makers these adoptive parents had every right to kill her as a suicide by proxy.

Another case involved a child who was starved to death by a mother already under investigation for neglect of her other children. The death was ruled a homicide but the prosecutor simply chose not to lay charges. Local prosecutorial guidelines permit such actions where prosecution is not deemed to be in the public interest.

Still another case involved the murder of a young woman with a mental disability by two young men who said that they set out to commit a hate crime. After abducting her, they chased her and tried to shoot her with a crossbow, then shot her repeatedly with a pellet gun before finally killing her by shooting her in the head with a .22-calibre gun. After being apprehended they confessed their crime but suggested that since she had a poor quality of life, their act was "a gift" rather than a crime. Their argument is no more or less defensible than that of the bioethicists who present similar rationale. It is simply less eloquent.

The pervasive nature of such beliefs, that people with disabilities are lesser beings, can be seen in cases like the Glen Ridge rape case. After a group of high school athletes raped a classmate, the community was shaken. The dominant concern expressed by community members was not for the victim of the crime but how the futures of the young men who raped her might be jeopardized (Sobsey, 1994). In another New Jersey case, many people in the community knew who committed the arson that killed some of the men who lived in a group home but remained silent to protect the perpetrators. Many of those who knew who committed this crime had fought to keep the group home for people with mental retardation out of the community and saw those who torched it as heroes.

The intrusions on the human rights of people with disabilities are not limited to homicide. Many people with disabilities are unnecessarily segregated from society, subjected to torture in the name of treatment and subjected to a variety of other intrusions. For example, a recent series of articles in the *Hartford Courant* (Weiss, 1998) reports on 143 confirmed cases of death in restraints in mental hospitals, nursing homes and similar facilities. While the deaths are in themselves shocking, these deaths represent only a tiny tip of the iceberg of hundreds of thousands of people who, often for trivial reasons, spend significant amounts of their lives in restraint. For example, one of the women who died in restraint had been assaulted and restrained by staff because she refused to give up a photograph of her family when commanded to do so.

In considering the devastating implications of arguments against the personhood and basic human rights of people with disabilities, it is important not to assume that all bioethicists hold such values and views. Many hold views that are more consistent with human rights perspectives. Some have proven to be powerful advocates for the rights of people with disabilities. Nevertheless, even among many of those who do not share the more extreme views, there has been a passive tolerance for the depersonalization of people with disabilities that would not exist if the same propositions were made regarding other marginalized groups.

■ Conclusion

People with disabilities have been frequently denied basic human rights. The field of bioethics has contributed to that denial through the presentation of rationale supporting unequal treatment. The development of bioethical arguments that deny human rights has occurred in part because bioethics has operated in isolation from the mainstream of society and not been informed by the principles of human rights. Everyone who considers herself or himself to be an advocate for human rights needs to consider the human rights issues facing people with disabilities and to work for the equal protection of the rights of all human beings. The field of bioethics must not continue to function in isolation from human rights and ethical concerns that exist in all areas of human experience.

REFERENCES

Duff, R. S. and A. G. M. Campbell. "Moral and Ethical Dilemmas in the Special Care Nursery." *New England Journal of Medicine* 173 (1973): 890–894.

Fletcher, J. *Moral Responsibility: Situation Ethics at Work*. Philadelphia: Westminster Press (1967).

Human Rights Watch. The Chinese Orphanages: A Follow-Up. *Human Rights Watch* 8 1: (March 1996). [Internet version available at:
http://www.hk.super.net/~hrwhkweb/summaries/s.china963.2.html#US]

Human Rights Watch Asia. *Death by Default*. New York: Author (1996).

Lyman, R. "Tribal Customs can Mean Death in South Africa." *San Jose Mercury News* (31 Jan. 1992): 2A.

Shapiro, J. *No Pity: People with Disabilities Forging a New Civil Rights Movement*. New York: Times Books (1993).

Singer, P. *Practical Ethics*. Cambridge: Cambridge University Press (1979).

Singer, P. *Rethinking Life and Death*. Melbourne: The Text Publishing Co. (1994).

Sobsey, D. *Violence and Abuse in the Lives of People with Disabilities*. Baltimore: Paul H. Brookes (1994).

Wall, S. N. and J. C. Partridge. "Death in the Intensive Care Nursery: Physician Practice of Withdrawing or Withholding Life Support." *Pediatrics* 99 1 (1997): 64–70.

Weiss, E. M. "A Nationwide Pattern of Death." *Hartford Courant* (11 October 1998),
http://www.courant.com/news/special/restraint/day1.stm

RICHARD J. SOBSEY

SOLOMON R. BENATAR

The Biotechnology Era

A Story of Two Lives and Two Worlds

Solomon R. Benatar is a professor and chairman of the Department of Medicine at the University of Cape Town and the head of the UCT Centre for Bioethics. He is actively involved with the US National Academy of Sciences' Committee on Human Rights as well as the Commonwealth Medical Association's Project on Health and Human Rights.

A CONFERENCE CELEBRATING THE FIFTIETH ANNIVERSARY of the Universal Declaration of Human Rights is an important milestone event. Much has been achieved in advancing the quality of human life in the past fifty years and human rights has become a new standard of civilization by which nations are being judged.[1] However, it must be acknowledged that an enormous amount of work remains to be done to ensure the achievement of even basic human rights for a large proportion of the world's population.

While we celebrate the achievements of the past fifty years, we cannot be complacent with our successes. It is through an approach which is both critical and constructive that further progress can be made. Simply stated, the goals of human rights are to safeguard human dignity and the fundamental rights and freedoms of individuals. This much is hardly contentious. Neither is the value we place on the concept of human rights, as evidenced by this conference. However, we must surely concede that despite many thoughtful documents and statements, considerable debate continues on what counts as a human right, how such rights can be justified and, even more important, how they can be achieved in practice. This task will become more difficult as biotechnology provides information that has implications beyond the rights of individuals, making it possible to take decisions with implications for future people.

We have entered an era in which the application of advances in biotechnology will have a profound impact on human life. In order to understand how

245

the power of new biotechnology may affect our lives in the future I shall begin by describing two very different lives and then, in the context of these, reflect on the state of the world fifty years after the Universal Declaration.

Two Lives

The year is 1998, the place Zimbabwe, and the person is a twenty-eight-year-old black woman. She is emaciated, hungry, HIV positive, suffering from tuberculosis and pregnant with her fourth child. She has no hope of access to drug treatment for tuberculosis, one of the most cost effective treatments available in the world at one American dollar per year of life saved. She has lost two children from lack of access to a few days of appropriate treatment for malaria and diarrhoea. Her third child is stunted from malnutrition and is emotionally listless as a result of the social and intellectual deprivation which has characterized her life. This small family represents over 600 million people who live in Africa and a total of one billion people in the world who live on less than one dollar per day. Another three billion people live under marginally better conditions on about three dollars per day.

The year is 1998, the place Edmonton, the person a fifty-six-year-old white Zimbabwean-born physician. Access to regular insulin injections for over forty years has enabled him to survive childhood, to receive tertiary education, to enjoy a fulfilling family, academic and social life and to provide similar opportunities for his children. He represents one billion people in the world who have been able to achieve their human potential and live privileged lives without knowing hunger or deprivation of any kind. The gulf that separates the life experiences of these two people and their families makes it almost impossible for the one to truly understand the life-style of the other.

The State of the World

It is necessary to acknowledge with regret that gross violations of human rights continue on a massive scale around the world (including Europe and the US) in association with proliferating wars, torture, ethnic conflict, refugeeism, police brutality, exponential population growth, economic exploitation and widespread poverty which reflect the dark side of progress during the 20th century.[2-7]

As we approach the next millennium we need to ponder the view expressed by the recently deceased Sir Isaiah Berlin, a distinguished Western philosopher, that "the 20th century has been the worst in Western history."[2] The evidence for this deteriorating state of the world includes widening economic disparities between rich and poor, flagrant disregard for others (especially distant others) and for our natural environment, failure to achieve sustainable development in many countries, growth of the underclass in wealthy countries, recrudescence of infectious diseases such as tuberculosis which could have been conquered, the spread of several new infectious diseases, including HIV infection, across the globe and progressive ecological degradation which threatens future generations and planetary survival.[2, 3, 5, 7, 8]

The polarization of the world, into a shrinking core of people with access to all they want and an enlarging pool of people at the periphery who are denied even basic human rights, can be explained (at least in part) by the abuse of power. The privileged world needs to better understand and acknowledge this if there is to be any hope of even beginning to rectify such disparities and to ensure that new forms of power associated with control of biological processes will be used to enhance human well-being universally rather then selectively.[3, 5–7]

In the past, domination of some by others was overtly manifest within the power structures of empires, feudal states, religions, kingdoms and the institutions of slavery and racism. New and more sophisticated forms of power in successive eras have been covertly used to perpetuate the domination which was previously maintained through more overt processes. Expenditure on modern forms of warfare and weapons of mass destruction has diverted resources away from the development necessary to enrich human life. In addition, a considerable portion of the resources loaned to poor countries for the purposes of national development has been misused for the purchase of weapons.[3] Military and imperial oppression have been supplemented by increasingly powerful forms of economic oppression during the past fifty years. This has been achieved not only through the efforts of powerful nations, but also through major transnational organizations (such as the International Monetary Fund [IMF] and the World Bank) that are much less accountable than governments.

Control has been gained over the economies, lives, health and suffering of billions of people through such modern economic processes as the unscrupulous creation of massive and unpayable debt by the linkage of aid to the purchase of military weapons and repayment mechanisms which impose austere structural adjustment programs; the eclectic application of free trade and protectionist practices to facilitate the extraction of natural resources required for economic growth in the industrialized world; and the use of modern information technology to repackage money and manipulate massive transactions over vast distances almost instantaneously, with devastating effects on the currency of weak nations.[3, 5, 10] These processes, together with the support for despots by powerful nations merely to satisfy their foreign policy aspirations, form the substance of a history that in due course should be unravelled in the equivalent of a global Truth and Reconciliation Commission. While the poor are not themselves blameless, there is a need to examine more thoroughly the role of industrialized nations in creating a polarizing world, and the consequent moral obligations which must extend beyond interpersonal relationships to connect all the peoples and nations in the world.

Following his extensive travels through "the landscapes of modern ethnic war" in Serbia, Croatia, Bosnia, Rwanda, Burundi, Angola and Afghanistan, Michael Ignatief wrote eloquently about the mixture of moral solidarity and hubris which impels powerful nations to embark on a "brief adventure in putting the world to rights." With regard to exploitation he notes that, "[I]n the 19th century, imperial interests bound the two worlds together: ivory, gold and copper sent the imperial agents into the heart of darkness. During the fifty years of the cold war the presence of one superpower's agents, spies, or other mercenaries in any particular ethnic war guaranteed the presence of the other on the opposing side." He goes on to ask how, "[N]ow [that] there is no narrative of imperial rivalry or ideological struggle that compels the zones of safety to make the zones of danger their business...what is left of a narrative of compassion...?"[11]

The example of South Africa "making its arduous journey back from the abyss", is used to counter despair and he argues that "as weak and as narrow as the narrative of compassion and moral commitment may be, it is infinitely stronger than it was only fifty years ago.... We are scarcely aware of the extent to which our moral imagination has been transformed since 1945 by the growth of a language and practice of moral universalism expressed above all in a shared human rights culture."[11]

Hosle, a German philosopher, in reviewing the state of the Third World as a philosophical problem linked to progress in the industrialized world, concludes that rather than seeking solutions in compassion, altruism or reparations for past actions, rational self-interest provides sufficient reasons for wealthy nations to address these issues.[12] In his view, and others who have written similarly, the growing populations of deprived people within rich nations and within the poor periphery now pose threats from which none can escape and which therefore cannot be ignored. "Violence from below", massive refugeeism, the rise and spread of new and recrudescing infectious diseases, and adverse ecological effects threaten us all.

Medical advances have also imposed major modifications on human life. Prolongation of life through a range of life support systems and transplantation, control over the ways in which we die through new approaches to death and dying, and more recently the ability to initiate life and even create it *in vitro*, with all the new problems these bring, are part of such progress. The influences of multinational drug companies and of the technological imperative on medical practice have led to unsustainable forms of medical practice and to major injustices in access to health care, even within wealthy nations that claim or desire to be just societies.[13] Unless more rational approaches are devised for the delivery of health care within nations, two- or three-tier systems will be perpetuated through discriminatory rationing processes. This may be further aggravated by the exploitation of newly available genetic data.[14]

■ Human Rights and Biotechnology

When we speak of biotechnology and human rights we need to ask ourselves whether we are speaking about the rights of the four billion people who live under wretched conditions or the one billion who live so well and have so much to look forward to through the benefits of scientific progress.

It is necessary to ask this question firstly because the disparities between the two types of lives I have mentioned have been constantly widening over the past thirty years and there is little evidence that this pattern will be reversed; secondly, because the abuse of power has been a significant force in contributing to wide disparities in human lives and to gross violations of human rights; and thirdly, because there is little to suggest that the new power which will be available in the biotechnology era will be used any more wisely than other forms of power have been used in the past.

We also need to ask several other questions. What counts as a right, how are rights justified, and how they can be achieved in practice? What does the concept of human rights and the Universal Declaration mean to our young Zimbabwean woman, and why has she not enjoyed the benefits of even basic human rights in her life? While she may have been enfranchized and never unjustly detained or tortured, she has certainly not had access to the basic biological and social resources required for human flourishing. Even after her country acquired independence from its colonizing power, wealthy nations concerned about sustaining their own economic growth have relentlessly continued to extract resources from her poor country at low prices. Massive deprivation has been created for her and for citizens of other poor nations through the sale of arms to corrupt leaders, enabling them to accumulate vast wealth and to wage unnecessary wars, often against their own citizens. Global economic processes have also continuously eroded the value of her country's currency and placed the economy of poor countries at the mercy of such unaccountable organizations as the IMF and the World Bank.[3, 9, 10]

What will happen in the era of biotechnology to improve her life? Will advances in plant, animal or human genetic engineering be of any benefit to her? Will the sentiments expressed in the Universal Declaration of the Human Genome be respected? Is it possible that genetic data from some groups of people will be exploited for economic benefit, or even more horrifyingly, to develop genocidal weapons? Will major agrochemical companies enable cheaper food to be produced or will the insistence on intellectual property rights and reduction in the biological diversity of agricultural products disrupt the economies of poor nations and ensure that food prices continue to rise and malnutrition be aggravated? If drugs for malaria and tuberculosis have not been made available in poor countries is it likely that the poor will benefit from advances in biotechnology? These questions cannot be avoided as we celebrate the fiftieth anniversary of the Universal Declaration of Human Rights.

While the Universal Declaration on the Human Genome, the first universal instrument in the field of biology, sets out to safeguard human rights, fundamental freedoms and the freedom of research, it is clear that there are many obstacles to achieving the high ideals expressed in this document.[15] Despite the statement in Article 4 that "the human genome in its natural state shall not give rise to financial gains," and in Article 6 that "no one shall be subjected to discrimination based on genetic characteristics...," there is already evidence to suggest that these requirements will be ignored. Considerations of "who will offer what to whom and at whose expense in health care in the US" have been explored in detail and concern expressed that genetic information will be used adversely to influence access to health care in a nation with "a long and disturbing history of drawing sharp distinctions among [its] citizens on the basis of race and ethnicity" as well as "a long tradition of belief in biological determinism."[14]

The implications of genetic testing for medicine and for the rights of privacy and confidentiality of individuals are many, varied and problematic. Shifting the frontier of medicine from curing diseases and caring for individual persons, towards the public health goals of preventing suffering in future generations, and even to the possibility of enhancing physical and mental capacities, poses major challenges to the concept of human rights. The ability to improve public health through mandatory vaccinations, at the cost of potential suffering of some who may have adverse reactions to vaccines, is widely accepted. While this acceptance of social benefit over individual rights does not apply to predictive and carrier testing for genetic abnormalities—and indeed the analogy drawn here is not exact. It is possible that in time public health considerations may also achieve over-riding importance and that the coercion required for such programs will threaten the rights of individuals.

Another problem is the generation of massive amounts of genomics data which is driving megamergers by companies seeking patents. The US patent and trademark office has received thousands of requests for patents on nucleic acid sequences. Major biotechnology, chemical, pharmaceutical and agribusiness companies are investing in molecular technologies. Techniques that are paving the way to controlling farming and world food production by giant agrochemical companies may threaten subsistence farmers in poor countries. Reduction of the genetic diversity of agricultural products or excessive protection of intellectual property rights, locking farmers into corporate control of production, could have profoundly adverse effects on the economies of developing countries and the lives of their citizens.[16] Attempts to patent products developed from information derived from plants used by traditional healers in developing countries and eagerness to patent components of the human genome for exclusive economic gain are viewed by the less fortunate in our world as new forms of exploitation that ignore the plight of those living in economic and social misery.

There are at least three key risks associated with the new life science industry: that the excessively high valuation of some life science conglomerates could substantially influence the international stock market; that genetically engineered products may be widely used before they have been rigorously tested; and that developments in biotechnology are outstripping public understanding and hence eroding both the trust and confidence of the public.[16]

In 1991 when the Human Genome Diversity Project was proposed, critics of the project argued that minority populations struggling for survival needed economic support and not the preservation of their genes or "immortalization" in laboratories. Recently described plans to put the health records of every Icelandic citizen into a huge database and then grant a private company the right to analyze and market the data and to exploit the genetic composition of Icelanders are other examples of practices that cause great concern.[17]

During the Truth and Reconciliation Commission's investigations into biological warfare in South Africa it was revealed that there had been programs designed to investigate methods of interfering with the ability of Africans to reproduce. This gives some credibility to more widespread fear among the marginalized and oppressed of the world that knowledge gained from the Human Genome Project and the Human Genome Diversity Project may be used for genocidal purposes.

How will individual human rights be protected under these circumstances? More declarations will not be sufficient. Against the background of power abuse in this century, it can be justifiably concluded that human rights declarations, despite their best intentions, have not achieved as much as desired to guarantee widespread access to even the most basic requirements for a decent human existence. It therefore becomes necessary to ask whether in the era of biotechnology the language of human rights alone can enable achievement of the respect we desire for all individuals.

In defence of the human rights approach as the single most powerful means of promoting human well-being, it can also be argued that failure to achieve human rights more widely is not the result of an inadequate concept of human rights, but rather that the full potential of the human rights approach has not been achieved because of simplistic or insincere use of the term and a lack of commitment by powerful nations to what a more wholesome concept of human rights means and implies for them as well as for others. A more coherent and comprehensive approach to human rights is required, with full consideration of the conceptual logic of rights language, as well as its moral grip.[7, 18]

▬ Duties and Responsibilities:
Consolidating and Expanding the Notion of Human Rights

It is generally agreed that the human rights approach to achieving human well-being has been a powerful and necessary tool. Jack Donnelly, who has written extensively about human rights, has made a strong case for the concept of human rights as a "new international standard of civilization" which has replaced the "classic" (19th century) imperialistic concept, and the subsequent (inter-war) "state-centric" logic of the sovereign equality of states. Despite arguments regarding the "size of the step taken [or] the distance remaining from the ideal," he argues that the move towards a form of international norms and law represents moral progress.[1]

The continuing violations of human rights, however, even in wealthy industrialized countries, and the intensified polarization of our world in the 20th century illustrate that more is required to ensure the moral progress we desire.[4, 6] The human rights approach must be extended by asking ourselves what responsibilities we have to others. Are rights meaningful without responsibilities? Who has these responsibilities? How can we ensure that responsibilities are honoured and reintegrated into the rights approach? Can the aims of the human rights approach be complemented by the use of other moral languages?

Both the Universal Declaration of Human Duties, recently offered as a supplement to the Universal Declaration of Human Rights, and Audrey Chapman's detailed formulation of how rights and responsibilities (which are indeed inextricably related), can be reintegrated, illustrate how the power of human rights language could be enhanced.[19, 20] Chapman expands on Mary Ann Glendon's concern that political discourse is impoverished by a human rights discourse in the US which, "far more than in other liberal democracies, is characterized by hyper-individualism, exaggerated absoluteness and silence with respect to personal, civic and collective responsibilities."

In her thorough argument for reintegrating rights and responsibilities, Chapman draws attention to the three advantages claimed by James Nickel for paying greater attention to the duties related to specific rights: moving the human rights debate in the direction of who has to do what if these rights are to be realized; more focused and specific discussions of questions of priority among rights and other important social goals; and discussions of the inadequacies of the contemporary international political and economic order. She eloquently describes the shift required from an excessively liberal human rights paradigm to a social model of human rights which links benefits and entitlements with the acceptance of a series of responsibilities. This is the starting point for such rights is the principle of respect for all persons in the context of community.[20]

The languages of virtue, love, care and solidarity are also increasingly being articulated and we should not underestimate the power of these in helping to shape our perceptions of what sort of people we should be.[21] Nelson Mandela and Desmond Tutu have been inspirational models, demonstrating the power of moral behaviour that embraces respect for human rights, tolerance, a deep sense of virtue, the ability to show solidarity with others and a spirituality which allows vengeance to be tempered by forgiveness.[23]

Bioethics and Human Rights

Both bioethics and human rights are relatively new approaches to moral behaviour which have flourished independently over the past thirty years. In recent times there has been a growing interest in linking the work of bioethics with human rights activities. While these endeavours are disparate in their intellectual and social approaches, both are concerned with fostering human well-being. The human rights movement is driven predominantly by lawyers and focused on conflict situations. It has been, to a very considerable extent, prescriptive and activist in its orientation. It has indeed been a powerful movement in the context of fear of excessive state power over individuals, the escalation of war and the pervasiveness of conflict in the 20th century, even though its full potential has not been remotely achieved.[24]

Bioethics, driven predominantly by the critical and questioning approach of philosophers, with a special focus on the doctor–patient relationship, has had a powerful influence on the balance of power in the context of medical decision-making in the complex milieu of modern medical practice. Given that health care professionals may be the first to witness human rights abuses, for example in the intimacy of families, within mental institutions, in prisons, in times of war and increasingly in relation to genetic information, it is undisputed that they have a special role in responding to human rights violations and in extending advocacy for human rights. The universality of human rights and the universality of medical ethics are thus linked by their common goal of advocacy for individuals and the task of improving human flourishing.[24-27]

It should be noted, however, that neither the thrust of bioethics nor that of human rights have included sufficient attention to issues of social justice. The limited efforts to promote social justice have enjoyed a singular lack of success. For example, the admirable rights-based argument for universal access to health care in the US proposed by the American Association for the Advancement of Science and the advocacy of the American College of Physicians for such universal access have been dismal failures. The impotence of such a rights approach is especially noteworthy within a powerful nation in which the notion of human rights is championed.

Complacency and self-satisfaction with an approach to human rights which suffers from the defects described by Glendon, Nickel and Chapman and which focuses on the abuses perpetrated against identifiable individuals, especially in other nations, should not be allowed to eclipse a more comprehensive and self-critical approach which could have profound effects on the lives and well-being of many.[5,7] Of course a more comprehensive approach will be more difficult to implement than merely chastizing others. As Mark Twain wrote: "Tis noble to do good, and nobler still to teach others to do good, but also more difficult."

New Ways of Thinking Required to Make Moral Progress

More than bioethics and human rights advocacy will be needed to make moral progress. A deeper understanding of what it means to be a citizen in an increasingly interdependent world will need to embrace renewed concepts of civic citizenship, solidarity and concern for others, even those very distant from our own lives. New ways of thinking about ourselves, our relationships to others, including future generations and our ecological system, are necessary in order to link concepts of human rights to bioethics in its broadest interpretation and to promote social justice within and between nations.

Shifts in both mind-set and attitude are essential. This will involve going beyond mind-sets characterized by a narrow conception of human rights, egotistical forms of individualism, linear mechanistic formulations for societal functions, institutional ways of thinking that tend to become tyrannical and international relations based on "realism," power and short-term perspectives on human life and well-being.

A new paradigm would emphasize a broader conception of human rights closely integrated with responsibilities, a concept of individualism within a context of interdependence (solidarity) which includes concern for population well-being as well as individual well-being, a deeper understanding of the ways in which complex, interdependent systems function, an ethic for institutions which prevents them from eclipsing the moral lives of individuals, and an ethics of international relations which recognizes the responsibility not to harm weak and poor nations and groups of people through economic and other forms of exploitation.[3, 5, 7, 28, 29]

The Power of Moral Example

As powerful as human rights and other moral languages may be, setting a moral example is potentially much more influential. The need to set a moral example applies especially to powerful nations. Amnesty International's 1998 report on the extent of human rights violations in the US and Cassese's description of such violations in the prisons of Europe provide both insight into how such abuses can continue even in wealthy democratic countries, and a realization of the great need for setting moral examples.[2, 6]

Neglect of the poor within rich societies, perpetuation of unsustainable consumerist lifestyles, lack of universal access to health care within wealthy nations, and the continuing production of weapons of mass destruction, are also poor examples for other nations. A shift from the idea that "might is right" to the idea that "right is might" is needed. The Jubilee 2000 program to relieve poor nations of crippling debts exemplifies the need for moral leadership.[29]

Widespread support for this endeavour could provide concrete evidence of the power of rational persuasion in dealing with the intractable problem of poverty and human misery.

Operationalizing These Ideas

What will it take to build a more robust human rights framework and to foster greater human well-being on a global scale? First, it will be necessary to acknowledge that unbridled materialism and wasteful consumerism are associated with impoverishment of the human spirit and do not necessarily bring happiness. Perpetual economic growth for some cannot continue at the expense of others without sacrificing our humanity. Second, the root causes of poverty should be studied more seriously and openly debated. The poor are not poor because they are lazy, incompetent or corrupt. While the poor must also accept some blame for their condition, the causes of poverty are much more complex, and wealthy industrialized nations are deeply implicated in creating and sustaining poverty.

Third, powerful nations need to resolve to deal with the root causes of unconscionable economic disparity through such constructive processes as debt relief, more accountable methods of loans and repayments, progressive displacement of military goals, and expenditure towards programs of sustainable development and ecological preservation. If the gradual reduction in global arms expenditure from a peak of $1 trillion in 1987 to $750 million in 1997 can be accelerated and the resources rediverted to much needed sustainable development processes and effective peace endeavours, there will be optimism that some of the folly of the 20th century need not be perpetuated.[30, 31]

Crucial to this approach will be the recognition that it is not merely altruism which is called for but a long-term perspective of rational self-interest in an increasingly interdependent world. Sustainable development and the widespread achievement of respect for human rights is in the interest of all, and can only be achieved through the active promotion of solidarity and the avoidance of economic, cultural and ethical imperialism. We should also acknowledge that all cultures have something to contribute to the development of a true form of universalism. To achieve this will require a broader approach to morality that goes beyond the concept of human rights.

Conclusions

Considerable progress has been made in human relations in the past fifty years and the human rights approach has been of great value. But it has not been enough to improve the lives of billions of people in the world. Additional moral approaches and strategies will have to be used to supplement and strengthen human rights activities. These are not beyond us if we can avoid being complacent and self-satisfied. As Douglas Roche has pointed out, "The present political process perpetuates a double standard of gross proportions in which money is readily found to wage war but is unavailable to build the conditions for peace, including comprehensive social programs to benefit children. The result is a world fractured by countless alienations." He suggests that solutions lie in finding ways to operationalize the four main lofty objectives outlined in the UN Declaration on its fiftieth anniversary: peace, development, equality and justice.[31]

The new forms of power being unleashed by biotechnology will have to be harnessed and used with greater wisdom than power has been used in the past. Like nuclear power, biotechnology has the capacity for great harm and this must be avoided. The resources and energy being devoted to ethical aspects of biotechnology reflect our awareness and concern for potential abuse. But can we be successful? I would like to be cautiously optimistic that we can, but only if the forces moving toward some of the new ways of thinking and acting can be transformed into more widespread attitudes among citizens, governments and multinational organizations.[32]

REFERENCES

1. Donnelly, J. "Human Rights: A New Standard of Civilization?" *International Affairs* (1998) 74: 1–24.
2. Hobsbawm, E. *The Age of Extremes: A History of the World 1914–1991*. London: Pantheon Books (1994).
3. Kothari, R., R. Falk, M. Kaldor, L. T. Ghee, et al. *Towards a Liberating Peace*. United Nations University and Lokvani. Tokyo and New Delhi (1988).
4. Cassese, A. *Inhuman States: Imprisonment, Detention and Torture in Europe Today*. Cambridge: Polity Press (1996).
5. Benatar, S. R. "Global Disparities in Health and Human Rights: A Critical Commentary." *American Journal of Public Health* (1998), 88: 295–300.
6. *The United States of America: Human Rights for All*. Amnesty International, London (1998).
7. Benatar, S. R. "A Perspective from Africa on Human Rights and Genetic Engineering." *The Genetic Revolution and Human Rights*. Burley J. (ed.). Oxford: Oxford University Press (1999).
8. McMichael, A. *Planetary Overload*. Cambridge: Cambridge University Press (1993).
9. George, S. and F. Sabeli. *Faith and Credit: The World Bank's Secular Empire*. London: Penguin Books (1994).
10. Teeple, G. *Globalization and the Decline of Social Reform*. New Jersey: Humanities Press (1995).
11. Ignatief, M. *The Warrior's Honour*. London: Chatto and Windus (1998).
12. Hosle, V. "The Third World as a Philosophical Problem." *Social Research*, 1992; 59: 227–62.
13. Callahan, D. *False Hopes*. New York: Simon and Schuster (1998).
14. Murray, T. H., M. A. Rothstein, R. F. Murray (eds.). *The Human Genome Project and the Future of Health Care*. Bloomington: Indiana University Press (1996).
15. Universal Declaration on the Human Genome and Human Rights. UN Scientific and Cultural Organization (1997).
16. Enriquez, J. "Genomics and the World Economy." *Science* 1998; 281: 925–26.
17. Enserink, M. "Physicians Wary of Scheme to Pool Icelanders' Genetic Data." *Science* 1998; 281: 890–91.
18. Benatar, D. A Justification for Rights. PhD Thesis, University of Cape Town (1992).

19. Universal Declaration of Human Duties, Committee on Human Rights, US National Academy of Sciences, National Academy of Engineering and Institute of Medicine. "Correspondence." Fall 1995, p. 6.
20. Chapman, A. R. Reintegrating Rights and Responsibilities. In: International Rights and Responsibilities for the Future. Hunter, K. W., T. C. Mack (eds.) Praeger, Westport, Connecticut (1996), p. 3–28.
21. Macer, D. Bioethics is Love of Life. Eubios Ethics Institute, Christchurch, New Zealand (1998).
22. Van Hooft, S. "Bioethics as Caring." *Journal of Medical Ethics*. 1996; 22: 83–89.
23. Minow, M. *Between Vengeance and Forgiveness: Facing History After Genocide and Mass Violence*. Boston: Beacon Press (1998).
24. Health and Human Rights: A Call to Action on the Fiftieth Anniversary of the Universal Declaration of Human Rights. JAMA. 1998; 280: 462–464
25. *Medicine Betrayed: The Participation of Doctors in Human Rights Abuses*. British Medical Association. London: Zed Books (1992).
26. Medical Ethics and Human Rights. Report of the Commonwealth Medical Association Project on "The role of medical ethics in the protection of human rights." British Medical Association. London (1994).
27. Human Needs, Human Rights, Gender and Medical Ethics. Proceedings of The UCT Faculty of Medicine Bioethics Day, February 1996. Benatar, S. R. (ed.). University of Cape Town (1997).
28. Benatar, S. R. Millennial Challenges for Medicine and Modernity. J. Roy Coll Phys. London (1998), 32: 160–165.
29. The Debt-Cutters Handbook: A Debt-Free Start for a Billion People. Jubilee 2000, London (1996).
30. Holdstock, D. Towards the Millennium. Editorial. Medicine, Conflict and Survival (1998), 14: 83–85.
31. Roche, D. "The People's Millennium Assembly." Medicine, Conflict and Survival (1998), 14: 86–96.
32. Benatar, S. R. Streams of Global Change, In: Ethics, Equity and Health for All. Z. Bankowski, J. H. Bryant, J. Gallagher (eds.). Council for the International Organization of Medical Sciences, Geneva (1997), p. 75–85.

BARTHA MARIA KNOPPERS

Human Rights and Genomics

Bartha Maria Knoppers is a professor of law at the Université de Montréal and chairs the International Ethics Committee of the Human Genome Project. She is also a member of the International Bioethics Committee of UNESCO. In 1997 she was named Scientist of the Year by Societé Radio Canada and the newspaper *La Presse*.

"CHANGES THAT WILL HAVE EFFECTS comparable to those of the Industrial Revolution and the computer-based revolution are now beginning. The next great era, a genomics revolution, is in an early phase."[1]

Genomics is the science that decodes the genes of all living organisms. It allows us to study, design and build molecules for the development of new technologies and therapies. Crossing as it does the plant, animal and human genomes, it constitutes the base for the genomics revolution. On the occasion of the fiftieth anniversary of the Universal Declaration of Human Rights, I would posit that like the evolution from the industrial to the informatic and now, to the genomic revolution, we have entered a third generation of human rights. The first generation of human rights was one of political freedoms and civil liberties, the second that of socio-economic rights, and the third is that of bioethics.[2] These three generations of human rights have culminated in the adoption by the General Conference of the United Nations Educational, Scientific and Cultural Organization (UNESCO) of the Universal Declaration on the Human Genome and Human Rights on 11 November 1997. An understanding of the breadth of this latter bioethics generation of human rights requires a brief incursion into the world of biotechnology and genomics before describing the UNESCO Declaration and criticizing certain weaknesses of it.

■■■ The Genomics Revolution

Today, most biopharmaceutical products are natural proteins based on the cloning of human genes. As genetic engineering and, in particular, transgenics occupy biotechnology, the distinction between the products of nature and human-made inventions is increasingly difficult to trace in the chain of living

259

matter. The field of comparative genomics is discovering an abundance of shared genes among life forms. As a result, "[g]enomics is so intertwined with other technologies and products of the molecular revolution that it is hard to trace its influence in a single company or industrial structure."[3]

As the industry crosses over the genomes, transgenics will "pharm" genetically engineered animals to produce medicines (agriceuticals). Likewise, vaccines will be inserted in foods (neutraceuticals) while pharmacogenomics will permit strategies to manufacture drugs suited to the needs of the individual and not just the disease class (molecule drugs). Although it is evident that we share our DNA with other living organisms, will we become just another form of living matter in this new life-science industry?

The worldwide market for biotechnology-based products is expected to grow from $15 billion in 1995 to $38 billion in 2005.[4] Human therapeutics, which account for more than seventy per cent of US biotechnology product sales, are expected to grow at an annual rate of eleven per cent.[5] In Canada, the National Biotechnology Advisory Committee has issued a wake-up call for government leadership in the next millennium. The committee recognized that seizing the opportunity creates public policy challenges.[6] One of these challenges is that of respect for the inherent human dignity and diversity of all members of the human family in the quest for access to human genes, access that is essential to the continued growth of the biotechnology industry.

▮▮▮ The Universal Declaration on the Human Genome and Human Rights

In 1993 the International Bioethics Committee (IBC) of UNESCO was created. Its mandate includes the drawing up of normative instruments for the protection of human rights with regards to issues raised by genetics and biology. In its first four years of work, the committee drew up a draft Universal Declaration on the Human Genome and Human Rights. This draft was reviewed by governmental representatives convened by UNESCO in the summer of 1997. Certain modifications were made and the Universal Declaration was unanimously adopted by the General Conference of UNESCO in November 1997.

There is no doubt that this Universal Declaration, like the 1948 Declaration, is proclamatory and hortatory in nature. Its principles will serve to frame the decisions humanity must make concerning scientific developments. Yet, it should not only frame these developments but also guide their direction, the setting of priorities and eventual applications. While scientific freedom is a fundamental right, the core principle of the Declaration like its earlier 1948 counterpart is that of respect for human dignity. A brief overview of its main provisions will serve to demonstrate the translation of this source of human rights in the field of human genomics.[7]

The first part of the Universal Declaration propounds the core values of dignity and diversity in the human species—ideas which run through the entire text. The starting point is that "everyone has a right to respect for their dignity and for their rights regardless of their genetic characteristics" (Article 2(a)). No one is to be reduced merely to their genetic characteristics (Article 2(b)). Mutations in the genome are natural (Article 3). In its natural state, the genome is not to give rise to financial gains (Article 4).

The second part of this Declaration specifies a number of rights of the individual. These include the rule that research, treatment or diagnosis affecting an individual's genome shall be taken only after assessment of risks and benefits (Article 5(a)) and with the prior free and informed consent of persons concerned (Article 5(b)). This includes the right of each individual to decide whether or not to be informed of genetic outcomes (Article 5(c)). There is a general prohibition on discrimination based on genetic characteristics (Article 6). Any limitations on the principles of consent and confidentiality are strictly confined (Article 9).

The third section lays down rules governing research on the human genome. No research or its applications may prevail over respect for human rights, fundamental freedoms and human dignity (Article 10). The benefits of advances should be made available to all (Article 12). Practices which are contrary to human dignity such as "reproductive cloning of human beings, shall not be permitted" (Article 11).

The fourth part of the Universal Declaration lays down conditions for the exercise of scientific activity. It imposes on states obligations to foster freedom of research but also to consider ethical, legal, social and economic implications of such research (Article 14). The Universal Declaration also provides that states should recognize the value of promoting the establishment of independent, multidisciplinary and pluralistic ethics committees to assess the ethical, legal and social issues raised by research on the human genome and its application (Article 16).

The fifth section of the Declaration addresses states as well as the international community and contains provisions for upholding human solidarity in this matter of universal concern to our species as well as international cooperation in order to ensure, among other things, that developing countries benefit from and are not merely the object of the research (Article 19). The final parts of the Universal Declaration concern the promotion of the principles contained within it (Articles 20 and 21) and the machinery for implementation and follow-up (Articles 22–25). In 1998, a new and smaller committee was formed and charged with this implementation and follow-up.

Accepting both the need to respect and uphold human dignity and diversity but recognizing our interdependence and co-evolution with other living organisms is the human rights challenge of the next millennium. Is an international, normative tool such as the UNESCO Declaration a sufficient bioethics framework for the safeguarding of the human values of dignity and diversity in the genomics revolution?

While the Declaration constitutes a historical achievement and while it demonstrates both scientific, legal and philosophical rigour in spite of its comprehensive and international scope, three aspects of the Declaration merit further discussion.

The Declaration, in its opening article, states that: "The human genome underlies the fundamental unity of all members of the human family, as well as the recognition of their inherent dignity and diversity. In a symbolic sense, it is the heritage of humanity" (Article 1). At this "collective" level of the human genome, other international and regional policymaking bodies have also addressed the issue of its shared status. Some regard the human genome at this universal level, as the "common heritage of humanity[8]/mankind,"[9] or as "collective"[10] or "general property,"[11] or finally, as our "common heritage"[12] and the "prized possession of all humanity."[13]

Yet definitive, legal recognition of the common heritage concept remains uncertain. This could be due in part to a fear of state control and monopoly and also to the adoption of mistaken genetic bases for group identification for political purposes. These two critiques have neither a scientific nor a legal foundation: not scientific, because human genetic diversity ensures that there are no unique, inclusive haplotypes that can identify all the individuals who supposedly belong to a specific race; not legal, because the common heritage concept provides the potential for an international framework of responsible governance.[14, 15]

The five elements under international law are nonappropriation, common management, equitable sharing of benefits, peaceful use, and protection and preservation for future generations. Individual state sovereignty and possible abuse is thereby lessened, not increased. This legal concept then evokes the possibility of a more prospective form of international stewardship. It is unfortunate that the Declaration limits the recognition to a symbolic one. The importance of the collective, universal oversight that adherence to this common heritage concept provides should not be underestimated. It demonstrates a willingness to consider its universality as giving rise to common responsibilities particularly for future generations, a duty that requires further elaboration. The Declaration proclaims the evolutionary character of the genome (Article 3) and also states that at the level of the individual, a person should not and cannot be reduced to his or her genetic characteristics (Article 2). But the concept of transgenerational duties and justice should have been explicitly included and could have been reinforced by the adoption of the common heritage of humanity concept.

The second critique I would make is in regards to the weakness of Article 19 which concerns international cooperation with developing countries. It reads: "States should seek to encourage measures enabling: (iv) the free exchange of scientific knowledge and information in the areas of biology, genetics and medicine." This raises two issues which again merit further elaboration but are not mentioned, that of patenting and benefit-sharing.

While reference is made in the preamble to intellectual property and to the "international instruments which could have a bearing on the applications of genetics," the International Bioethics Committee deliberately decided not to adopt any substantive articles on the subject of patenting. This was due to the fact that under patent law the strict application of the traditional patenting criteria would preclude possible patents on human genes or any part thereof in their natural state, a position reiterated and reinforced in Article 4.

Unfortunately, the contradictory opinions of the Patents and Trademarks Office of the United States, straying as they do from traditional clarity, have led to a slowdown in the availability of biomedical and therapeutic products reaching the international market.[16] An explicit reference to the traditional criteria of inventiveness, novelty and utility, while not sufficient for those who oppose on moral grounds any "patents on life," may have served to stem the harmful effects of the current gold rush of conflicting patents. Furthermore, the drafting of an international declaration would have been an opportune occasion for the inclusion of the ethical filter of the prohibition of patents whose commercial exploitation would be contrary to public policy and morality as found in the European Patent Convention since 1973 and, more recently, in the 1998 Directive on the Legal Protection of Biotechnological Innovations of the European Commission.

The Declaration also fails to address the issue of benefit-sharing and state sovereignty, though again reference is made in the preamble to the Convention on Biological Diversity. That Convention concerned genetic resources such as plants and animals but not humans. Such oblique, preambular reference to the genetic diversity of humanity fails to address the need for mechanisms that recognize the contribution of populations to the eventual commercial rewards that patenting provides. While such rewards should not become an inducement to participate, some compensation to the public infrastructure that made it possible is an idea that should be promoted.

Indeed, the ethics committee of the Human Genome Organization in its 1996 Statement on the Principled Conduct of Genetic Research suggested that benefits to participating communities include "agreements with individuals, families, groups, communities or populations that foresee technology transfer, local training, joint ventures, provision of health care or of information infra-structures, reimbursement of costs, or the possible use of a percentage of any royalties for humanitarian purposes."[17]

My third critique concerns the naming of specific scientific techniques in a declaration. Pressures from the governmental representatives sent to review the Declaration in July 1997 resulted in last-minute additions to the final draft, mentioning in Articles 11 and 24 practices considered contrary to human dignity. These include "reproductive cloning of human beings" (Article 11) and "germ-line interventions" (Article 24). The International Bioethics Committee, during its four years of work and much discussion, decided that a declaration should not name any specific scientific techniques. Why? Because of its universality, its future viability and the hortatory nature of a declaration as well as the human rights mandate. The committee considered that this mandate precluded mentioning specific techniques because of its definitional dangers, to say nothing of creating time limits on the Declaration's effectiveness.

The strength and influence of international principles in a declaration can only be weakened by the naming of certain techniques as contrary to human dignity. A declaration should proscribe the goals of scientific research which the international community considers morally reprehensible. Naming techniques implies that the concept of human dignity is either too narrow to be understood to prohibit germ-line or cloning, or that cloning and germ-line interventions are the only techniques contrary to human dignity.

■ Conclusion

In this third generation of human rights, that of bioethics, the challenge lies in continuing this initial bold step of the UNESCO Declaration. Its dissemination and implementation require concerted effort and courage. While we have criticized some of its inadequacies, the Declaration constitutes a landmark in human rights instruments. As we face increased consumerism and commercialization in the health care sector, the genomics revolution risks turning human genetic "resources" into commodities. With regard to the current emphasis in industrialized countries on autonomy and free choice as a factor in this international commercialization, one author notes with some pessimism that, "Many concerns associated with the genetic revolution may be beyond the reach of human rights instruments. The genetech industry will be propelled forward by social forces imbedded in the fabric of Western culture. It seems certain that the cumulative pressure of these forces will prove too much for the most sharply crafted declaration."[18]

I do not share this pessimism. Similar concerns were voiced about the future effectiveness of the 1948 Declaration. Yet no one can deny its force, influence and vitality. Surely, the UNESCO Declaration that promotes and frames human genome research that "seek[s] to offer relief from suffering and improve health of individuals and humankind as a whole" (Article 12) will not fall prey to this "marriage between commerce and human genetics."[19]

Like all international human rights instruments, the life and future of this "bioethics" Declaration depends on the goodwill of all peoples and individuals and on the fundamental belief in the need to ensure respect for human dignity and diversity. This international consensus on shared values reflected in UNESCO's Declaration is not a mirror but a beacon. We are free to choose to steer our scientific endeavours by its light. As the French philosopher François Rabelais said in 1534: "Science without conscience is but the ruin of the soul."

REFERENCES

1. Abelson, P. H. "A Third Technological Revolution." *Science* 279 (27 March 1998): 2019.
2. Elizalde, J. "Bioethics as a New Human Rights Emphasis in European Research Policy." *Kennedy Institute of Ethics Journal* 2 (1992): 159.
3. Enriquez, J. "Genomics and the World's Economy." *Science* 281 (14 August 1998): 925.
4. Bio-Industries Branch. "Bio-industries; Part 1: Overview and Prospects." (Draft) Industry Sector, Industry Canada (1997): 5.
5. Shamel, R. and M. Macbeth. "Outlook for Biotechnology Industry Remains Strong for Next Year and Beyond." *Genetic Engineering News* (Dec. 1997).
6. National Biotechnology Advisory Committee. "Leading in the Next Millennium." Industry Canada (1998): 4.
7. The overview that follows was provided by the Honourable Justice Michael Kirby, "Bioethics and Human Rights: The Role of UNESCO," paper presented to the Second International Summit of National Bioethics Advisory Commissions, Tokyo, Japan, 3 November 1998. The author wishes to thank Justice Kirby for permission to use this overview.
8. Ethical, Legal, and Social Issues Committee. "Statement on the Principled Conduct of Genetic Research." *Genome Digest* (May 1996): 2.
9. Latin American Human Genome Program (PLAGH). "Declaration of Manzanillo." *International Digest of Health Legislation* 48 (1997): 424, art. 1.
10. European Commission, Working Group on the Ethical, Social and Legal Aspects of Human Genome Analysis. Report of 31 December 1991 (WG-ESLA), also in *Bulletin of Medical Ethics* (June 1993): 19.
11. World Medical Association. "Declaration on the Human Genome Project (1992)." *International Digest of Health Legislation* 44 (1993):150.
12. FIGO Committee for the Study of Ethical Aspects of Human Reproduction. "Recommendations on Ethical Issues in Obstetrics and Gynaecology—Patenting Human Genes." *International Digest of Health Legislation* 48 (30 May 1997): 447.
13. First South–North Human Genome Conference. "Declaration on Patenting of Human DNA Sequences." *International Digest of Health Legislation* 44 (1993): 362.
14. Marshall, E. "DNA Studies Challenge the Meaning of Race." *Science* 282 (1998): 654; See also Juengst, E. "Group Identity and Human Diversity: Keeping Biology Straight from Culture." *American Journal of Human Genetics* 63 (1998): 673.
15. Baslar, K. *The Concept of the Common Heritage of Mankind in International Law.* The Hague: Martinus Nijhoff Publishers, 1998; Knoppers, Bartha Maria, *Human Dignity and Genetic Heritage.* Ottawa: Law Reform Commission of Canada, 1991.
16. Heller, M. and R. Eisenberg. "Can Patents Deter Innovation? The Anticommons in Biomedical Research." *Science* 2 80 (1 May 1998): 698.
17. HUGO International Ethics Committee. "Statement on the Principled Conduct of Genetic Research." *Genome Digest* (May, 1996): 2.
18. Caufield, T. "Keeping up with Science." *UNESCO Courier* (Oct. 1998): 36.
19. Ibid.

Recognizing the Inherent Dignity and Rights of Women

A MIRAGE IN THE DISTANCE?

Women of the Millennium

Pamela A. Jefferies is the chief human rights commissioner in New Zealand and represents her country on the Coordinating Committee of National Institutions for the Promotion and Protection of Human Rights. In 1993 she received the New Zealand Suffrage Centennial Medal and was made a Member of the Order of the British Empire.

E TE TANGATA WHENUA. Tena Koutou. To the people of the land, I greet you. *E nga Mana, E nga reo, E nga waka, Tena koutou katoa.* To the leaders, to all the cultures around the world, I greet you. I greet you in Maori and in English, the two official languages of New Zealand. The recent United Nations Human Development Report stated we were the fourth most gender-empowered nation in the world. Coming from there, I am in a good position to talk about whether recognizing the inherent dignity and rights of women is really just a mirage in the distance.

New Zealand has a female prime minister and a female leader of the opposition. Women hold one-third of seats in Parliament, and make up nearly fifty per cent of professional and technical workers. It sounds pretty good, yet somehow women's share of earned income is only thirty-nine per cent. Moreover, when we look at the same United Nations report's rankings for gender-related development, New Zealand slips to eighth ranking (Canada, by the way, is ranked first).[1]

In July 1998 the Committee on the Elimination of Discrimination Against Women (CEDAW) released its draft concluding comments on New Zealand's progress in implementing the CEDAW Convention. Although they were generally positive, they were concerned about the impact of the free market and economic restructuring on women. They were also concerned about the situation of indigenous Maori women who continue to leave school earlier, have higher rates of teenage pregnancy, poorer health, less access to employment and a decent income, and less political power than the general population.[2] Maybe some of this sounds familiar to you?

I am sure that many Maori women in New Zealand would say that recognition of their inherent dignity and rights is a mirage in the distance. Many

269

women of the Pacific Islands and other ethnic minority women would probably agree, as would women with disabilities who are unable to find employment, and lesbian and bisexual women who still experience legal and practical discrimination.

The first draft of the Universal Declaration of Human Rights stated, "All men are created equal." Fortunately, the female members of the commission, led by Mrs. Hansa Mehta of India, pointed out that some might interpret this to exclude women.[3] So the final version stated, "All human beings are born free and equal in dignity and rights." The next sentence is still sexist, stating, "They are endowed with reason and conscience and should act toward one another in a spirit of brotherhood," but the universal intent is clear.

Fifty years on it is still necessary to proclaim that as human beings we are all born free and equal in dignity and rights, and to urge that we act toward one another with a spirit of humanity. Women make up roughly half of humanity. The rights of women are not tack-ons to other human rights. As the fourth World Conference on Women held in Beijing in 1995 proclaimed, "Women's rights are human rights."[4] No country in the world appears to have achieved equality for women and men. But the extent and nature of the challenge differs from nation to nation. From time to time I experience a defining moment. One of these was recently, at the fourth meeting of the Asia-Pacific Forum of National Human Rights Institutions in Jakarta. I made an impassioned statement on the subject of women's human rights and asserted that women are not victims. Nor are we minorities. We are the majority of the population. I argued that the issues are not about giving us a few rights but about sharing power to enable us to develop our own solutions.

I was immensely humbled when the speaker who followed me, Commissioner Dayal of the National Human Rights Commission of India, said, "I wish I could say that women are the majority in my community—they do not survive."

With the diversity of women's experiences and lives throughout the world it can be difficult to see what women have in common besides the fact that we are women. But if we look at what is important to women, we can find common aspirations throughout all our cultures. For example, the aspirations to be nurtured and cared for as part of a family during childhood, to receive an education to at least the high school level, to have food and shelter, to work, to participate in decision-making and political life and live in a democracy, to found a family, to live in a world without discrimination based on sex. All of these aspirations can be found in the Bill of Rights.

These aspirations are, of course, also shared by men. Yet women face particular difficulties getting our human rights acknowledged and taken seriously. International instruments and meetings do not necessarily translate into changes on the ground for women living in remote villages, in megatropolises, or in the towns and cities of my own country, New Zealand. The gains that have been made in women's rights come from the concerted efforts of activists, organizers, governments and ordinary women. We all know that how these are realized in each of our countries is very different.

The efforts need to be continued and adapted for the new millennium so that women will experience respect for their rights and dignity as a reality, not a mirage. The women leaders of the millennium generation have probably already been born. They will be different to us. They will live in a world which is increasingly globalized, and yet arguably even more tribal.

One of the most pressing challenges for women's rights in the millennium is to acknowledge that overcoming disadvantage suffered by women cannot and should not have to be solved by women alone. It is a challenge to be met by all in society. Those most affected by gender discrimination—very poor women, refugee women and girl children—have the least resources to fight it. They may know what needs to be changed but not have the power to change it. It is important that more powerful women, men, businesses, NGOs, governments and international agencies also take up the issues of gender discrimination.

There are a number of legislative methods to reduce gender discrimination. This may start with removing overt discrimination, for example in inheritance laws. Electoral system reform—either through moving to a proportional system as New Zealand has done, or through reserving a number of seats for members of each gender, as has been done in a number of Scandinavian countries. These measures may give women a greater voice in government. Affirmative action approaches have been the subject of much debate, particularly in the US where they have been constitutionally challenged. They may, however, be the most effective way to address historical disadvantage in some circumstances.

Another challenge is to end the endemic violence against women that occurs in all cultures and in all states. Progress in this regard comes on a number of levels. There has finally been international recognition that the use of mass rape and sexual violence is an appalling war crime. On another level, many states including New Zealand are now recognizing family violence as serious crime. Police are being retrained to deal with domestic violence situations, laws are being passed to protect women from violent partners and, despite limited funding, women's refuges continue to provide shelter for women and children.

There is the challenge of education. Two-thirds of the world's children not in school are girls. Similarly, two-thirds of the people who can neither read nor write are female. Women need education to allow them to make informed decisions about their lives. Women's empowerment through education has important consequences for the future of the world. Educated women are able to make decisions about their fertility and family size. Where coercive policies have failed to affect population growth, educated women are making their own decisions to have smaller families based on their own assessment of their best interests.

In a number of countries, including New Zealand and Canada, the number of women receiving university degrees now exceeds that of men. Young women have seized higher education as a means to overcome the barriers that still exist for them, barriers which prevent them from having jobs and economic and political power that are equal to that of their male counterparts. They know that they will have to work harder than their male peers if they are to both participate in paid work and have families. It is vital that the education women receive keeps pace with technological progress so that women can be equal partners in society.

There is the challenge of globalization and tribalization. With the age of global business, there is a danger that it will be harder and harder for women to influence the world around them. It is wrong for Nike to offer unsatisfactory terms and conditions of work in Asia. It is also wrong that New Zealanders are asked to accept that Australian, Canadian or British companies provide a lower standard of protection for their workers in New Zealand than in their home countries because we have lower standards in our laws.

New ways of viewing the world are needed. We need to write clear, enforceable provisions related to human rights into trade treaties and to create an environment where workplaces operate at international standards. Despite the encroachment of globalization, or perhaps because of it, it is now more important than ever to allow for and respect diversity. We must ensure that particular groups of women are not excluded from women's rights. Developed nations must address the ghettos of disadvantage that exist within them. Human rights are not a reality when young single mothers or indigenous and ethnic minorities are excluded from access to the power and wealth of the dominant culture.

We must also address the two extremes of the ages of women, to recognize the human rights both of the large populations of girl children in many developing countries and growing populations of ageing women in developed countries. Eliminating arbitrary age discrimination while meeting the specific needs of the very young and very old is a challenge.

We have the challenge of reconnecting women and their aspirations with the world of economists. A rethink of economics is needed on a number of levels to ensure that economics takes account of the realities and aspirations of women as well as men. The unpaid work done predominantly by women must be included in economic calculations. Women's access to capital must be enhanced and issues such as the value we put on raising children and caring for the ill or elderly in the community must be faced.

Finally, there is the challenge of finding the balance between work outside the home, caring for children and dependants, the individual sense of self worth for the women and fulfilling partnership and parenting. In New Zealand there have been several recent conferences about men taking an active role in parenting. We need to discover ways for women and men to realize their rights to work, as well as their rights to form relationships and to have and raise families.

Are these suggestions merely part of a mirage? Much of the emphasis in the fifty years since the Universal Declaration has been on achieving civil and political rights. In many countries women now enjoy equal *de jure* rights. But we must guard against thinking that this is enough. Sometimes developed countries point the finger at developing countries while ignoring human rights issues at home. Many appear to have decided that the visions of equality expressed in the Universal Declaration are an unattainable mirage. If we accept that this is so, it will become so. Western-style democracies must not become a hollow shell of human rights. Academic centres conducting discourses on human rights theory are useful, but it may be more important to ask why the majority of Americans did not exercise their fundamental right to vote in their last election or the one before.

Why do we tacitly accept that poverty is the fault of the poor, even though most of the poor are children or their mothers struggling to care for them? As more and more services are privatized, do we absolve governments of their responsibility to protect the rights of citizens? Have we decided that some human rights issues, such as access to justice, are too hard? Developed countries still have difficulty recognizing the humanity of all their members. As prison incarceration rates spiral upwards, there appears to be less and less understanding of the human rights of prisoners. Yet we know that nearly all of the women in prison are themselves victims of serious physical or sexual abuse and few are in fact a danger to society. The rising youth suicide rates in developed countries should cause us to ask whether we truly recognize the inherent dignity and rights of the young people in our societies.

At the start of this essay I suggested that many women in New Zealand, the fourth most gender-empowered nation in the world, may feel that recognition of their rights and inherent dignity is indeed a mirage far off in the distance. And yet, in the final analysis, I would have to disagree with that point of view. For to speak of a mirage is to imply that something has no real existence. A mirage is a hazy vision which is unreachable.

In the fifty years since the Universal Declaration, the world has come so far in recognizing women's rights that even relatively recent restrictions seem ludicrous. For example, the New Zealand Human Rights Commission recently held a party to celebrate its twenty years of existence at which a video of our history was shown. The audience laughed heartily when reminded of how the local builders' association had chosen to cancel its annual dinner rather than admit women less than twenty years ago. Attitudes have changed so much in that time. As New Zealand's chief human rights commissioner, chair of the Asia-Pacific Forum of National Human Rights Institutions and as a member of the International Co-ordinating Committee of National Human Rights Institutions, I believe the role of national human rights institutions in protecting women's rights is very important. This was recognized in the Beijing Platform of Action which calls on governments to "create or strengthen independent national institutions for the protection and promotion of [women's] rights."

Two examples indicate the range of ways in which national human rights institutions enhance women's rights. One is the pay equity case taken on by the Canadian Human Rights Commission in relation to public service pay rates. In an entirely different sphere, Komnas HAM, the Indonesian Human Rights Commission, has documented the rapes and violence against Chinese-Indonesian women and brought them to the attention of the world. When Komnas HAM was set up there were concerns that it might not be sufficiently independent to take a strong stance on issues. But in the recent turmoil in Indonesia it has bravely fulfilled its mandate.

United Nations High Commissioner for Human Rights Mary Robinson has shown leadership in emphasizing the role of effective national human rights institutions in turning human rights norms into reality. This has made me optimistic about the potential for the women of the millennium to enjoy real rights and freedoms. I am reminded of the words of Nelson Mandela, in relation to the struggle against apartheid in South Africa: "We have merely achieved the freedom to be free, the right not to be oppressed. We have not taken the final step of a journey, but the first step on a longer and even more difficult road. For to be free is not merely to cast off one's chains, but to live in a way that respects and enhances the freedom of others. The true test of our devotion to freedom is just beginning."[5]

To those who are tired of hearing about women's rights, who think we live in a post-feminist age where these issues are no longer important, I say that the journey is just beginning. For women of the millennium, *de jure* rights must translate into real equality. Women must be able to realize their potential free from violence, free from sexual harassment and discrimination. And women and men must discover how to use their freedom to shape a society which meets their aspirations, values diversity and guards against oppression.

A famous Maori proverb asks: What is the most important thing of all? The answer is: *He Tangata. He Tangata. He Tangata.* It is people. It is people. It is people. *Kia Kaha. Kia Manawanui.* Be strong. Be of Brave Heart.

REFERENCES

1. United Nations Development Programme, Human Development Report, 1998.
2. Committee on the Elimination of Discrimination Against Women, 22 June–10 July 1998, 9 July 1998, advance unedited version.
3. Cited in Hillary Rodham Clinton, 12/10 Human Rights Day Address, United States Information Agency, Washington Daily File, East Asian and Pacific Affairs Version, Article #: EPF310.
4. United Nations, Report of the Fourth World Conference on Women, Beijing, 4–15 September 1995, A/CONF.177/20.
5. Mandela, Nelson. *Long Walk to Freedom*. London: Abacus (1994): 751.

Turning the Rhetoric into Reality

Michelle Falardeau-Ramsay is chief commissioner of the Canadian Human Rights Commission. She is also Queen's Counsel and a member of the Canadian Human Rights Foundation, the Canadian Institute for the Administration of Justice and the Canadian Council on International Law. In 1997 she was awarded the Arthur L. Green Civil and Human Rights Award.

IS THE RECOGNITION OF THE INHERENT DIGNITY AND RIGHTS OF WOMEN just a mirage in the distance even now, in 1998, as we mark the fiftieth anniversary of the Universal Declaration? Is the recognition of the rights of women still some distant goal that seems to move further away each time we take steps toward it? The simple answer is "yes" and "no."

It is certainly true that much of the overt discrimination against women that existed in 1948 and prior to the Declaration is now gone. In some senses at least, the recognition of the inherent dignity and rights of women is not a mirage at all. The rights of women have, in fact, been recognized time and time again. The UN Declaration of Human Rights and all the covenants attached to it over the years are clear proof of that recognition. The greatest value of the Declaration, for its time, was that it gave every government in the world a vision for its own society and citizens. At the same time, it gave the citizens themselves the hope that their own society could be built on the values of equality, freedom and justice for all.

Fifty years on, the Universal Declaration of Human Rights remains an eloquent and far-reaching document. Its message is just as powerful today as it was then. It is that societies function better, create more wealth, become more prosperous and make better use of the intellectual power of their citizens if all the people—including women—are treated with equality. They must be free from repressive abuse and allowed to participate fully in society and the economy. Respect for human rights is not only a fundamental human value. It is

275

central to the development of democratic societies which are at peace with one another and at peace with their own citizens.

But all the declarations, resolutions and laws the world has to offer are worthless unless they are backed up by people who are resolved to maintain them. We have to make a clear distinction between the rhetoric and the reality when we talk about progress in the protection of the rights of women or the protection of any individual rights for that matter. It is one thing to sign on to the Universal Declaration, but it is quite another to have the ability or the inclination to uphold its provisions.

As the title of this conference states, the Declaration has been a blueprint for peace, justice and freedom. And like the blueprint for a new house, it is only the plan, not the completed house itself. The house still has to be built. Nations which have accepted the blueprint—the principles set out in the Universal Declaration of Human Rights—must also have the workable mechanisms in place to enforce its provisions. The Universal Declaration contains a series of commitments with regard to women. These include equal protection against discrimination, the right to work, free choice of employment, just and favourable conditions of work, and the right to a standard of living adequate for the health and well-being of the worker and her family.

In Canada, these principles are expressed in our Constitution and through legislation. The Canadian Constitution, for example, incorporates the Charter of Rights and Freedoms which states clearly that discrimination on the basis of sex is against the law. Our federal human rights legislation says the same thing, as does legislation in the provinces and as do various charters and human rights laws in countries around the world. In large part we can say that we are winning the rhetorical battle. There are plenty of blueprints in place, plenty of statements of the best intentions. But the real question is, are we winning the reality battle? Is the house being constructed on a solid foundation, or are we just building castles in the air? How do these high-sounding sentiments translate into real help for the woman who is facing barriers to working in a nontraditional occupation? Or the woman who is receiving less than her male counterpart for the same job? Or the woman who faces sexual harassment in the workplace?

Progress toward full equality for women requires more than just great words and more than just general statements of intent; it requires a commitment to act. There are several key actors working to ensure that the rights of women are enhanced and protected. There are many outstanding leaders in the women's movement around the world. There are also national and international labour organizations, national and international human rights organizations, as well as many community and advocacy organizations which play significant roles. Some governments have designated ministers and created departments as watchdogs and advocates for women's concerns such as the Status of Women

Office here in Canada, which does excellent work on behalf of the women of this country.

But the protection of the rights of women must also be integrated into the mainstream mechanisms protecting human rights in general. This point has been made many times before. Both the World Conference on Human Rights in Vienna in 1993 and the fiftieth session of the Commission on Human Rights meeting in Tunis later that year made reference to the central role played by national institutions in enhancing the rights of women within all societies. The third International Workshop of National Human Rights Institutions in Manila in 1996 also stressed the need for national institutions to promote the Convention on the Elimination of all Forms of Discrimination Against Women.

National human rights commissions, such as ours here in Canada, help give practical effect to the equality rights of women because commissions like ours operate independently of government and have both a legislative and funding base to support their activities. I would like to give you two or three short examples related to the activities of my own commission. I don't want to imply that we are all-powerful or perfect, either in our structure or actions. But I do believe we have contributed significantly to the advancement of women's rights in this country, particularly in the areas of employment equity, pay equity and preventing harassment in the workplace. We not only take complaints of discrimination in employment and services in the federal government and the federally regulated private sector, we also monitor the state of equality rights in Canada and report to Parliament on an annual basis. With the revised Employment Equity Act of 1996, we ensure that the employers in the federal sector provide equal employment opportunities for women, aboriginal people, visible minorities and people with disabilities. Attitudes have changed. Some of the roadblocks to equality have been removed and, statistically at least, some things are moving in the right direction.

Recent studies by the International Labour Organization and the Conference Board of Canada show that while women are still largely excluded from senior management and top level professional positions in both the private and public sectors, women in the federally regulated workforce are beginning to break through the glass ceiling. One of our employment equity successes was the *Action Travail des Femmes v. CN Rail* case in 1987, which dealt with the underrepresentation of women in nontraditional occupations. Following hearings, CN Rail was ordered to ensure that twenty-five per cent of its new hires in these types of jobs were women. The decision in this case not only helped women at CN Rail, it also established important precedents in employment equity for women across Canada.

In the case of sexual harassment, one of our more important milestones is the case of *Robichaud v. the Department of National Defence*. In addition to the remedy given to Ms. Robichaud, this case established the principle that employers have a duty to provide a working environment that is free of harassment. When we deal with sexual harassment cases we often go beyond simple restitution to make sure, for example, that employers provide antiharassment training for their managers and employees. We also have extensive promotion efforts designed to prevent sexual harassment from happening in the first place. Many large Canadians employers now have policies in place and a process for handling sexual harassment incidents quickly and effectively. For those who don't, we have developed model policies as guides for large and small employers. Our regional offices across the country provide training and information on harassment issues to business, labour and community organizations.

We have also had some success, and some very large frustrations, in pay equity cases. In most cases the roots of the problem reach back into the era of overt discrimination against women, when occupational segregation was the order of the day, and have been carried forward over the years for a variety of different reasons. In many cases, usually those affecting smaller groups of employees, we have been able to bring the parties together to work on a solution. But not every case has proceeded in that spirit, in particular, the now-famous case involving the Public Service Alliance of Canada (PSAC) and the federal government. It was originally proceeding in a cooperative way, with both sides agreeing to an independent study by experts in the field. The government, however, chose a very narrow interpretation of the study's findings and the two parties ended up arguing their cases in front of a human rights tribunal.

In July 1998 the tribunal found that the study provided an adequate basis for settlement. However, the federal government decided to seek judicial review. Over the years, other federally regulated employers have also used the courts as a way to delay or derail pay equity cases. Meanwhile, the women affected by these cases—among the lowest-paid employees in Canada—continue to wait. Recently, there seems to be some movement on the collective bargaining front, but we have yet to see how the pay equity claims made on behalf of women will be affected.

Our role also includes raising issues that are cause for broad public concern. We do this in various ways, through media opportunities and public meetings. But one method we have found particularly effective is using our annual report to Parliament as a kind of "bully pulpit" to bring public attention to issues, as we did in our last report on the pay equity situation of women in the public service of Canada and the problem of sexual harassment in the workplace.

There are other matters that don't fit neatly into our mandate but which are clearly linked to human rights principles. With respect to women, one such issue is poverty. I have spoken out many times on this issue because I believe that a country like Canada should not ignore a problem which affects many women and children. I have been criticized for it, but the issue is important and I plan to continue making this point whenever and wherever I can. In all of these actions, an important realization for us as a commission is that we do not, and indeed we cannot, work alone.

We highly value our partnerships with others involved in the protection of human rights and we act as a kind of resource body for several Canadian nongovernmental organizations committed to these issues. We offer advice and work collaboratively to promote the understanding and acceptance of both the intrinsic and practical value of protecting human rights within Canada. At the international level, commissions such as ours have created their own network to trade information and advice. We encourage our sister national institutions to make women's issues central to their work if they have not already done so.

For all of us, the world is changing rapidly. Globalization, the new world economy and the high-tech revolution have forever altered the way we interact with one another. My fear is that as societies we may allow these new phenomena to wash over us without noticing the important consequences; or worse, we may use them as excuses to deny people, particularly women, their full rights. The framers of the Universal Declaration clearly intended that human rights be taken into account when addressing economic issues and that economic issues be part of our consideration of human rights. We must have a real discussion about the role of human rights legislation and women's rights in the context of the world economy. Do we really believe in fundamental human rights for women or are we content to let market forces make our decisions for us?

As national boundaries become less significant, the spectre of international corporations "shopping" the world for the lowest-paid, least-protected labour force—usually made up of women, but sometimes consisting of child or even slave labour—is not an appealing prospect. We must, as national institutions, speak and act together on human rights in general and women's rights in particular, on a more global basis and on a more collaborative basis. We must continue to stand with the victims of discrimination—the least advantaged, the disenfranchised and the dispossessed—wherever they may be. Discrimination, intolerance, exploitation and hatred wound the community's bond of solidarity. We are all the poorer for it. And we are all the richer for it when we take positive steps to bring it to an end.

In closing, I want to say that in this country we are proud of the fact that it was a Canadian, John Humphrey, who drafted the original version of the Universal Declaration of Human Rights and took part in the lobbying effort that got other nations to sign on. When South African President Nelson Mandela recently came to Canada, he unveiled a plaque at the Canadian Tribute to Human Rights monument in Ottawa in recognition of Mr. Humphrey's contribution. President Mandela left us with a chilling reminder that at an international level, our progress on human rights is not what it should be. I would like to quote his words: "Though we can celebrate many advances in the frontiers of political freedom in the past fifty years, millions still live in conditions that prevent them from the full enjoyment of the rights they have been formally accorded. In many respects the gap between those who are secure in their rights and those who are not is growing."

It is to these millions—most of whom are women—that we must direct our efforts in the coming years. We must continue our work to close that gap, both within our own societies and throughout the world. We must show a renewed commitment to continue the struggle to make the rhetoric of human rights protection a reality in the life of every woman, no matter where she lives on this planet.

The Practice of Female Genital Mutilation in Mali

A Violation of Physical Integrity

Fatoumata Siré Diakité is president of l'Association pour le Progrès et la Défense des Droits des Femmes Maliennes, which she founded in 1991, and a member of the Women's Committee of the International Confederation of Free Trade Unions. She was awarded the Chevalier de l'Ordre National du Mali in 1996 and France's highest distinction, the Chevalier de la Légion d'Honneur de France, in 1997.

CREATED ON 6 APRIL 1991, the Association pour le Progrès et la Défense des Droits des Femmes Maliennes (APDF) aims to promote, protect and defend of the rights of women and girls and combat all forms of violence against them. Of particular concern are traditional practices that are harmful to the health of women and girls and violate their rights. This is particularly true of female genital mutilation (FGM), commonly known as excision. Since its formation, most of the association's work at the local, regional and national levels have focused on achieving concrete results regarding these objectives.

The APDF has adopted a three-pronged strategy for the adoption of a law which prohibits the practice of FGM and ensures its eradication. The strategy focuses on three areas: the legal rights of women and girls; economics, including socioeconomic support of the women who perform FGM and who voluntarily put down their knives; and health, recognizing the long-term consequences of FGM on the physical and mental well-being of women and girls. Those targeted were women who perform FGM, women in general, young people, religious leaders, schools, media, locally elected officials and health personnel.

Why is it women who perform the excisions? They are crucial to the success or failure of our campaign yet, in previous programs to eradicate FGM, they were ignored. We brought them together and listened to them to find out the real reasons why they practise FGM. More than ninety per cent of women in

Mali have undergone excision. Two major reasons were identified: the practice of FGM is a tradition handed down by grandmothers, mothers, mothers-in-law, etc. It is also for economic reasons: the women carry out FGM in order to survive, receiving money or payment in kind (grain, animals, poultry, soap, cloth, etc.) for every excision performed. Why target women in general? Clearly, they are the ones who most often subject their daughters to this odious practice. In more than sixty per cent of the cases, the reason for carrying out excision was based on religious belief. They believe that the Koran requires it. As well, the decision is taken because it is the custom in the family and because it ensures the girl's marriageability.

Why the young people? They are the adults of tomorrow: the objective is to help them adopt a new attitude towards FGM and prepare them for the end of this custom. They can then save their children from having to undergo this practice. The young boys and girls are a powerful and active ally in terms of lobbying the other target groups. Why religious leaders? In a country where more than eighty per cent of the people are Muslim and more than ninety per cent are illiterate and poor, religion is the liferaft to which everyone clings. The religious leaders are the people's consciences. What they say, whether right or wrong, is accepted as the truth by the trusting believers. Consequently, the religious leaders have a very important role to play and they know it. Because of this, the APDF decided to make them part of its fight, inviting them to speak at workshops which it organizes. The hope is to create a strong partnership, even a climate of trust, so that we can fight together to protect the physical and mental health of the women and girls of Mali.

Why the school? It is the place where the citizens of tomorrow are shaped. Teachers are supposed to have knowledge and through them the school is perhaps the most important place to affect change. Why the media? They are increasingly becoming the number one power for change: they play a central role in providing information and educating the whole population and can be a catalyst for change. It is common to hear such statements as, "But the radio said it," and "I even heard it on the radio." This shows that messages carried by the media have a definite impact on the population. They reach a wide audience and influence decision-makers, especially politicians.

Why elected officials? They are the spokespersons for the grassroots, for the people that they represent and on behalf of whom they make decisions and vote on the laws that will guide their futures. Why health workers? They have a mission to inform and to educate, but also and especially to ensure prevention and to offer advice. Unfortunately, this mission is not always understood by all health workers. We are now experiencing a transfer of "skills" and "technology" whereby some health officials are taking the place of the women who formerly performed excisions and are now receiving money for their services.

Training on the rights of women and girls, with respect to national legislation and international instruments (whether or not they have been ratified by Mali), has been provided to all of these target groups. The purpose of this work is to familiarize them with existing legal provisions related to violence and FGM and to build awareness of the content of these documents, an awareness that could lead to grassroots acceptance and the adoption of a law against FGM. Comments by health workers on the dramatic short- and long-term consequences of FGM on the physical and mental health of women and girls were collected and presented, along with testimony from victims of FGM (e.g., problems excised women have giving birth compared to those who have not undergone excision).

Religious leaders spoke on very specific issues: Does the Koran require the practice of FGM? Is there a passage in the Koran which says that FGM is mandatory? Is it possible for someone who doesn't comply with the practice of FGM to be a good Muslim? Why is FGM not practised in Morocco, Tunisia and Algeria, all of which are Islamic countries? Is the practice of FGM part of the five fundamental tenants of Islam? Why was the daughter of the Prophet not subjected to this practice? This series of questions produced the desired result: namely, a realization that there is no mention of the supposedly mandatory practice of FGM anywhere in the Koran.

After hearing answers to these questions, those who had taken part in training programs to stop FGM in Mali uttered a collective sigh of relief. The rightness of our position was reinforced and there was a renewed conviction to end this practice. This conviction grows and grows as horrific stories confirm the urgency of abandoning this practice. The showing of the CIAF film *La duperie* reaffirmed the necessity for Mali to adopt a law against FGM.

What are the problems? There is still no real political commitment by the necessary authorities. Many feel that it is too early or that it is not the solution after more than thirty years of building awareness that produced few concrete results. Only in the past six years, thanks to the work of certain NGOs, have women who perform excisions voluntarily set aside their knives. There is also the problem of certain fundamentalist Muslim religious groups which use the issue of FGM as a means of blackmailing authorities, criticizing and making threats against the government in the media. Without adequate funds, NGOs in general and the APDF in particular are unable to take their programs aimed at ending excision to the entire country. There is also a real lack of cooperation between the NGOs on this issue, some of which do not think it is necessary for Mail to adopt a law against FGM.

Nevertheless, there is cause for hope. Mali does have national legislation which, while it does not make explicit reference to FGM, could be used or strengthened to achieve the desired outcome. These provisions include the Mali

Constitution of 25 February 1992, which states in its preamble, and I quote: "The sovereign people of Mali proclaim their determination to defend the rights of women and children."

As well, safeguards for women's rights could be protected by the following articles:

Article 1: The human person is sacred and inviolable.... An individual has a right to life, liberty, security and the integrity of his or her person.

Article 3: No person shall be subject to torture, nor to inhuman, cruel, degrading or humiliating abuse or treatments. Any individual or any officer of the State who is found guilty of such acts, by his own initiative or as a result of following orders, shall be punished in accordance with the law.

The Criminal Code goes even further:

Article 166, paragraph 1: Any individual who wilfully attacks or causes injury to or commits any form of violence or assault, which results in illness or inability to work for a period exceeding twenty days shall receive a prison term of between one and five years and a fine of between Fr 20,000 and 500,000.

Paragraph 3: When such violence, injury or assault results in mutilation, amputation, loss of the use of a body part or a sense, blindness, loss of an eye or some other infirmity or illness, the penalty will be from five to ten years of hard labour.

Article 163: Cracks down on fatal attacks, cases where the victim dies as a result of an attack. In such cases, the offence becomes a crime punishable by five to twenty years of hard labour and, optionally, local banishment for one to twenty years.

Article 167: Provides for cases in which the attack or injuries do not lead to illness or incapacity for a period exceeding twenty days. The penalty in such cases is between eleven days and two years in prison and/or a fine of between Fr 20,000 and 100,000.

Article 168: Refers to attacks or injuries of an unintentional nature and provides as follows: "a person who through blunder, carelessness, inattention, negligence or failure to adhere to regulations unintentionally strikes or injures or causes illness to another shall be punished with imprisonment of between three months and two years and/or a fine of between Fr 20,000 and 300,000."

In addition to these national provisions, it should be remembered that Mali ratified the Convention on the Elimination of All Forms of Discrimination Against Women without any reservation (1985) and the Convention on the Rights of the Child (1990), as well as other international instruments such as the

International Covenant on Economic, Social and Cultural Rights (1974) and the African Charter on Human and Peoples' Rights (1985). Despite all of this, there is still hesitation to adopt specific legislation against the practice of FGM. Could this mean that FGM does not constitute an offence according to Mali law? And if it does, why have Mali legislators not pressed for the application of the law to punish those committing this offence?

What is the responsibility of parents who submit their children to this practice? What is the responsibility of the people who perform excisions? What is the responsibility of the health worker who knows the consequences but continues to perform FGM for money? FGM is a serious violation of the physical and emotional integrity of women and girls and, as such, is a criminal act which should be punished. Because it is a criminal act, the government is obliged to adopt legislation against FGM. Experience has shown that the disapproval of NGOs and individuals is not enough to end this practice. There must be political will from the decision-makers.

Mali should honour its international commitments and bring an end to FGM. After all, we have known for more than thirty years that it should be stopped. The adoption of legislation is now an urgent matter. The experience of countries like Burkina-Faso, Egypt and Togo are good examples for Mali. Now is the right time to save the futures of thousands of girls in Mali. Let's do it.

Sexuality, Discrimination and Human Rights

Lesbian and Gay Rights[1]

Martha A. McCarthy practises general, family and equality rights law at the firm of McMillan Binch in Toronto. She's the author of *Family Law for Every Canadian* and a speaker and writer on gay and lesbian equality issues. She represented 'M.' in the case of *M. v. H.* which is presently before the Supreme Court of Canada. That case concerns whether a former partner in a lesbian relationship is entitled to interim spousal support.

IN 1992, when I was in my second year of law practice, a client walked into my office and changed my career. She told me the following story. She had met her partner in 1980, while travelling with a group in Nepal. They started an immediate love affair which continued when they returned to Toronto. In 1982 they moved in together and started their own business. They cohabited for the next ten years, sharing virtually every part of their lives, acquiring property together, pooling income and sharing expenses. Each year they celebrated October 15th as their anniversary.

They had just separated. My client had $5.64 in her bank account, no assets apart from a jointly owned country property and no source of income apart from the jointly owned business. She took a few personal possessions with her, leaving behind all of the property that they had acquired together. When she went back the next day, the locks to both homes had been changed and the business was being answered with a new name. She was denied access to the business' answering service and cut off from business contacts. The accountant told her that he was not authorized to give her information. In a telephone call that same day, her partner had told her that she was not entitled to anything— that the law didn't recognize her because she had been in a lesbian relationship.

It didn't take much to see that my client, who later came to be known as M. in the case of *M. v. H.*, was discriminated against because of her sexual orientation.[2] If she had been in an opposite-sex relationship she would have had immediate access to family law remedies. She could have obtained spousal support on an interim basis within weeks of separation. Little did we know that six years later we would have argued the constitutional issue at trial, an appeal and had more than fifty other judicial attendances in the case without M. ever receiving any relief from the financial stress of separation. Little did we know that because the case was fundamentally so simple, this woman's struggle would culminate in a decision from the Supreme Court of Canada that stands to truly achieve equality for gays and lesbians in Canada. And little did I know that I would have learned enough along the way to have the privilege of addressing sexual orientation discrimination at the Edmonton conference.

■■■ How Far Have We Come? Then and Now

Since we are celebrating the fiftieth anniversary of the adoption of the Universal Declaration of Human Rights by the United Nations, I will begin by looking at the Universal Declaration.[3] Although it did not include a provision prohibiting discrimination on the basis of sexual orientation, five provisions were included which held some promise for gays and lesbians who sought equality: (i) the essential human rights provision about being free and equal in dignity and rights;[4] (ii) the equality before the law provision;[5] (iii) the right of recognition as a person before the law;[6] (iv) freedom from interference with a person's right to privacy;[7] and, (v) the right to marry and found a family.[8] Unfortunately, these were false hopes for gays and lesbians, who were told by various court decisions in the ensuing years that they had no right to equality, no right to privacy, no right to marry, no right to found a family. In all, gays and lesbians have gained little direct assistance from the Universal Declaration over the last fifty years. Certainly, gays and lesbians can be counted among its beneficiaries, to the extent that the Declaration is responsible for a general attitude shift over inalienable human rights. At the current time, however, this is more of an abstract, spiritual effect than a substantive one.

■■■ Then

If we look at the social context of the Universal Declaration from the perspective of gays and lesbians, it isn't surprising that the document excludes sexual orientation discrimination from its guarantees. The gay and lesbian equality movement was clearly in its infancy in 1948. The Kinsey Report, the first major survey about sexual orientation, had just been released, showing a continuum between heterosexuality and homosexuality.[9] "Homosexuality" was still regarded as a psychiatric illness.[10] In 1956 Dr. Evelyn Hooker released her groundbreaking research that showed that there was no difference in adjustment, psychological or otherwise, between gays, lesbians and heterosexuals.[11] In 1957 the United Kingdom's famous Wolfenden Report concluded that it is not the function of the law to intervene in the lives of private citizens or to seek to enforce any particular pattern of behaviour.[12]

While many forms of discrimination were in the midst of revolution, sexual orientation discrimination was the legal norm at the time of the Universal Declaration. Here in Canada, for example, Everett Klippert was sentenced to "preventative detention" as a dangerous offender after he was diagnosed as "an uncurable homosexual" in 1959.[13] He lost his appeal before the Supreme Court of Canada in 1967 and his case created such an outcry that Canadian politicians were moved to repeal laws against same-sex sexual relations. Klippert was released from jail with the decriminalization of consensual "gross indecency" and "buggery" in 1969.

Starting in the late 1950s, a wave of change swept across North America. Birth control was made available, weakening the notion that the only acceptable grounds for sex were procreative. Unmarried heterosexual couples lived together openly. Civil rights, anti-war, student and women's movements each challenged societal norms in different ways. These movements raised questions about authoritarianism, the construction of gender, and the ability of the government and the legal system to promote justice for all. Courts rejected laws that failed to respect the principles of equality, even when these laws expressed long-standing religious and social traditions. In 1953, the seminal desegregation case *Brown v. Board of Education* began the process of healing racial inequality in the United States.[14] In 1958, in *Loving v. Virginia*, the US Supreme Court overturned the laws in sixteen states containing same-race restrictions on people's choice of a marriage partner.[15] In the midst of all of this evolution, gay and lesbian concerns were not necessarily a priority. It wasn't until many years later, in 1969, that the Stonewall Riots in Greenwich Village, New York, marked the birth of the modern gay and lesbian equality rights movement. A full twenty years after the Universal Declaration, the gay and lesbian equality rights movement began to take shape.

Now

Coming to the present day, what has been achieved? The average person's answer to this question would be extremely positive. After all, it seems that every day we hear another news story about the evolution of equality for gays and lesbians, and most of us believe that there have been significant gains. The following is a brief summary of where we are now.

While the United Nations has still yet to amend the UN Declaration to include sexual orientation as a prohibited form of discrimination, many countries have adopted human rights protection for gays and lesbians[16] and European decisions are beginning to show recognition of sexual orientation discrimination as a societal wrong.[17] Constitutions in South Africa, Germany and Poland all include sexual orientation protection. The European Parliament passed a resolution on Equal Rights for Homosexuals and Lesbians in the European Community in 1995, and resolved in 1994 that gays and lesbians should have access to marriage or domestic partnerships.[18] Many countries have registered domestic partnership schemes.[19] Several American and Canadian courts have provided adoption rights to same-sex couples.[20] Several countries include same-sex couples in immigration sponsorship provisions.[21]

In 1996, in the case of *Romer v. Evans*, the United States Supreme Court found that a constitutional amendment that denied human rights protections to gays and lesbians "defies" the equality guarantee of the US Constitution.[22] Following this decision, two successful trial decisions in Hawaii and Alaska concluded that same-sex marriage restrictions are unconstitutional.[23] In response, many state legislatures rushed to judgement, passing legislation that refused to recognize same-sex marriages performed in other states.[24] The American federal government passed the Defence of Marriage Act, which says that the term "spouse" in all federal legislation does not include gays and lesbians and allows states to refuse to recognize same-sex marriages performed in other states.[25] In 1998, the Hawaiian and Alaskan governments passed constitutional amendments specifically prohibiting such unions.[26] Notwithstanding the clear message of *Romer v. Evans*, the popular American attitude seems to be, if our constitution allows for same-sex marriage then we'll change our constitution. These legislative and constitutional efforts are the latest conceptual barrier in the legal battle over the human rights of gays and lesbians.[27]

In Europe, Denmark was the first to provide recognition of same-sex "domestic partnerships" in 1989. Many other Scandinavian nations have followed Denmark's example.[28] Registered partners enjoy all of the rights and responsibilities of marriage except for adoption and in some cases other restrictions relating to children. Denmark has recently removed the adoption restriction on domestic partnerships so that now there is separate, but at least relatively equal, treatment in that country.[29]

Two Australian territories and one Canadian province, British Columbia, have taken a different approach and provided simple equality in family law terms to same-sex couples on the same terms as unmarried opposite-sex couples.[30] While this remedy does not contemplate the issue of same-sex marriages, it provides the same treatment to the two groups over a range of issues.

▬ Now in Canada

The Canadian struggle for same-sex equality has moved slowly and has centred on court decisions after some staggering failures at legislative reform.[31] While decriminalization of sexual acts was achieved early, comprehensive human rights protection and general spousal recognition are still unrealized. Litigants have slowly and successfully obtained, through piecemeal constitutional challenges, sexual orientation protection in employment, spousal employment benefits, step-parent adoption, public health coverage and conjugal visits in jail.[32] However, with the very notable exception of the comprehensive British Columbia family law legislation,[33] gays and lesbians continue to reach for meaningful equality in Canada.

In the 1992 case, *Layland v. Beaulne*,[34] the Ontario Divisional Court considered the issue of same-sex marriages and concluded that the two men who had been denied a marriage licence were not discriminated against because each of them was free to marry a woman. An appeal was launched but was later abandoned after two Supreme Court of Canada cases left gays and lesbians with the distinct impression that the courts were not ready for the marriage issue.

Those cases were *Miron v. Trudel* and *Egan v. Canada*.[35, 36] In *Miron*, the Supreme Court of Canada found that it was unconstitutional to distinguish between unmarried and married opposite-sex spouses in the payment of automobile insurance benefits. Marriage, according to the Court, was not a relevant marker for the legislature's purpose of reducing economic hardship after a family member had been injured. The marriage requirement was, therefore, unconstitutional.

Egan, which was released the same day as *Miron*, involved a challenge to the exclusion of same-sex spouses from the Old Age Security Act. A majority of the Supreme Court determined that this treatment was discriminatory but constitutional. Four justices held that there was no discrimination, because sexual orientation was relevant to fundamental social norms and values rooted in biology, morality and tradition.[37] The ninth Justice, holding the "swing vote," found that the legislation violated the equality guarantee but stated that the government should be granted some time to respond to the widespread discrimination against gays and lesbians, because their claims to equality were "novel." Although the recognition of sexual orientation as an analogous ground in *Egan* may be seen as important, the irony between the progressive result of *Miron* and the reliance on historical prejudice in *Egan* was not lost on gay and lesbian equality-seekers. Heterosexism seemed to be alive and well.

Three years later, the Supreme Court of Canada had an opportunity to consider the basic human rights of gays and lesbians in the case of *Vriend v. Alberta*.[38] In *Vriend*, a gay university employee was fired because of his sexual orientation and told that he had no human rights protection under the Alberta human rights code.[39] The appeal decision had aggressively supported the government's refusal to provide any human rights protection on the basis of sexual orientation.[40] Before the Supreme Court, the Alberta government continued to argue that the courts should not interfere when the legislature has specifically decided to exclude certain groups from protection. Mr. Justice Iacobucci, writing for the unanimous Court, wrote a powerful judgement that holds out real promise that the rights of gays and lesbians will be protected by the judiciary:

Groups that have historically been the target of discrimination cannot be expected to wait patiently for the protection of their human dignity and equal rights while governments move toward reform one step at a time. If the infringement of the rights and freedoms of these groups is permitted to persist while governments fail to pursue equality diligently, then the guarantees of the Charter will be reduced to little more than empty words.[41]

Two weeks after the decision in *Vriend* was released, a unanimous Ontario Court of Appeal ordered the government to include same-sex couples in the definition of spouse for the purposes of registered pension plans under the Income Tax Act in *Rosenberg v. Canada* (Attorney General).[42] The decision, written by Madam Justice Abella, forcefully recognizes the human rights of gays and lesbians. It marks a major victory over the tax system's blatant heterosexism, hopefully suggesting an end to the requirement that gays and lesbians subsidize a tax scheme that does not even recognize them.[43]

We argued *M. v. H.* before the Supreme Court of Canada on 18 March 1998, and the decision continues to be under reserve.[44] The case concerns spousal support rights and obligations, and more generally, access to the justice of family law. It is about responsibility and the relationship between the couple, not just access by the couple to some public benefit. While so many other cases that came before it have considered the relationship in the context of some government benefit, *M. v. H.* considers only the economic and emotional interdependency of the couple. In this way, the case addresses the factual centre of most claims to gay and lesbian equality—the loving unions of gay and lesbian couples—free from the complications of government decision-making or budgetary concerns. In its simplicity, and given the backdrop of the recent equality decisions in Canada, *M. v. H.* is expected to have very broad implications for the rights of gays and lesbians in this country.

When we look at *Miron, Egan, Vriend* and *Rosenberg* together, it appears that Canadian courts are moving towards the equal treatment of all intimate relationships. The marker of marriage between opposite-sex married and unmarried couples is unconstitutional. Differential treatment of opposite-sex and same-sex couples is highly suspect. Whether we do it now or by persistent case-by-case attack, it seems that any law that is extended in favour of opposite-sex couples is going to have to be extended in favour of same-sex couples. As one British judge recently wrote on the subject, "to conclude otherwise would be to stand like to King Canute, order the tide to recede, when the tide in favour of equality rolls relentlessly forward and shows no sign of ebbing."[45]

◼ Reality

One of the common themes of this conference is that while the Universal Declaration must be celebrated, we must remember how far we still have to travel in order to achieve its goals. And while a seminar on sexual orientation discrimination at this Conference is itself an accomplishment, the theme of continuing struggle rings particularly true for gays and lesbians, who are still denied full membership in our society fifty years after the Declaration.

While there have been some positive court decisions recognizing the dignity of gays and lesbians, and while a select number of governments have actually moved in that direction, there is so much important work yet to be done. Many legislatures continue to react with homophobic efforts to hush the judiciary. Governments continue to vigorously fight equality claims by gays and lesbians in the courts. Same sex marriage is a wildly controversial issue. And as a rule, our society continues to denigrate, marginalize and exclude gay and lesbian relationships from our conception of friends, family and religion.

We need look no further than the crime sections of our newspapers to see reality. Hate crimes are on the rise. The *Globe and Mail* recently reported that, in Toronto alone, "gay-bashing" has increased by twenty per cent since 1997.[46] On 7 October 1998, Matthew Shepard, a 21-year-old student, was brutally murdered in Wyoming simply because he was gay.[47] Harvey Fierstein, the noted American playwright and gay activist, wrote a moving tribute to Matthew Shepard that seemed particularly suitable to this discussion:

> Where do we express our outrage? Who can we count on to extract our revenge? How could this happen in our America? Why is that beautiful, brave, caring, bright and loving gay boy dead?
>
> The easiest to answer of these questions are "how" and "why": Because we are represented by politicians who feel free to call our lives a disease, an illness, a maladjustment, even a crime—and they do so with impunity.... That's why Matthew Shepard was beaten bloody.
>
> Because we turn for moral leadership to priests and pastors, ministers and rabbis who daily refer to our lives as an "abomination."...That's why Matthew Shepard was robbed and crucified on a fence.
>
> Because talk show hosts get laughs making jokes at our expense.... Because newspapers and articles lose no readership addressing their audience as if everyone of us is straight. That's why Matthew Shepard was set on fire and left to die.
>
> Because WE, in vast numbers, refuse to come out of the closet, thereby sending a clear message that even WE believe that's something to hide; that our lives are shameful; that being gay or lesbian is wrong. That is why Matthew Shepard is dead.[48]

A Vision of Change

Rather than conclude on this melancholy note, I thought I should briefly make some suggestions of ways to continue to breathe life into the Universal

Declaration's message from a gay and lesbian perspective. I have four very general concepts in my vision of change.

The first is that courts have to continue to play an aggressive role in cases involving gay and lesbian equality issues. These cases are not about legislatures versus the courts and they are not about democracy.[49] We often hear people say that democracy is at stake when courts make decisions about society and that courts are interfering with the democratic process when they intervene. This is an age-old argument. The Governor of Alabama made it when he refused to comply with the US Supreme Court decision in *Brown v. Board of Education*.[50] In fact, whenever courts step in to recognize the oppression of a minority group, the anti-change majority has shouted about democracy.

The principle behind the democracy argument is that political power should be in the hands of the people. However, the argument ignores the fact that no democracy provides genuine equality of political power. That is why we have a Universal Declaration, constitutions and human rights codes. Respect for the inherent dignity of the human person, commitment to social justice and equality, accommodation of a wide variety of beliefs, respect for cultural and group identity, and social inclusiveness and participation are among the values and principles essential to a "free and democratic society." A true vision of democracy is only achieved where all members of society have equality of political power. Judicial review enhances the democratic ideal by providing a forum for uniquely sound and principled conclusions about rights, free from the pressure of political popularity. It is a necessary pre-condition to a healthy, functioning democracy. As Ronald Dworkin has written, equality and democracy are "aspects of the same ideal, not, as is often supposed, rivals."[51]

Second, although equality cases often dwell what might seem to be the small details of medical benefits or gay pride parades or one woman's job security, much more is at stake. Human rights are at issue whenever and wherever homophobia is operating. Sexual orientation discrimination strikes at the core of humanity and freedom. It denies individuals the fundamental right to live life with the mate of one's choice in the fashion of one's choice.[52] It is, truly, about the right to love. What could be more essential to our conception of human rights?

Discrimination on the basis of sexual orientation denies the dignity and worth of individuals. Laws which differentiate between opposite- and same-sex couples cannot be defended by legislative reform, constitutional amendment or judicial deference to history, tradition, biology or morality.[53] The Universal Declaration and all of its subsequent achievements clearly indicate that a human rights conception of our society must be the governing morality.

Third, our goal must be the achievement of substantive equality. A substantive equality analysis is directed at preventing the violation of human dignity and freedom, and the promotion of a society in which all persons enjoy equal recognition at law, equally capable of and equally deserving of concern, respect and consideration.[54] It is aimed at changing the material conditions, or the "substance," of people's lives. Because it focuses on lived realities, it considers the effects of government action, in the larger social and historical context, from the perspective of the disadvantaged rights holder. Since *Andrews v. The Law Society*,[55] the first major decision under Canada's constitutional guarantee of equality, our nation has been a leader in promoting substantive equality. However, the Supreme Court of Canada has not been consistent in protecting the rights of lesbians and gay men. In *Egan,* a majority of our highest court refused to recognize same-sex spouses by reverting to a formal equality analysis, with its emphasis on biology, sectarian morality, and tradition.[56] Hopefully, *M. v. H.* will confirm the Court's commitment to advancing substantive equality for lesbians and gays.

Finally, the family unit must be addressed. To date, the approach in Canada has been to work "from the outside in." We have talked about the importance of prison visits yet we have failed to address the spousal relationship itself. It is crucial that we address the concept of family head-on if we are going to achieve substantive equality—if we are going to aim to remedy and remove discrimination from our society. As Alistair Nicholson, the Chief Justice of the Family Court of Australia, recently wrote:

> Prejudicial community attitudes only change when society truly recognizes the humanity of the group who have been enduring discrimination and, to my mind, nothing can be more central to a definition of humanity than respect for the importance that each of us places on enduring relationships.[57]

If we address the family—if we get people not just to understand but to truly appreciate that gays and lesbians are family, that they love each other, that they have healthy, positive intimate relationships—then, and only then, can people truly appreciate the humanity, and thus the human rights, of gays and lesbians.

These issues really need to be dealt with in a comprehensive way, preferably by positive law reform. Because the possibility of legislative change seems unlikely to occur, at least in North America, it will have to be achieved by court challenge and ongoing efforts at changing discriminatory attitudes. This requires continued bravery and tenacity by individual gay and lesbian litigants, their advocates and their judges. It requires hours of labour (often, unfortunately, unpaid) and reams of paper dedicated to compiling evidence, building strategies, crafting arguments and educating the public. For now at least, this seems to be the only path available if gays and lesbians are to truly share in the celebration of the achievements of the Universal Declaration on its next anniversary.

■ Postscript

On 20 May 1999, the Supreme Court of Canada released its decision in *M. v. H.* In an eight-to-one decision, the highest court in Canada declared the opposite-sex definition of "spouse" in section 29 of the Family Law Act (FLA) to be unconstitutional because it excludes same-sex couples.

In the majority judgement, Justices Cory and Iacobucci stated that the opposite-sex definition of "spouse" in s. 29 of the FLA led to differential treatment on the basis of sexual orientation and that this violated the human dignity of individuals in same-sex relationships. The Court concluded that this differential treatment was discriminatory and infringed the right to equality under s. 15 of the Canadian Charter of Rights and Freedoms. It held that this infringement could not be justified under s. 1 of the Charter, as there was no rational connection between the objectives of the spousal support provisions and the means chosen to further the objectives. As a result, the Court declared s. 29 of the FLA to be of no force or effect, suspending the declaration for six months to allow for legislative reform of the Act.

The ruling will require the federal and provincial governments to amend all legislation in Canada which contains an opposite-sex definition of "spouse" to include same-sex couples. Justices Cory and Iacobucci wrote that "declaring s. 29 of the FLA to be of no force or effect may well affect numerous other statutes that rely upon a similar definition of the term 'spouse'. The legislature may wish to address the validity of these statutes in light of the unconstitutionality of s. 29 of the FLA."

Following the decision, the federal government has passed survivor pension legislation for gays and lesbians, and Québec has introduced an omnibus bill overhauling all legislation to include same-sex couples. All Canadian premiers except Ralph Klein of Alberta have said they will comply with the decision, many announcing plans to introduce omnibus legislation that will change all definitions of spouse in provincial legislation. The Supreme Court's decision in the *M. v. H.* case truly stands to achieve substantive equality for all gays and lesbians in Canada.

REFERENCES

1. This paper is adapted from Ms. McCarthy's address on the topic of Sexuality, Discrimination and Human Rights delivered to the International Conference on Universal Rights and Human Values: A Blueprint for Peace, Justice and Freedom (Edmonton, 26 November 1998).

2. *M. v. H.* (1996), 132 D.L.R. (4th) 538 (Epstein J.), aff'd (1996), 142 D.L.R. (4th) 1 (Charron J. A. and Doherty, J. A. concurring; Finlayson J. A. dissenting). Heard by the Supreme Court of Canada on 18 March 1998; decision under reserve [hereinafter *M. v. H.*].

3. G.A. res. 217A (III) UN DOC A/810 at 71 (1948) [hereinafter the "UN Declaration"]. The UN Declaration was adopted on 10 December 1948 by the General Assembly of the UN without dissent.

4. According to Article 1: "All human beings are born free and equal in dignity and rights. They are endowed with reason and conscience and should act towards one another in a spirit of brotherhood."

5. According to Article 7: "All are equal before the law and entitled without any discrimination to equal protection of the law. All are entitled to equal protection against any discrimination in violation of this Declaration and against any incitement to such discrimination."

6. According to Article 6: "Everyone has the right to recognition everywhere as a person before the law."

7. According to Article 12: "No one shall be subjected to arbitrary interferences with his privacy, family, home or correspondence, nor to attacks upon his honour and reputation. Everyone has the right to the protection of the law against such interference or attacks."

8. According to Article 16(1): "Men and women of full age, without any limitation due to race, nationality or religion, have the right to marry and to found a family. They are entitled to equal rights as to marriage, during marriage and at its dissolution."

9. Alfred C. Kinsey, Wardell B. Pomeroy, Clyde E. Martin, *Sexual Behaviour in the Human Male* (Bloomington IN: Indiana University Press, May 1998). The Staff of the Institute for Sex Research, Indiana University, Alfred C. Kinsey, Wardell B. Pomeroy, Clyde E. Martin and Paul H. Gebhard, *Sexual Behaviour in the Human Female* (Bloomington IN: Indiana University Press, May 1998). Paul H. Gebhard and Alan B. Johnson, *The Kinsey Data: Marginal Tabulations of the 1938–1963 Interviews Conducted by the Institute for Sex Research* (Bloomington IN: Indiana University Press, May 1998).

10. American Psychiatric Association (1973). "Position Statement on Homosexuality and Civil Rights." *American Journal of Psychiatry*, 131 (4) 497.

11. E. Hooker. "The Adjustment of the Male Overt Homosexual." *The Journal of Projective Techniques*, 1957 and 1958.

12. The Wolfenden Report on Homosexual Offences and Prostitution recommended that homosexual behaviour in private between consenting adults (i.e., over the age of twenty-one), should be decriminalized. The Wolfenden Report. *Report of the Committee on Homosexual Offences and Prostitution*. American Edition. New York: Lancer Books (1964).

13. *Klippert v. The Queen*, [1967] S.C.R. 822, 2 C.R.N.S. 319, discussed in D. C. Casswell, *Lesbians, Gay Men, and Canadian Law*. Toronto: Emond Montgomery (1996) at 108–109.

14. *Brown v. Board of Education*, 347 US 483, 74 S. Ct. 686, 98 L. Ed. 873.

15. 385 US 986; 87 S. Ct. 595; 17 L. Ed. 2d 448 (1966). Mildred Jeter and Richard Loving faced up to five years in prison for getting married until the inter-racial marriage laws were struck down.

16. Including Canada, Denmark, France, the Netherlands, Norway, Ireland and Spain.

17. *Grant v. South-West Trains* C-249/96. Judgement of 17/02/1998, (Rep. 1998, p. 1–621); and *P. v. S. & Cornwall County Council*, Case C-13/94 (Court of Justice of the European Communities, Luxembourg) and "Sex change dismissal discriminatory," Times Law Reports (7 May 1996).

18. European Parliament Resolution on Equal Rights for Homosexuals and Lesbians in the European Community (A3-0028/94) available on the Internet at http:/www.qrd.org/qrd/world/europe/ec/parliament.resolution.equal.rights-02.08.94.

19. Including Denmark, the Netherlands, Norway, Sweden, Hungary and Iceland. See James D. Wilets, "International Human Rights Law and Sexual Orientation" (1994) 18:1 Hastings Int'l & Comp. L. Rev. I. at 96; M. Bailey, "Hawaii's Same Sex Marriage Initiatives: Implications for Canada" (1998) 15 C.J.F.L. 153. *The Norwegian Act on Registered Partnerships for Homosexual Couples*, The Ministry of Children and Family Affairs, Oslo, Norway (April 1993) and the *Danish Registered Partnership Act* are available on the Internet at http:/www.qrd.org.

20. *Re K.* (1995), 23 O.R. (3d) 679 (Prov. Div.); *In re Adoption of a Child by J. M. G.*, 267 N. J. Super. 622 A.2d 550 (1993); *Adoption of Evan*, 153 Misc. 2d 844, 583 NY 2d 997 (1992).

21. Australian has a visa and permit category for "Nonfamilial Relationships of Emotional Interdependency" which may be used by opposite- or same-sex couples to achieve residency. See, Wilets, *supra*, at 104–105. British citizens may bring their same-sex spouses to join them in Britain under the *Concession Outside the Immigration Rules for Unmarried Partners* as announced by the Honourable Mike O'Brien, Minister of Immigration, 10 October 1997 (effective 13 October 1997). In Canada, there are new guidelines under the Inland Processing Manual for immigration officers, which are available on the Internet at http://cicnet.ci.gc.ca (go to What's New, March 5) and Citizenship and Immigration Minister Lucienne Robillard recently announced that gays and lesbians would be able to sponsor their partners into the country. See "Civil service to get same-sex benefits: Ottawa to overhaul pension plans in bid to head off court battle" Tuesday, 16 March 1999, Daniel Leblanc (Parliamentary Bureau). The sponsorship provisions under the regulations to Canada's *Immigration Act*, R.S.C. 1985, chap. 1–2, currently do not include same-sex couples under the definition of spouse, section 5 of Reg. SOR/97–145 s. 3.

22. *Romer v. Evans*, 517 US 620, 116 S. Ct. 1620 at 1628–29 (1996) Kennedy J.

23. *Baehr v. Lewin*, 8522 P. 2d 44 (1993); *Baehr v. Miike*, 910 P. 2d 112 (1996); *Braise and Dugan v. Bureau of Vital Statistics, Alaska Dept. of Health & Social Services, and the Alaska Court System* (Case NO. 3 AN-95-6562 CI; In the Superior Court for the State of Alaska, Third Judicial District at Anchorage).

24. Anti-marriage measures have been widely adopted: WA, AR, FL, HI, IN, ME, MN, MS, MT, ND, VA, AK, AZ, DE, GA, ID, IL, KS, MI, MO, NC, OK, PA, SC, SD, TN, UT.

25. *Defence of Marriage Act*, Pub. L. 104–199, 110 Stat. 2419 (1996). Passed by House of Representatives (7/12/96) and the Senate (9/10/96), signed into law by President Clinton under cover of darkness on 21 September 1996. Many academics have since suggested that this statute may be unconstitutional: see e.g., Lawrence Tribe, "Toward a Less Perfect Union," *New York Times* (26 May 1996) A11; J. M, Donovan, "DOMA: An Unconstitutional Establishment of Fundamentalist Christianity," 4 Mich. Gender & L. 335 (1997).

26. See Dan Foley, "A loss that moves us forward is in the end a victory," *Frontiers Newsmagazine* (23 November 1998) A-1.

27. There is still a Vermont marriage case that remains to be decided. *Baker v. State of Vermont* (Vermont Supreme Court Docket No. 98–32), materials available at http://www.vtfreetomarry.org. It was argued on 17 November 1998 and the earliest date for a constitutional conditional amendment would be the year 2002. Accordingly, even if somebody tries to fix the constitution later, there may be some window of time during which gays and lesbians can get married in Vermont.

28. See, e.g., Sweden's *Registered Partnership (Family Law) Act* and Norway's *Norwegian Act on Registered Partnerships for Homosexual Couples.*

29. The Dutch Government has announced that it will examine upgrading registered domestic partnerships to marriages in the next three years. See, *Commissie inzake openstelling van het burgerlijk huwelijk voor personen van hetselfde geslacht* (Den Haag, October 1998).

30. See *Domestic Relationships Act 1994*, available on the Internet at http://www.austlii.edu.au. *Family Relations Act*, R.S.B.C. 1996, c. 128, as am. by *Family Relations Amendment Act, 1997* (proclaimed 4 February 1998); *Family Maintenance Enforcement Act*, R.S.B.C. 1996, c. 127 as am. by *Family Maintenance Enforcement Amendment Act, 1997* (proclaimed 4 February 1998).

31. The most notable of which was Ontario's *Bill 167, Equality Rights Statute Law Amendment Act*, an attempt to remove discrimination by amending the definition of spouse in fifty-seven statutes to include same-sex couples. When the bill was defeated by a narrow margin, the legislative gallery erupted with screams of protest. Legislative security guards and provincial police wearing rubber gloves moved in to remove the protesters.

32. *Veysey v. Correctional Service of Canada* (1990), 109 N.R. (F.C.A.), aff'g on different grounds

(1989), 20 F.T.R. 74 (F.C.T.D.); *Knodel v. British Columbia (Medical Services Commission),* [1991] 6 W.W.R. 728 (B.C. S.C.); *Holmwood* (November, 1992) (BC Work. Comp. Bc.); *Jeffs* (1993, U.I. Bd. of Ref.) under appeal; *Re Canada (Treasury Board-Environment Canada) and Lorenzen* (1993), 38 L.A.C. (4th) 29; *Coles and O'Neill v. Ministry of Transportation and Jacobson,* File No. 92-018/09 (October, 1994) (Ont. Bd. Inq.); *Re K.* (1995), 23 O.R. (3d) 679 (Ont. Prov. Div.); *Re C.E.G.* (No. 1), [1995] O.J. No. 4072 (Gen. Div.) (QL); *Re Yarrow and Treasury Board (Agriculture and Agri-Food Canada)* (1995), 43 C.L.A.S. 309 (Pub. Serv. Staff Rels. Bd.); *Re Metro Toronto Reference Library and C.U.P.E., Local 1582* (1995), 51 L.A.C. (4th) 69; *Moore and Akerstrom,* supra note 12; *Dwyer v. Toronto (Metropolitan),* File No. BI-0056-93 (27 September 1996) (Ont. Bd. Inq.); *Re Treasury Board (Canadian Grain Commission) and Sarson* (1996), 42 C.L.A.S. 337; *Kane v. Attorney General (Ontario),* [1997] O.J. No. 3979 (Gen. Div.) (QL); *Bewley v. Ontario,* [1997] O.H.R.B.I.D. No. 24 (File No. BI-1014096) (Ont. Bd. Inq.).

33. *Family Relations Amendment Act,* 1997, supra.

34. (1993), 104 O.L.R. (4th) 214 (Ont. Div. Ct.)

35. [1995] 2 S.C.R. 418 [hereinafter *Miron*].

36. [1995] 2 S.C.R. 513 [hereinafter *Egan*].

37. This minority judgement with respect to section 15 was adopted by Lamer, C. J., La Forest, Gonthier and Major J. J.

38. [1998] 1 S.C.R. 493 [hereinafter *Vriend*].

39. The Court was unanimous except with respect to remedy. On that issue, Major J. dissented; he would have declared the sections denying protection to gays and lesbians unconstitutional but would have granted a declaration of invalidity, suspended for a period of one year. "Reading in" was inadvisable since it was clear that the Alberta Legislature was opposed to including sexual orientation as a prohibited ground of discrimination. The Legislature might prefer no human rights statute over one that included sexual orientation as a prohibited ground of discrimination or it might want to invoke the notwithstanding clause.

40. *Vriend v. Alberta* (1996), 132 D.L.R. (4th) 595 (Alta. C.A.). McClung J. A. wrote at 609: "I am unable to conclude that it was a forbidden, let alone a reversible, legislative response for the Province of Alberta to step back from the validation of homosexual relations, including sodomy, as a protected and fundamental right, thereby, 'rebutting a millennia of moral teaching': *Bowers v. Hardwick,* 92 L. Ed. 2d 140 (U.S.S.C., 1986), per Burger C. J. at 150." *Vriend* C.A. at 611: "I say nothing as well of the respondent's answer to the appellant's concerns that the term 'sexual orientation' is limited to 'traditional' homosexual practices shared by consenting adults, and its IRPA inclusion would never be raised as a permissive shield sheltering other practices, both heterosexual and homosexual, commonly regarded as deviance in both communities. It is pointless to deny that the Dahmer, Bernardo and Clifford Robert Olsen prosecutions have recently heightened public concern about violently aberrant sexual configurations and how they find expression against their victims."

41. *Vriend* (S.C.C.), supra, at para. 122.

42. (1998), 158 D.L.R. (3d) 664 (Ont. C.A.) [hereinafter *Rosenberg*].

43. The tax benefit awarded to heterosexuals, on the basis of their heterosexuality, was approximately $5 billion dollars in 1993, comprising the sixty-seventh largest government expenditure. It is estimated that same-sex couples loses between $16.2 million and $165 million by subsidizing a system which does not benefit them. See, K. Lahey, "The Political Economies of 'Sex' and Canadian Income Tax Policy" (Address to the Canadian Bar Association (Ontario), (1998)) [unpublished].

44. The Supreme Court's decision is expected at any time.

45. *Fitzpatrick v. Sterling Housing Association Ltd.* (unreported) (23 July 1997), per Ward L. J. (U.K. C.A.).

MARTHA A. MCCARTHY

46. T. Appleby. "In the tolerant 90s, attacks on gays Persist." *Globe and Mail*, Saturday 17 October 1998. For a disturbing summary of recent hate crimes committed in the US, see www.wired-strategies.com/shepardx.html.

47. See "Matthew Shepard On-line Resources": www.wiredstrategies.com/shepardx.hmtl.

48. H. Fierstein. Speech at Matthew Shepard Memorial Rally. Hartford, CT, 15 October 1998.

49. The inappropriateness of legislative deference in the context of equality rights claims is discussed in a paper I wrote with Joanna Radbord, "Foundations for 15(1)" presented to the CBAO Institute on Constitutional/Civil Litigation (30 January 1998). Revised version forthcoming in the *Michigan Journal of Gender and the Law*.

50. (1955), 349 U.S. 294.

51. Ronald Dworkin, *Freedom's Law: The Moral Reading of the American Constitution* (Cambridge Harvard University Press, 1996) [hereinafter *Freedom's Law*] at 29. See also R. Dworkin, *A Matter of Principle* (Cambridge: Harvard University Press, 1985), particularly pages 24–28; Martha Jackman, "Protecting Rights and Promoting Democracy: Judicial Review Under Section 1 of the *Charter*" (1997) 34:4 Osgoode Hall L. J. 661; Morton J. Horwitz, "Foreword: the Constitution of Change: Legal Fundamentality Without Fundamentalism" (1993) 107 *Harvard Law Review* 30 at 63–64; John H. Ely, Democracy and Distrust: A Theory of Judicial Review (Cambridge: Harvard University Press, 1980); and *Vriend per* Iacobucci J.

52. *Miron*, supra, at para. 151.

53. Discussed by M. McCarthy and J. Radbord, supra.

54. Law v. Canada File No: 25374 at para. 51; Available on the Internet at http://www.droit.umon-treal.ca/doc/csc-scc/cn/rec/html/law.en.html.

55. [1989] 1. S.C.R. 143.

56. Under a formal approach to equality, equality is theorized as treating likes alike. There must be sameness of treatment on the face of legislation. The famous Canadian example is *Bliss v. Canada (Attorney General)* [1979] 1 S.C.R. 183. In that case, a woman was denied unemployment benefits because she was pregnant. The Supreme Court held that the treatment of the complainant was not discriminatory, because she was treated the same as other "pregnant persons." Women as a group were not treated differently from men as a group. The decision in *Bliss* graphically illustrates the difficulties with a formal equality approach: the exercise of determining the relevant comparator is arbitrary; there is no consideration of the adverse effects of government action; the approach demands sameness to current rights holders. The relevance of the comparator group is often determined by reference to biology, tradition and dominant morality, the "basic tenets" so often used to justify discrimination—the tenets that equality rights are supposed to allow us to reevaluate.

57. Nicholson, A. (The Honourable Chief Justice of the Family Court of Australia). "The Changing Concept of Family: The Significance of Recognition and Protection." Conference Paper from "Sexual Orientation and the Law" presented September 1996. (1997) 6 *Australasian Gay and Lesbian Law Journal* 13 at 13.

DANIEL BORRILLO

Sexual Orientation and Human Rights in Europe

Daniel Borrillo is a professor with the Judicial
Sciences Department at the University of Paris in Paris,
France. He is also the director of the Judicial Group of
the AIDES Association of Paris and the author of
numerous articles on sexuality and the law. He
received the Fondation de France award in 1990.

AFTER WORLD WAR II, when the main international human rights instruments were being drafted, no provision was dedicated to protection against discrimination based on sexual orientation. Today, if one were to search for a specific reference to homosexuality in one of these instruments, one would search in vain. Neither instruments with universal application, such as the United Nations Universal Declaration of Human Rights of 1948 or its International Covenant on Civil and Political Rights of 1966, nor regional instruments such as the Organization of American States' American Convention on Human Rights of 1969 or the Organization of African Unity's African Charter on Human and Peoples' Rights of 1981, deals with the question.

Over the years the list of rights protected by the Council of Europe's European Convention on Human Rights has been extended through additional protocols but no new norm or provision deals addresses homosexuality as such. Despite the numerous homosexual victims of persecution, especially as a result of the Nazi policy of extermination, the main international human rights conventions have not found it advisable to establish legal mechanisms for protecting homosexuals.

The paradigm of homosexuality as an illness and the homosexual as a pervert represented the most progressive concept of homosexuality at the time. But because discrimination based on disability was not yet widely prohibited, gays and lesbians could not even invoke this form of protection. As a result, abandoned to the shadows outside the law, millions of homosexuals had to protect themselves by leading a double life, involving the apparent respectability of a marriage of convenience or a family formed in most cases against their will.

It is only recently that protection against sexual orientation discrimination has seen the light of day. Whether it is by the indirect route of a recourse to classical notions of "private life," a right to "nondiscrimination," or "freedom of expression," or by appeals to the application of the principle of equality without regard to one's sexual leanings or tendencies, or by the introduction of a specific reference to the notion of sexual orientation in the 1997 Treaty of Amsterdam (which amends the 1957 European Community Treaty), both "Greater Europe" (the forty-member Council of Europe) and the "Europe of 15" (the fifteen-member European Union) are beginning to build (a still embryonic) area of legal protection of sexual orientation.

In order to present this embryonic legal protection of persons without regard to their sexual orientation, I have structured my analysis around four variables: hard law of the Council of Europe (the Europe of forty members, European Convention on Human Rights, case law of the European Court and European Commission of Human Rights in Strasbourg); hard law of the European Community (the Europe of fifteen members, European Union Treaty and European Community Treaty, case law of the European Court of Justice in Luxembourg); soft law of the Council of Europe (recommendations of the Parliamentary Assembly of the Council of Europe in Strasbourg); and soft law of the European Community (resolutions of the EC's European Parliament in Strasbourg and Brussels).

▆▆▆ Hard Law of the Council of Europe

The first step in a slow and incomplete evolution towards equality of rights was the decriminalization of same-sex sexual activity. Even though the French Revolution caused the removal of the offence of "sodomy" from the Penal Code of 1791 (which was confirmed by the Napoleonic Code of 1810), many European countries continued to punish sexual acts between consenting adults of the same sex. Thus, between 1955 and 1977, the European Commission of Human Rights in Strasbourg considered that, although a person's sexual life was a part of their "private life" protected by Article 8 of the Convention, complete criminalization of same-sex sexual activity between consenting adults was not a violation of the Article 8 right to "respect for private life," because it could be justified as necessary for the "protection of health or morals," or for the "protection of the rights and freedoms of others." Indeed, the Commission declared that "the Convention allows a High Contracting Party to punish homosexuality since the right to respect for private life may, in a democratic society, be subject to interference as provided for by the law of that Party for the protection of health or morals."

It was only in 1981, twenty-six years after the rejection of the first application submitted to the Commission, that the European Court of Human Rights finally held in *Dudgeon v. United Kingdom* that criminalization of all sexual activity between men in Northern Ireland violated Article 8. In order to comply with the court's judgement, the United Kingdom decriminalized sexual acts between consenting men over twenty-one. Nonetheless, as the court reminded us, decriminalization does not imply approval, and a fear that some sectors of the population might draw misguided conclusions in this respect from reform of the legislation does not afford a good ground for maintaining it in force with all its unjustifiable features." In 1988 in *Norris v. Ireland*, and in 1993 in *Modinos v. Cyprus*, the court applied Dudgeon, finding that criminalization in the Republic of Ireland and in Cyprus also violated Article 8.

Even though the European Court of Human Rights established in 1981 that criminalization of sexual acts between consenting adults of the same sex is an unjustifiable interference with private life, the European Commission of Human Rights held repeatedly that a higher age of consent for sexual acts between men, compared with sexual acts between men and women or between women, could be justified. However, in 1997 in *Sutherland v. United Kingdom*, the Commission concluded for the first time that the maintenance of different ages of consent for same-sex and different-sex sexual activity could not be justified in a democratic society. The *Sutherland* case was referred to the court, but is on hold under an agreement between the Stonewall litigation and lobbying group in London and the United Kingdom government, which requires the government to permit a free vote in the House of Commons on equalizing the age of consent. Such a vote was held in June 1998 and produced a large majority in favour. But the amendment was rejected in July 1998 by the unelected House of Lords. On 24 November 1998, the government outlined its legislative programme in the Queen's Speech. It will include an Age of Consent and Abuse of Trust Bill, which will equalize the age of consent at sixteen but criminalize sexual activity between persons between sixteen and eighteen and persons in positions of trust or authority over them, such as schoolteachers.

In other areas, no such progress has been made. In *Bruce v. United Kingdom* in 1983, the European Commission of Human Rights upheld the dismissal of gay and lesbian members of the armed forces, finding it justifiable under Articles 8 (private life) and 14 (nondiscrimination) of the Convention. In *Johnson v. United Kingdom* in 1986, the Commission permitted criminalization of sexual acts involving more than two men. Similarly, in *Laskey v. United Kingdom* in 1997, the court found a justification for the criminalization of sado-masochistic sexual acts in private involving a group of consenting adult men.

Apart from "private life" in Article 8, homosexuals have been unsuccessful in finding protection for their unions or partnerships. The Commission (but not yet the court) has decided that gay and lesbian couples do not have a "family life," which must be respected under Article 8, or a right to marry and to found a family" under Article 12 *(C & L.M. v. United Kingdom* in 1989). In three cases dealing with transsexual persons, the court has held that the right to marry in Article 12 refers "to the traditional marriage between persons of opposite biological sex:" *Rees v. United Kingdom* (1986), *Cossey v. United Kingdom* (1990), *Sheffield & Horsham v. United Kingdom* (30 July 1998).

The current state of the "hard law" of the Council of Europe is that decriminalization of sexual behaviour involving two consenting persons over eighteen of the same sex is required. As a result, every country joining the Council of Europe and signing the European Convention must decriminalize: Opinion No. 176 (1993) of the Parliamentary Assembly regarding Romania's application to join the Council of Europe. But, as the court indicated, decriminalization does not mean in any way the recognition of homosexuality as a source of rights, or its being rendered so commonplace that it ceases to be a hindrance to the enjoyment of Convention rights. The refusal to include gays and lesbians within the right to marry in Article 12 or the right to respect for "family life" in Article 8, is used to justify in particular their exclusion from family law and from immigration rights.

This minimal protection, which arises more from a concept of tolerance that one of strict application of principles of equality and nondiscrimination, is the result of a "consensus-oriented approach" which interprets and applies the Convention with regard to the legal situations existing in the member states of the Council of Europe. It is clear that the new member states, in most of which same-sex sexual activity has only recently been decriminalized, have preferred an extremely conservative interpretation of notions such as "private life," "family life," "right to marry" and "discrimination based on sex" (interpretation was conservative pre-1989, before these states joined, when there were only twenty-three member states, all from western Europe). To improve protection under the Convention, three reforms can be proposed.

First, the Convention countries could consider adopting a specific protocol on sexual orientation discrimination; second, Article 14 of the Convention could be amended so as to add "sexual orientation" as a specific prohibited ground of discrimination, alongside "sex;" and third, the European Community could sign the European Convention, thereby bringing European Community law and European Community institutions clearly under the jurisdiction of the European Court of Human Rights in Strasbourg (the European Court of Justice in Luxembourg already applies the Convention to EC law and EC institutions itself). Of these three reforms, the second seems to me to be both the most realistic and the most effective.

Hard Law of the European Community

For many years, European Community law took no interest in the lot of gays and lesbians, whose cases were traditionally dealt with by the European Court of Human Rights in Strasbourg. In *P. v. S. & Cornwall County Council* in 1996, the situation changed significantly when a transsexual woman succeeded in convincing the European Court of Justice in Luxembourg (the highest court of the European Community), that her dismissal constituted discrimination based on sex. It therefore violated the 1976 Equal Treatment Directive (76/207/EEC), which prohibits sex discrimination in employment in relation to hiring, promotion, dismissal and working conditions. If the notion of discrimination based on sex protects transsexual persons, one would imagine that the same legal protection would be extended to gay, lesbian and bisexual persons. This reasoning was adopted by the lawyer for Lisa Grant, a lesbian woman who invoked Article 119 of the European Community Treaty (the 1957 Treaty of Rome), which requires equal pay for men and women, and had her case referred to the Luxembourg Court. She claimed that her employer's refusal to provide free rail travel benefits to her female partner, as the employer did to the unmarried female partners of male employees, was a violation of Article 119. A similar argument was used by the lawyer for a gay employee of the Royal Navy, Terence Perkins, who had been dismissed, and who invoked the same 1976 Equal Treatment Directive on which the transsexual woman, P., had relied.

In the *Grant v. South-West Trains*, advocate General Elmer considered that the notion of discrimination based on sex could also include the notion of discrimination based on sexual orientation. Thus, by comparing the situation of Lisa Grant and her female partner to that of a heterosexual man with a female partner (with whom he was living outside of marriage), Advocate General Elmer concluded that the sex of Lisa Grant was also the cause of the discrimination, and not only the fact that she is lesbian. Even though the Luxembourg Court often follows the opinion of the Advocate General, and did so in the *P.* transsexual case, in *Grant* the Court rejected this opinion and adopted a traditional analysis under which there is no discrimination based on sex, but only discrimination based on sexual orientation. This analysis precluded the application of European Community law, which currently prohibits employment discrimination only when it is based on sex, and not when it is based on race, religion, disability, age or sexual orientation.

The Grant decision makes it clear why specific European Community legislation on sexual orientation discrimination is needed. This is the approach taken by the new Article 13 which will, after the ratification of the 1997 Treaty of Amsterdam by all fifteen member states, be inserted into the European Community Treaty. This new Article 13 provides as follows: "Without prejudice to the other provisions of this Treaty and within the limits of the powers conferred by it upon the Community, the Council (the effective legislature of the

DANIEL BORRILLO

EC), acting unanimously on a proposal from the Commission (the executive of the EC) and after consulting the European Parliament, may take appropriate action to combat discrimination based on sex, racial or ethnic origin, religion or belief, disability, age or sexual orientation."

Once Article 13 comes into force it will give specific power to the European Community institutions authorizing them to adopt legislation banning discrimination based on sexual orientation. However, there is no obligation for the Commission to exercise this power by making a proposal to the Council, or for the Council to agree to any proposal. New legislation will require the consent of all fifteen member states. Although Article 13 represents an important symbolic advance, it is unlikely to lead to effective legal protection in the immediate future. Indeed, given the variations between the current laws of the fifteen member states in this area, it is hard to imagine a consensus in favour of a European Community directive on sexual orientation discrimination.

■■■ Soft Law of the Council of Europe

In 1979 a commission of the Council of Europe directed by Mr. Voogd presented a proposed recommendation (document 4436), which aimed to provide "moral and legal protection to homosexuals," the "elimination of discrimination in employment and other areas" and the "enjoyment of the rights and opportunities granted to other citizens." The proposal was accepted and a report on discrimination against homosexuals was issued in 1981. The report proposed a draft recommendation to the member states of the Council of Europe, and a draft resolution to the World Health Organization asking it to remove homosexuality from its international classification of illnesses. The report's argument had a liberal tone which sought "equality of human beings and the defence of human rights" by respecting an individual's sexual preferences. After having considered the history of the question and a synthesis of the social, political and legal situation in Europe, the report tried to define homosexuality. It criticized strongly the notions of "mental problems," "sexual problems" or "deviation," and proposed the rejection of any type of medical or psychiatric definition by speaking simply of "sexual preference."

The report ended with a number of suggestions. It proposed: (a) the amendment of Article 14 of the European Convention by adding the notion of "sexual preference" (*penchant sexuel* or "sexual leaning or tendency" in French). The current text of Article 14 reads as follows:

> The enjoyment of the rights and freedoms set forth in this Convention shall be secured without discrimination on any ground such as sex, race, colour, language, religion, political or other opinion, national or social origin, association with a national minority, property, birth or other status.
>
> (b) the destruction of police files on homosexuals.

(c) equality of treatment for homosexuals with regard to employment, pay and job security.

(d) an end to all medical research or activity seeking a compulsory modification of the sexual preferences of adults.

(e) the removal of any discrimination against lesbian and gay parents with regard to custody of children, or rights of access to children.

(f) the payment of reparations to homosexuals who suffered in concentration camps.

(g) vigilance by prison directors and other public authorities to prevent homosexuals from being the victims of rapes and acts of violence in prisons.

The report did not take a position on the age of consent to same-sex sexual activity: "Every society must fix this limit with regard to the degree of social and cultural maturity. It is hard to understand why the age selected should be different for boys and girls who are heterosexual or homosexual." But the report did propose (in an informal way) better information for the public. Following the report, Recommendation 924 (1981) and a resolution regarding discrimination with respect to homosexuals reproduce in part the report's proposals, emphasizing the decriminalization and demedicalization of homosexuality.

In 1984 the Legal Affairs Division of the Council of Europe published a study on "Sexual Behaviour and Attitudes and Their Effects on Criminal Law," by D. J. West, director of the Institute of Criminology at the University of Cambridge. The study contained a chapter on homosexuality.

▬▬ Soft Law of the European Community

Within the European Community institutions, it is the European Parliament that has dealt most with the question of discrimination against gays and lesbians. On 13 March 1984 (O.J., C 104, p. 46, published on 16 April 1984), the Parliament adopted a "Resolution on sexual discrimination at the workplace," proposed by Vera Squarcialup. The term "sex" was given a broad meaning, in that the resolution dealt with discrimination against homosexuals. The resolution called on member states to abolish national laws discriminating against homosexuals and to pass laws prohibiting discrimination against them. On 11 June 1986, the Parliament urged member states to apply, in their national legislation, the principle of nondiscrimination based on sex, marital status and sexual preference. Unlike the Legal Affairs Division of the Council of Europe, the Parliament proposed an explicit reference to "sexual preference." The Parliament also proposed that member states prevent any discrimination in certain occupations, such as the armed forces, the civil service or the diplomatic service.

On 27 May 1990 the Council of Ministers adopted a resolution (O.J. 1990, C 157/3) recommending that employers take action against sexual harassment in the workplace. Thanks to the work of the International Lesbian and Gay Association, a special clause on harassment based on sexual orientation was inserted into the resolution.

On 8 February 1994, a "Resolution on equal rights for homosexuals and lesbians in the EC" was approved by the Parliament. It urged all member states to establish the same age of consent to sexual activity, whether same-sex or different-sex, to protect homosexuals against any form of discrimination, and to encourage and support financially associations of homosexuals. The resolution also proposed that the Commission of the EC present "a draft recommendation on equal rights for lesbians and homosexuals," which should seek to end "the barring of lesbians and homosexual couples from marriage or from an equivalent legal framework," and "any restrictions on the rights of lesbians and homosexuals to be parents or to adopt or foster children."

▬ Conclusion

To date, no European country has been able to eliminate discrimination based on sexual orientation. The advances made by the European Court and Commission of Human Rights in Strasbourg have been limited to requiring decriminalization of sexual activity between two consenting adults of the same sex and equalization of the age of consent or sexual activity, whether same-sex or different-sex. These tribunals have adopted extremely restrictive interpretations of "private life" as an intimate sphere surrounding an atomized individual, of "family life" as exclusively heterosexual, of "discrimination based on sex" as independent of and unconnected to sexual orientation, and the "right to marry" as applying only to unions between one man and one woman. As for the European Court of Justice in Luxembourg, by also concluding that discrimination based on sexual orientation in not discrimination based on sex, it has closed the door to the application to gays and lesbians of the huge body of European Community sex discrimination law. In view of the failure of the case law of the Strasbourg Court and Commission and the Luxembourg Court to develop mechanisms for protecting gays and lesbians, the solution would seem to be the use by the European Community of the new Article 13 of the EC Treaty, hoping that the necessary political will on the part of the member states will be there.

Things are better at the national level in Europe. Countries such as France, Denmark, Norway, the Netherlands, Luxembourg, Spain and Ireland have legislation expressly prohibiting sexual orientation discrimination, especially with regard to employment. As for recognition of same-sex couples, the European Parliament's resolution of 8 February 1994 is unambiguous. It requires access to marriage or to forms of partnership granting the same rights as those of married couples and to adoption and medically assisted procreation. The first country to have passed legislation granting rights to same-sex couples was Denmark in 1989. Since then, Norway, Sweden, Hungary, Iceland, the Netherlands, Belgium,

Catalonia and Arapón (Spain) have followed. In most of the fifteen member-states of the European Union, bills providing for the registration of civil partnerships by same-sex couples are being proposed and debated. Despite the strong opposition of conservative groups, both secular and religious, and even though much remains to be done, the dynamic of equality seems to be spreading gradually throughout the continent of Europe.

DANIEL BORRILLO

The Fragile Progress of Human Rights and Sexuality

Svend Robinson is a member of the Canadian
Parliament and a former spokesperson on foreign
affairs and international human rights for the federal
New Democratic Party. He has served on the
Parliamentary Human Rights Committee and the
Special Committee on Equality Rights. He is the recip-
ient of the Edith Adamson Award for Leadership in
Issues of Conscience and the Order de la Pléiade.

ONE OF THE HIGHLIGHTS OF MY LIFE was in 1994, having been able to visit
and observe the first free elections in South Africa, to meet a young man there.
Simon Nkoli, a young black South African, shared with me his story of imprisonment and beating, solely because he was gay. Simon was a supporter of the
African National Congress. It was wonderful that out of the evil of apartheid and
the destruction of apartheid, out of that tyranny, South Africa was one of the
first countries in the world to include in its constitution a prohibition of discrimination based on sexual orientation.

I remind you that it was similarly out of the horrors of the Holocaust that
peoples from around the world gathered in 1948 to frame the Universal
Declaration of Human Rights, with its fundamental theme that all human
beings are born free and equal in dignity and rights. In addition to the yellow
stars of six million Jews who were killed in the Holocaust and the gypsies, there
were also pink triangles on the homosexuals who were victims of that same
Holocaust. Despite that, in the fifty years since the adoption of the Universal
Declaration, there has largely been a conspiracy of silence about the human
rights of sexual minorities.

Despite the fact that Article 1 of the Universal Declaration talks about all
human beings and other UN human rights instruments spell out many rights,
too often the United Nations, other world bodies, most governments and NGOs
are silent or worse. There is no protection. What that means is that we, as gay

313

and lesbian people, are treated as somehow less than human. If we are not part of that universality then, of course, we are less than human. The implication of that is an invitation to violence and abuse.

In Beijing thirty countries put the rights of lesbians on the agenda. At the Vienna Plus Five Conference, in Ottawa in 1998, an important part of the final declaration was a reference to the rights of lesbians, gay men, bisexuals and transgendered peoples. Since 1991 Amnesty International has included us as well, as prisoners of conscience.

But much more remains to be done at the international level. I am a member of the International Advisory Board of the International Gay and Lesbian Human Rights Commission and too many times I have heard stories of widespread discrimination and violence. When, as a member of Parliament, I raise these issues with government officials, I'm frequently met with incredulity, with denial, with anger.

It is not always as bad as it was when I had a meeting with the foreign minister of the Ukraine in the early 1980s. I asked about the legal status of homosexuals in the Ukraine and, with an air of astonishment, he told me that there were no homosexuals in the Ukraine. "Our men like women," he said. As I pursued the subject, my interpreter warned me that I better not go there, but I did, and so the foreign minister asked me, "Why are you asking me these questions, Mr. Robinson?" I said, "Well, I'm the foreign affairs and human rights critic for my party. I'm also a gay man. I would like to know what's legal in this country." He looked surprised and then he said, "Well, I was wrong. There are a few ballet dancers in the Ukraine."

Too often, gay men, lesbians, bisexuals and transgendered people are forced into invisibility and denial. When we are "out," we are fired from our jobs and thrown out of our homes. Our children are taken from us. We are harassed, tortured, imprisoned and murdered. This violence and discrimination knows no political boundaries. I fought hard in support of the people in Zimbabwe in their struggle against oppression. That made it particularly sad to hear President Robert Mugabe saying that homosexuality degrades human dignity, suggesting that homosexuals behave worse than dogs and pigs and throwing people in jail.

A Brazilian member of Parliament, Marta Suplecy, has noted that just in the two years from 1992 to 1994 there were over 180 documented assassinations of homosexuals in Brazil. Romania has still not repealed Article 200 of its constitution. Malaysia is charging Anwar Ibrahim as a criminal, among other things because they say he's guilty of homosexual conduct—a crime in that country.

In the United States in October 1998 a beautiful and innocent young man, Matthew Shepard, was beaten and left dangling on a fencepost just because he was gay. Here in Canada, I am proud to say we have made significant progress in the last decade, particularly since the coming into force of our Charter of Rights. As a result of Supreme Court of Canada decisions, our constitution also prohibits discrimination based on sexual orientation. Further, by a narrow majority our Supreme Court has said that discrimination against gay and lesbian relationships also constitutes discrimination based on sexual orientation.

We have made progress in the Canadian Human Rights Act, finally amending it to explicitly include sexual orientation, hate crimes legislation, ending discrimination in the Canadian Armed Forces, not with a "Don't ask, don't tell" policy but with full equality. Indeed, the Canadian Armed Forces recently extended same-sex benefits to its members.

Refugees to Canada who have fled oppression on the basis of sexual orientation are recognized. There is also much more visibility for members of the homosexual community. I am delighted that here in the city of Edmonton, for example, an outstanding city councillor, Michael Phair, who also happens to be an out and proud gay man, was just reelected with one of the biggest majorities anywhere. Recently Winnipeg, the fourth largest city in Canada, elected an out gay mayor, Glen Murray. When I came out publicly on national television in 1988, I said I longed for the day that the response would be, "So what, who cares?" We're moving in that direction. It wasn't the response in my case: my office was smashed and destroyed. Bullets have been fired through the windows on more than one occasion, but certainly we have made process.

But I want to say how incredibly fragile this progress is. Yes, we have a Charter of Rights but that Charter can be overridden by the stroke of a legislative pen. We saw it here in Alberta with people who were sterilized, an attempt to override the most basic and fundamental rights. We heard strong arguments from elected people here in Alberta to do the same thing. To hell with the Charter of Rights—override it—in the case of sexual orientation after the *Vriend* decision.

Alberta is the only province in Canada that still hasn't amended its legislation to conform with the Charter of Rights. It is not just an abstract problem. Not that long ago I was invited to speak in Calgary to a group of gays and lesbians. They called themselves, discreetly, Calgarians Networking. They were still in the process of coming out. They booked a banquet room at one of the biggest and poshest hotels in Calgary. When the hotel found out who they really were and, by God, who their guest speaker was to be, they cancelled the booking. They said, and I quote: "Management and staff do not feel comfortable having you here."

When the group asked me, "Well, what can we do about that?", I said, "Well, in Alberta you can't do anything about that legally. You have no protection under the Individual Rights Protection Act and remember, if you have no protection against being fired from your job or being thrown out of your home, and if somebody beats you up or harasses you, you're not going to report that to the police, are you? You're not because you're afraid you might lose your job or your home, or you might be outed to your family."

Alberta has the highest level of youth suicide in Canada. I remind you that gay and lesbian bisexual youth are at particular risk because of the alienation and fear they face. They alone among all minorities too often have no support from the three traditional sources of support for those who are victimized. Often one of the greatest fears is coming out to your family. I spoke just two days ago to a man who told me about when he finally told his mother and father, that his father had refused to speak to him and wouldn't talk to him for a year and a half afterwards. That hurts. The family is too often not there. The school too is silent. The church, instead of being a supportive and nurturing environment, is too often a condemning environment. The Pope talks about intrinsic moral evil. The death penalty for homosexuals is prescribed in the Bible.

Everywhere, including Canada, major challenges remain around recognition of our relationships. We have made major progress in British Columbia and elsewhere. British Columbia has changed its law, for example, to allow full adoption rights and recently our Human Rights Commission recommended full recognition of the rights of transgendered people as well. So we are making progress in trying to help people understand that our relationships are just as strong and just as powerful, just as real and just as loving as other relationships.

After I recently spoke about relationships, I received a letter from a twelve-year-old boy who wrote to me about his two dads. His father sent me a covering letter in which he talked about his relationship with his partner of ten years. His partner, Frank, had been diagnosed with cancer in 1989. When his partner was hospitalized, the man's devoutly religious family suddenly appeared on the scene and refused him access to the hospital room. They even hired a security guard to keep him and the son away from his partner.

They never visited him. He wrote to me, saying, "(Frank) spent his last months of life hollering through the door that he loved us and we did the same. He begged the security officer to let him say goodbye and he was refused. To this day Joshua and I don't know where he was buried or if he was even buried at all." And his son wrote to me about this. And he said: "Please let other kids like me see their mommies and daddies." There can be nothing more cruel than the denial of our relationships. They talk about special rights. I don't want special rights. I just want equal rights. They talk about pedophilia and how we're a threat to their children. I remind you, they used the same thing against Jews. Jews were going to convert our children. They said gypsies were going to abduct our children. And we, of course, will seduce our children. It is an evil lie. In fact, in a study that was published not that long ago in the *Journal of Pediatrics,* the American Academy of Pediatrics looked at 269 cases of pedophilia and found that in two of those cases the offenders could be identified as being gay. In eighty-two per cent of cases, 222 cases, the alleged offender was a heterosexual partner of a close relative of the child.

I appeal to all of you to work hard in your own communities and your own countries and with your families, NGOs, universities, unions and governments to put an end to the invisibility and the silence. Put the issue of equality and justice for gay lesbian, bisexual and transgendered people front and centre on the political agenda. For those of you who are not gay or lesbian, who ask, "Well, why me, why is this my struggle?", I want to remind you of two things Desmond Tutu said on this subject. He was recently asked, if there was one injustice that he could undo in the world, what would it be. And he replied in typical Desmond Tutu fashion: Would you give me two? And the interviewer said, sure. Desmond Tutu said number one is forgiving Third World debts. And then he said number two is the importance of equal treatment for gays and lesbians. He called the persecution of gays and lesbians as unjust as apartheid and said it is a matter of human rights and a deeply theological issue, and that they are as much God's children as anyone.

Remember the words of Martin Luther King when you're wondering: Why me? Why is this my struggle? He was talking about the history of the oppression of African Americans and he said: "History will not judge this time by the viciousness of our enemies so much as it will by the silence of our friends." Let us together break that silence and work for a world in which, in the words of Article 1 of the Universal Declaration, every human being—gay, lesbian, bisexual, transgendered and straight—is truly equal in dignity and in rights.

Effective Remedies for Violations of Fundamental Rights

The Responsibilities of the State

Rosalie Silberman Abella is justice for the Ontario Court of Appeal and a director of the Canadian Institute for the Administration of Justice and the International Commission of Jurists. She was the first Jewish woman to be named as a judge in Canada and the first non-American to be appointed as a member of the American Bar Association's Standing Committee on World Order Under Law.

THE UNIVERSAL DECLARATION OF HUMAN RIGHTS, and its spiritual sibling, the Genocide Convention, were the wings of the Phoenix that rose fifty years ago from the ashes of Auschwitz. In conceptual solidarity against the ravages of intolerance, they were the powerful legal symbols of a world shamefully chastened.

The Declaration was a document of magisterial indignation, a powerful statement that human rights is the essence of justice and that justice is the essence of the world we want to see. These are clearly millennial aspirations, but spoken as they are on the eve of a millennium, they are spoken with a sense of wistfulness at the distances not yet travelled.

There is, it seems to me, no argument that one can offer against governments playing a decisive role in the delivery of rights. It is they who decide which rights to turn into laws, what remedies will accompany those laws and how accessible those laws and remedies will be. Governments decide which covenants and treaties to sign, what resources will be available to implement them and how determinative they will be permitted to be. They choose the ministers who set the priorities and the timing for delivering them. They pick the judges and the quality of the administration of justice. There can be no remedies without the state because there can be no rights without the state. This is the heart of the story.

But of course there is more to the story, more because the international community is so breathtakingly disparate in its collection of states and their sense of responsibility. Despite fifty years with the Declaration as an illuminating vision, it is difficult to say with confidence that the commitment to tolerance is fastened to the spirit of our times. All over the world the arteries that pump justice into the hearts of our nations are growing sclerotic, clogged by a diet too rich in intolerance, the very substance we thought we banished in disrepute after World War II. Less and less is the intricate social blueprint we collaboratively designed after World War II being followed.

There are, of course, spectacular successes: the Land Mines Treaty, the International Criminal Court and Pinochet's pierced immunity being the three most obvious. But the Land Mines Treaty was started on the ground by one member of the public and transformed into an international commitment by the fortuitously timed appointment of Lloyd Axworthy as Canada's tenacious foreign affairs minister; the International Criminal Court took almost a whole generation to bring into being, and then only with last-minute diplomatic delicacy; and the original Pinochet judgement was the singular creation of three British judges who, to their enormous credit, disagreed with their two colleagues and decided to bring the common law in line with international ideals. Not one of these initiatives started from any state's sense of responsibility.

We have no international mechanism to prevent the ongoing slaughter of children and other innocent civilians, and no overriding sense of moral responsibility that informs us and helps develop a consensus for when responsive military action is required to protect human rights. We have, in fact, no consensus on what our international moral responsibilities are, period, and that is why we are so desperately lacking in enforcement mechanisms, legal and otherwise.

We have the language, the people, the organizations, the ideas and the ideals, but not enough states have enough courage to put remedies at the top of the international agenda, leaving those who care to watch the relentlessness of the abuse with despair.

As for those states who do care, there is much they could do but have not yet done. They could create a single International Human Rights Court; they could streamline the well-meaning but hopelessly ineffective reporting systems on human rights at the UN; they could speak out in a way that signals to their domestic populations that human rights is not a peripheral social policy; and they could allocate budgets accordingly.

But there is now at the international level what seems to be a sustained discourse about the importance of international human rights, at least about its most excessive abuses. It is a discourse we can only hope is not merely the international discourse *du jour*. Rather, it is, with luck, a discourse that will reenergize governments to create at last the enforcement mechanisms for delivery of the remedies the Declaration's noble rhetoric so enticingly promised five decades ago.

Beyond the truism that we need international enforcement mechanisms to provide effective remedies for human rights abuses at the international level, there are still serious human rights issues to address closer to home. Fifty years later, aside from the occasional exuberance for rights that is reflected in a conference such as this, we seem to have allowed human rights to move from its confident primacy in the centre of the justice picture to the defensive margins of the canvas.

When I went to law school and started practising law, people who believed in human rights were called progressive; those who didn't were called regressive. Today, human rights proponents are called biased radicals and opponents are called impartial realists. What happened to the human rights parade we thought was unstoppable a generation ago, now a casualty of thinning crowds and unpopular floats?

Part of what turned our rights vision so myopic—a big part—was that we were allowing the premise behind civil liberties to checkmate the moves human rights wanted to make. Unless we understand that there is a difference between civil liberties and human rights, we won't know what remedies to seek from governments. Civil liberties is a concept of rights that requires the state not to interfere with our liberties; human rights, on the other hand, cannot be realized without the state's intervention.

But we have to start at the beginning of the story. The human rights story in North America, like many of our legal stories, started in England. The rampant religious, feudal and monarchical repression in 17th-century England inspired new political philosophies like those of Hobbes, Locke and eventually John Stuart Mill, philosophies protecting individuals from having their freedoms interfered with by governments. These were the theories of civil liberties which came to dominate the "rights" discussion for the next three hundred years. They were also the theories which journeyed across the Atlantic Ocean and became firmly planted in American soil, receiving confirmation in the Declaration of Independence that guarantees that every "man" enjoyed the right to life, liberty and the pursuit of happiness, and that government existed only to bring about the best conditions for the preservation of those rights. Thus was born the essence of social justice for Americans—the belief that every American had the same right as every other American to be free from government intervention. To be equal was to have this same right. No differences.

Individualism is at the core of the political philosophy of rights articulated in the American Constitution, ascribing equal civil, political and legal rights to every individual regardless of differences. The Constitution became America's most significant international export and the exclusive rights barometer for countries in the Western world. It was formal equality, it ignored group identities and realities and, indeed, regarded collective interests as subversive of true rights. Concern for the rights of the individual monopolized the remedial endeavours of the pursuers of justice all over the world.

It was not until 1945 that we came to the realization that having chained ourselves to the pedestal of the individual, we had been ignoring rights abuses of a fundamentally different and at least equally intolerable kind; namely, the rights of individuals in different groups to retain their different identities without fear of the loss of life, liberty or the pursuit of happiness.

It was World War II which permanently jolted us from our complacent belief that the only way to protect rights was to keep government at a distance and protect each individual individually. What jolted us was the horrifying spectacle of group destruction, a spectacle so far removed from what we thought were the limits of rights violations in civilized societies that we found our entire vocabulary and remedial arsenal inadequate. We were left with no moral alternative but to acknowledge that individuals could be denied rights not in spite of, but because of their differences, and started to formulate ways to protect the rights of the group.

We had, in short, come to see the brutal role of discrimination; a word we had never and could never use in a concept like civil rights that permitted no differences. We invented the term "human rights" to confront it. We clothed governments with the authority to devise remedies to prevent arbitrary harm based on race or religion or gender or ethnicity, and we respected government's new right to treat us differently to redress the abuses our differences attracted. We saw how the neutral purpose of civil libertarian individual rights had an unequal impact on the opportunities of many individuals, and eventually we saw that all the goodwill in the world could not protect us from our own prejudices and stereotypes, or from restrictively designing systems and institutions accordingly.

So we blasted away at the conceptual wall that had kept us from understanding the inhibiting role group differences played, and extended the prospect of full socioeconomic participation to women, nonwhites, aboriginal people, persons with disabilities, the elderly and those with different sexual preferences. And, most significantly, we offered this full participation and accommodation based on, and notwithstanding, group differences.

It was as if we had awoken from a three-hundred-year sleep, looked around us, realized how limited our rights vision had become and, with stunning energy and enthusiasm, acknowledged more rights and remedies in one generation than we had in all the centuries since the Glorious Revolution in England in 1688–89, starting with the remarkable consensus found in the Universal Declaration of Human Rights.

But having decided half-way through this century to endorse a commitment to diversity as integral to our understanding of rights and justice and community, why do we now appear to be abandoning the commitment as the century closes?

What we appear to have done, having watched the dazzling success of so many individuals in so many of the groups we had previously excluded, is concluded that the battle with discrimination had been won and that we could, as victors, remove our human rights weapons from the social battlefield. Having seen women elected, appointed, promoted and educated in droves; having seen the winds of progress blow away segregation and apartheid; having permitted parades to demonstrate gay and lesbian pride; having constructed hundreds of ramps for persons with disabilities; and having invited aboriginal people to participate in constitutional discussions we had started to protect other distinct cultures, many were no longer persuaded that the diversity theory of rights was still relevant and sought to return to the simpler rights theory in which everyone was treated the same. We became nostalgic for the conformity of the civil liberties approach and frightened by the way human rights had dramatically changed every institution in society, from the family to the legislature.

And this, I think, is at the heart of why we are marginalizing human rights. Unlike civil liberties, which rearrange no social relationships and protect our political ones, human rights is a direct assault on the status quo. It is inherently about change—in the way we treat each other, not just in the way government treats each of us. And so, in North America, we tend to yearn for the rights that are less expensive, less confusing and less frightening. The intellectual baskets into which we place information once again take the shape of civil rights, and we end by dismissively calling a differences-based approach reverse discrimination, or political correctness, or an insult to the goodwill of the majority and to the talents of minorities, or a violation of the merit principle. Personal aspirations, we are now convinced, will be realized by those who deserve them and no one who is qualified will be turned away. Civil rights trumps human rights. Social and economic Darwinism trumps social and economic reality.

The irony is that having dedicated the last five decades to promoting human rights and tolerance, we have done such a good job that we have learned to tolerate even intolerance. The creeping forces of intolerance have watched as, over the past fifty years, new roles were given to women, minorities, and religious and linguistic groups. While these new roles gave dignity to many, they also altered the status quo.

The backlash to change grew accordingly, accompanied by a strident chorus of those who felt their status quos had been too severely violated by our rearrangements. Anxious to squelch the realigning generosity of opportunity, the forces of intolerance proclaimed that their patience had run out and that it was time to return to truth, as they understood it.

The real truth is that the newly emergent forces of intolerance are really promoting the right to be free from tolerance and threatening to turn the "rights" revolution of the past fifty years upside down, using the rights discourse as the operative script, no less. They use the language of the right to freedom of association to defeat our sense of community; they use the language of the right to freedom of religion to defeat religious choice; they use the language of the right to equality to defeat diversity; they use the language of the right to freedom of the press to defeat our intelligence; and they use the language of the right to freedom of expression to defeat our opinions.

Somehow we have let those who have enough say, say "Enough is enough," allowing them to set the agenda while they accuse everyone else of having an "agenda" and leaving thousands wondering where the human rights they were promised are, and why so many who already have those rights think that the rest of the country doesn't need them.

The reality is there are still built-in headwinds for those who are different, who are thwarted in their conscious choices by stereotypes unconsciously assigned, and who cannot be expected to understand why the evolutionary knowledge we came to call human rights has suffered such swift, Orwellian obliteration. We have forgotten the courage our outrage after World War II gave us to expand our understanding. We have, I fear, been lulled into a false sense of complacency by the formidable human rights successes that resulted from our post-war courage.

Many of us have benefited from that courage. We are the people who know the gratitude and energy and commitment which are the legacy of that generosity. But we are also, as people who grew up in the shadow of the promise of the Universal Declaration of Human Rights, the people who know that the successes this generation proudly claims for human rights are, as civil rights were three hundred years ago, just the beginning of a new era.

We know from history that all rights, especially in their infancy, are fragile and need nurturing. Democratic communities need their civil liberties rigorously protected, but unless they also protect their human rights, they do a disservice to justice. Of course we need the right to vote and think and speak freely, but no less do we need the right to eat and work and aspire freely. Before we relinquish the lessons of history to those who fear its transforming vision, before we allow the civil libertarian spirit to hold us in exclusive thrall, and before we are lured into intellectual lassitude by the successes of the lucky and the tenacious, we need to remember the human rights lesson of World War II: the enormity of its intolerance shocked us into a new understanding of diversity; we should need no more shocks to retain that understanding. Ignoring the contributions our diversity offers to the social texture is incomprehensible, but ignoring the lessons of history is unforgivable.

Our memory of World War II inspired us to create a Universal Declaration of Human Rights. This memory should be all we need to keep the fire lit under human rights—the memory of the horror when human rights do not exist. The memory inspires us, but it is an inspiration we should never knowingly let anyone experience.

M.N. VENKATACHALIAH

Human Rights Are Our Inalienable Inheritance

M.N. Venkatachaliah is chair of the National Human Rights Commission of India. He is a professor of law and the former chief justice of India.

IN THE EVOLUTION OF THE POLITICAL ORGANIZATION OF HUMANKIND, there has been a continuous yearning for a higher law as a touchstone for the ethical and moral content of our domestic laws. Written constitutions are intended to realize this aspiration. A constitution is intended to control governmental power, so essential to the realization of societal values, in order that it does not destroy the very values it is intended to protect.

A written constitution is a charter of limited government. It serves as the fundamental law. It limits and binds the organs of the state as a matter of law. It seeks to avoid concentration of power by built-in checks and balances and constitutes the foundation of the legal system. The purpose of a bill of rights is to entrench certain cherished democratic and political values so that they are not affected by the unpredictable nature of democratic rule.

"The very purpose of a bill of rights," said Justice Jackson, "was to withdraw certain subjects from the vicissitudes of political controversy, to place them beyond the reach of majorities and to establish them as legal principles to be applied by the courts. One's right to life, liberty and prosperity, to free speech, a free press, freedom of worship and assembly and other fundamental rights may not be submitted to a vote. They depend on the outcome of no elections" (See *West Virginia State Bd v. Barnette*, (1943) 319 US 624 (638)).

The Declaration of American Independence exhorted: "We hold these truths to be self-evident; that all men are created equal; that they are endowed by their creator with certain inalienable rights; that among these are life, liberty and the pursuit of happiness." Natural rights of man became entrenched rights under the Constitution. Declared fundamental rights have also invoked the theory of "penumbras" or "emanations" as auxiliary rights. Right to privacy, right to dignity, right against torture, right to speedy trial, to legal aid, to shelter, to emergency medical relief, to a clean environment, to education of the child and (in

India) freedom of the press are indeed some of the emanations from the declared specific rights.

Fundamental rights are not conferred rights but are the inalienable inheritance of man. They are above ordinary laws. Ordinary laws cannot change them. They are not built into the law but are placed above the law. But a bill of rights is not an automatic guarantee of liberty. Its efficacy depends on the integrity and sensitivity of the institutional mechanisms that apply and enforce it. These rights are not self-executing. They require human agencies—courts, lawyers, press and a whole host of government agencies—to implement them. This needs the spirit of constitutionalism, a conducive political climate and tradition. Most of all, there must be the spirit of liberty in the hearts of men and a willingness to pay the price of liberty.

■■■ Bill of Rights and Parliamentary Supremacy: English Debate

The idea of declaration and incorporation of a bill of rights with entrenched rights operating as limitations on state power has evoked mixed reactions in the Anglo-Saxon tradition. The proposal to introduce a clause on "life, liberty, property and due process of law" in the Irish Home Rule Bill, 1912, provoked Mr. Asquith to object on the ground that those expressions "abounded in ambiguity and pitfalls" and were "provocative of every kind of frivolous litigation." Even a provision for "Equal Protection of Laws" was considered a matter of opinion, bias or inclination or judgement which cannot be acted on under anything like settled rules of law. There was also the criticism of the American experiment with the Bill of Rights, that it had converted the Supreme Court of the United States into a "Third House of Legislature."

The debate in the United Kingdom on the merits of a bill of rights is still on. The jurisdiction of the Strasbourg Court has indirectly influenced the debate (See: A. W. Bradley "United Kingdom before the Strasbourg Court: 1975–1990"). The fundamental rights in England are protected by common law. Magna Carta extolled the "law of the land" which implied an independent body of law that every authority must obey.

When James I claimed that he was above the law, Chief Justice Sir Edward Coke exhorted that the "King ought not to be under any bet under God and the Law." In Dr. Bonham's case, Coke asserted: "When an act of Parliament is against common right and reason it is void." This went against the notion of parliamentary supremacy. Judicial review of legislation was not the English legal tradition. Bonham was an insular episode. But, ironically, it seems to be returning through the backdoor of the European Court of Strasbourg. Common law insisted on the most anxious scrutiny of deprivation of life and liberty, the protection against self-incrimination, search and seizure procedures and of free speech.

In the recent *Derbyshire* case, the House of Lords denied a local authority the right to sue a newspaper for libel, stating: "It is of the highest public importance that a democratically elected body should be open to uninhibited criticism. The threat of a civil action for defamation must inevitably have an inhibiting effect on free speech."

Earlier there was a sharp divergence of views on the need for a bill of rights in the UK. It was apprehended that a bill of rights would expand the courts' jurisdiction and increase judicial law-making. It was also said that a bill of rights would create high expectations in the minds of the people and be regarded as a panacea for all grievances, which could not, in reality, be possible to satisfy in practice. It was also apprehended that a bill of rights might promote an activist judiciary which might "hamper strong and progressive government" and "result in important public issues being discussed and resolved in legal or constitutional terms rather than in moral or political terms."

Lord Denning himself expressed great reservations about a bill of rights. He said, "If judges were given the power to overthrow sections of the Act or Acts of Parliament, they would become political, their appointments would be based on political grounds and the reputation of our judiciary would suffer accordingly. One has only to see, in the great Constitution of the United States of America and of India, the conflicts which arise from time to time between judges and the legislature. I hope we shall not have such conflicts in this country." But Lord Scarman, the pillar of the alternative argument, said, "When times are normal and fear is not stalking the land, English law sturdily protects the freedom of the individual and respects human personality. But when times are abnormally alive with fear and prejudice the common law is at a disadvantage; it cannot resist the will, however frightened and prejudiced it may be, of Parliament.

Lord Halsham said, "One of the main purposes of law and justice, courts, judges, governments and parliaments is to protect the weak against the strong, the few and even, in extreme cases, the individual against the many, the unpopular against the popular. The 'greatest happiness of the greatest number' may serve well enough as a slogan. But, in a democracy, it becomes a charter for elective dictatorship, the denial of justice in the interests of a shifting and perhaps amoral majority. If nonsense walks on stilts it is under the banner of populist utilitarianism, and not of natural, that is individual or minority rights." (Lord Halsham's "Values, Collapse and Cure.") Democracy can degenerate into a mere game of numbers. It may become necessary to protect the minority from the power of numbers. A majority may tend to become amoral. A bill of rights is an entrenched provision with which all legislative and executive action must comport. Courts will uphold the rights even against the will of the parliament and its supremacy must yield.

Fundamental Rights and International Human Rights Law

The meanings of expressions like civil liberties, human rights and fundamental rights overlap. This is because of their common pedigree and source. They are not given by any human agency. They inhere in man. The humanitarian base of fundamental human rights assumed prominence fifty years ago when, chastened by the capacity of the human species to destroy its own kind through acts of war and barbarous inhumanity, the peoples of the world gave themselves two instruments designed to prevent forever the recurrence of such unconscionable behaviour: the Charter of the United Nations and the Universal Declaration of Human Rights. These were not devised by impractical or utopian minds. They represented the hard-headed conclusions of a generation that twice in its time had witnessed global war as well as the horrors of the Holocaust.

One is not left with a particularly strong idea of the kindness of our species to itself. Not without reason ours has been the bloodiest century in human history, a less than enviable distinction: According to an estimate made for the Carnegie Commission on Preventing Deadly Conflict, some one hundred million people have been killed in armed conflict this century. Politically related violence (in which race, ethnicity, religion or political opinion has been a factor) has led to another 120 million deaths.

The UN Human Development Report of 1998 notes that, whereas civilian casualties in situations of armed conflict were some five per cent at the start of the century, by the 1990s they were more than ninety per cent, with children as the principal victims (as Grace Machel's report for UNICEF has made evident). Further, some fifty million people are refugees or displaced persons, having been forced to flee their homes. Never before has human rage been directly so vehemently against its own species. Never before has the destructiveness taken such a toll, in addition, on other forms of life and on the very ecosystems on which life itself depends.

The Charter of the United Nations was adopted to save succeeding generations from the scourge of war. The Declaration was adopted to proclaim and establish the equal and inalienable rights of all members of the human family—great or small, rich or poor—and their inherent dignity, regardless of birth or status, race, colour, sex, language, religion or political or other opinion. Article 55 of the Charter of the United Nations requires the United Nations to promote "universal respect for, and observance of, human rights and fundamental freedoms for all without distinction as to race, sex, language or religion." Article 56 enjoins that "All members pledge themselves to take joint and separate action in cooperation with the organization for the achievement of the purposes set forth in Article 55."

Human rights and humanitarian norms have progressively emerged as new rules of the customary international law. It is now recognized that relatively extensive participation in a treaty, coupled with a subject matter of general significance and stipulations which accord with the general sense of the international community, do establish for some treaties an influence far beyond the limits of formal participation in them. These factors give such a treaty something of the complexion of a legislative instrument and assist the acceptance of the treaty's provisions as customary international law, in addition to their contractual values for the parties. The process whereby a treaty's provisions may also come to be rules of customary law is of considerable significance for the role of treaties in international law.

Indian Constitutional Experience

In India, the Universal Declaration greatly influenced the drafting of the constitution. The Indian Constitution was adopted shortly after the Universal Declaration. Article 51(c) of the Constitution enjoins the "state to endeavour to foster respect for international law and treaty obligations." Because of this, the Indian courts have endeavoured to interpret Indian Statutes in consonance with the international covenants ratified by India.

The subject of human rights as part of the inalienable heritage of man has inspired the philosophy of entrenched rights in the Indian Constitution. The Indian Supreme Court observed that fundamental rights are merely the modern name for what have traditionally been known as "natural rights." The fact that an international convention has not been incorporated in the domestic laws of India does not mean that its ratification holds no significance in Indian law.

The hope for collective survival depends on how successful we are in making collective rights universal. International human rights philosophy seeks to extol the individual and place him or her at the centre of the Universe. As it is written in the Talmud: "A man may coin several coins with the same matrix and all will be similar, but the King of Kings, the Almighty, has coined every man with the same matrix of Adam and no one is similar to the other. Therefore, every man ought to say the whole world has been created for me."

Freedom of Expression in a Multimedia Universe

RIGHTS, LIMITS AND DANGERS

The Principles of Freedom of Expression

Irwin Cotler is a professor of law at McGill University in Montréal. In his role as international legal counsel, he has advised such political prisoners as the imprisoned Indonesian labour leader Muchter Pakpahan; Wole Soyinka in Nigeria, winner of the Nobel Prize for literature; Nobel laureate Andrei Sakharov in the former Soviet Union; and in South Africa, President Nelson Mandela when he was a political prisoner. He has intervened on free speech issues and international tribunals covering crimes in the former Yugoslavia and Rwanda. Professor Cotler is also the international legal counsel to the Palestinian Human Rights Monitoring Group.

335

IN SPEAKING OF FREEDOM OF EXPRESSION, I am reminded of the words of John Stuart Mill—the intellectual apostle of free speech—who began his famous essay "On Liberty" with an apology as follows: "Those to whom nothing which I am about to say will be new, may therefore, I hope, excuse me, if on a subject which for now three centuries has been much discussed, I venture on one discussion more."[1]

Speaking some 140 years after John Stuart Mill uttered his apology, I too must beg your indulgence for venturing on "one discussion more" on freedom of speech. But I want to suggest that there are "compelling considerations" for "one discussion more," not the very least of which is the theme of Freedom of Expression in a Multimedia Universe: Rights, Limits and Dangers—let alone the over-arching theme of this conference, Universal Rights and Human Values.

We meet at an important moment of remembrance and reminder, of witness and warning. Indeed, this conference takes place not only on the eve of the fiftieth anniversary of the Universal Declaration of Human Rights—the Magna Carta of humankind—and the fiftieth anniversary of the Genocide C- with its motif of "Never again." It also convenes on the fiftieth anniv

Nuremberg trials and the Nuremberg judgements. Indeed, what is called the *double entendre* of Nuremberg—the Nuremberg of jackboots, of hate, and the Nuremberg of principles and of judgements.

The fundamental lesson of Nuremberg is that Nazism almost succeeded not only because of its industry of death and technology of terror, but because of the ideology of hate. This teaching of contempt, this demonizing of the other: this is where it all begins. As the Supreme Court of Canada affirmed in upholding the constitutionality of anti-hate legislation, the "Holocaust did not begin in the gas chambers. It began with words."[2]

Fifty years later we are witnessing a growing trafficking in hate from Central America to Central Asia, a murderous teaching of contempt which in the Balkans and Rwanda, for example, has taken us down the road to ethnic cleansing and genocide. You only have to read the transcripts of trials before the international criminal tribunals in the former Yugoslavia and Rwanda to get a sense of the dangers, not only of incitement to discrimination, but with state-orchestrated incitement to discrimination.[3] Read the transcripts of the judgement earlier this year in Canada in the *Mugasera* case, which ordered the deportation of Léon Mugasera for incitement to genocide in 1992, and you will see the dangers of assaultive speech.[4]

The witness testimony and documentary evidence of survivors of ethnic cleansing and genocide in the Balkans and Rwanda are only too clear. As survivors themselves told me in the course of my preparation of *Amicus* briefs before these tribunals, "They are killing us with words." Nor is this assaultive hate speech limited to the Balkans or Rwanda.

There is, in North America, a growing web of hate reflected in the following message sent on the Internet of the e-mail system of the University of Missouri:

Dear Friend, Please be correctly advised. Tutsis are the only enemies of mankind on the face of this earth. Kill all the Tutsis and there you get an ever-lasting peace upon the face of this earth. The bloodthirsty, warmongers, empire-prone Tutsis have now conquered: Uganda, Rwanda, Burundi. Next on their long lists of conquests are the following: Congo, Kenya, Tanzania, Sudan, Ethiopia and Somalia. This is just not to mention their ambition to conquer and control: Zambia, Zimbabwe, Angola, Madagascar, etc. All these are the dirty work of the stupid punkhead the tutsi yoweri kaguta the already established conqueror of Uganda. So be informed, all Tutsi must be wiped off the face of the earth in order to save humanity from Tutsis's mass massacre, atrocities, calamities and so on. Yes, that is the only formula for peace for the world to adopt before it is too late. An unexamined life is not worth living. JUST KILL THE OPPRESSIVE TUTSIS (all of them) AND LIFE FREE! Got it? That is the truth. Truthfully, Human Peacer Lover.[5]

And so there are compelling considerations that warrant "one discussion more," and distinguish this discussion—on the eve of the fiftieth anniversaries of the Universal Declaration of Human Rights, the Genocide Convention, and the Nuremberg Judgements—from that of John Stuart Mill and the successor liberal theory that invokes his legacy.

First, there is the very real and existential character of the discussion. In other words, we are not simply discussing the abstractions of freedom of speech, or speech *in abstracto,* or freedom of expression as a matter of political theory or philosophic inquiry alone. We are discussing the balancing, or even the confrontation, of two core values: the principle of freedom of speech on the one hand, and the right of minorities to protection against group vilifying speech on the other. The philosophic and normative inquiry, while owing much to Mill, emerges as a more profound and more compelling one, than that addressed by Mill.

Second, there are important legal, indeed constitutional, considerations which did not even arise for Mill, or would only be averted to in the framework of political theory, but which today have not only a national but international juridical resonance and are anchored in the dynamics of constitutional and international legal theory.

More particularly, is anti-hate legislation—the panoply of civil and criminal remedies developed to combat hate propaganda—constitutional? How does one address, let alone determine, its constitutionality? Is such anti-hate legislation necessarily over-broad and all-encompassing given the enormity, but ephemeral character, of the evil it seeks to combat? Will it be rendered void because of this very overbreadth or vagueness? Or, conversely, if it is narrowly tailored so as to meet a constitutional challenge, can it be effective in combating the evil? Can constitutional theory and practice coexist? Is there a dissonance between validity and efficiency? And what principles, and precedents, exist to guide us in our deliberations?

Third, there are important socio-technological considerations which Mill did not face or could not even imagine. On the one hand there is the development of the information superhighway, where the technology of cyberspace emerges as a megaphone for freedom of expression and for advancing the promotion and protection of human rights. At the same time, the information superhighway that can "transport the best—can also transport the worst."[6] In a word, there is a veritable explosion today of racist hate speech, a global web of hate, not only of a kind and character that Mill could not envisage, but conveyed by a technology of cyberhate that even postmodernists did not foresee.

Fourth, there is the dialectical, or what I would call dynamic, encounter in Canada and elsewhere between the rise in hate speech and the existence of a comprehensive legal regime to combat it. The constitutionalization of rich
as in the Canadian Charter of Rights and Freedoms—and the interna

of rights, as in the Universal Declaration of Human Rights, emerges as a double-edged human rights sword. This sword is invoked by both the purveyors as well as the targets of hate propaganda.

The hate mongers shield themselves behind the freedom of expression principle in constitutional law, invoking also Article 19 of the Universal Declaration of Human Rights. The victims shield themselves behind the right to protection against group vilifying speech, similarly anchored in both domestic and international law.

It is an encounter and litigation that would have been alien to Mill. But it is an encounter and experience that culturally, as well as legally, has international significance and which makes the Canadian experience a constitutional model for the validity and efficacy of legal remedy.

Fifth, there is also a psychological consideration that underpinned Mill's analysis from the perspective of philosophic inquiry and political theory, but whose psychological fallout was unknown to Mill and is only now becoming known to us. I am referring to the serious individual, group and societal harm resulting from this scurrilous speech, harm that is only now being appreciated as a veritable assault on our psyches with catastrophic effects for our polity— harm which if it were known to Mill would make the hate-speech issue, even for this classical liberal theorist, a hard case. Indeed, it is arguable that Mill's own philosophic concern with harm, revisited today in the context of the trafficking in hate at the *fin de siècle*, might well have led him to exclude hate speech from the ambit of protected speech.

Sixth, there are considerations of an international juridical character that were neither existing, nor even foreseeable, in Mill's time. There exists today an international legal regime, anchored in international treaty and customary law, which not only prohibits racist hate speech and excludes it from the ambit of protected speech, but obliges state parties to these international treaties, like Canada, to enact measures to combat such scurrilous speech. If countries like Canada had not enacted such measures, they would now be obliged to do so. Having enacted them, they cannot lightly be set aside.

Seventh, there is a jurisprudential movement beyond the liberal legal theory and perspectives on free speech reflected in Mill and Rawls, and which finds expression today in the rethinking of freedom of expression or, more particularly, hate speech, in critical race theory, feminist legal theory and international legal theory.

One can see, therefore, that there are a variety of considerations of an existential, philosophical, legal, sociological, psychological and international character that simply were not party of Mill's analysis some 140 years ago. These considerations alone warrant one discussion more, and must necessarily be factored into any discussion of free speech and hate propaganda today.

Moreover, this discussion may also be said to be warranted by its taking place today against the backdrop of the most celebrated hate speech litigation in the history of Canadian jurisprudence. It includes most notably, the historic trilogy of the *Keegstra*, *Andrews* and *Taylor* cases, decided together by the Supreme Court of Canada in 1990, and for which *Keegstra* has become both metaphor and message, and including the ultimate disposition of the *Keegstra* case (*Keegstra*, No. 2) in 1996.[7, 8, 9]

The *Zundel cause célèbre* involved one of the world's foremost Holocaust deniers.[10] There was still another famous case lodged under the province of New Brunswick's Human Rights Act against the New Brunswick school teacher and hate propagandist Malcolm Ross which was the most recent hate speech judgement by the Supreme Court in 1996.[11] The judgement was organized around the principle of hate propaganda as assaultive of equality, if not the underlying liberal rationale for free speech itself.

There have also been numerous lower court decisions under the federal and provincial human rights codes involving hate propaganda, notably the *Heritage Front* case in Ontario, the *Harcus* case in Manitoba, the *Bell* case in Saskatchewan, the *Aryan Nations* case in Alberta and the *Liberty Net* cases in British Columbia, which are again organized around the notion of hate propaganda as a discriminatory practice.[12-16]

But what makes this Canadian jurisprudential experience particularly significant for us, and for those seeking to construct a comprehensive legal theory for democracies generally, is that it has generated one of the more instructive and compelling sets of legal precedents and principles in the world today respecting freedom of expression and this genre of hate speech. It may help explain what American First Amendment scholar Fred Shauer has called "the multiple tests, rules and principles...reflecting the [extraordinary] diversity of communication experiences," a matter of particular importance as the rise in racist hate propaganda is now an international and not just a domestic phenomenon.[17]

What follows is a distillation of some of these interpretative principles and perspectives. This should help advocates, activists, judges and scholars appreciate the considerations that should be factored into any analysis of freedom of expression, hate speech and nondiscrimination and any attempt to balance competing normative principles.

◼◼◼ Principle 1—
Chartering Rights: The Constitutionalization of Freedom of Expression

From the perspective of constitutional theory, or that of the "first amendment" doctrine, the notion that Canadian constitutional theory and doctrine dilute and diminish freedom of expression as the "life-blood of democracy" is misinformed and misleading. For the notion of freedom of expression as a fundamental right not only underpinned the Canadian free speech jurisprudence under the Charter of Rights, but it pervaded the free speech jurisprudence even in the pre-Charter era. As the Supreme Court of Canada put it in the *Switzman* case, itself reflective and representative of this pre-Charter free speech jurisprudence, "Liberty in these things (i.e., freedom of expression) is little less vital to man than breathing is to his physical existence."

In the most recent free speech case decided by the Supreme Court of Canada in 1996, involving New Brunswick Holocaust denier Malcolm Ross, the court reaffirmed, as it had in the *Keegstra* case, that "it is difficult to imagine a guaranteed right more important to a democratic society than freedom of expression; as such it should only be restricted in the clearest of circumstances." The court invoked the classical dictum of Holmes J. in the *Schwimmer* case as follows:

> As Holmes J. stated over sixty years ago, the fact that the particular content of a person's speech might 'excite popular prejudice' is no reason to deny it protection for 'if there is any principle of the Constitution that more imperatively calls for attachment than any other it is the principle of free thought—not free thought for those who agree with us but freedom for the thought that we hate.'[18]

But what distinguishes the Canadian from the American approach, and locates it closer to the European and international perspective, is the constitutionalization of a configurative "balancing" principle of rights and limits in Section 1 of the Charter. This section guarantees the rights and freedoms set out in the Charter, such as freedom of expression, subject only to "such reasonable limits prescribed by law as can be demonstrably justified in a free and democratic society."

Accordingly, while Canadian jurisprudence regards freedom of expression as "the life-blood of democracy," it acknowledged that it may be subject to reasonable and demonstrably justified limits and, as will be seen below, this balancing act involves existential as well as legal questions, rights in collision as well as rights in the balance. On the one hand, there is the "fundamental" right of free speech, a core principle. On the other hand, there is the right to protection against group vilifying speech, also a core principle. What is at stake is the litigation of the values of a nation.

Accordingly, one cannot say that those who challenge anti-hate legislation are the only civil libertarians, or the ones promotive of free speech, or that those who support anti-hate legislation are not really civil libertarians, or are against free speech. Rather, there are good civil libertarians and good free speech people on both sides of the issue. In a word, one can adhere to the notion of free speech as the lifeblood of democracy and still support anti-hate legislation.

■ Principle 2 —
Freedom of Expression: Fundamental but not an Absolute Right

Freedom of expression, as Professor Abraham Goldstein has put it, "is not absolute, however much so many persist in talking as if it is."[19] In every free and democratic society certain forms and categories of expression are clearly regarded as being outside the ambit of protected speech. In the US, certain categories of speech—obscenity, personal libel and "fighting words"—are not protected by the First Amendment. Such utterances, said the US Supreme Court in *Chaplinsky*, "are no essential part of any exposition of ideas, and are of such slight social value as a step to the truth that any benefit…is clearly outweighed by the social interest in order and morality," while some American scholars argue that *Beauharnais v. Illinois*, which upheld of the constitutionality of a group libel ordinance, is still good law.[20, 21]

In summary, all free and democratic societies have recognized certain limitations on freedom of expression in the interest of protecting fundamental human values, such as prohibitions against perjury, to protect the right to a fair trial, or prohibitions against treasonable speech to protect national security, or prohibitions against pornography to protect the human dignity of women and children, or prohibitions respecting libellous and defamatory speech, to protect privacy and reputation, or prohibitions respecting misleading advertising to protect consumers and the like. The prohibitions against hate speech partake of this genre of limitations.

■ Principle 3—
The Scope of Freedom of Expression and the Purposive Theory of Interpretation

In the view of the Canadian Supreme Court, the proper approach to determining the ambit or scope of freedom of expression and the "pressing and substantial concerns" that may authorize its limitation is a purposive one. This principle of interpretation was set forth by then Chief Justice Dickson in the *Big M. Drug Mart Ltd.* case as follows: "The meaning of a right or a freedom guaranteed by the Charter was to be ascertained by an analysis of the purpose of such a guarantee. It was to be understood, in other words, in the light of the interests it was meant to protect."[22]

In the *Keegstra* case, the court reiterated the three-pronged purposive rationale for freedom of expression that it had earlier articulated in the *Irwin Toy* case as follows: seeking and attaining truth is an inherently good activity; participation in social and political decision-making is to be fostered and encouraged; and diversity in forms of individual self-fulfilment and human flourishing ought to be cultivated in a tolerant and welcoming environment for the sake of both those who convey a meaning and those to whom a meaning is conveyed.[23]

Hate-mongering, however, according to the court, constituted an assault on these very values and interests sought to be protected by freedom of expression as follows: hate-mongering is not only incompatible with a "competitive market-place of ideas which will enhance the search for truth," but it represents the very antithesis of the search for truth in a marketplace of ideas.[24] Secondly, it is anti-thetical to participation in democratic self-government and constitutes a "destructive assault" on that very government.[25] Thirdly, it is utterly incompat-ible with a claim to "personal growth and self-realization." It is analogous to the claim that one is "fulfilled" by expressing oneself "violently."[26] Citing studies showing that victims of group vilification may suffer loss of self-esteem and experience of self-abasement, the court found that incitement to racial hatred constitutes an assault on the potential for "self-realization" of the target group and its members.[27] It is not surprising, then, that the court anchored its reasons for judgement in the "catastrophic effects of racism."[28]

■ Principle 4 —
Freedom of Expression and the Contextual Principle

A fourth principle of interpretation, or "building block," as then Supreme Court Justice Bertha Wilson characterized it, is the contextual principle.[29] Again, the contextual principle, as with the purposive principle, is relevant both in the interpretation of the ambit of a right and the assessment of the validity of legis-lation to limit it.

As the Supreme Court put it in *Keegstra*, "It is important not to lose sight of factual circumstances in undertaking an analysis of freedom of expression and hate propaganda for these shape a court's view of both the right or freedom at stake and the limit proposed by the state; neither can be surveyed in the abstract."[30] As Wilson J. said in the *Edmonton Journal*, referring to what she termed the contextual approach to Charter interpretation: "a particular right or freedom may have a different value depending on the context. It may be, for example, that freedom of expression has greater value in a political context than it does in the context of disclosure of the details of a matrimonial dispute."[31]

In a recent retrospective on the case, Justice Wilson commented that "there was, for example, no point in assessing the value of freedom of speech for balancing purposes in the context of our political institutions if it had come before the court in the context of advertising aimed at children."[32]

One might equally argue that it makes all the difference in the world if the freedom of expression principle at issue comes before the court in the context of political speech, or in the context of hate speech aimed at historically disadvan-taged minorities and against the backdrop of "the chilling facts of history." As Justice Wilson concluded on this point, "A contextual as well as purposive inter-pretation of the right was required for purposes of Section 1 balancing."[33] In the matter of hate-mongering, whether the principle of interpretation adopted is the purposive or the contextual one, both interpretations converge in favour of the right of the disadvantaged minorities to be protected against group vilification, while maintaining an "expansive" and "liberal" view of freedom of expression itself as a core right.

■ Principle 5 —
Freedom of Expression in a Free and Democratic Society

According to Supreme Court doctrine, the interpretation of freedom of expression must involve not only recourse to the purposive character of freedom of expression (Section 2(b)), but "to the values and principles of a free and democratic society." This phrase, as the court put it, "requires more than an incantation...[but] requires some definition...an elucidation as to the values and principles that [the phrase] invokes."[34]

Such principles, said the court, are not only the genesis of rights and freedoms under the Charter generally, or democratic societies, but also underlies freedom of expression (Section 2(b)) in particular. These values and principles include "respect for the inherent dignity of the human person...[and] respect for cultural and group identity."[35] Accordingly, anti-hate legislation should not only be seen as not infringing upon freedom of speech but as promoting and protecting the values and principles of a free and democratic society.

■ Principle 6—
Freedom of Expression in Comparative Perspective

In determining whether incitement to racial hatred is a protected form of expression, the Supreme Court reasoned that resort may be had not only to the values and principles of a free and democratic society such as Canada, but to the legislative experience of other free and democratic societies. It concluded that an examination of the legislative experience of other free and democratic societies clearly and consistently supports the position that such racist hate speech is not entitled to constitutional protection.[36]

By 1966, the Special Committee on Hate Propaganda (the Cohen Committee) had already recorded the existence of legislation in a number of countries which sought to proscribe incitement to group hatred. The countries concerned were demonstrably "free and democratic." An analysis of the legislative experience of other free and democratic societies supports the view, as the court put it, that not only is such legislation representative of free and democratic societies, but its very purpose is to ensure that such societies remain free and democratic. Indeed, free and democratic societies in every region of the world have now enacted similar legislation, including countries in Asia, the Middle East and Latin America, as well as the countries of Scandinavia and Western and Eastern Europe. Such legislation can also be found in the countries of the former Soviet Union.

Freedom of Expression in Light of Other Rights and Freedoms

The Supreme Court has also determined that the principle of freedom of expression must be interpreted in the light of other rights and freedoms sought to be protected by a democracy like Canada. In the words of the court: "The purpose of the right or freedom in question [freedom of expression] is to be sought by reference to...the meaning and purpose of the other specific rights and freedoms with which it is associated."[37]

It should be noted that the purpose, if not also the effect, of hate speech is to diminish, if not deny, other rights and freedoms, or the rights and freedoms of others. Such hate-mongering is the very antithesis of the values and principles underlying these rights and freedoms. Any reading of freedoms of expressions in the light of other rights and freedoms admits of not other interpretation than that such hate speech is outside the ambit of protected expression.

Principle 8—
Freedom of Expression and the Principle of Equality:
Hate Propaganda as a Discriminatory Practice

If freedom of expression is to be interpreted in the light of other rights and freedoms, a core and underlying associated right is that of equality. The denial of other rights and freedoms, or the rights and freedoms of "the other," makes freedom of expression or group defamation not just a speech issue but an equality issue. In the words of Professor Kathleen Mahoney: "In this trilogy of cases, the majority of the Supreme Court of Canada articulated perspectives on freedom of expression that are more inclusive than exclusive, more communitarian than individualistic, and more aware of the actual impacts of speech on the disadvantaged members of society than has ever before been articulated in a freedom of expression case. The court has advanced an equality approach using a harm-based rationale to support the regulation of hate propaganda as a principle of inequality."[38]

Principle 9—
Freedom of Expression, Group Libel and the Harms-Based Approach

According to the Supreme Court in *Keegstra*, the concern resulting from racist hate-mongering is not "simply the product of its offensiveness, but stems from the very real harm which it causes."[39] This judicial finding of the "very real harm" from hate-mongering is not only one of the most recent findings on record by a high court, but may be considered a relevant and persuasive authority for other democratic societies.

The following excerpt from the *Keegstra* case, anchored in the analysis and findings of the Cohen Committee, is particularly instructive in this regard: "Essentially, there are two sorts of injury caused by hate propaganda. There is harm done to members of the target group. It is indisputable that the emotional damage caused by words may be of grave psychological and social consequence....[40] A second harmful effect of hate propaganda which is of pressing and substantial concern is its influence upon society at large. The Cohen Committee noted that individuals can be persuaded to believe 'almost anything' (p. 30) if information or ideas are communicated using the right technique and in the proper circumstances (p. 8)."

The Supreme Court's conclusion on this point is particularly relevant today. In the words of the court: "The threat to self-dignity of target group members is thus matched by the possibility that prejudiced messages will gain some credence, with the attendant result of discrimination, and perhaps even violence, against minority groups in Canadian society. With these dangers in mind, the Cohen Committee made clear in its conclusions that the presence of hate propaganda existed as a baleful and pernicious element, and hence a serious problem, in Canada (p. 59)."[41]

Again, in the words of the Cohen Committee as quoted by the Supreme Court of Canada: "The amount of hate propaganda presently being disseminated [is] probably not sufficient to justify a description of the problem as one of crisis or near crisis proportion. Nevertheless the problem is a serious one. We believe that, given a certain set of socioeconomic circumstances, such as a deepening of the emotional tensions or the setting in of a severe business recession, public susceptibility might well increase significantly. Moreover, the potential psychological and social damage of hate propaganda, both to a desensitized majority and to sensitive minority target groups, is incalculable. As Mr. Justice Jackson of the United States Supreme Court wrote in *Beauharnais v. Illinois*, such sinister abuses of our freedom of expression...can tear apart a society, brutalize its dominant elements, and persecute even to extermination, its minorities."[42]

■ Principle 10—
Freedom of Expression, Hate Propaganda and International Law

In the words of the Supreme Court, international law may be regarded as "a relevant and persuasive source" for the interpretation of rights and freedoms under the Charter.[43] As then Chief Justice Dickson wrote in *Keegstra*, "No aspect of international human rights has been given attention greater than that focused upon discrimination.... This high concern regarding discrimination has led to the presence in two international human rights documents of articles forbidding the dissemination of hate propaganda."[44]

Reading the freedom of expression principle in light of international human rights law generally, and under these two international human rights treaties in particular, requires that such racial incitement be excluded from the protective ambit of freedom of expression.[45] Any legislative remedy prohibiting the promotion of hatred or contempt against identifiable groups on grounds, of their race, religion, colour or ethnic origin would be in compliance with Canada's international obligations, and have the effect of implementing these international obligations.

Accordingly, the Supreme Court reasoned in *Keegstra*, "It appears that the protection provided freedom of expression by CERD and ICCPR does not extend to cover communications advocating racial or religious hatred."[46] Of crucial importance was the conclusion of the court that, in assessing the interpretative importance of international human rights law, the "CERD and ICCPR demonstrate that prohibition of hate-promoting expression is considered to be not only compatible with a signatory nation's guarantee of human rights, but is as well an obligatory aspect of this guarantee."[47]

■■■ Principle 11—
Freedom of Expression and the Multicultural Principle
The increasing multicultural features of the liberal democracies invite consideration or interpretation of hate speech in light of the multicultural principle. Section 27 of the Charter mandates that the rights guaranteed therein, including freedom of expression, be interpreted "in a manner consistent with the preservation and enhancement of the multicultural heritage of Canadians."

This interpretative principle admits of no other reading than that such hate-mongering is not only an assault on the members of the target group singled out on grounds of their identifiable race or religion, but it is destructive of a multicultural society as a whole. As such, it falls outside the protection of freedom of speech. Conversely, and again to paraphrase Mr. Justice Cory in *Smith and Andrews*, anti-hate legislation is designed not only "to protect identifiable groups in a multicultural society from publicly made statements which wilfully promote hatred against them," but are designed to "prevent the destruction of our multicultural society."[48]

■■■ Principle 12—
Freedom of Expression and the Principle of Abhorrent Speech
It is important that one distinguish between political speech—where the government, its institutions and public officials are the target of offensive speech—and abhorrent, racist speech, intended to promote hatred and contempt of vulnerable and targeted minorities. The hate-mongering at issue in *Keegstra*, and in analogous cases, is not the libel of public officials as in the *Sullivan* case; or directed against "the world at large" as in the *Cohen* case, but is hate-mongering wilfully promoted against disadvantaged minorities with intent to degrade, diminish, vilify.[49, 50] This is not a case of a government legislating in its own self-interest regarding its political agenda, but an affirmative

responsibility of governments to protect the inherent human dignity and equal standing of its citizens.

■ Principle 13 —
Freedom of Expression and the Slippery Slope

Those who reject anti-hate legislation on the grounds that such group libel legislation leads us inevitably down the slippery slope to censorship ignore a different slippery slope—"a swift slide into a marketplace of ideas in which bad ideas flourish and good ones die."[51] It is submitted that the more the hateful speech is tolerated, the more likely it is to occur. As Karl Popper put it, the "paradox of tolerance" is that it breeds more intolerance, so that the tolerance of hateful speech results in more, not less, hate speech; in more, not less harm; and in more, not less hateful actions. Tolerance of hate speech risks legitimizing such speech on the grounds that "it can't be all bad if it is not being prohibited." The slippery slope is there, but it may lead not in the direction of more censorship—which the Canadian experience does not demonstrate—but in the direction of more hate, which it does.

■ Conclusion

These constitute the principles respecting freedom of expression, hate speech and non-discrimination as articulated by the Supreme Court of Canada in the historic case law symbolized by *Keegstra*. But an appreciation or invocation of these principles or factors need not be limited to the Canadian jurisdiction only. Just as Canadian courts and counsel appearing before them have drawn upon principles grounded in comparative and international perspectives to help strike a balance, so too may courts and counsel of other free and democratic societies draw, and those aspiring to become ones, draw on the Canadian experience.

It is important to realize that we are not talking about freedom of speech in the abstract. We are talking about a particular genre of speech—hate speech. Nor are we talking about hate speech in the abstract, or the general limitation of any hate speech directed against anyone at anytime. We are talking about the regulation of a specific series of hate propaganda in a specific sense: of hate speech that is not only disseminated but promoted, not just promoted but promoted wilfully and not against just anyone but against an identifiable if not historically oppressed minority. And not just anywhere but in a public place only. We are talking about a narrowly tailored circumscription of a particular genre of assaultive speech.

From the time that we were young, one of the refrains that we heard was that "sticks and stones may break my bones but words will never harm me." As we grew up, we began to understand that words can maim, that words can wound, that words can exclude, that words can vilify, that words—as happened in the former Yugoslavia and Rwanda—can take us down the road to genocide. Free speech is one of the most compelling of universal rights and human values. But racist hate speech gives that hallowed freedom of expression a bad name.

REFERENCES

1. John Stuart Mill. *On Liberty*. Representative Government. The Subjection of Women. London: Oxford University Press (1969): 21.
2. *Andrews and Smith v. R.* (1988) 65 O.R. (2d) 161 (Ont C.A.) at 179.
3. *The Prosecutor v. Jean Paul Akayesu* (2 September 1998), International Criminal Tribunal for Rwanda, Case No. ICTR-96-4-T. See also *The Prosecutor v. Anto Furundzija* (10 December 1998), International Criminal Tribunal for the Former Yugoslavia, http://www.un.org/icty
4. *Mugasera v. Minister of Citizenship and Immigration* (6 November 1998), Immigration and Refugee Board (Appeal Division), Case no. M96-10465.
5. Sender. Student@showme.missouri.edu/Content ID: <0907553941@inet_out.Mail.showme.missouri.edu.2>. Text errors in original message.
6. L. Axworthy, notes for an address to the NGO forum on "The Internet and Human Rights," Montréal, 11 September 1998 at p. 1.
7. *R. v. Keegstra*, (1990) 3 S.C.R. 697.
8. *R. v. Andrews and Smith*, (1990) 3S.C.R. 870.
9. *Canada (Human Rights Commission) v. Taylor*, (1990) 3 S.C.R. 892.
10. *Zundel v. R.*, (1992) 2 S.C.R. 731.
11. *Ross v. New Brunswick School District #15* (1996) 1 S.C.R. 825.
12. *Canada (Human Rights Commission) v. Heritage Front* (1994) 1 F.C. 203 (T.D.); *Canada (Human Rights Commission) v. Heritage Front* (1994), 78 F.T.R. 241 (Fed. T.D.)
13. *League for Human Rights B'nai B'rith Can. (Midwest Region) v. Man. Knights of the Ku Klux Klan* (1993), 18 C.H.R.R. D/406 (Can. Human Rights Trib.).
14. *Saskatchewan (Human Rights Commission) v. Bell* (1994), 114 D.L.R. (4th) 370 (Sask. C.A.).
15. *Kane v. Church of Jesus Christ Christian-Aryan Nations* (No. 3) (1992), 18 C.H.R.R. D/268 (Alta. Bd. of Inq.).
16. *Khaki v. Canadian Liberty Net* (1993), 22 C.H.R.R. D/347 (Cdn. Human Rights Trib.); *Canada (Human Rights Commission) v. Canadian Liberty Net*, (1992) 3 F.C. 155 (T.D.); *Canada (Human Rights Commission) v. Canadian Liberty Net*, (1992) 3 F.C. 504.
17. F. Schauer, book review, 56 *Univ. Chicago L. Rev.* 397, 410 (1989).
18. *United States v. Schwimmer* (1929) 279 US 644, at 654–655.
19. Abraham Goldstein. "Group Libel and Criminal Law: Walking on the Slippery Slope." Paper presented at the International Legal Colloquium on Racial and Religious Hatred and Group Libel, Tel Aviv University, 1991, 3.
20. *Chaplinsky v. New Hampshire*, 315 US 568, 571–72 (1942).
21. *Beauharnais v. Illinois*, US 250 (1952).
22. *R. v. Big M. Drug Mart Ltd.*, (1985) 1 SCR 295.
23. *Keegstra*, supra, Note 2 at 728.
24. *R. v. Zundel* (1987), 580 R (2d) 129 at 155–56, and quoted with approval on this point in *R. v. Andrews and Smith* (1988) 28 O.A.C. 161, to the effect that "the wilful promotion of hatred is entirely antithetical to our very system of freedom" (emphasis added).
25. *R. v. Andrews and Smith*, ibid., per Grange J.A. at 181–4.
26. See *Irwin Toy Ltd. v. A.-G of Québec* (1989) 1 SCR 927, 970.
27. See empirical date respecting the harm to target groups as summarized in Report of Special Committee on Hate Propaganda in Canada (the Cohen Committee) (1966), 211–215; findings of

the Ontario Court of Appeal in *R. v. Andrews and Smith,* supra note 2, per Cory, J., 171; and empirical data cited in M. Matsuda, "Public Response to Racist Speech: Considering the Victim's Story," 87 *Michigan Law Review,* 2320 (1989).

28. *Keegstra,* 725.

29. See Justice B. Wilson, "Building the Charter Edifice: The First Ten Years," conference paper, Tenth Anniversary of the Charter (Ottawa, April 1992), 6.

30. *Keegstra,* 737.

31. *Edmonton Journal v. Alta.* (AG), (1989) 2SCR 1326 at 1355–6.

32. Supra, Note 29.

33. Ibid.

34. *Keegstra,* 736.

35. *R. v. Oakes* (1986) 24 C.C.C. (3d) 321 (S.C.C.) 346.

36. See, for example, the Study on the Implementation of Article 4 of the International Convention on the Elimination of All Forms of Racial Discrimination (a report on the United Nations Committee on the Elimination of Racial Discrimination, submitted in May 1983) A/CONF. 119/10 18 May 1983.

37. *R.W.D.S.U. v. Dolphin Delivery Ltd.* (1986) 2 SCR 573, per McIntyre, J., 583.

38. K. Mahoney, "*R. v. Keegstra:* A Rationale for Regulating Pornography?" 37 *McGill Law Journal* 242.

39. *Keegstra,* 746.

40. Ibid., 746.

41. Ibid., 748.

42. Ibid.

43. Reference re Public Service Employees Act (Alta.) (Dickson CJC dissenting, but not on this point) (1987) 1 SCR 313 per Dickson CJ, at 349. See also *R. v. Videoflicks,* (1984) 14 DLR (4th) 10 (Ont. CA) 35–6.

44. *Keegstra,* 750.

45. International Convention on the Elimination of All Forms of Racial Discrimination. See especially Article 4 (a) of the convention; and the International Covenant on Civil and Political Rights. See especially Article 20(2) of the convention.

46. *Keegstra,* 752.

47. Ibid., 753.

48. *R. v. Andrews and Smith* (1988) 43 C.C.C. (3d) 193 (Ont. C.A.O. 211).

49. *New York Times v. Sullivan,* 376 US 254 (1964).

50. *Cohen v. California,* 403 US 15 (1971).

51. This principle and perspective find expression in A. Goldstein, *supra,* note 19.

Freedom of Speech in Israel

Dan Yakir is the legal counsel of the Association for Civil Rights in Israel. He specializes in civil rights of people in the occupied territories, freedom of speech and gay and lesbian rights. He has defended the freedom to publish and successfully overturned a ban imposed by the Israeli government on the broadcast of a program about gay and lesbian youth.

FREEDOM OF SPEECH IN ISRAEL does not enjoy an explicit constitutional protection. First of all, we don't have a written constitution. After the establishment of the State of Israel in 1948, merely six months before the adoption of the Universal Declaration of Human Rights, the Knesset, our Parliament, decided not to adopt a constitution for various reasons. One of them was the hope that all of the Jewish people would immigrate to Israel, a hope which was not fulfilled. The other problem was the tension between religion and state, another problem that is not solved to this day. So it was decided to pass piecemeal legislation, called Basic Laws, regarding various aspects of a regular constitution.

Until 1992 no Basic Law regarding a bill of rights or any civil rights or civil liberties had been enacted by the Knesset. The Knesset had, however, enacted various basic rights regarding the branches of government. We had Basic Law: the government, the Knesset and judiciary—but no basic rights. Only in 1992 did the Knesset enact the first two basic laws in regard to basic human rights. One of them is Basic Law: Freedom of Occupation and the other one, the most important one, is Basic Law: Human Dignity and Liberty.

There are shortcomings for this Basic Law. The main one is that it covers only the specific rights that are enumerated in it and some of the most important rights are not included for various reasons. It covers the right to life, the right to integrity of the body, the right of personal liberty, the right of property and the right of privacy. But there is no mention of freedom of speech, freedom of religion or equality.

There is a dispute among Supreme Court judges whether the concept of human dignity encompasses those missing rights. Some say that this cannot be interpreted other than to include those basic rights. Others contend that the legislator clearly decided to delay the enactment of constitutional protections of those rights and that it is not the task of the judiciary to include them in current legislation. This is still an open question.

Since the inception of the State of Israel, the Supreme Court has been instrumental in protecting basic rights without a written constitution. As early as 1953 the Supreme Court, in a landmark decision, overturned the decision of the minister of interior to close down a communist newspaper for publishing an article that was deemed by the government to be inciteful. The minister of interior had relied upon a draconian press ordinance of the 1930s, an inheritance we were left by the British mandate which governed Palestine before the establishment of the State of Israel, which include the power to close down newspapers for publications that are deemed by the government to endanger public order. The court decided that only a near probability of endangering public order can justify the use of such an extraordinary measure and overturned the decision.

I would like to give you three examples of cases I dealt with in recent years. They are good examples of the problems we confront in Israel regarding the protection of freedom of speech. The first is the case of Mohamed Jabarin. Mohamed Jabarin is an Arab Israeli. When I say Arab Israeli, I mean an Arab citizen of the State of Israel. Arab Israelis comprise a minority of twenty per cent of the citizens of Israel. Mohamed Jabarin is a journalist and an educator who published articles from time to time in the local Arab-language newspapers.

In 1992 charges were brought against him for publishing three articles regarding the *Intifada* or uprising in the West Bank. In those articles he described an imaginary dialogue between two persons, two Palestinians in the West Bank. One accused the other of being a coward for sitting at home, for not participating in the uprising. The charges were that those articles were contrary to the Prevention of Terrorism Act of 1948 which includes an offence of publishing praises for deeds of violence. The case was heard in 1994 and the Magistrate Court convicted Mohamed Jabarin. The District Court dismissed our appeal and finally we got to the Supreme Court. Although the case was in regard to articles published in 1991 and the case was tried in 1993 and 1994, the case got to the Supreme Court only in the spring of 1996.

Six months before that Prime Minister Yitzhak Rabin had been assassinated and the aftermath of this assassination was a reconsideration by the attorney general and the prosecution of their traditional policies against prosecuting freedom of speech offences. I'm afraid that those events also affected the outcome of the Supreme Court decision. The Supreme Court dismissed our appeal, interpreting this offence broadly and rejecting our argument that near probability to do danger or violence must be proven by the prosecution before a person can be convicted of this offence. Not only did the prosecution not bring evidence at all regarding those articles and the circumstances of their publication, but we brought ample evidence to show that there wasn't the slightest chance of any violence occurring from these publications. I must note that our Supreme Court sits usually in panels of three and is comprised of fourteen judges. The president of the Supreme Court granted our petition for a rehearing before an enlarged panel of seven judges and this is still pending. I am cautiously optimistic about the results of this hearing.

The second case is that of Mike Eldar. Mike Eldar is a retired high-ranking officer of the Israeli navy. After retiring from the navy he started a career as a journalist and author of books about the Israeli navy. He wrote a book about the submarine unit of the Israeli army. There are two hard rules in publishing anything about the army or national security matters in Israel. First of all, there is military censorship. Any publication, whether in a newspaper or a book, regarding the army or national security issues or security services, must get pre-approval by the military censor before publication. The book was submitted to the military censor and he approved it completely.

The other hard rule is for civil servants and army officers. If they want to publish any book regarding their service that includes information that they obtained during that service, they must submit this publication to a ministerial committee that has the power to approve or reject the publication. Without this approval it is an offence for a civil servant to publish any information regarding his or her service.

Mike Eldar never served in the submarine unit in the navy (it is quite a classified unit) and all of the material in his book he got by independent research after his retirement. He notified the authorities that he was not willing to give this book to the ministerial committee and that he was going ahead in publishing it. The authorities did nothing and on the same day he held a news conference announcing the publication of the book, the Ministry of Defence filed a civil suit against him quickly received a temporary injunction order *ex parte* prohibiting the publication and distribution of the book. The next day soldiers from the navy swept through the book stores and confiscated all copies of the book. The police came and searched the home of Mike Eldar, taking his personal computer and all his files regarding the book.

A few months later we filed an appeal with the Supreme Court against this temporary injunction. We argued that the military censor had approved this book, that no danger to national security was posed by this book and that the dispute over whether information contained in this book was acquired during the author's military service was not a sufficient basis for a temporary injunction, that it was a prior restraint on speech.

A few months after that, Mike Eldar opened a website called com.mikeldar (don't look for it; it isn't there anymore) and promised to publish a few chapters from the book on the Internet. He also published a thirty-year-old classified report about the disappearance of the submarine *Dakar*. It was a new submarine that was built in the United Kingdom for the Israeli navy and disappeared in the spring of 1968 on its way to Israel. It is still a mystery where this submarine is and what happened to it.

Sure enough, the police came with an arrest warrant. Mike Eldar was investigated for opening this site and, under threat of imprisonment, the investigators from the computer offences unit instructed him how to wipe out this website and he did so. He was released later the same day but may still face criminal charges both regarding the publication of the book and the Internet site.

This fight took a great personal toll on Mike Eldar and especially his family, his wife and children. He decided he had enough and started negotiating a settlement of the case. He decided to agree to submit the book to this ministerial committee and hoped that the criminal charges would be dropped. But the negotiation failed and we are waiting for the hearing at the Supreme Court.

To conclude with a more optimistic case, I would like to tell you about Avi Golan. He had earlier received a sentence of eight years for a long series of fraud offences against banks in Israel. In 1994, as a prisoner, he wanted to publish a personal column in a local newspaper near the prison. He was to tell about his own experiences in prison. The prison authorities denied his request. He filed a petition of his own with the District Court and the court dismissed the case. Then he somehow found out about the Association for Civil Rights. One day I got a call from him and he asked us to file an appeal with the Supreme Court to try to secure his freedom of speech in prison.

At the hearing I referred to various writings of prisoners to show the court the important artistic, social and political value of writings of prisoners such as Oscar Wilde, who wrote *De Profundis* after he was imprisoned for sodomy. There is also the famous letter by Martin Luther King in the 1960s when he was in prison, *The Letter from Birmingham Jail*.

After the hearing was concluded I got word from a friend of mine in Toronto, sending me the first instalment of a series of articles called "Life in Prison" that had been published by the *Globe and Mail* in December 1994 and January 1995. With the help of a generous lady at the Canadian embassy in Tel Aviv, I got the other instalments of this illuminating series written by a prisoner convicted of murder. The articles had thought-provoking ideas about the shortcomings of the prison service in Canada, about its lack of ability to rehabilitate prisoners.

I sent a letter to the legal counsel of the Canadian Prison Service asking whether there were any limits on the freedom of speech of prisoners, whether they needed a permit to publish articles in the newspapers. I was told there are no regulations regarding freedom of speech of prisoners and any limitations must take into account the Canadian Charter of Rights and Freedoms.

I filed this series of articles and the correspondence with the Canadian Prison Service with the Court. After a waiting period of about eighteen months the Supreme Court overturned the decision of the District Court. It is a very important decision, both regarding freedom of speech and the rights of prisoners. At the end of the decision the Court referred to the series of articles in the *Globe and Mail* as one of the grounds for its decision.

Fortunately, for Avi Golan, he received early release for good conduct a few months after the decision was rendered. So, after waiting eighteen months, he was able to publish only one column after the decision. The case was so important to him that he might have been glad to stay in prison just to write a few more columns. But that is another problem of the delays in justice in Israel.

What do I make from these examples? First of all, that even in a free and democratic society committed to freedom of speech—and I believe that Israel by and large is such a society—freedom of speech is under constant danger. Secondly, we owe the protection of freedom of speech to those brave people— people like Mohamed Jabarin and Mike Eldar—who are willing to sacrifice their own personal liberty in their fight for freedom of speech.

DAN YAKIR

WILLIAM THORSELL

Rights, Limits
and Dangers of
Freedom
of Expression

William Thorsell is editor-in-chief of the *Globe and Mail* newspaper. He has served as associate editor of the *Edmonton Journal,* executive officer of the University of Alberta Senate and external reviewer of the graduate program at the Woodrow Wilson School at Princeton University.

AROUND THE WORLD, freedom of expression is a generally acknowledged right that is often unjustly limited and which generates dangers, both for those who speak it and for those who listen. I offer one proposition each about the rights, the limits and the dangers of free expression in a multimedia universe.

The right, first of all, is the right to free expression. I hold that the freedom of expression is not equal in weight to other fundamental human rights. Freedom of expression is the superior or core human right among many others that are listed in its presence. Almost every other human right is dependent for its achievement and defence on freedom of expression. I realize that as a journalist I carry a brief for freedom of expression, but let me make my case. Freedom of expression is listed in Article 19 of the Universal Declaration of Human Rights, which states: "[T]his right includes freedom to hold opinions without interference and to seek, receive and impart information and ideas through any media and regardless of frontiers."

Let's scan a few of the eighteen articles in the Universal Declaration of Human Rights that precede this one on freedom of expression. Article 1 says that all humans are endowed with reason and conscience. I would argue that neither can be developed, tested or known without freedom of expression. Article 2 says that no one shall be discriminated against on the basis of race, sex, opinion or nationality, among other things. Without freedom of expression, I would argue, how could we know the circumstances that are contrary to these guarantees and how could we campaign against them in places such as this and many other forums?

Article 3 says everyone has the right to life, liberty and security of the person. Without publicity these rights can be overridden by the state or criminal elements with relative ease. Article 4 says no one shall be held in slavery or servitude. Again, without freedom to describe such things, the right can be stripped of its life with relative impunity. Article 5 says no one shall be subjected to cruel, inhuman or degrading punishment. It is first of all, I would argue, the reporting of such things that makes them unsustainable over time and practice. In fact, the same general argument applies to most of the thirty articles in the Universal Declaration, from the right to a fair trial to freedom of religion. Freedom of expression is a necessary, if not always sufficient, condition of most other basic human rights.

We used to say that the human rights guarantees in the constitution of the former Soviet Union made that document among the most inspiring in the world to read. Of course, it was inspiring to read, but it was drained of all life or nullified by the effective absence of one right alone in the Soviet Union: the right to free speech. More profoundly still, it should be obvious that the very life-blood of democratic politics is the right to free expression. Without free speech there can be no contesting ideas or political parties in effective practice on which to make democratic choice, and without free speech there can be no opportunity to change the choice in the future.

Call your countries democracies if you wish. Celebrate declarations of basic human rights with bands and balloons, if you will, but do not claim to tell the truth about these things in the absence of free expression. So let us not weigh rights against rights, starting with the assumption that all rights are born equal. Freedom of expression is a seminal, germinal, essential, necessary prior right in the pantheon of rights, most of which depend for their very life-blood on free speech. Yes, that means that freedom of the press is particularly important in a humane and democratic society, but that is true despite the fact that I happen to be an editor.

There are rights, limits and dangers of freedom of expression. Regarding limits, I hold that freedom of expression should not be absolute, but should be limited by law retrospectively. While I argue in the first proposition that freedom of expression is the prior and superior human right, I do not argue that its exercise should be immune from legal limits or social sanction. The very power that gives free expression such pride of place in the pantheon of rights gives free expression the potential to do considerable harm. Surely anyone who does unjustified harm to another must be accountable, whatever the instrument of that harm-doing may be.

The most familiar harm in our society in this context is the obvious one of defamation of character. The destruction of another person's reputation, relationships, business or employment through lies, publicly expressed, is as consequential to them as the same destruction through physical acts. Another example is misleading advertising, which is properly subject to legal sanctions. Unjustified harm is a proper constraint on freedom of expression as long as three conditions are met: that the legal limits be imposed through a free and democratic process; that the limits and the penalties be reasonable; and that the limits do not generally apply a priori, that is, in advance of speaking out.

Without an open democratic process the case for limits will be taken to extremes and the substance of free speech will be lost. Some countries still make it a criminal offence, for example, to insult the president, which fails every test of reasonable limits for its vacuity. It is not a reasonable limit. It is desirable and maybe necessary that the reasonableness of limits on free speech be subject to appeal to independent courts, even in well-functioning democracies.

It is one thing to be warned against publishing a story for fear of legal conse-quences under a law. It is quite another to be prevented from publishing by an injunction in advance. In most cases, the onus in speaking must lie with the speaker, not with the state. That said, I do not support all the current legal limits on free speech that exist in Canada. For example, we have opposed our criminal hate laws from the day they were proposed in the 1970s. The Alberta human rights law, for example, prohibits discrimination in public statements or publi-cations which has a negative effect on any individual or group.

Such well-intentioned, barn door language shows very little understanding of the fundamental importance of free speech. I wouldn't be surprised if that part of the human rights laws of Alberta, of British Columbia and some other provinces will be found to be unconstitutional for their overgenerality. Prohibition on reporting opinion poll results just before elections came under the Criminal Code that Parliament brought in several years ago. I thought it was a completely unjustified infringement on freedom of the press and freedom of speech.

The *Globe and Mail*, among other papers, took it to court and we had the Supreme Court throw it out. We threw that law out of court under the Charter of Rights as unconstitutional in June 1998. But I do respect the potential of free expression to do harm and, therefore, as long as a healthy democratic process and a legal process offers the opportunity to contest what limits should exist, I would argue that reasonable limits on free expression actually reflect the significance of free expression itself.

The third argument regards the dangers that have to do with free expression. I would hold that in a multimedia global universe it both increases the wonderful range of free expression and the danger of inaccurate, malicious information capable of doing harm without the normal, effective constraints described in my earlier argument. If information is power, corrupt information can constitute malevolent power indeed.

Traditionally, the quality of information is regulated by the standards of those who gather and disseminate it through competitive media backed, as I have outlined above, by legal penalties for certain harmful behaviours or abuses. Even so, the quality of information in our society varies enormously across the media, and information consumers in most advanced democracies need to be on constant guard against error and spin. Indeed, I would say it is a duty of citizenship to be media-wise. There are even courses now in schools to learn how to be sceptical about media. I think that is a very good idea. If the printing press allowed one person to reach many, the Internet allows many to reach many. New media such as the Internet allow millions of individuals to be their own writer, editor and publisher and potentially reach millions more. The Internet also allows for publication beyond national borders and national regulation and can allow for anonymity.

The danger comes in freedom of a malicious and inaccurate expression that is not effectively challenged by competing messages or subject to even the most basic legal accountability in a sovereign democratic state. Without the normal correctives working as they should, corrupted information has the much greater potential to incite irrational and bad behaviour. As rumours planted to drive down a stock price, sell a product or influence an election arise from nowhere and everywhere, they are very hard to check or to refute. Over time one assumes that an ever more sceptical public will learn to weigh the quality of information it receives depending on its source around the world. But there is great scope for misinformation in a world that seems perpetually gullible, especially when it comes to dark conspiracy theories or promises of heavenly rewards.

Perhaps the greatest implication of this is that those of us working in the imperfect but accountable traditional media will have to act with much more alacrity to recognize dubious claims, assess them and respond when such issues arise. There is another area of dangers to freedom of expression that can arise even in the most functioning and open democratic society, and I will speak of Canada here. There is danger in the overconcentration of ownership of certain media, whether from public ownership of certain media or from the overregulation or the regulation of licensed media by government commissions such as the Canadian Radio-Television and Telecommunications Commission (CRTC).

In my view we have considerably too much concentration of ownership in the newspaper industry in Canada, and it threatens to worsen with the current proposals of the *Toronto Star* to take over the Sun Media chain. Indeed, we have heard that Southam is now interested in the Sun Media chain. I believe that the current concentration of ownership under Conrad Black (Southam) has gone too far as it is. The prospect of him owning the Sun chain is unacceptable to me and should be rejected by the competition bureau.

Second, we have too little independence in the publicly owned media that we do have, particularly the Canadian Broadcasting Corporation (CBC), even in the recent change in the government's methodology of appointing the president and so on. It seems to me that if we are going to have publicly owned news media their independence and the degree of their autonomy from government has to be absolutely clear. Certain things that are happening regarding the CBC and its relationship to government now are iniquitous. We need to go much further in granting the CBC effective autonomy from public control.

Finally, we have far too much regulation of content on electronic media, radio and television through the CRTC. Can you imagine the government licensing commission going into your local newsstand and the magazine stand and saying, "Well, there should be four magazines on culture, three magazines on international politics, six for children, and we will regulate the content mix of all the magazines." The only reason we even accept such a ludicrous thing when it comes to electronic media was the old-fashioned constraints of analogue technology, which meant there were only so many bands available. With digital technology we can have our magazine stand of electronic media. I would say to the government and its regulatory agencies, "Get out of the newsstands."

Freedom of expression is the single most important human right, a defining condition of being human. It is inherent and can only be denied, never granted, by the state. It is essential for the realization of most other human rights and a condition of democracy itself. The right to free expression of all rights should be the most fiercely defended from state or private intimidation. When in doubt, publish. At the same time; precisely because freedom of expression is so powerful and germane a right, its potential to do harm must be acknowledged. Limits on its exercise are appropriate in democratic societies as long as there are conditions for those societies to function correctly. It does not mean that we all agree in a democratic society what the limits should be, but we can argue it out in court and in a political arena.

Finally, new media increases the probability that an explosion of free speech, a wonderful explosion of free speech around the world, will be effectively unaccountable and the balance that must attend the exercise of all rights will be threatened and compromised. We know how to campaign for and defend free expression. We know what limits on free expression are generally appropriate in a free and democratic society. We do not know how to weigh in against errors and lies and malicious misinformation that have the potential to do great harm in the global media.

The Challenge of Different Cultures, Different Religions

A COMMON STANDARD OF ACHIEVEMENT FOR ALL PEOPLES AND NATIONS?

The Universality of Human Rights

Maxwell Yalden is a member of the United Nations Human Rights Committee. After joining Canada's Department of External Affairs in 1956, he served in numerous positions including chief commissioner of the Canadian Human Rights Commission. He is an Officer of the Order of Canada and a Commandeur de l'Ordre de la Pléiade.

THE QUESTION OF WHETHER THERE CAN BE A COMMON STANDARD of achievement for all peoples and nations is enormously complex. It goes to the heart of the international human rights order. The wide range of religious and cultural values—the clash of cultures and values, as some would have it—is something which all of us hear about on an almost daily basis and often in terms which challenge the whole notion underlying the Universal Declaration, that there is a "common standard of achievement" applicable to all.

Why should Western ways of thinking prevail, one is asked. Why should a Declaration that was put together half a century ago, largely by colonial powers, or Western and communist states, pretend to universality as we enter the new millennium? In short, should the developed world occupy the moral high ground? Why should we not revise the whole business, as the prime minister of Malaysia, Mahathir Mohamed, and others have suggested?

These are good questions and like all good questions they are easier to ask than to answer. But complexity is not going to allow us to run away from them. One cannot avoid taking a stand on them, and I might as well declare my own colours before I go any further: I think there is a lot more life in the concept of universality than many would have us believe. Why that is so and what it means in practice I shall try to explain.

To begin with, we need to look more closely at two separate but related matters: first, the universality of the human rights and value systems themselves; and second, the universal applicability of those systems, through engagements accepted under the United Nations charter, the Declaration and domestic law. And in all cases we need to keep in mind international and national mechanisms designed to monitor their implementation. Let me deal with each in turn.

365

On the universality of values, I suggest we look briefly at the matter from four perspectives—the historical background, the contemporary situation, the normative angle and the future in light of these considerations.

Historically speaking, have there in fact been universal or near-universal values and practices? I think the answer has to be in the affirmative. On the positive side, civilized views of political responsibility and equity, for example, go back a very long way. At the same time, paradoxically, what one might call negative values also have a lengthy history behind them.

We have no cause to rejoice about it, but it cannot be gainsaid that value systems which posit the inferiority of a race or caste, religion or ethnic group, or one sex against another, have been with us for a long time, in all corners of the world, and show no signs of disappearing to this day. Of course it can be argued that such things should not count in the calculus of values: man's inhumanity to man may be a given, but by its nature it is not a "value." That one may wish to define it out of the way, I can understand, but my point is a different one: it is simply that there are and always have been widely followed practices and values, to the point of being universal for all practical purposes.[1] If one has doubts on the positive side of the ledger, they are starkly evident on the negative side.

None of this should be taken to mean, however, that the particular brand of Western-style individual liberalism that has evolved over the years, and is so vigorously promoted in our contemporary world, has the same historical pretensions.[2] Locke and Rousseau give us two hundred years of history, it is true, but the practices and on-the-ground values of much of 19th, and even post-war 20th-century Europe and America are hardly consistent with many of those high ideals.[3] We should make no mistake about it: a genuine commitment to freedom of expression or to equality of sexes or races is decidedly a Johnny-come-lately.

What does this say for the historical perspective? That there are some fine principles with a lengthy pedigree, and some beastly practices, worldwide and going back a long way. And that there is a relatively new preoccupation with individual freedoms and meaningful equality rights that are still honoured more in the breach than in the observance.

Given all this, from the contemporary vantage point, it is hardly surprising that there has been more than a little scepticism in the developing world over what are called Western values, let alone the West's propensity for attaching them as conditions for international civility and cooperation. But, once again, that does not mean that these countries are necessarily out to assert a brand-new set of values, markedly different from those that have been endorsed by the international community. We should not be looking to the fifty-odd states that were in San Francisco in 1945, but at the 171 that were in Vienna in 1993. There they approved a modern-day Declaration that reaffirms on something approaching a universalistic basis the values that most governments are prepared to accept as their own.[4]

That those values are challenged is also evident, most notably in the Muslim community.[5] However, there is no such thing as a monolithic Islamic approach, any more than elsewhere in this diverse world. Not all Muslims believe in the fatwah against Salman Rushdie; not all Muslims accept the extremes of Taliban discrimination against women.[6] There is, in short, very little reason to believe that the Muslim and non-Muslim worlds must inevitably be in conflict with one another or that what was achieved in Vienna is a smoke-screen behind which the West has erected a false value system that it will force on others if they let down their guard.

To the contrary, as Miriam Budiarjo, my sometime colleague from the Human Rights Commission of Indonesia, the largest Muslim country in the world, has put it in criticizing the Malaysian prime minister's views, "The Vienna Declaration reflects the effort to bridge the gap between the views of the West and the nonwestern countries."[7] Or, as Professor Thomas Franck has pointed out in a recent article in the *American Journal of International Law,* some of the Islamic members of the UN Human Rights Committee "have been among the most outspoken in rejecting the notion of incompatibility between Muslim law and the global law of the human rights treaty system."[8] Or again, as the daily press these past few months has shown very clearly, there are major divisions in Iran between so-called conservatives and moderates over a number of matters of concerns to us.

That there are obviously more extreme views on both sides of the line is perfectly true, but that is quite another matter; their ideas cannot be used to characterize an entire religious or cultural community. I say "both sides of the line" advisedly, by the way, for it was only a few weeks ago that I read in the press that the Southern Baptist Convention, apparently the largest Protestant denomination in the United States, had endorsed as part of its Faith and Message Statement that a woman should "submit herself gracefully" to her husband's leadership, and that he in turn should "provide for, protect and lead his family."

Other cracks in the clash-of-cultures thesis are so numerous they are hard to keep up with. I take only a few as illustrations. What could be more remote from one another on the face of it than the situation in India and the Canadian experience? Yet Canadian and Indian human rights legislation assert the same principles and mandate essentially the same requirements for freedom and equality. Of course that does not mean that the caste system disappears with a wave of the magic wand, and it does not mean, to our shame, that the plight of Canada's native peoples disappears either. But it does mean that we are a lot closer to universality than many think, when thirty million Canadians can share large elements of a value system with almost a billion people of a vastly different cultural background half a world away.

Or let us look squarely at the most difficult case from the Western—or at least the North American—point of view: China. There is not enough time for an in-depth assessment of China's human rights record. In many respects, one may simply reaffirm the obvious: it is bad. But in others, particularly in raising standards of education and health or equality of women—which, given China's situation and stage of development, are just as important as individual freedoms for many hundreds of millions of people—it is much better than the demonizing oversimplifications that some Western journalists might have us believe.[9]

China has also signed the Covenant on Economic, Social and Cultural Rights and, in October 1998, the Civil and Political Rights Covenant. This may not signify a great deal by itself but it does mean two things of some consequence: first, that the authorities representing one-fifth of the world's population are prepared to accept—at least in principle—the same broad range of values as the rest of the world, which can hardly fail to bolster the universalistic thesis; and, second, that they are apparently willing to submit themselves in some measure to the reporting requirements and the potential for worldwide scrutiny that goes with them, which are imposed by the two treaties. I know as well as anyone else, of course, that the mere act of adding another international treaty to one's collection, so to speak, does not establish political freedoms or improve the rights of the minorities or the disabled or women, or anyone else for that matter. But that is not the point. The point is that it is hard to go on defending a West-versus-the-rest, clash of cultures theory in the face of this kind of evidence.

From the normative perspective, the tableau is much the same. It is obviously not for me as an individual to pass moral judgements; what matters is what the international community thinks. And what it thinks and says is increasingly universalistic. Article 5 of the Vienna Declaration states quite unequivocally that "human rights are universal," and that "it is the duty of States, regardless of their political, economic and cultural systems, to promote and protect all fundamental rights and freedoms."

This does not mean, to repeat, that anyone would argue that they are universally and consistently implemented, or indeed, in some states, that they are implemented at all. Human rights workers may be idealists but they are not blind to reality. They know, we all know, that these principles are often ignored in practice. But it does mean that they are accepted as principles and that few if any countries are prepared to challenge them directly.

This analysis does of course leave out of account the other half of Article 5, which asserts that "the significance of national and regional particularities and various historical, cultural and religious backgrounds must be borne in mind." And obviously this can be regarded by some as potential licence for all manner of violations, ostensibly in the name of national or cultural "particularities." But in fact this is rarely the case; my experience on the UN Human Rights Committee suggests the contrary. States do not attempt to justify a poor record, say, on freedom of expression or association, on this basis; what they cite are national security considerations, which is precisely what any country would do in the circumstances, including Canada if one remembers the events of October 1970 and the War Measures Act. Nor do they argue, to take only one other illustration, that child labour is acceptable or desirable; they say that they have little choice in the economic circumstances in which they find themselves. Or that the law requires that it be eradicated and that it will be, but that "these things take time" given a traditionalist society in which it is hard to break old patterns of behaviour. Again, I suggest, this is a line of argument that is not entirely foreign to traditional Western ways of thinking.

Finally, what do these conclusions portend for the future? In my view, an increasing convergence, a slow but steady movement towards more-or-less universal acceptance of a set of basic normative rules, such as those set down, for example, in the Universal Declaration, as determinative of state policy in the matter of rights. At the same time, however, disputes over "contextualization," to use a current jawbreaker, will continue and many observers in the developing world will continue to show their irritation with what they perceive—with some reason, I might add—as Western arrogance and insensitivity to genuine cultural, historical and material differences which must of necessity temper any monolithic approach to rights. In other words, we should expect to see a reasonable degree of suppleness in applying the Declaration's "common standard," though evidently not to the extent of justifying gross violations. At the same time, there will be general agreement that such a standard exists and can in fact be applied.

All this is very fine in principle, it might be argued, but in practice the fiftieth anniversary year has been a pretty grim one. Pierre Sané, the secretary general of Amnesty International, recently observed that the Universal Declaration is "little more than a paper promise" for many unfortunate people in all parts of the world.[10] To change that situation is the real challenge—in the fullest sense of that overworked word—at the close of the millennium. How to pull it off is far from clear, but what is manifest is that values mean very little unless states are committed to them. That in turn requires, as a minimum, universal or near-universal acceptance of the major international instruments and a genuine willingness by states parties to uphold the principles they entail.

There are numerous roadblocks in the way of universal ratification of, and respect for, the covenants. There are states which have bad records and don't want anyone looking at them. Such is the case, for example, with Myanmar, which is not a party to the Covenant on Civil and Political Rights or the Covenant on Economic, Social and Cultural Rights, or those dealing with torture or racial discrimination. In fairness, however, it should be noted that it is a party to the Convention on the Rights of the Child and has recently ratified the Convention on Women's Rights.

Second, there are countries whose authorities do not readily accept international supervision that may call into question domestic law or the actions of domestic legislators. Regrettably, as world leaders, the United States is in this category and as a result is not a party to the Covenant on Economic, Social and Cultural Rights or on Women's Rights, or the Convention on the Rights of the Child. Moreover, it became a party to the Covenant on Civil and Political Rights relatively recently and is still not a party to the Optional Protocol which permits individuals to bring human rights complaints against governments to the UN Committee. One might observe, by the way, that there has recently been evidence of the same kind of reasoning at work in the negotiations surrounding the International Criminal Court.

Third, there are states which, one assumes, do not accede to certain instruments because they perceive their terms as being in conflict with traditional values or religious precepts. Such appears likely to be the case, for example, with Saudi Arabia, which is not a party to the Convention on Women's Rights.

And fourth, there are very small states which may not (or at least believe they do not) have the capacity to cope with various treaty requirements with respect to reporting or responding to complaints. Without wishing to ascribe motives to any particular national authorities, one has to suppose that states like Bhutan, Tuvalu and Vanuatu, which are parties to very few of the major instruments, have been influenced at least partly by considerations of this nature.

How can the international community attempt to deal with these problems? To take the last first, it ought to be a simple enough matter, if the rich, developed world were to practise what it preaches on human rights, to establish technical assistance programs through the High Commissioner's Office, or regionally, to help a number of these states appreciate better what is involved and assist them with reporting as required. It would also be helpful to look to a reform of treaty body procedures that would reduce the reporting burden, but that is a matter which leads far beyond our subject.

As to the problem of religious or cultural differences, it should be possible to present a forceful argument that there is nothing in any of the major instruments which is inherently inimical to any of the world's religions or cultural traditions. I grant that this is hardly likely to convince anyone who does not wish to be convinced, but it should be tried nonetheless, regionally as well as within the United Nations.

Those who traditionally go their own way, whatever the international community may think, are obviously more difficult to deal with. I certainly have no prescription for bringing Senator Helms or others in the US Congress who share his views to see reason. But one can hear many voices from our neighbour to the south and one has to hope that patience will bring its reward, as it did in the end with the Covenant on Civil and Political Rights.

Finally, there are the irredeemable bad actors. Fortunately, however, they are few in number. I am not talking, obviously, about states which in fact have poor records but do not admit it, and try to justify their actions on the grounds of poverty or state security. They are regrettably altogether too numerous. I mean genuine hard-liners, the scofflaws, so to say; and these I contend, as I did earlier, are not numerous and have very little support, unless perhaps in the face of what their neighbours may regard as unjustifiable bullying by the West. Evidently there is a lesson to be learned there as well; that it may be better to outwait them than to try to bring them down by sanctions or megaphone diplomacy, but that too goes well beyond our subject matter.

At all events, at least as I see it, it is entirely possible to bring most if not all states on board for most if not all of the major international covenants. And that would be no small thing. It would then remain to beef up the monitoring systems, both international and national, to try to ensure that the treaties and the standards they entail actually produce something concrete in the real world, outside the debating rooms in Geneva and New York.

This is in part, once again, a matter of money. That the United Nations' human rights effort is woefully underfunded is a commonplace; something less than two per cent of the regular budget of the organization.[11] That this is entirely unacceptable in a world in which the powers great and small—and particularly countries like the United States and, for that matter, Canada—remind us on a daily basis of the fundamental importance of human rights, should be even more evident. What can be done about it, however, is less obvious. I personally find it very doubtful that significant sums of new money will be found in the regular budget, especially at a time of financial crisis, when the secretary general is obliged to squeeze every penny for all it is worth.

What realistic options does that leave us? Essentially three, I suggest. First, those states that have a genuine commitment to human rights, among them I again include Canada, should be lobbied hard to consider more substantial voluntary funding. Second, countries that do not have domestic monitoring agencies, which will likely include smaller states as well as those which have traditionally been less than enthusiastic about rights-related issues, should be encouraged by their neighbours and friends to set up human rights or ombudsman offices. And, finally, international human rights institutions, whether the High Commissioner's Office or the treaty bodies themselves, should make a renewed and sustained effort to improve their output within existing resources, and to streamline their procedures to reduce the burdens involved in adhering to the treaties and respecting their requirements once a state has done so.

To recapitulate, the values set own in the UN Declaration of Human Rights are largely universal in the sense that they are accepted in principle by most countries, although some allowance must obviously be made for differing modes of implementation, to take account of different national situations.

Most countries will accede to most of the international covenants, even if some of them show little interest at this time, and they would do so more readily and sooner if they were lobbied harder by their allies, neighbours and friends— and not, one might add, hectored by the West.

Further, the *sine qua non* of effective defence and promotion of human rights lies in improving the monitoring systems, both international and domestic; while this is partly a matter of the human rights community being accorded a more appropriate share of the financial pie, it also involves making better use of the resources we have.

Finally, there is more cause for optimism, notwithstanding egregious setbacks and a grim outlook in many areas, than we might be entitled to expect; and that is perhaps all one can ask for in a less than perfect world. If so, we may truly allow ourselves to look forward, one day, in spite of the many differences that divide humankind, to what the Universal Declaration calls "a common standard of achievement for all peoples and all nations."

REFERENCES

1. On what one might call the consistency of man's inhumanity to man, note that "The church council of Arles (France) in 1235...ordered all Jews to wear a round yellow patch, four fingers in width, over their hearts as a mark of identity." (Henry Kamen. *The Spanish Inquisition*. Folio Books (1998): 9.)

2. For an excellent analysis of this entire issue, see Thomas Franck, "Is Personal Freedom a Western Value?" *American Journal of International Law* 91 4 (October 1997): 593–627.

3. One cannot fail to be amazed, for example, that the great powers accepted and promoted the Charter and the Universal Declaration while maintaining regimes that in several respects were hardly compatible with the engagements entailed by either.

4. It is worth noting that more than eight hundred NGOs were also represented at the Vienna meeting, resulting in a total of over seven thousand participants.

5. See Ann Elizabeth Mayer, "Universal Versus Islamic Human Rights: A Clash of Cultures or a Clash with a Construct?" *Michigan Journal of International Law* 15 307: 308–404.

6. Indeed, there are sometimes surprising statements on this matter from unexpected quarters. For what it is worth, consider, for example, the following declaration from the Libyan Great Green Charter of Human Rights: "The members of Jamahiriyan society, whether men or women, are equal in every respect. The distinction of rights between men and women is a flagrant injustice that nothing whatsoever can justify."

7. Statement entitled "Should the Declaration of Human Rights be Revised?," 30 August 1997.

8. Op. cit., p. 607.

9. Walter Russell Mead, senior fellow for US foreign policy at the Council of Foreign Relations, goes much further. In an article written for the *International Herald Tribune* (26 June 1998), on the occasion of President Clinton's visit to China, he observed that "It would be hard to find any country on earth where human rights conditions and economic prosperity have improved so dramatically in the last generation."

10. As reported by Reuters, 22 June 1998.

11. The human rights program was allotted 1.74 per cent of the UN regular operating budget in the past biennium, which has been reduced to 1.67 per cent.

The International Community and Human Rights

Lim Kit Siang is secretary general of the Democratic Action Party, leader of the opposition in the Malaysian Parliament and author of numerous publications on politics and human rights. During his long struggle for democracy in Malaysia, he was detained twice under the Internal Security Act and adopted as a prisoner of conscience by Amnesty International of Toronto, Canada.

OVER THE PAST TWO DAYS (25–26 November 1998), two events taking place in two completely different corners of the world have given special meaning and significance to this international conference in Edmonton, Canada, to commemorate the fiftieth anniversary of the Universal Declaration of Human Rights. The rejoicing of human rights activists in different parts of the world at these events powerfully underscores the timeless universality of human rights. One of these events is the House of Lords decision in the United Kingdom on the Pinochet case. This decision establishes the great precedent that there can be no diplomatic immunity for genocide and crimes against humanity like mass murders and tortures.

The second event is the Singapore government's lifting of all restrictions on one of the longest-serving prisoners of conscience in the world, Chia Thye Poh. His twenty-three-year detention once put him in the same league as Nelson Mandela. He was also subject to a variety of restrictions and disenfranchisement of his civic rights for another nine years after his formal release from detention under the Internal Security Act in 1989. Chia Thye Poh's reaction that the Singapore government's release of all restrictions on him had come too late was most apt. The best part of his life—thirty-two years—has been taken away from him without so much as a charge or trial. This is a gross injustice of iniquitous legislation like the Internal Security Act, which allows for detention without trial in Singapore and Malaysia.

On 26 November 1998 the Singapore Home Ministry threatened that, despite the lapse of the restriction order, Chia would be "dealt with firmly under the law" should he in future reinvolve himself in activities "prejudicial to Singapore's security." The Singapore government owes the international community a full explanation as to how it could be so cruel, heartless and inhumane. It has politically detained a person and restricted his political and civil rights on the grounds of "activities prejudicial to Singapore's security" for over three decades. This is all the more troubling given that the island republic has undergone major changes in its political, economic and security in the thirty-two years since Chia's first arrest.

Progress in the international human rights scene has never been a smooth and easy passage. These two positive developments cannot relieve the long and sad tale of continued flagrant human rights abuses in many countries in the world—whether west, east, north or south—or the emergence of new black spots of human rights violations. Malaysia is one such example. Since September 1998, Malaysia has suddenly become the new "bad boy" in the world of human rights. Events in the country have been hogging the international media. The long-running saga raises disturbing questions about fundamental principles like the state of democracy, human rights and the rule of law. Half a century ago these principles were accepted as universal rights in the Universal Declaration of Human Rights. They include:

Article 5 - No one shall be subjected to torture or to cruel, inhuman or degrading treatment or punishment.

Article 9 - No one shall be subjected to arbitrary arrest, detention or exile.

Article 10 - Everyone is entitled in full equality to a fair and public hearing by an independent and impartial tribunal, in the determination of his rights and obligations and of any criminal charge against them.

Article 11(1) - Everyone charged with a penal offence has the right to be presumed innocent until proved guilty according to law in a public trial at which they have had all the guarantees necessary for their defence.

Article 12 - No one shall be subjected to arbitrary interference with their privacy, family, home or correspondence, nor to attacks upon their honour and reputation. Everyone has the right to the protection of the law against such interference or attacks.

Article 19 - Everyone has the right to freedom of opinion and expression; this right includes freedom to hold opinions without interference and to seek, receive and impart information and ideas through any media and regardless of frontiers.

Article 20(1) - Everyone has the right to freedom of peaceful assembly and association.

Anwar Ibrahim had just held the second-highest political office in the land, was heir apparent to the prime minister of Malaysia, and a well-known international advocate for human rights and the civil society. Yet within twenty-four hours of his ouster from government and the ruling party, he was stripped of the most basic rights and fundamental liberties embedded in the Universal Declaration of Human Rights. When such action can be taken against such a prominent person, how can there be justice, honour, dignity and respect of human rights for the ordinary people of the country? There is a widely held international perception that Malaysia has transformed overnight from a civil society into a rogue society, a society which has stopped according respect for basic human rights and fundamental liberties.

The shabby treatment of Anwar Ibrahim in Malaysia and the deprivation of his most fundamental rights were in the news in the international media almost every day. The local media effectively tried and convicted him of the most terrible charges, ranging from sexual misconduct to corruption, of being a pawn of foreign powers to high treason. There was an utter disregard of the principle that a person is presumed innocent until proven guilty. Overnight he was transformed from the No. 2 leader in the country to the No. 1 criminal in the country.

Although Anwar's lawyers had earlier offered to co-operate with the police in any arrest, the police carried out a commando-style arrest. It was as if his private residence had become the headquarters of an international terrorist network. Anwar was detained under the infamous Internal Security Act, then released under this law but denied bail and then charged in court under another law. He turned up in court with a black eye which he alleged was the result of a police assault when he had been handcuffed and blindfolded. He said he had been assaulted until he lost consciousness on the first night of his arrest ten days earlier. The government has refused to commission an independent investigation into Anwar's black eye or to release the report of the police investigations into the assault.

The police action to deal with the peaceful assembly of people demonstrating in support of Anwar was high-handed. They used cannons with chemically laced water, tear gas and downright violence. There was an indiscriminate use of the Internal Security Act and abuse of police powers to systematically humiliate detainees. During the trial of Anwar, top police officers admitted that they have special techniques to "turn over" and "neutralize" people who are recalcitrant, to force those arrested to alter or retract their earlier statements given to the police.

Futurist Alvin Toffler wrote about the plight of his Pakistani scientist friend, Dr. Munawar Ahmad Anees, who was detained under the Internal Security Act. After only a few days under arrest he was broken so completely that he appeared in court to plead guilty to a serious offence. His plea got him jailed for six months and made him the sole key witness in a serious charge levelled against Anwar Ibrahim. The statutory declaration made by Munawir two months later, which is available on the Internet, is a most damning indictment of the blatant violation of human rights and dignity. And all this in the year dedicated to the commemoration of the fiftieth anniversary of the Universal Declaration of Human Rights.

Malaysia is a microcosm of multireligious and multicultural diversity, with strong followings of the great religions of the world, including Islam, Buddhism, Christianity, Hinduism, Sikhism and Confucianism. It is legitimate to ask how a country with an economy, which until the recent international financial meltdown, made it an Asian tiger, and which had enjoyed generally high regard in the international community, could degenerate with such suddenness. All the basic freedoms and fundamental liberties enshrined in the Universal Declaration of Human Rights have been trampled upon. In actual fact, the state of democracy, human rights and the rule of law in Malaysia had long been under siege, well before the arrest of Anwar. Although all the facts were there for those who have eyes to see and ears to hear, Malaysia's lack of human rights had not attracted international attention.

Malaysia is undergoing a multitude of crises. It is experiencing not only the worst economic and political crisis in the nation's history, but also a crisis of confidence in the independence of the judiciary, the rule of law and the entire system of democratic governance. This is highlighted and symbolized by the cases and trials of Anwar; the woman activist Irene Fernandez who is now on trial because she took up the case of the ill-treatment of migrant workers; and the case of the opposition member of parliament Lim Guan Eng, who is in jail because he fought for the honour of women's rights and against a series of gross violations of human rights including freedom of assembly and freedom of expression.

The Vienna Declaration and Program of Action (VDPA), adopted by the World Conference on Human Rights in 1993, made the important statement that the promotion and protection of human rights is a legitimate concern of the international community—whether international organizations, national players or individuals. This statement has been profoundly reinforced by the Pinochet case. It establishes the principle that the violation of human rights—whether those of individuals or the peoples of a community—cannot be the sovereign right of nation states but is a legitimate concern of the international community. How can the protection of human rights be implemented? How can this mandate be given substance?

The time has come for the international community to develop new international standards and norms so the international community can carry out the VDPA mandate to promote and protect human rights without receiving the classic reaction that these are interferences in the domestic affairs of nations. The development of new international norms and standards for the promotion and protection of human rights by the international community will be a significant step forward for the next half-century of the Universal Declaration of Human Rights.

Religion, Ethnicity, Culture and the Common Standard

Ujjal Dosanjh is the attorney general of British
Columbia, Canada, and minister responsible for multi-
culturalism, human rights and immigration. He has also
served on the Select Standing Committee for
Aboriginal Affairs and worked with the BC Civil
Liberties Association and the BC Multicultural Society.

A S WE CELEBRATE THE FIRST FIFTY YEARS of the Universal Declaration of
Human Rights and, more importantly, look to the next fifty years, we face some
very important issues. What we have seen over the past fifty years gives reason for
both hope and despair. We should be encouraged to see that the impasse in the
Middle East may have been broken, that the peace talks in Northern Ireland show
real promise of achieving significant progress. The fall of the Berlin Wall and the
end of apartheid in South Africa were remarkable events and there are many, many
other examples from the last fifty years that make us optimistic about the future.

Sadly, there has also been cause for despair, manifested in places such as
Rwanda, Bosnia, Indonesia and Kosovo. There have been far too many examples
around the world of that disturbing nature. Thus we see reason for both hope
and despair. We must never lose sight of the fact that human rights are indivisible, that the oppression experienced by other people in other places weighs
heavily on you and me, as well. Another person's loss of human rights—be it
here in Canada, in India, in Bosnia—is also our loss.

Religion, ethnicity and culture have played a part in both the creation of hope
on the one hand, and violence and despair on the other. But in response to the
question posed—whether religion and culture across the world can provide a
common standard of achievement—I can tell you from my experience that the
emphatic answer would be no. And that is not because traditions and spirituality in many religions don't provide cohesive forces or cohesive bases of
equality. Far too often, however, ethnicity, culture and religion have emphasized
separateness, exclusivity and division and been used as an excuse for hostility,
violence and oppression.

377

As we look forward to the next fifty years, there are some very serious questions that we need to pose. One of the most important of those has to do with how we live together and build a multicultural society. In Canada we pride ourselves on being a culturally diverse country. But contrary to what some people have said, Canada is not some sort of new experiment in multiculturalism. The First Nations of this country were multicultural. In British Columbia alone there were thirty-three languages spoken before the European diversity came to Canada. They were multicultural and they were multilingual. Then European and non-European immigrants came to North America with their many cultures and languages and increased the diversity. Let no one say that multiculturalism in this country was somehow plucked out of the air, an abstract concept imposed on Canada. It is reflected in our entire history.

No doubt we in Canada have done things for which none of us is proud. We imposed a "head tax" on Chinese immigrants. We took away their right to vote and only returned those voting rights to Chinese-Canadians in 1948. Members of First Nations in this country did not have the right to vote until 1960. We should not forget those injustices. We've come a long way in the past fifty years. But have no doubt there is still strife in the world, still violence in the world, still oppression in the world. And quite often it is carried on in the name of ethnicity, in the name of culture, in the name of religion. We need to recognize that.

If religion and culture create hope on the one hand and despair on the other, what makes the difference? I believe the difference comes from great leadership. The leadership of Mandela and Tutu in South Africa, of Trimble and Hume in Northern Ireland, and of the countless others who have gone before and those who are active today. So it is important that we recognize, as political leaders and as activists from all over the world, that we have a very specific duty that compels our compliance.

The leaders I mentioned are notable for their desire to bring different cultures together and for emphasizing spirituality instead of the kind of sectarian religion that tries to impose exclusivity and separateness. The most important work we can do to support these goals is to provide institutions that guarantee equality, that guarantee justice, that guarantee fairness and compassion on the part of the state *vis-à-vis* the individual. As a Canadian and a British Columbian, it is important that I raise issues we are facing here in Canada and the work we need to do in Canada to live up to the spirit of the Canadian Charter of Rights and Freedoms which this country adopted in 1982. If we are to build a province and country where human rights are a paramount value, surely we must start with youth, the young people who will be our leaders tomorrow.

British Columbian schools and communities are a wonderful blend of diverse faces, costumes and languages. Even a few minutes spent in the neighbourhood of a typical school shows that most young people mix comfortably in diverse groups. Unfortunately, some prejudice and negative attitudes toward

those who are different persists. It may only be a small minority that perpetuates this prejudice, but it is often a vocal and destructive minority. In BC we have
developed a number of initiatives for countering these negative attitudes among
youth, programs which help celebrate diversity and promote awareness around
racism, hate bias, homophobia and racially motivated crime.

These programs also raise awareness of the potential consequences of
discrimination and prejudice. Our government has worked with the community
to develop a program called TROO (Total Respect of Others) to assist schools
and community agencies in declaring their school or community a place where
there is total respect for everyone. This program is designed to give youth the
opportunity to take ownership of their actions and attitudes and provide all
youth with the skills to be respectful towards others. We have also created
drama groups for youth, such as 841-KOZ (Eight for One Cause), that allow
young people to address issues of violence in schools and the community, and
TCO^2 (Taking Care of Ourselves, Taking Care of Others), that helps youth recognize their responsibilities to themselves and their peers. These youth-led teams
travel to schools around the province and use role playing, games and audience
participation in interactive workshops to bring the message home.

In BC we have also embarked on the important task of bringing peace and
justice to our relationships with the aboriginal people of our province. Our
provincial government is about to become a party to the first modern treaty
with a First Nation, the Nisga'a, in what is now the province of BC. The Nisga'a
Treaty is one of the many treaties that are needed. These treaties will be crucial
to the future of the province. All British Columbians, whether born here or
immigrant, young or old, bear part of the responsibility for the injustices visited
on the aboriginal people of this province, for the theft of their culture, their
language, their children. We have done great harm to First Nations and we have
an obligation to repair that harm. They have been wronged and we must make it
right. The Nisga'a Treaty is an important first step along that road.

The Nisga'a Treaty is part of our pursuit of social justice, equality and human
values in British Columbia. It is not a perfect treaty, nor is it a perfect instrument
for resolving all the problems in relations between the Nisga'a people and the
rest of Canada. It is the product of human effort, with all the compromise and
imperfection that entails. The Nisga'a Treaty is the result of many years of negotiation. It redresses more than a hundred years of injustice. No matter that it is
imperfect, it is an effort to come to terms with our sorry history and to say we
will redeem ourselves. With this treaty the Nisga'a people will be full and equal
British Columbians and Canadians. Together we will pursue social justice and
build a society of equals.

Our efforts to help youth educate themselves and their peers and our efforts
to redress the harm we have done, both past and present, in our relations with
First Nations are part of a larger effort to make human rights a priority in British

Columbia. To make this goal a reality, we need effective human rights mechanisms. In BC this has required changes to both the structure of our human rights bodies and the content of our human rights law. In 1997 we put in place a new, more effective structure for dealing with human rights abuses in areas for which the province has responsibility. Prior to then, human rights complaints in BC were handled through a Human Rights Council that both investigated and adjudicated those complaints. The council's mandate was almost exclusively driven by the individual complaints process and the council accepted, investigated and adjudicated each separate case. The new structure provides for a separate Human Rights Tribunal to adjudicate individual cases and gives the Human Rights Commission a more effective, more preventive mandate.

The commission now not only investigates specific complaints but can also identify systemic complaints and pursue a resolution that applies to entire classes of people. This will eliminate the need for many individuals to pursue individual complaints. The commission also offers mediation of disputes to reduce the ill-will that formal adjudication often engenders. Perhaps most importantly, the commission will be a much stronger voice for educating British Columbians about human rights in the province. We have also made changes to ensure that the protections enshrined in our legislation are the best they can be. In 1993 we expanded BC's human rights coverage to prohibit publication or display of any statements that indicate discrimination against a person or class or which are likely to expose them to hatred or contempt because of race, colour, religion, sexual orientation or other characteristics.

Some people have criticized us for this provision, claiming it limits freedom of speech, but I disagree. Freedom of speech is a fundamental right, one that is enshrined in the Canadian Charter of Rights and Freedoms. As citizens of a democratic society we have a right, indeed a duty, to exercise free speech, but we have an obligation to exercise it with a degree of responsibility. We are also called upon to oppose the intolerance and violence engendered by hate and hate speech whenever and wherever we see it. I find it ironic that, according to our laws, if I were to call someone a cheat or a thief, I would leave myself open to a criminal charge of libel and if convicted could be imprisoned for up to two years. In addition, I could be sued for damages in civil court. Yet if I call someone by a racist or other hurtful epithet—often more damaging to the dignity of the person—there is little recourse in our legal system. I believe it is time we accorded the same dignity and importance to human rights that we accord to property rights.

In BC we have also acted to deal with more serious situations where hate and prejudice become criminal matters. Over the past year and a half we have created a hate-crime team to deal with crimes of hate whether based on religion, ethnicity, culture, sexual orientation, gender or other grounds. The team is made up of police officers, crown prosecutors and other resources to help police and courts around the province deal with these issues. We have been active in proposing to the federal government our view that we need a change in the hate laws in Canada—that we need amendments to the Criminal Code. BC has succeeded in putting these issues on the national agenda.

At an October 1998 meeting with my federal, provincial and territorial counterparts, I was pleased to receive support for the five key elements of BC's proposal: make possession of hate propaganda for the purposes of distribution a Criminal Code offence; allow seizure of computer hard drives storing hate propaganda; provide definitions of both "possession" and "public place" as they relate specifically to computers; establish a definition of hatred in the Criminal Code; and make the identifiable groups protected from hate propaganda in the Criminal Code. The groups should then include race, national or ethnic origin, language, colour, religion, sex, age, mental or physical disability, and sexual orientation.

We need to do still more. It is important that we recognize that our record on apprehending war criminals and successfully prosecuting them is dismal. We have failed in Canada to appropriately apprehend war criminals and prosecute them. So we need to review the Criminal Code provisions dealing with war crimes and also those dealing with torture. The House of Lords recently made a progressive decision in the Pinochet case, but the issue is that another court in another country could have arrived at a different decision. These decisions must not be left to be decided by the courts. The whole notion of diplomatic immunity ought to be reconsidered on a global scale to determine whether or not we want to be able to adequately punish torturers in any jurisdiction, no matter where they might be, where they may come from or who they might have tortured.

Here is what I propose: The United Kingdom has Section 134 of the Criminal Justice Act of 1988. Section 134 says that any torturer, no matter where he or she is from, no matter who he or she has tortured, no matter what the location of the crime might be, that individual, that torture, can be tried in Britain before the British courts. While the Criminal Code of Canada has several provisions that taken together might be judged to have the same effect, we do not have a single provision that states so clearly or holds so unequivocally that crimes against humanity will not be tolerated by Canada. I believe that we must ensure that we have a similar if not stronger provision in our Code.

The International Criminal Court is still in its infancy and I don't know what it will ultimately look like or what its powers may ultimately be, but I am hopeful that is will enable us to hold international criminals to account. However, it is important for each and every state across the world to create its own mechanisms to give meaning and concrete shape to instruments such as the Universal Declaration of Human Rights. We need to create those mechanisms so that in each and every jurisdiction we are able to punish war criminals and torturers. I believe this should be a priority for all of us.

It is important for us to pay tribute to those who have gone before, fighting for these kinds of universal rights, fighting for justice, fairness and compassion on behalf of all of us. It is important for us to pay tribute to them in concrete shape by bringing into our domestic laws those principles that would make sure that we have justice and fairness across our borders and across the world.

FRANCINE FOURNIER

UNESCO and Human Rights

Francine Fournier is assistant director general of
UNESCO, responsible for the Social and Human
Sciences Sector. She has served as secretary general
of the Council on the Status of Women, president of the
Québec Human Rights Commission, chairperson of the
Canadian Equality Rights Panel and secretary general
of UNESCO's Canadian Commission.

As an organization for international cooperation and a forum for world dialogue, the United Nations Educational, Scientific and Cultural Organization (UNESCO) has specific responsibility for the promotion, defence and deepening of human rights. This responsibility is formulated in Article 1 of the UNESCO Constitution, which states that, "The purpose of the Organization is to contribute to peace and security by promoting collaboration among the nations through education, science and culture in order to further universal respect for justice, for the rule of law and for human rights and fundamental freedoms."

383

Since the adoption of the Universal Declaration, there has been progress. Some mass violations of human rights have ceased. We have seen the end of official colonialism and the end of apartheid. Democratic regimes have replaced bloody dictatorships, in particular in Latin America and in some countries of Africa. National, regional and international institutions for the protection and implementation of human rights have been created. The Berlin Wall has fallen, ending some authoritarian regimes in eastern and central Europe.

Yet continuing violations of human rights in all parts of the world are a permanent reminder of how much remains to be done to ensure the full and universal exercise of the right to education (particularly for girls and women), freedom of opinion and expression, the right to cultural life, and freedom of thought, conscience and religion. Discrimination on the grounds of race, national or ethnic origin, language and belief, intolerance and violence, extreme poverty and exclusion are a persistent reality in many societies.

At this end of the century we have witnessed genocide in Rwanda and ethnic cleansing in Bosnia. We are witnessing the total negation of the human rights of women in Afghanistan. We know of children's exploitation, including sexual exploitation. We know that extreme poverty is in itself a violation of human rights and that an unbearable proportion of the world's population lives in that condition.

The fiftieth anniversary of the Universal Declaration of Human Rights is an occasion for redoubling our efforts to combat human rights violations and promote respect for human life, security, dignity and basic rights for all. In addition to the activities realized within the plan of action for the United Nations Decade for Human Rights Education, UNESCO has set up a plan of action for the celebration of the anniversary. The purpose of this plan is to mobilize public opinion in favour of universal human rights. Our goal is to create a new momentum for human rights education, formal and nonformal, and to review the state of implementation of human rights. For UNESCO, particular rights fall specifically within its responsibilities: the right to education; the right to enjoy the benefits of scientific advances; the right to participate in cultural life; the right to the protection of moral and material interests resulting from scientific, literary or artistic production; the right to freedom of opinion and expression and information.

Because all human rights are interdependent and indivisible, as was firmly recognized at the Vienna World Conference on Human Rights, UNESCO is, as we all are, challenged by all of the rights affirmed by the Universal Declaration. From its very conception, the Universal Declaration of Human Rights was meant as a solemn recognition for all human beings of their fundamental rights. This is not to say that the institutions set up to promote and protect these rights must be the same throughout the world, but it does mean that human rights form part of the common heritage of humanity. Human rights are universal because they transcend cultural differences and political systems and should be guaranteed without exception. "All human rights for all" is the stated objective of the commemoration of the fiftieth anniversary.

In recent debates concerning human rights, cultural relativism has been presented as a challenge to their universality. In its extreme interpretation, cultural relativism can lead to theories like that of "conflict of civilizations." According to this opinion, the globalization of the modern world has given rise to a conflict between basic cultural systems. This theory about the beginning of an age of irreconcilable battles between powerful civilizations does not, however, correspond to reality. Within a culture of human rights, cultural diversity and plurality of cultures are in fact positive factors which will lead to intercultural dialogue.

The question of the universality of human rights was discussed during the 1993 World Conference on Human Rights. In preparation for this conference, African states in the Tunis Declaration, adopted in November 1992, stressed that "the universal nature of human rights is beyond question," but added that "no ready-made model can be presented at the universal level since the historical and cultural realities of each nation and the traditions, standards and values of each people cannot be disregarded." Asian states, in the Bangladesh Declaration of April 1993, stated: "While human rights are universal in nature, they must be considered in the context of a dynamic and evolving process of international norm, setting, bearing in mind the significance of national and regional particularities and various historical, cultural and religious backgrounds."

The analysis of statements made during the Vienna Conference shows that the universality of human rights was not in the end openly challenged, whereas cultural relativism was in fact rejected. Universality and cultural specificity were seen, after debate, as being fully compatible notions. The argument that the existence of specific values in specific regions justifies adopting an understanding of human rights and democracy which is different from that prevailing in the West was criticized by governments, nongovernmental organizations and activists as an excuse for gross violations of human rights. In fact, as Mary Robinson quite rightly put it, "It was never the people who complained of the universality of human rights, nor did the people consider human rights as a Western or northern imposition. It was often their leaders who did so."

The Vienna Declaration adopted by consensus at the World Conference confirmed the universality of human rights and rejected the notion of cultural relativism. The Declaration reaffirms the solemn commitment of all states to fulfil their obligations to promote universal respect for the observance and protection of human rights and fundamental freedoms for all. As it stated: "The universal nature of these rights and freedoms is beyond question." The problem of national and regional peculiarities was referred to in paragraph 5 of the Declaration, which states: "All human rights are universal, indivisible and interdependent and interrelated. While the significance of national and regional particularities and various historical, cultural and religious backgrounds must be borne in mind, it is the duty of states, regardless of their political, economic and cultural systems, to promote and protect all human rights and fundamental freedoms." So this is a given now.

The mention of particularities and various historical, cultural and religious backgrounds is sometimes interpreted as a sort of escape clause, as an argument for the failure to comply with human rights standards. This understanding of paragraph five does not take into account the last part of the Declaration which underlines that states are duty-bound—regardless of their political, economic and cultural systems—to promote and protect all human rights. In line with this formulation—and this is important—cultural specificities should be taken into account in the promotion and protection of human rights. They should help to determine the most effective ways and means to overcome difficulties in the implementation of human rights and fundamental freedoms.

All cultures can contribute to the discussion concerning human rights. The establishment of a balance between rights and responsibilities, between individual

FRANCINE FOURNIER

rights and their collective dimension, between individuals and groups, is far from being achieved in all regions of the world. It is not accidental that, in recent years, attention has been given to the preparation of various declarations of human duties and responsibilities and the elaboration of a global ethics. This is seen as a reinforcement of the concept of universal human rights.

One day after the 1948 adoption of the Universal Declaration by the General Assembly, on December 11, the General Conference of UNESCO requested its director general to promote human rights in all of UNESCO's programs and particularly in its education programs. UNESCO's long-term goal is the establishment of a comprehensive system of education and training for peace, human rights and democracy that is intended for all groups of people and embraces all levels of education, whether formal or nonformal. As an intergovernmental organization, UNESCO collaborates first and foremost with governments. The organization supports the framing of national policies and the design of strategies, in particular, to improve the human rights content of curricula and textbooks, teaching methods and the functioning of educational institutions.

The preparation of educational aids for higher and nonformal education is a priority. A manual on human rights designed for universities has been published in English. Further editions in French, Spanish and Russian will follow. The manual covers a range of themes and takes into consideration current developments and trends in the field of human rights. It is important to have this education on human rights at the university level because, in most countries, an important proportion of the leaders are university trained.

Two other important educational aids on democracy and human rights have been prepared and published. One is called *Democracy: Questions and Answers,* and the other, *Human Rights: Questions and Answers.* The two titles are published in over twenty languages. They are scientifically sound and rigorous, but are written in a style that is readily accessible to what we could call actors in the social sphere, including parliamentarians.

A new issue of *Major International Human Rights Instruments* was also recently published. This publication includes data on the state of ratification of human rights instruments, both universal and regional, and has proved to be a valuable reference for human rights education. It is also used as a kind of incitement for ratification for those states that have not ratified one or the other of the instruments. Since 1987 UNESCO has also published the *World Directory of Human Rights Research and Training Institutions.* The *Directory,* now in its fifth edition, provides information on research themes, specialists working in the field of human rights and international co-operation.

UNESCO chairs on human rights, democracy and peace are being established to promote an integrated system of research, training and information activities and to facilitate subregional and regional cooperation between researchers and teachers. Already, thirty-six chairs have been created in different regions—Africa, Europe, eastern and central Europe, Arab states and Latin America. These chairs are aimed not only at developing expert knowledge on human rights but to make this knowledge and understanding available to nonexperts.

The approach of UNESCO to human rights education is centred on the conviction that the shaping of attitudes and behavioural patterns requires not only knowledge and instruction about human rights, but everyday practice in and out of school and in public life. A human rights culture can only be built with an in-depth understanding of the implications of the respect of human rights for all and by all, and with the participation of all social actors.

387

FRANCINE FOURNIER

Global Security and Human Rights

THE CASE FOR DISARMAMENT

DOUGLAS ROCHE

Nuclear Weapons and the Right to Peace

Douglas Roche is a member of the Canadian Senate, chair of the United Nations Disarmament Committee and special advisor to the Holy See on disarmament and security. The author of fifteen books on peace, security and related issues, he is a recipient of the UN Association's Medal of Honour and the Papal Medal, and an Officer of the Order of Canada. He is visiting professor at the University of Alberta. His most recent book is *Bread Not Bombs: A Political Agenda for Social Justice.*

WE ARE ABOUT TO LEAVE the bloodiest century in the history of humanity. What can provide a basis of hope that the world community will move beyond war in the new millennium? More than one hundred million people were killed in wars during the 20th century. At least twenty-five million people—ninety per cent of them civilians—have been killed in 170 wars since the end of World War II. Thirty wars are now taking place, most inside national boundaries.

In addition to the tragic loss of life and limb, these conflicts breed international terrorism, and they have huge economic costs. World military expenditures in 1998, almost a decade after the end of the cold war, are still at an incredibly high level of $780 billion. The development, deployment and maintenance of nuclear weapons from their inception has cost $8 trillion, of which the US share alone was $5.5 trillion.[1]

Government spending priorities for the prosecution of war and to clean up its aftermath are gargantuan. But the priorities for the prevention of war are Lilliputian. Governments spend billions of dollars on economic rehabilitation of war-ravaged areas, humanitarian aid, refugee relief and peacekeeping forces. But they invest little in the prevention of war. For the sake of a world that has become technologically united and where human rights are indivisible, we must do better in the next century.

Although the discordance, enmity and vile acts of a twisted section of humanity are all too evident, there are, fortunately, new signs of hope that a comprehensive approach to war prevention can be developed. A culture of peace is possible. Already, innovative concepts for the prevention of war are being advanced by the United Nations system, the Organization for Security and Cooperation in Europe and other regional bodies. A new nongovernmental initiative, Global Action to Prevent War, is under way. It provides the details for a phased program for government and grassroots effort to stop war, genocide and other forms of deadly conflict.[2]

At this remarkable international conference on the fiftieth anniversary of the Universal Declaration on Human Rights, we should shift our focus upward and outward to concentrate on a new right that is coming into view: the human right to peace. I am greatly encouraged by the findings of the Carnegie Commission on Preventing Deadly Conflict, which recently reported that deadly conflict is not inevitable.[3] Violence on the scale of what we have seen in Bosnia, Rwanda, Somalia and elsewhere does not emerge inexorably from human interaction.

It is also stated that the need to prevent deadly conflict is increasingly urgent. The rapid compression of the world through breathtaking population growth, technological advances and economic interdependence, combined with the readily available supply of deadly weapons and easily transmitted contagion of hatred and incitement to violence, make it essential to find ways to prevent disputes from turning violent. Preventing deadly conflict is possible, the commission reported. The problem is not that we do not know about incipient and large-scale violence; it is often that we do not act. Examples from "hot spots" around the world illustrate that the potential for violence can be defused through the early, skilful and integrated application of political, diplomatic, economic and military measures.

Though terrible sufferings occurred, it is a fact that warring parties have put down their arms in El Salvador, Namibia, Mozambique, Angola, South Africa, Guatemala and the Philippines. The peace accords in Northern Ireland and the Middle East, though precarious, illustrate that the human desire for peace can overcome the histories of conflict. These lessons have taught us that violence and war are not inevitable. Rather than intervening in violent conflicts after they have erupted and then engaging in postconflict peace-building, it is more humane and more efficient to prevent such violence by addressing its roots. This is the essence of a culture of peace approach.

The current work of UNESCO, in promoting knowledge of a culture of peace, is inspiring.[4] Responding to a request by the United Nations General Assembly to develop the concept of a culture of peace as an integral approach to preventing violence and armed conflicts, UNESCO succeeded in defining norms, values and aims of peace. This work has led to a Declaration on a Culture of Peace issued by the General Assembly.

The Declaration states that a culture of peace is the set of values, attitudes, traditions, modes of behaviour and ways of life that reflect and inspire: respect for life and for all human rights; rejection of violence in all its forms and commitment to the prevention of violent conflicts by tackling their root causes through dialogue and negotiation; commitment to full participation in the process of equitably meeting the developmental and environmental needs of present and future generations; promotion of the equal rights and opportunities of women and men; recognition of the rights of everyone to freedom of expression, opinion and information; devotion to the principles of freedom, justice, democracy, tolerance, solidarity, cooperation, pluralism, cultural diversity, dialogue and understanding between nations, between ethnic, religious, cultural and other groups, and between individuals.

It can readily be seen that a culture of peace is a process of individual, collective and institutional transformation. It grows out of beliefs and actions of the people themselves and develops in each country within its specific historical, sociocultural and economic context. A key is the transformation of violent competition into cooperation based on the sharing of values and goals. In particular, it requires that conflicting parties work together to achieve objectives of common interests at all levels, including the development process.

Reciprocity can be a moral value with universal application. As Confucius taught: "What you do not want done to yourself, do not do to others." The rule of reciprocity is defined by the followers of Christ as the Golden Rule. In the new age of interdependence, this means that governments should take as a starting point in the formulation of their policies the impact of those policies on other states. As the nuclear deterrence doctrine so pointedly illustrates, one nation's security can cause another's insecurity. Mountains of UN global strategies could be categorized by the simple dictum: States should treat others as they wish to be treated in return.

Reciprocity may not lay claim to a high level of altruism. But it is a valid and effective base to find and express human values for common security. Reciprocity has moved from the realm of idealism to the most basic realism: survival. Here we find common ground between spirituality and technology. What spirituality tells us we ought to do (love one another), technology tells us we must do so that we do not destroy one another. If love is deemed by some to be too strong (given the ideological, cultural and racial divides that still exist), at least acceptance and tolerance are demanded as the price of life, liberty and happiness in a world that has become one. If we need reminding of the oneness of the world and the integrity of all life, look again at the photo of the planet sent back by the astronauts. In previous centuries we did not even know one another, let alone care. Now technology has united us, at least in our knowledge of one another.

Through the United Nations and its systems, we possess for the first time in the history of the world a catalogue of information about how our planet works and treaties to protect the rights of individuals and the environment itself. Both people and governments are learning that they must cooperate for many purposes: to maintain peace and order, expand economic activity, tackle pollution, halt or minimize climate change, combat disease, curb the proliferation of weapons, prevent desertification, preserve genetic and species diversity, deter terrorists, ward off famines, etc.

All this has prepared us for the formulation of a new global ethic, which can be essentially expressed as a new attitude of discharging our responsibilities for caring for ourselves and for the earth. The abolition of nuclear weapons becomes part of this new global ethic of enlightened realism. A peace consciousness does not appear overnight. It is evident that constructing a culture of peace requires comprehensive educational, social and civic action. It addresses people of all ages. An open-minded, global strategy is required to make a culture of peace take root in people's hearts and minds.

The General Assembly has helped to foster this ethical transformation by proclaiming the period 2001–2010 as the International Decade for a Culture of Peace and Nonviolence.[5] The General Assembly called on UN bodies, NGOs, religious groups, educational institutions, artists and the media to actively support the Decade for the benefit of every child in the world. This is a fitting way to begin the new millennium in which a culture of war and violence my finally give way to a culture of peace. For this to become a reality, however, the peoples of the world must learn to live together on the basis of universal values of peace.

Mobilizing public opinion and developing new education programs, at all levels, are essential to permeating society's rejection of war. The recent series of roundtables for community leaders conducted across Canada by Project Ploughshares came to the same conclusion: education programs in schools must be strengthened because children today learn little about the culture of peace.[6] The school system is the perfect place to develop this culture. Past campaigns for environmental protection and non-smoking first gained hold in schools and the permeated society.

Federico Mayor, the director-general of UNESCO, has eloquently called for activating the immense potential of youth so that each young person can become the master and architect of his or her own destiny. As he said, "We cannot give to youth what we no longer possess in youthful vitality but instead we can offer what we have learned through experience, the fruit of our failures and successes, of the burdens, joys, pain and perplexity and the renewed inspiration of each new moment."[7]

Mr. Mayor holds that the best way to celebrate the fiftieth anniversary of the Universal Declaration is to promote the newly understood "right to peace—the right to live in peace." The new delineation of the right to peace has particular relevance in the current nuclear weapons controversy. The protection of the right to life and bodily security are at the heart of the Universal Declaration. It is argued by some that the right to life is not an absolute right and that the taking of life in armed hostilities is a necessary exception to this principle. However, when a weapon has the potential to kill between one million and one billion people, as the World Health Organization informed the International Court of Justice, human life becomes reduced to a level of worthlessness that totally belies human dignity as understood in any culture. No weapon invented in the long history of warfare has so negated the dignity and worth of the human person as the nuclear bomb. This recognition has led the UN Human Rights Committee to advocate that the use of nuclear weapons be categorized as a crime against humanity.[8]

The famous Advisory Opinion on Nuclear Weapons of the International Court of Justice did not go this far but did uphold the cardinal principles of humanitarian law. These are the following: In order to protect the civilian population, states must never use weapons that are incapable of distinguishing between civilian and military targets. Also, it is prohibited to cause unnecessary suffering to combatants, and hence states do not have unlimited freedom of choice of weapons. The President of the Court, Mohammed Bedjaoui, in his personal statement, gave a stinging indictment of nuclear weapons: "The very nature of this blood weapon...has a destabilizing effect on humanitarian law which regulates discernment in the type of weapon used. Nuclear weapons, the ultimate evil, destabilizes humanitarian law."[9]

President Bedjaoui added that even if it uses a nuclear weapon only in defence of its very survival, a state cannot exonerate itself from compliance with the "intransgressible" norms of international and humanitarian law. Yet, the nuclear weapons states continue to ignore the court's call for the conclusion of negotiations leading to the elimination of nuclear weapons.

We who have gathered here to reaffirm the principles of the Declaration on Human Rights must recognize that the most devastating attack on the Declaration comes from those who would assault the very existence of human life on the planet. The right to peace demands the abolition of nuclear weapons. This is a hard truth, violently resisted by the nuclear retentionists. We who affirm the right to life and the right to peace can never give in. Through this international conference we must gather our strength anew. For the sake of our children and grandchildren and the future of life on the planet, we dare not relax our commitment to life. When we fully understand our own potential to make a culture of peace the ruling norm in society, nuclear weapons will then be discarded into the ashbins of history.

REFERENCES

1. See Schwartz, Stephen I., *Atomic Audit*, Brookings (1998), for a complete review of the economic costs of nuclear weapons.
2. "Global Action to Prevent War;" a coalition-building project initiated by Amb. (Retd.) Jonathan

Dean, Dr. Randall Forsberg and Prof. Saul Mendlovitz, Institute for Defence and Disarmament Studies, 675 Massachusetts Ave., Cambridge, MA 02139.

3. "Carnegie Commission on Preventing Deadly Conflict," Carnegie Corporation of New York, 1979 Massachusetts Avenue, N.W., Suite 715, Washington, DC 20036–2103.

4. See "Preliminary Consolidated Report to the United Nations on a Culture of Peace," UNESCO Document 155ex/49, Paris, 11 August 1998.

5. UN Document GA/9500, 10 November 1998.

6. Nuclear Weapons: The Problem, the Solution, Canada's Role, Report of Discussions with Community Leaders Across Canada, 8–26 September 1998, Project Ploughshares.

7. Federico Mayor, "The Human Right to Peace," UNESCO, January 1997.

8. See Ginger, Ann Fagan, *Nuclear Weapons Are Illegal*, Apex Press, an imprint of the Council on International and Public Affairs, 777 United Nations Plaza, Suite 3C, New York, NY 10017.

9. See Roche, Douglas, *The Ultimate Evil: The Fight to Ban Nuclear Weapons*, Lorimer (1997).

GEOFFREY A.H. PEARSON

The Need to Control Conventional Weapons

Geoffrey A.H. Pearson is the national vice president of the United Nations Association of Canada. He served as the first executive director of the Canadian Institute for International Peace and Security and as special representative of the prime minister for arms control. He is the author of *Seize the Day: Lester B. Pearson and Crisis Diplomacy.*

Human rights and disarmament are usually considered as separate subjects for analysis and action at the United Nations. Perhaps the links between them are taken for granted. The UN Charter and most conventions on human rights appear to do so. The Charter was the work of the victors in 1945, especially those who were determined to learn the lessons of the events leading to the war. Thus, they put emphasis on the need for collective security, not disarmament, as the best way to prevent war.

The Charter notes the principles of "peaceful settlement" and the non-use of force, but it gives to the Security Council the power to impose sanctions, including the use of force, to ward off threats to the peace and to repel acts of aggression. The Council is also required to "formulate" plans for the establishment of "a system for the regulation of armaments," not for disarmament; a system that took some twenty years before plans were put on paper by East and West, and then shelved as the cold war made agreement impossible.

So, too, while the Universal Declaration of Human Rights refers to "friendly relations between nations" and to "the right to life, liberty and security of person," there is no exhortation to disarm. Nor is there in the two principal conventions which give effect to the Universal Declaration, bearing on civil and political, and economic and social rights, and adopted later.

Growing concern about the effects of the testing of nuclear weapons in the 1960s led to treaties on the control of such weapons and in Latin America to their prohibition. Since then, treaties on biological and chemical weapons and further restrictions on the development and testing of nuclear weapons have strengthened the process of multilateral disarmament. But despite the repeated desire of the General Assembly to eliminate nuclear weapons, neither the goal itself nor the means of doing so has been agreed by the nuclear weapon states. There is still no light at the end of this tunnel—indeed, the tunnel grows longer as the capacity to produce nuclear weapons spreads to other states.

Agreements to control or ban conventional weapons have been given less priority, except in the case of certain weapons deemed "excessively injurious." The Register of Conventional Arms was established in 1992 on a voluntary basis to deal with the transfer of heavy weapons from state to state, but less than half of UN members have reported. Expert studies of the use of small arms have called for ways and means of destroying stocks and preventing illicit transfers; in some cases, e.g., West Africa and Latin America, efforts are being made to comply. But it was not until the Ottawa conference on land mines in 1997 that a convention aimed at universal compliance was agreed.

Whether and, if so, when, it will rid the world of land mines is an open question. Most armed conflicts in this decade have taken place within states and have, therefore, drawn attention to the plight of civilians. One estimate of such conflicts, defined as those leading to at least one thousand deaths, puts the number at thirty-seven in 1997, taking place in thirty-two countries (thirteen in Africa). UN missions, military or civilian, are present in only fifteen countries, underlining the difficulty for the UN to obtain consent for intervention in the internal affairs of member states.

Nevertheless, the boundaries between domestic and inter-state conflict have become so blurred that the concept of sovereignty embedded in the Charter has had to be increasingly ignored and the emergence of so-called "failed states," accompanied in some cases by egregious violations of human rights, has been deemed to justify action under Chapter Seven of the Charter. This is despite UN failure to prevent acts of genocide in Rwanda and Bosnia, failures attributable to a lack of will rather than a lack of authority.

If armed conflict is now to engage the lives of civilians as much or more than the lives of soldiers (and with some three hundred thousand child soldiers now active this distinction too is breaking down), then the link between disarmament and human rights takes tangible form. It does so mainly in the form of weapons, small arms in particular. Both demand and supply are growing. Total sales of both heavy and small arms were estimated to be some $46 billion in 1997, a twelve per cent increase over the year previous, with the US supplying almost half the total. Those sales are followed by the United Kingdom, France and Germany (Russian sales seem to have decreased significantly). Two-thirds of sales went to the Middle East and East Asia (Saudi Arabia and Taiwan, in particular), and while these estimates refer mainly to sophisticated weapons, such as aircraft, they include the much cheaper small arms, e.g., less than ten dollars for an AK–47 in some markets.

According to the secretary general, in fifteen or more of current armed conflicts, "the primary or sole tools of violence are small arms or light weapons." He has proposed a UN conference on the illicit arms trade in order to build "a global consensus on monitoring and controlling illicit arms transfers and their links with trafficking in other contraband goods." Efforts to reach such a consensus are now under way, especially on the issue of illicit sales. An Organization of American States (OAS) convention on the subject has already been agreed, and on 19 November 1997 the Security Council urged Africa to consider similar measures.

Consensus on measures to control the transfer of weapons by governments to non-state actors, a proposal advocated by Canada and Norway, will be more difficult to reach. A meeting of twenty-one countries in Oslo in July 1997 began to examine the subject, and consultations will no doubt continue.

The control of small arms, not to mention heavy arms, is the responsibility of states. States, however, prize their sovereignty, a major component of which is the capacity for self-defence and thus the use of force. The concept of collective security is also based on the use of coercion by states, including the use of armed force. The common answer to the question of how to prevent or deter the illegal use of force, either by states or by non-states actors, is therefore the legal use of force, not disarmament.

Moreover, in cases of state failure, whether by internal division or by social destitution, arms are usually available and may be necessary if only for self-defence. In such cases, states need to be rebuilt in order to give them the capacity to control violence and thus to procure arms. In other cases, state monopoly of the use of force may be used to suppress democracy and human rights. In these cases, is armed resistance legitimate if other means fail to change the situation? It was thought to be so in South Africa. Is it true in Kosovo?

Despite these kinds of questions, and perhaps because of them—and they are likely to become more acute as poverty and population pressures in parts of Asia and Africa combine to exacerbate racial and religious tensions—the impetus to ban the production and use of certain weapons and to limit the availability of others is bound to continue. Modern methods of communication make the dangers of the use of weapons of mass destruction apparent to citizens everywhere and allow many of them to organize opposition across borders. The key question is one of legality. The Charter vision is one of the collective and, therefore, legal (in UN terms) use of force to prevent or stop the illegal use of force, a concept that citizens of democracies accept in the form of law enforcement by police. If the agencies of the UN can slowly build consensus about the rule of law as it relates to the use of certain weapons, and if civil society takes hold in more countries, then the obstacles to arms control mentioned will lose importance.

Meanwhile, UN members can and should be encouraged by Canada and others to take measures to register and regulate the ownership of small arms, destroy surplus stocks, and develop codes of conduct for arms transfers to other states; e.g., prohibit transfers to areas of conflict and to gross violators of human rights. Guidelines of this kind have already been accepted in principle by the General Assembly. Canada is consulting with other like-minded governments to develop a "Global Convention Prohibiting the International Transfer of Military Small Arms and Light Weapons to Non-State Actors."

Moreover, some sixty NGOs from both the North and South have agreed to form an international network to promote action by governments. It is likely to be the strength and effectiveness of this group that will determine, in the end, the rate of progress towards making disarmament an integral component of the campaign to make the Universal Declaration "a common standard of achievement for all peoples."

Teaching the Public About Weapons of Mass Destruction

Fernando de Souza Barros is a professor at the Physics Institute of the Federal University of Rio de Janeiro, Brazil and a member of the International Network of Engineers and Scientists Against Proliferation. He is also a member of the International Steering Committee for the Middle Powers Initiative, which encourages nuclear weapons states to negotiate nuclear disarmament. **Susana de Souza Barros** is a researcher in physics education and a member of the International Commission of Physics Education of the International Union of Pure and Applied Physics.

401

THE CASE OF DISARMAMENT within the framework of human rights is a timely question. The fragility of current international agreements against weapons of massive destruction prevents the realization of human rights for a large part of humankind. One should discuss the reasons why the continuing stalemate regarding the elimination of these weapons hinders human rights.

In order to achieve the technological capabilities required to acquire and maintain these weapons, an enormous bill has been and is being paid by civilians all over the world. This is a heavy penalty for the manufacture of weapons which if used would only magnify the already immense social problems. World resources destined for building sophisticated weapons of massive destruction could provide education and health for all.

Human rights are universally denied to the majority of the world's people when they are kept unaware of how these weapons could effect their lives through wars, famine, destruction and suffering. The secrecy surrounding these weapons is clearly against Article 19 of the Universal Declaration of Human Rights which protects the right to freedom of opinion, expression and information.[1] There is an urgent need for the public to understand nuclear issues and, in particular, the urgency of disarmament. The world will need informed citizens in the third millennium.

We propose the preparation of an agenda to develop educational materials so that the public will understand both the technical and political aspects of weapons of massive destruction, including nuclear weapons. This requires a careful reflection on how this proposal should be implemented as it deals with complex forces that drive the politics of knowledge in our "risk society."[2]

"Most assertions of human rights, arguably not all, are qualified by the limitation that the rights of any particular individual or group in any particular instance are restricted as much as is necessary to secure the comparable rights of others and the aggregate common interest."[3] It is our understanding that this necessary limitation imposes two basic questions for this agenda: Is there any justice in having countries armed with nuclear weapons in order to ensure their security? Can the international order be set forth upon the fear of nuclear weapons?

Article 28 of the Universal Declaration of Human Rights proclaims that "everyone is entitled to a social and international order in which the rights set forth in this Declaration can be fully realized." We submit that the full realization of these rights require that the above two questions must eventually be answered by a universal "No." Should the agenda be aimed at schools? Again we find a basis for this ultimate objective in the Universal Declaration of Human Rights. Article 26 (paragraph 2) reads: "Education shall be directed to the full development of the human personality and to the strengthening of respect for human rights and fundamental freedoms. It shall promote understanding, tolerance and friendship among all nations, racial or religious groups, and shall further the activities of the United Nations for the maintenance of peace." We would like to emphasize that this belongs to the realm of universal education for all.

What should be the essential components for an agenda directed to the public understanding of nuclear issues?[4] The agenda should deal with the reality of having to live in, what has been appropriately termed a "risk society."[5] Such a society has an awareness that there are nuclear, biological and chemical technologies that can lead to weapons of massive destruction. The same facility that produces vaccines for children can be equipped to make material for biological bombs.

The agenda should also recognize available channels for public knowledge and what the common citizen knows about the risks and benefits of modern technologies. How does media convey information? Are common citizens prepared to take a critical stand about nuclear-related issues? A public understanding of nuclear issues, as related to civilian and military applications, is imperative for the containment of the political and social consequences involved with weapons of mass destruction. One should recall that some sixty years ago President Franklin D. Roosevelt was perhaps the first lay citizen to become aware of the power of nuclear weapons.[6] Should the world's common citizens be entitled to this same awareness at the threshold of the third millennium?

Since World War II the technical aspects involved in such an understanding have become quite formidable. Creating learning materials which will illuminate the complexities will be a difficult task. But it is necessary if we are to achieve "scientific literacy for all." There are many questions to take into consideration when planning an education program. They include: How much relevant information should be available to students and teachers in order to understand the limits, risks and benefits that the use of nuclear technologies could bring to humanity? Are lay citizens aware of the possibilities/consequences of the use of nuclear technologies by intent or by accident? Would a non-nuclear posture prevent applications of nuclear technologies in areas of social relevance?

For the case of nuclear weapons, educational materials should include specific information about nuclear issues that will help people form their opinions. For instance, a nuclear-weapon-free world is no longer a fanciful idea.[7] It is being taken seriously by strategists, military men, even former US secretaries of defense. This is because they now concede the point—one which peace movements have been making for years—that nuclear weapons diminish, rather than enhance, the security of nuclear weapon states. The reduction and dismantlement of nuclear warheads should be irreversible and requires a cut-off of the production of weapon fissile material (e.g., cut-off convention). There are formidable arguments—economic, ecological, security and waste disposal—against extraction (i.e., reprocessing of spent fuel) and use of plutonium.

The ballistic missile threat could be removed most effectively by a Ballistic Missile Convention (BMC). An international control body could be set up to verify that space technology was not used for the development and production of ballistic missiles. Regional approaches towards a nuclear-free world are an important way in which the non-nuclear weapon states can seize the initiative in the nonproliferation arena, by declaring their regions to be off-limits for nuclear weapon deployment, use or threat of use. As such off-limit regions spread around the world, international pressure will build for nuclear weapons states to accept the idea of weapon-free zones.

The educational agenda should emphasize the vital role of international treaties and international law must have in the quest for a weapon-free world. It should explicitly present the struggles that characterize their implementation. The present situation of the Non-Proliferation Treaty (NPT) is a case in point. The second preparatory conference for the 2000 review of the NPT collapsed in 1998 with no agreement on substance, recommendations or rules of procedure.[8]

The agenda should also stress that international law now recognizes the unique characteristics of nuclear weapons. In its Advisory Opinion of 8 July 1996, the World Court cited the uniquely destructive characteristics of nuclear weapons: "in particular their destructive capacity, their capacity to cause untold human suffering, and their ability to cause damage to generations to come."[9] It continued, "Any threat or use of nuclear weapons must conform to international humanitarian law.... One cannot legally use weapons of mass destruction such as chemical and biological weapons. Through the Court's decision, nuclear weapons are now in the same category."[10, 11]

Disarmament should be presented as both feasible and urgently needed. A recent report by the International Network of Engineers and Scientists Against Proliferation states: "If complete nuclear disarmament is to become a reality and not remain just a Utopian dream, we need to describe in detail what a world free from nuclear weapons would look like; we need to be quite clear about our goals and we need to devise a strategy which sets out the steps by which those goals can be reached."[12]

Robert D. Green, in *Fast Track to Zero Nuclear Weapons*, writes: "Even if the treaty START II is ratified and fully implemented by Russia and USA, there will still be at least 10,000 nuclear weapons of all kinds remaining on each side at the end of 2007. Besides, over half the START II reductions would have come to the end of their useful lives in that time. Even full compliance with START III would leave about 2,000 strategic warheads on each side and would not touch the British, French or Chinese arsenals. Finally, there are still no plans to include the thousands of tactical nuclear weapons in any disarmament negotiations, yet these are the ones most likely to be used first in a future regional conflict, and to be coveted by paranoid regimes or terrorist groups."[13] Insecure nuclear-weapon materials compound the problem. Moreover, there also exists a growing risk of accidental nuclear war.

In the near future, technologies related to testing and design of nuclear weapons shall be refined in laboratory environments. A major step in that direction was taken in the US and the US is not alone in planning new generations of nuclear weaponry.[14] There are great difficulties in influencing the decisions of key nuclear-power states (and those of *de facto* nuclear states). Thus the preparation of the proposal for this campaign should highlight special problems arising from "frozen postures" and ideologies that oppose disarmament initiatives. One can mention several instances that substantiate this concern.

To date, NATO has taken no position on the World Court Opinion. The NATO nuclear states, however, have each baldly asserted that they are "confident" that it requires no change to their nuclear policies. Weapon states also ignore public opinion.[15] Recently we witnessed cases of public demonstrations in the Third World celebrating their countries' achievement of nuclear-weapon-state status.[16] Author Robert D. Green has pointed out some of the main arguments, revealing their weaknesses in justifying nuclear weapons. Some of those arguments include: "Nuclear weapons cannot be de-invented.... Deterrence works!... Nuclear weapons are essential for my country's ultimate security.... Nuclear weapons are essential for my country's status in the world."[17]

The main objective of scientific knowledge generated through the centuries has been man's well-being and quality of life. At this end of a millennium, we have yet to ask why science education has not yet been liberalized and made accessible for all people. Society's engagement should be considered as essential. As Hazen and Trefill put it: "Science education for all should mean that it would be possible to prepare citizens that are able to foresee consequences and achieve the wisdom to save themselves from their own actions."[18]

The time has come when we need to make adequate choices for the education of citizens so that they are able to have a role in a world dominated by science and technology, in a world where politics and economy are in the hands of the powerful few. Nowhere in the science curriculum are weapons—chemical, biological or nuclear—mentioned. Students finish secondary instruction without ever having discussed (during their science lessons) the social and technical implications of that science or the ethical and moral implications of weapons of mass destruction.

The main objectives of an educational agenda should be to prepare information on modern technologies associated with weaponry and corresponding statistics about the costs of their development and destruction; to introduce to science education elements that will ensure that citizens recognize the implications of technical development for society as a whole; and to motivate students about the need to be conscious of their rights to the peace and freedom assured by the Universal Declaration of Human Rights.

REFERENCES

1. The authors would like to express their thanks to Prof. J. A. Mignaco, of the Physics Institute - UFRJ, Rio de Janeiro.
2. Beck, Ulrich. *Risk Society: Towards a New Modernity*. Sage Publications (1992).
3. 1994–1998 Encyclopaedia Britannica.
4. de Souza Barros, Susana, ICPE Conference, Ballaton, Hungary (1989).
5. In 1939 Leo Szilard, Edward Teller and Eugene Wigner persuaded Albert Einstein to write the famous letter to President Franklin D. Roosevelt advocating the immediate development of an atomic bomb. After the atomic bomb was first used, Szilard became an ardent promoter of the peaceful uses of atomic energy and the international control of nuclear weapons, founding the Council for a Liveable World. See *The Making of the Atomic Bomb*, Richard Rhodes, Simon & Schuster (1988), pg. 526–527.
6. In 1939 Leo Szilard, Edward Teller and Eugene Wigner persuaded Albert Einstein to write the famous letter to President Franklin D. Roosevelt advocating the immediate development of an atomic bomb. After the atomic bomb was used, Szilard became an ardent promoter of the peaceful uses of atomic energy and the international control of nuclear weapons, founding the Council for a Liveable World. See note 5.
7. "Beyond the NPT: An Executive Summary." International Network of Engineers and Scientists Against Proliferation, INESAP Study Group-APRIL (1995).

8. The Strategic Defence Review, Cm 3999, London: The Stationery Office (July 1998), para. 64.

9. 8 July 1996, World Court Advisory Opinion, para. 36.

10. Ibid., paras. 78–87.

11. Green, Robert D. *Fast Track to Zero Nuclear Weapons*. Middle Powers Initiative, Cambridge, Massachusetts, USA (1998).

12. "Beyond the NPT: An Executive Summary." International Network of Engineers and Scientists Against Proliferation, INESAP Study Group-APRIL (1995).

13. See note 11.

14. Lichterman, Andrew and Jacqueline Cabasso. *A Faustian Bargain: Why 'Stockpile Stewardship' is Fundamentally Incompatible with the Process of Nuclear Disarmament*. Western States Legal Foundation (April 1998).

15. See note 11.

16. Private communication of Dr. Zia Mian (now at Princeton University): "At a press conference on 2 June 1998, organized in a hotel in Islamabad by the Pakistan–India People's Forum for Peace and Democracy, A. H. Nayyar, Eqbal Ahmad and Samina Ahmad (no relation) were supposed to talk about the current nuclear crisis in South Asia. About fifty to sixty journalists attended the press conference and most were hostile. Instead of questions from the floor, there were long inflammatory statements attacking the speakers. This incident was described to Dr. Mian by Dr. A. H. Nayyar (associate professor of physics at Quaid-i-Azam University in Islamabad, Pakistan).

17. See note 11.

18. Hazen, Robert M. and James Trefil. *Science Matters*, Doubleday/USA (1991).

Meeting the Challenges

DISABILITY, POVERTY AND CHILDREN IN NEED

ZUHY SAYEED

The Elusive Quest
for Human Rights

Zuhy Sayeed is the president of the Alberta Association
for Community Living and a member of the Canadian
Association's Inclusion Steering Committee, chairing
its International Affairs Committee. She has received
the Governor General's Commemorative Medal and the
Immigration Award for Contributions to Social Issues.

THE FIFTIETH ANNIVERSARY of the Universal Declaration of Human Rights is
a time for celebration, a time for reflection, a time to challenge our commitments and ourselves. It is also a time to think about the thousands of children
and adults in our communities and countries who have been deprived of their
rights because they have a disability. We should think about labels and they way
they are used to segregate and exclude.

Our celebrations and reflections must include a review of our commitment
to the UN Declaration of Human Rights, which is a powerful foundation by
which people of the world can be nurtured. Human rights are indivisible.
Different sets of human rights do not exist for different people. Issues relating
to persons with a disability cut across all sectors and all walks of life. They relate
to gender, poverty, age, religion, justice, effects of war and oppression, employment, education, economic prosperity and health. This is only a partial list.

Persons with a disability are the most marginalized, the poorest and the most
discriminated members of our communities. For persons with a disability, their
marginalized status is rooted in political, social, economic and cultural conditions rather in the nature of their disability. Too often human rights are thought
of only in terms of protecting people from the atrocities of war and repression.
But wars do happen and are the single biggest cause of disabilities.

This is 1998, one short year before the dawn of a new millennium. It is a time
when we are all seriously taking stock of what we have achieved during the 21st
century. For human rights activists, there are still many questions and many
challenges. How do we examine the lives of the vulnerable citizens of the world?
What lens do we use to get true experiences and stories by which we can judge
our own record of applying the principles of human rights? How much further

do we have to go to achieve the Declaration of Human Rights? How well have we done so far?

The Declaration gives us guarantees of citizenship, of belonging. Other UN instruments which have followed say that the nations of the world must protect the rights of people with different abilities. From the early 1960s, beginning with the Geneva Declaration, persons with disabilities have been reassured that their needs will be met, that they will receive the supports necessary to lead lives of quality. The thinking since then, with the backing of various UN instruments and conventions, has evolved from support based on charity, to one of full citizenship. That progress has been reflected in many UN conventions, instruments and declarations since the 1970s.

The International Year of Disabled Persons and the subsequent decade vocalized the evolution of that shift in thinking. The theme "Full Participation and Equality" gave expression to the growing realization that it is only if all citizens are included and can participate and contribute to everyday life, that true democracy can flourish. And that only then will the world live in peace.

The UN Convention on the Rights of the Child forces us to examine the way we protect the very vulnerable lives of our little ones—the citizens and leaders of tomorrow. They will, in their lifetimes, be the keepers of the great instruments that will someday lead to peace. Their experiences will have proven to them that inclusion strengthens society and enables members of their communities to belong and to contribute.

Midway through the decade, the international disability community, in partnership with other organizations, demanded stronger UN instruments. In 1993 the Standard Rules on the Equalization of Opportunities for Persons with Disabilities was adopted by the General Assembly of the UN. The rules state: "In all societies of the world, there are still obstacles preventing persons with disabilities from exercising their rights and freedoms and making it difficult for them to participate fully in the activities of their societies. It is the responsibility of the States to remove such obstacles...." This must be with the collaboration of international nongovernmental organizations representing families and individuals with disabilities. The rules further state that this should be done by both empowering persons with disabilities and by creating an accessible society. Above all, the Standard Rules strongly emphasizes the human rights perspective.

Because of this, some countries that are at the beginning point of democratization have embraced the philosophy of inclusion for all citizens. In Panama inclusive education is enshrined in law. Nicaragua is looking to Canada for electoral reform which will include citizens with disabilities and enable them to exercise voting rights. The Polish Republic recently passed the Charter of Rights of Persons with Disabilities. South Africa has also passed legislation recognizing the rights of people with disabilities. India has adopted new legislation, replacing legislation in effect since the 1930s. The list goes on. Indeed, within Canada, the Charter of Rights and Freedoms gives us the promise of equality under the law.

But experiences in real life been different. Different, as families with children and adults with developmental disabilities and individuals with disabilities struggle every day to live in a society that has not understood the shift in thinking. The traditional "fix the child" attitude, has been overtaken by a broad approach that works with civil society to include all citizens into the community. This simple concept of creating a society that will be good for us all seems to be most misunderstood. The inclusion of persons with developmental disabilities has taught us that the provisions of the Universal Declaration can be applied to the most vulnerable citizens and not just to the majority.

For fifty years, individuals with disabilities and their parents and families have been working together to create the recognition of basic human rights. But there still remains a gap for persons with disabilities: the fundamental rights that are applied to issues of gender, age, colour, race and ability are not applicable to citizens with disabilities and their families.

Despite the guarantees of freedom, despite the protection that is awarded to citizens, we encounter horrific examples of prejudice and discrimination. There are examples of double discrimination, where people are mistreated not only because of a developmental disability, but also because of race, gender, religion, economic status or sexual orientation. We have learned about the vulnerability of disabled women to sexual abuse and violence. They also receive fewer educational opportunities than their male counterparts. Yet very few human rights organizations representing a defined group also advocate for those among their number who are disabled.

In a world that is celebrating fifty years of universal and fundamental freedoms, we are still denied opportunities to go to school and to learn skills that will assure us security as citizens. We are saddened by the contradictions that this very celebration signifies. At the same time that we celebrate this historical UN Declaration, members of society are working to legitimize the eradication of human diversity.

In 1998 we are having a debate about whether we should apply the law to a father who murdered his child. Would we debate justice if his little one did not have a disability? Yesterday I heard of a child who has suffered intense abuse in a system that has never accepted or understood his differences and has caused him to be forever locked in a system that will try to cure his behaviour. Last month, we heard yet again stories of undeniable horrors in our own province of the kinds of abuse that occurred while in the caring hands of a large institution. We thought that medical experiments happened during a grim part of the history of the world, far away and a long time ago. Let us think about that again.

In 1998, in spite of the security of the United Nations, we still have to negotiate to prove that diversity is indeed part of the rich heritage of humankind. We have heard devastating testimony about the absence of informed consent. We will pay a price for generations to come, the devastation and the years lost because of being labelled "defective." The Leiliani Muir case, a case of compulsory sterilization in a Canadian province, graphically illustrates the results of labelling. How do we know that denial of opportunity or the effects of experimental drugs did not in fact cause the conditions that we traditionally label as "defective"?

According to UN statistics, there are three hundred million people with disabilities in the world. Even this figure may be underestimated. The Universal Declaration speaks to us of having "the right to life, liberty and security of person." Yet, cleansing and massacres begin with the most vulnerable of our family members: people with disabilities. On the one hand in the 1990s, we have been aggressive in our search for "perfectness." And on another, we have thousands of children being hurt, maimed or killed by the minute in active warfare. And the world's backing and promotion goes to elimination of "humanness"—instead of eliminating war—and to "prevention" in the name of disease and sickness. It isn't about sickness. It is about the value judgements that are going to be used to measure the worth of my son today and maybe yours tomorrow. And we talk of prevention from only a health point of view. And health? In the name of eradicating disease and illness, scientists have embarked on the slippery slope of creating the perfect human being.

When cancer and diabetes and heart or lung disease is being equated to the loving, perfect characteristics of my sons—maybe your daughters, siblings, parents, cousins, uncle, aunts or our friends—we are researching ways that would eradicate the very personalities and the strengths that our children possess. And that governments, health and other insurance companies and the pharmaceutical industry will all be on the bandwagon of the so-called "cost-factor"—which is the biggest threat to all our lives?

Let me explain clearly what I mean by all of this. To allow our children to exist is looked as an expense to society. Hence their complete absence would save money. Today it will be our children; tomorrow it will be children with diabetes, asthma, a genetic predisposition to heart disease, and the list goes on and on. In developing countries, this would mean the choice of aborting female babies and infanticide would be reaffirmed and legalized. For once this picking and choosing begins on the basis of so-called health, how long would it be before this would spread to eliminating those citizens of the world who are considered racially inferior by some? The atrocities of World War II will be resurrected.

The challenge is how to pursue genetic research that does not threaten the acceptance of diversity as a fundamental characteristic of humankind. It is not only scientists whom we must question: we must also look to ourselves. What is the message we are giving to our sons and daughters and our friends? That their lives have all been in vain? There is a big difference between promoting health by ensuring that each individual is able to grow and develop to his or her potential, and judging human characteristics by deciding which ones to preserve, and which to eliminate.

At the recent Congress of Inclusion International in The Hague, The Netherlands, over one thousand people from sixty-nine countries gathered. The theme of the congress was Partners in Action: Working Towards Human Rights and Social Justice for All. For the first time, persons advocating on their own behalf participated fully and actively. Their number-one issue was the threat of biotechnology and their concern that current research does not recognize persons with a disability as part of the human family. Their message was simple: Don't prevent us, include us. Eugenics attempted to create the perfect society. Have we really progressed? Fifty years later, we have not given up.

This seems as though I am speaking of future scientific progress. In fact, I am speaking about the present and about today. It is horrifying to realize that in 1998, as we celebrate the anniversary of the Universal Declaration of Human Rights, a specialized agency within the UN would be working to rid mankind of diversity—and that too in the name of human rights. How do we explain this to the UNESCO bioethics committee which is searching for ways to officially sanction the eradication of children like yours and mine?

Today the Universal Declaration of the Human Genome has been signed and instructs the world to go forth and promote the principles of the Declaration. It is only because of the concern and the action of persons with disabilities, their families and international advocates that there have been some clauses included which will protect the rights of groups of vulnerable people, including people with a disability. All over the world there have been historic declarations signed by numerous governments and parent organizations that promote equity for persons with disabilities.

The Declaration of Managua was endorsed by governments and family associations in more that thirty countries. Almost five hundred people came together in Canada to confirm our beliefs and recognize the need for a society that welcomes the diversity of all people and the need for the richness of inclusive communities. The Saint John's Declaration serves as the blueprint to guide the Canadian Association for Community Living towards the new millennium. Yet all the power of these statements, the wealth of experiences, has not changed the conditions of discrimination and the control under which people with disabilities are living. What would our experiences be if the societies using the visionary human rights instruments of the UN paved for us—families with sons, daughters, family members or friends—the realization of an inclusive community? A warm, caring community, free from war and violence, and truly embracing of diversity and potential?

Mothers around the world hold their newborn babies in their arms and with emotion and tears of joy and promise that they will move the earth for their children. The same dream that we, as parents of children with different abilities share with the hundreds of parents I have met through my years of experience as a teacher and, I daresay, with millions of parents around the world. Children don't see differences, they see gifts. As a preschool educator for over sixteen years and an elementary school teacher for some years prior to that, I can attest from an educator's point of view, that children are by nature accepting and loving. I can tell many stories of the unconditional acceptance through the eyes of a young child. Personally, as a parent of a young man with different abilities, I can attest to the fact that the young people around our sons in school, in the community, in scouts and in soccer, have an innate sense of fairness and inclusion. The cynicism and the prejudice come from the biases that we as adults pass onto our children. And there are too many examples of that.

There are prerequisites to being able to contribute to and participate in community life. Inclusion must occur from the very beginning. It is vital to support parents and assist the community to realize the strengths that each child has within him or her. It is a way of life. I will submit to you that every child has potential. That it is the limitation of opportunity and the environment that prevent this potential from being realized. Indeed, the UN itself, in the preamble to the UN Standard Rules, defines "handicap" as a relationship of a person with his/her environment.

In a truly inclusive society, all members have accepted the innate differences of all its citizens. All citizens are given opportunity to contribute, and disability is not seen as a condition that needs a cure or treatment that is isolated. We as a society would have fulfilled our responsibilities and would be taking our roles seriously. We would have asked ourselves the hard questions. How many times have we thought about being injured or our abilities being hampered by illness or circumstance? Would we then not appreciate a world that would treat us all with equity, dignity and respect? We have begun but, while there are successes, there are also threats.

The Universal Declaration of Human Rights evokes the best humankind has to offer. Its vision is the fulfilment of human potential. But the words of the those persons who were in The Hague advocating on their own behalf keep ringing in my ears: Don't prevent us, include us. And the delegates from Africa telling us how the first victims of genocide were persons with a disability—people who were too weak or too slow to flee their pursuers. I cannot help but recall that the very reason for developing the Universal Declaration was in response to the Holocaust, where persons with a disability were among the first to be exterminated.

That is the ultimate result of not respecting the rights of persons with severe disabilities: their exclusion from the human family. There are other less extreme forms of exclusion, which also take a toll on their victims and debase the rest of us for our complicity. Exclusion has a high price. The benefit of inclusion is a society that is tolerant of diversity, that truly embraces and understands the principles and ideals expressed in all the instruments and conventions. The benefits of inclusion are obvious and for most of us, the ethical, moral and right reasons are enough.

Fifty years after the Declaration we now have a breakthrough. For the first time, in 1998, the UN has included the issues of persons with a disability within the UN Human Rights (UNHR) Commission framework. Recently, Ireland introduced a resolution, co-sponsored by Canada, to the UNHR Commission that called for the inclusion of disability into the UNHR agenda. This was adopted at the UNHR Commission meetings in March 1998. In the words of Bengt Lindqvist, Special Rapporteur to the UN Standard Rules on the Equalization of Opportunities for Persons with Disabilities, "an important and rich resolution on human rights and disability....[It is m]ost important that the disability issue will from now on be recognized as a dimension of human rights by all UN entities....The Standard Rules become a recognized human rights instrument....And that the disability dimension will be included in the work of the Special Rapporteurs of the UN."

This is a result of international partnerships, collaboration and awareness that has occurred as people around the world have realized that true democracy can only happen if all citizens are included, that the accommodations of the past have been limited to surface adjustments. That nothing will change if we continue to focus on the limitations of persons with a disability, instead of the limitations within our communities, systems, laws, policies and programs. Instead of systemic human rights violations against persons with disabilities, we would be engaged in more pro-active work which will benefit all people.

There are statements from the special agencies of the UN, all compelling in their direction, to include—and not just include, but include with dignity and respect—and provide full opportunities to reach unlimited potential. The World Health Organization is now examining how people with disabilities will access a more just system of health care. With this resolution and with the potential will of human rights activists all over the world, once and for all, the second class of citizenship for persons with disabilities could be overturned.

Let me quickly review our new challenges. The biggest challenge is to learn to study the world around us through the lens provided by the Declaration and by the resolution adopted by the UN Human Rights Commission. The challenge is in how to change our own thinking to really understand what it means to have disability as part of the human rights agenda. The challenge is full access to systems that were previously designed to exclude and apply unrealistic criteria, definitions and labels and systems designed to forever relegate persons with disabilities to a life of poverty.

The challenge is to think about what it means for human rights advocates to include issues of disability in all our deliberations. The challenge is to learn from the *Eve* case in Canada, which is about the right of a woman with a disability to have a child. The challenge, as we learned through the *Eaton* case, another case in Canada, is about equity in education. The challenge is to understand the case of Leiliani Muir, which ends up not only being about forced sterilization, or more broadly—informed consent—and what it means to have been labelled as a "defective". The *Eldridge* case in Canada has assisted us to understand that it is not simply about access to services, or in this case interpreters for people with hearing impairments but about the basic right to health care. It has helped us understand what institutionalization means to people who are innocent and yet incarcerated and what the denial of opportunity really means.

The challenge is to think about what guardianship orders mean: the stripping away of an individual's right to self-determination, which is the most fundamental right to citizenship. How can we change the control that the system imposes? Most often it is easier to have substitute decision-makers, rather than to work with a person or to find the best way to communicate. How do we deal with the fact that people are denied the right to decide where and with whom they will live and that people who will provide personal support are chosen for them, just as it has been decided in the past who would be sterilized or who should be celibate?

We need to think about influencing systems to provide services for us all together, so that we can all benefit from quality inclusive services, rather than perpetuating the creation of special services designed to keep people out. Of course then, physical barriers would have to be addressed, which again would benefit all members of society. The challenge to the human rights world is to expand our own notions and to include a group of people that even we have ignored. The challenge is to ensure individual learning. We must ask what democracy truly means and what the equality of outcomes will be for people who have different needs. How do we really figure out what self-determination will be within this new context? How is "right to access" defined?

I would like to share with you a conversation with a gentleman with a developmental disability in New Zealand. When asked, "What should we call you?", his instant reply was, "Call me Mister!" Labels are hurtful. This is what the Canadian Association for Community Living, our provincial and territorial associations, over 450 local associations in Canada, and Inclusion International, our world federation of over 179 national associations in over 109 countries, promote. This is the vision of the past fifty years and the vision that will lead us into the next millennium. This is the legacy we will leave for our children. Our hope is that the power of many voices coming together will form that which is invincible—the power of one.

Think of the children to whom the Universal Declaration promised that they would receive special attention and that the future lay in their hands. Think of the children who were assured of being able to go to the same school as their brothers, sisters or friends, as "education shall be directed to the full development of the human personality and to the strengthening of respect for human rights and fundamental freedoms."

Our children deserve all this and more. They deserve the chance to live their lives in warm, welcoming communities, where abilities and strengths matter and not disabilities and weaknesses. Our families need the warmth and protection to carry out the precious roles of bringing up children who teach us valuable lessons, lessons of hope, of joy, of strength and indomitable courage in the face of the harshness of the world. Let us reaffirm today the commitment and the promises of all the declarations, conventions, instruments and the Universal Declaration of Human Rights.

A human rights framework for all the world's citizens would lead to tolerance, understanding, to a gentler society and a kinder world and ultimately to sustained peace. Our challenge is to create a society that protects and enhances the lives of all its citizens and confirms that human rights are unequivocal and indivisible. As it has been said time and time again, true democracy is judged by the way in which a society promotes the equity and protection of its most vulnerable citizens.

ZUHY SAYEED

Beyond the
Rhetoric

Midge Cuthill is the coordinator of Poverty in Action,
Canada, and a director of the National Anti-Poverty
Organization Board. She organized the 1996 Cross
Canada Women's March for Bread and Roses and the
1997 Western Canada Poor People's Conference.

ON 10 DECEMBER 1948 the General Assembly of the United Nations
proclaimed the Universal Declaration of Human Rights. Today, fifty years later,
we are here to celebrate our accomplishments and explore our shortcomings. It
is important to remember that human rights are ideals and do not easily translate into laws. They require a commitment by all people to go beyond the
restrictions of legislation in reaching towards those ideals. It's not an easy task
but a necessary one, so that we can truly say, "All human beings are born free
and equal in dignity and rights."

Considering the relative wealth of Canada and the commitment that was
made fifty years ago, there has been very little work done to achieve the standards set out in the declaration, specifically articles 23 to 26. The examples I will
share are people who I have talked with or are people who have sent information to organizations which I work with.

Article 23 Section 1 states: "Everyone has the right to work, to free choice of
employment, to just and favourable conditions of work and to protection
against unemployment." Currently, the provinces of Alberta, BC, Ontario, New
Brunswick and Québec have adopted various workfare programs that are linked
to provincial social programs. Policy states that you must accept any opportunity for employment and many people are being forced into low-paying
part-time jobs. For example, a family man here in Alberta was cut off social
assistance for quitting a job when he was told he would have to work seventy
hours a week, with a half-hour break per day and no paid overtime.

Article 23 Section 2 states: "Everyone, without any discrimination, has the
right to equal pay for equal work." The federal government has recently lost in
the Supreme Court decision for federal female employees who were paid less
than their male counterparts. As a result of this decision, the federal government

has been ordered to pay backwages and correct the pay scale to reflect equality. The federal government has appealed this decision.

Article 23 Section 3 states: "Everyone who works has the right to just and favourable remuneration ensuring for themselves and their family an existence worthy of human dignity, and supplemented, if necessary, by other means of social protection." There is no federal standard ensuring a minimum standard of living and minimum wage. As a result, many families are surviving on less than half of the Statistics Canada low-income cut-off lines (LICO). The LICO for 1996 in Edmonton for a family of six is $37,787. A typical instance of this violation would be a local family of six which has been refused financial assistance. One of their children has special needs because of a behavioural disorder. Their total family income for 1997 was $13,600. Alberta Family and Social Services consider this family ineligible for social assistance. The question of what is a "just" wage is being answered by the economic sector when we should be listening to the social sector which is concerned with human dignity.

Article 23 Section 4 states: "Everyone has the right to form and to join trade unions for the protection of his interests." A shocking example of a violation of this article is that in Ontario it is now illegal for welfare recipients on workfare placements to belong to a union. They are also specifically excluded from all Employment Standards Legislation.

Article 24 states: "Everyone has the right to rest and leisure, including reasonable limitation of working hours and periodic holidays with pay." When I think of this article and recall my own circumstances, I personally know that my rights are not realized. I worked a full-time plus a part-time job at minimum wage to support my two sons and myself. Even at this level of effort, at minimum wage I needed help from social services. My leisure time and stress relief were being allowed a small amount of time: one or two days off from one of these jobs. Rest and holidays were not a possibility. I saw my children early in the morning when getting them ready for daycare. My children were in bed by the time I returned from work in the evening.

Article 25 Section 1 states: "Everyone has the right to a standard of living adequate for the health and well-being of themselves and their family, including food, clothing, housing, medical care and necessary social services and the right to security in the event of unemployment, sickness, disability, widowhood, old age or other lack of livelihood in circumstances beyond their control." Due to cuts and the altering of regulations in social program funding, many people are being denied basic necessities. The public and our government has been made aware of the alarmingly rise in food bank usage and of the necessity for some people to choose between buying food or paying for shelter. Changes in regulations across the country mean that many people have been made ineligible for social assistance. At the same time, we have seen an increase in demand for child welfare services because families can longer meet their children's basic needs.

Article 25 Section 2 states: "Motherhood and childhood are entitled to special care and assistance. All children, whether born in or out of wedlock shall enjoy the same social protection." Some parents have been denied the opportunity to raise their children. For instance, families in Alberta who have no income or are of low-income find it necessary to rely on public assistance or are forced into low-paying jobs when their children are as young as six months old. They can no longer depend on a stressed and inadequately subsidized daycare system.

Article 26 Section 1 states: "Everyone has the right to education. Education shall be free, at least in the elementary and fundamental stages. Elementary education shall be compulsory. Technical and professional education shall be made generally available and higher education shall be equally accessible to all on the basis of merit." In Canada, education is no longer free. School fees and charges for field trips place low-income children at an immediate disadvantage. In Edmonton, school fees for elementary children are close to $100 per year. Social assistance policy allots $50 per child per year to cover school fees, supplies and clothing.

There are children who are excluded from school-related activities because of fees attached. Some school sport teams have uniform or participation fees. Some poor children are socially isolated from a very early age by the very structures that are supposed to be supporting them. These children are left out of activities such as pizza days, hot-dog days and many other events. Other children in the classroom know that they are poor and often tease the children. Even if there is a subsidy, some parents often don't know or are ashamed to ask for it.

Poverty is presently one of Canada's biggest problems. Canada made a commitment on 24 November 1989 to eliminate child poverty by the year 2000. Since that date, child poverty has increased an alarming fifty-eight per cent. We must not forget the fact that children are poor because their parents are poor. Children are not poor in isolation. There have been many studies done that prove the long-term costs of poverty are a terrible drain on health care, remedial education and judicial costs. We need to stop analyzing the obvious aspects of poverty. We know the problems. It's time to actually deal with it.

Landlords, utility companies, the media and banking systems regularly discriminate against low-income individuals and families. There is currently a bill before the House of Commons, which was passed by the Senate on 5 June 1998. Bill S-11, introduced by Senator Ermine Cohen, seeks to add "social condition" to the list of prohibited grounds of discrimination in the Canadian Human Rights Act. However, the Minister of Justice and Attorney General, Anne McLellan, and the government has not supported this change and so it is questionable whether it will pass the Commons.

Over the past ten years our social programs have been steadily eroded and on 1 April 1996 we lost our most basic human rights due to the elimination of the

Canada Assistance Plan (CAP). For thirty years we had the right to an adequate amount of welfare when in need, the right to appeal decisions about welfare provisions and could not be forced to work for a welfare cheque (i.e., workfare). Currently, the provinces are pushing for even more control of social programs that will result in a total elimination of any type of national standards through a proposed social union.

People on social assistance who have children are experiencing discrimination through the new National Child Tax Benefit. Families on assistance receive the national benefit and then it is deducted from their welfare cheques dollar for dollar. This new benefit was supposedly put in place to fight child poverty; however, those who need assistance the most are being denied the money. Their situation has not been improved by these policies. Some working people who were being supplemented by social assistance have now been pushed off assistance because of the National Child Tax Benefit. When the child benefit is added to their employment income it puts them over the cut-off line which means they also loose their medical benefits and their drug plan.

In November 1998 Canada appeared before the UN Committee on Economic, Social and Cultural Rights to answer specific questions—questions about the country's commitment to upholding the UN Covenant dealing with increased food bank usage, questions about the decrease in the amount of unemployed people receiving employment benefits, questions about the lack of funding for social housing when there is homelessness. Municipalities across Canada have passed resolutions declaring homelessness a national disaster.

The Canadian government is quite proud that the UN has named Canada as the best country in the world to live in. But they have failed to respond to the other part of the same UN report which states that homelessness, poverty and particularly child poverty are serious issues which Canada must address. It is time for the Canadian government to realize that, as well as accepting praise, it must be ready to deal with Canada's deficiencies in its treatment of poverty and of those who live in poverty.

We need to push for a return of the basic human rights as outlined in the Canada Assistance Plan (CAP) and push for the higher standards of the Covenant if we are to achieve zero poverty within the next five years. In a country as rich as Canada this is possible if we are willing to take a hard look at the issues and if, after doing so, we are willing to respond through action. We need action by individuals, by politicians responding to the lobbying power of the citizens, by responsible businesses and corporations, by communities and by the country.

Poverty in Action is a grassroots group of people who live or have lived in poverty and are actively working towards the changes necessary to eliminate poverty. Through membership empowerment and public education we promote community connections, build skills, share resources and support a collective voice to educate and to challenge people about the myths of poverty. Our membership empowerment provides for workshops, leadership training and opportunities to network and share skills.

Poverty affects all people regardless of economic status. We must all work together if we desire change. Poor is an economic term, just like wealthy. Poor is not a personal characteristic. It is a circumstance, a situation and not a person. When we work together, there will be zero poverty.

423

MIDGE CUTHILL

Universal Declaration of Human Rights

On 10 December 1948, the General Assembly of the United Nations adopted and proclaimed the Universal Declaration of Human Rights. Following this historic act the Assembly called upon all member countries to publicize the text of the Declaration and "to cause it to be disseminated, displayed, read and expounded principally in schools and other educational institutions, without distinction based on the political status of countries or territories."

Universal Declaration of Human Rights

Preamble:

Whereas recognition of the inherent dignity and of the equal and inalienable rights of all members of the human family is the foundation of freedom, justice and peace in the world. Whereas disregard and contempt for human rights have resulted in barbarous acts which have outraged the conscience of humankind, and the advent of a world in which human beings shall enjoy freedom of speech and belief and freedom from fear and want has been proclaimed as the highest aspiration of the common people. Whereas it is essential, if human beings are not to be compelled to have recourse, as a last resort, to rebellion against tyranny and oppression, that human rights should be protected by the rule of law. Whereas it is essential to promote the development of friendly relations between nations. Whereas the peoples of the United Nations have in the Charter reaffirmed their faith in fundamental human rights, in the dignity and worth of the human person and in the equal rights of men and women and have determined to promote social progress and better standards of life in larger freedom. Whereas Member States have pledged themselves to achieve, in cooperation with the United Nations, the promotion of universal respect for an observance of human rights and fundamental freedoms. Whereas a common understanding of these rights and freedoms is of the greatest importance for the full realization of this pledge.

Now, therefore, the General Assembly proclaims the Universal Declaration of Human Rights as a common standard of achievement for all peoples and all nations, to the end that every individual and every organ of society, keeping this declaration constantly in mind, shall strive by teaching and education to promote respect for these rights and freedoms and by progressive measures, national and international, to secure their universal and effective recognition and observance, both among the peoples of Member states themselves and among the peoples of territories under their jurisdiction.

Article 1: All human beings are born free and equal in dignity and rights. They are endowed with reason and conscience and should act towards one another in a spirit of brotherhood.

Article 2: Everyone is entitled to all the rights and freedoms set forth in this Declaration, without distinction of any kind, such as race, colour, sex, language, religion, political or other opinion, national or social origin, property, birth or other status. Furthermore, no distinction shall be made on the basis of the political, jurisdictional or international status of the country or territory to which a person belongs, whether it be independent, trust, non-self-governing or under any other limitation of sovereignty.

Article 3: Everyone has the right to life, liberty and security of person.

Article 4: No one shall be held in slavery or servitude; slavery and the slave trade shall be prohibited in all their forms.

Article 5: No one shall be subjected to torture or to cruel, inhuman or degrading treatment or punishment.

Article 6: Everyone has the right to recognition everywhere as a person before the law.

Article 7: All are equal before the law and are entitled without any discrimination to equal protection of the law. All are entitled to equal protection against any discrimination in violation of this declaration and against any incitement to such discrimination.

Article 8: Everyone has to right to an effective remedy by the competent national tribunals for acts violating the fundamental rights granted them by the constitution or by law.

Article 9: No one shall be subjected to arbitrary arrest, detention or exile.

Article 10: Everyone is entitled in full equality to a fair and public hearing by an independent and impartial tribunal, in the determination of their rights and obligations and of any criminal charge against them.

Article 11: (1) Everyone charged with a penal offence has the right to be presumed innocent until proved guilty according to the law in a public trial at which they have had all the guarantees necessary for their defence. (2) No one shall be held guilty of any penal offence on account of any act or omission which did not constitute a penal offence, under national or international law, at a time when it was committed. Nor shall a heavier penalty be imposed than the one that was applicable at the time the penal offence was committed.

Article 12: No one shall be subjected to arbitrary interference with their privacy, family, home or correspondence nor to attacks upon their honour and reputation. Everyone has the right to the protection of the law against such interference or attacks.

Article 13: (1) Everyone has the right to freedom of movement and residence within the borders of each state. (2) Everyone has the right to leave any country, including their own, and to return to their country.

Article 14: (1) Everyone has the right to seek and enjoy in other countries asylum from prosecution. (2) This right may not be invoked in the case of prosecution genuinely arising from non-political crimes or from acts contrary to the purposes and principles of the United Nations.

Article 15: (1) Everyone has the right to a nationality. (2) No one shall be arbitrarily deprived of their nationality nor denied the right to change their nationality.

Article 16: (1) Men and women of full age, without any limitation due to race, nationality or religion, have the right to marry and to found a family. They are entitled to equal rights as to marriage, during marriage and at its dissolution. (2) Marriage shall be entered into only with the free and full consent of the intending spouses. (3) The family is the natural and fundamental group unit of society and is entitled to protection by society and the State.

Article 17: (1) Everyone has the right to own property alone as well as in association with others. (2) No one shall be arbitrarily deprived of their property.

Article 18: Everyone has the right to freedom of thought, conscience and religion; this right includes freedom to change their religion or belief, and freedom, either alone or in community with others and in public or in private, to manifest their religion or belief in teaching, practice, worship and observance.

Article 19: Everyone has the right to freedom of opinions and expression; this right includes freedom to hold opinions without interference and to seek, receive and impart information and ideas through any media and regardless of frontiers.

Article 20: (1) Everyone has the right to freedom of peaceful assembly and association. (2) No one may be compelled to belong to an association.

Article 21: (1) Everyone has the right to take part in the government of their country, directly or through freely chosen representatives. (2) Everyone has the right to equal access to public service in their country. (3) The will of the people shall be the basis of the authority of government; this will shall be expressed in periodic and genuine elections which shall be universal and equal suffrage and shall be held by secret vote or by equivalent free voting procedures.

Article 22: Everyone, as a member of society, has the right to social security and is entitled to realization, through national effort and international cooperation and in accordance with the organization and resources of each state, of the economic, social and cultural rights indispensable for their dignity and the free development of their personality.

Article 23: (1) Everyone has the right to work, to free choice of employment, to just and favourable conditions of work and to protection against unemployment. (2) Everyone, without any discrimination, has to right to equal pay for equal work. (3) Everyone who works has the right to just and favourable remuneration ensuring for themselves and their family an existence worthy of human dignity, and supplemented, if necessary, by other means of social protection. (4) Everyone has the right to form and to join trade unions for the protection of their interests.

Article 24: Everyone has the right to rest and leisure, including reasonable limitation of working hours and periodic holidays with pay.

Article 25: (1) Everyone has the right to a standard of living adequate for the health and well-being of themselves and their family, including food, clothing, housing and medical care and necessary social services, and the right to security in the event of unemployment, sickness, disability, widowhood, old age or other lack of livelihood in circumstances beyond their control. (2) Motherhood and childhood are entitled to special care and assistance. All children, whether born in or out of wedlock, shall enjoy the same social protection.

Article 26: (1) Everyone has the right to education. Education shall be free, at least in the elementary and fundamental stages. Elementary education shall be compulsory. Technical and professional education shall be made generally available and higher education shall be equally accessible to all on the basis of merit. (2) Education shall be directed to the full development of the human personality and to the strengthening of respect for human rights and fundamental freedoms. It shall promote understanding, tolerance and friendship among all nations, racial or religious groups, and shall further the activities of the United Nations for the maintenance of peace. (3) Parents have a prior right to choose the kind of education that shall be given to their children.

Article 27: (1) Everyone has the right freely to participate in the cultural life of the community, to enjoy the arts and to share in scientific advancement and its benefits. (2) Everyone has the right to the protection of the moral and material interests resulting from any scientific, literary or artistic production of which they are the author.

Article 28: Everyone is entitled to a social and international order in which the rights and freedoms set forth in this declaration can be fully realized.

Article 29: (1) Everyone has duties to the community in which alone the free and full development of their personality is possible. (2) In the exercise of their rights and freedoms, everyone shall to subject to such limitations as are determined by law solely for the purpose of securing due recognition and respect for the rights and freedoms of others and of meeting the just requirements of morality, public order and the general welfare in a democratic society. (3) These rights and freedoms may in no case be exercised contrary to the purposes and principles of the United Nations.

Article 30: Nothing in this Declaration may be interpreted as implying for any State, group or person any right to engage in any activity or to perform any act aimed at the destruction of any of the rights and freedoms set forth herein.

The Edmonton Resolution

The Edmonton Resolution was presented and unanimously adopted on 28 November 1998 at the International Human Rights Conference on Universal Rights and Human Values: A Blueprint for Peace, Justice and Freedom in Edmonton, Alberta, Canada.

The Edmonton Resolution reads as follows:

Whereas, in the words of the Universal Declaration of Human Rights, "recognition of the inherent dignity and of the equal and inalienable rights of all members of the human family is the foundation of freedom, justice and peace in the world;"

Whereas many states have yet to sign or ratify the International Covenant on Civil and Political Rights, the International Covenant on Economic, Social and Cultural Rights, and Optional Protocols, which together with the Universal Declaration constitute the International Bill of Human Rights;

Whereas many states have yet to sign or ratify other important international human rights agreements regarding matters such as freedom from torture, the rights of women, the elimination of racial discrimination and the rights of children and refugees;

Whereas, public education and awareness strengthen the commitment of nations to the human rights;

Be it resolved that the International Conference in Edmonton:

Reiterates and reaffirms its commitment to the universal and inalienable rights enshrined in the Universal Declaration and the other international human rights instruments; and calls on all states, without further delay, to sign and/or ratify the International Covenants and other international human rights instruments and to subscribe to the optional mechanisms designed to monitor implementation of these instruments;

Calls on all states to remove all declaration and reservations that limit the application of human rights instruments within their jurisdiction;

Calls on all states, in cooperation with the United Nations and civil society to implement comprehensive National Human Rights Education Programs and Plans of Action, and to this end, to commit the material, human and financial resources necessary;

Calls on all states to promote and protect the human rights of all citizens, and especially those of women, girl children, racial and religious minorities, person with disabilities, and indigenous peoples;

Calls on all states to take steps to ensure the protection of human rights under the rule of law by, among other means: enacting domestic legislation designed to protect rights; ensuring that there is an effective and independent judiciary; establishing national human rights institutions; and promotion and strengthening the role of citizens and Non-Governmental Organizations in the promotion and protection of human rights.

Presented and moved by R O B I N S O N   K O I L P I L L A I, C.M.
Commissioner, Canadian Human Rights Commission
Seconded by R I C A R D O   C Á M A R A
Executive-Secretary, National Human Rights Commission of Mexico

The following additions were suggested to the Resolution Committee by two conference delegates:

Re: Indigenous Peoples
To call on all states to honour existing treaties and existing instruments relating to indigenous peoples.

Re: Caste System in India
The caste system, based upon inequality by birth, and practice of Untouchability has dehumanized, created destitution in more than a quarter billion population in India and affects a quarter of the world's population in South Asia. It is also the root cause of half of the world's child labour in India.

"Even though all the laws and constitutional provisions are on the books their implementation is missing with the will of governments of India and South Asia to do the following immediately: compulsory free education for every child till the age of fourteen; total abolition of child labour and bonded labour in all its forms and their rehabilitation and revocation; total eradication of caste system through long-term human rights education as per UN CERD Report #CERD/C/304/Add.13, 17th Sept. 1998; full implementation of constitutional provisions and laws for the marginalized people, the Dalits of India and South Asia. We are very concerned that failure to implement these will result in the loss of democracy and explosion into civil wars thus affecting peace and security of South Asia and the world.

About the Editors

GURCHARAN S. BHATIA chaired the Universal Rights and Human Values Conference held in Edmonton, Canada, in 1998. He is a former director of the Canadian Human Rights Foundation and Canadian Human Rights Commissioner. He has served as editor and publisher of *Canadian Link*, a national newspaper promoting multiculturalism.

J.S. (JACK) O'NEILL was co-chair of the Universal Rights and Human Values Conference. He is a former chief commissioner of the Alberta Human Rights Commission and deputy minister of Culture and Multiculturalism in the Alberta government. He holds degrees in education from the University of Manitoba and Fordham University in New York and was a member of the Jesuit Order of Canada from 1943 to 1973.

GERALD L. GALL is a professor of law at the University of Alberta where he teaches constitutional law and civil liberties. He is a barrister and solicitor in the province of Ontario and has served on several boards of directors including the Legal Education Society of Alberta and the Centre for Constitutional Studies. He is a former executive director of the Canadian Institute for the Administration of Justice and the author of the first, second, third and fourth editions of *The Canadian Legal System.*

PATRICK D. BENDIN is a lawyer with the Canadian Department of Justice where he currently practices in the area of civil litigation. He is a sessional instructor in the Faculty of Law at the University of Alberta and a member of the Alberta Bar.